UTAH POLITICS

THE ELEPHANT IN THE ROOM

At a rally in Provo in support of Senator Reed Smoot (R–Utah), one placard calls former Senator Frank J. Cannon (D–Utah) a Judas. Another message condemns the Women's Christian Temperance Union for its opposition to polygamy. "Go back to your knitting," it says. Two of the messages hint at religious persecution: "Roger Williams still lives" and "Our country is larger than its religious bigots." *O. Blaine Larson Collection, Utah State Historical Society, ca. 1903*

UTAH POLITICS

THE ELEPHANT IN THE ROOM

ROD DECKER

SIGNATURE BOOKS | 2019 | SALT LAKE CITY

For Ben, Megan, and Rachel

Cover design by Ron Stucki
Photo of Rod Decker on back cover by Amanda Anderson Cooney

Utah Politics: The Elephant in the Room was printed on
acid-free paper and was composed, printed, and bound
in the United States of America.

FIRST EDITION | 2019

LIBRARY OF CONGRESS CATALOGING-IN-PUBLICATION DATA

Names:	Decker, Rod, 1941– author.
Title:	Utah politics : the elephant in the room / Rod Decker.
Description:	Salt Lake City : Signature Books, 2019.	Includes bibliographical references and index.
Identifiers:	LCCN 2019002573	ISBN 9781560852728 (pbk. : alk. paper)
Subjects:	LCSH: Utah—Politics and government.
Classification:	LCC JK8416 .D43 2019	DDC 320.9792—dc23
	LC record available at https://lccn.loc.gov/2019002573

CONTENTS

ILLUSTRATIONS

Graphs

Maps

Photographs

Tables

THIS BOOK'S ARGUMENT

This book comes from my career as a political reporter in Salt Lake City. When I began it, I thought I knew Utah politics. But as I proceeded, my ideas changed. I started out to write a book describing Utah politics and government, the kind of book a political scientist would write.[1] But as I proceeded, my inclination was to tell stories from political history, for example, how Utah became so Republican (the elephant in the room), why federal ownership of land has been so controversial, and how social disorder rose and fell. The book divides into three parts. The first six chapters tell how politics changed in the 1970s, so that Utah became different from the rest of America. The next four show how land and climate have affected politics. And the last six describe a state government run by Republican members of the Church of Jesus Christ of Latter-day Saint, perpetually in power because of Utah's conservatism.

I argue that a key to understanding Utah politics is resistance by the Latter-day Saint Church and its members to American social change. Latter-day Saints choose differently from most Americans in matters of morals, sex, and families. They refused the sexual revolution that swept not only the United States but developed countries generally after World War II, as people married less and had more

---

1. There are four such books: Adam Brown, *Utah Politics and Government*; JeDon Emenhiser, *Utah's Government*; Charles P. Schleicher and G. Homer Durham, *Utah: the State and Its Governments*; and George Thomas, *Civil Government of Utah*.

sex and more babies outside of marriage. Old laws designed to promote traditional families by forbidding abortion, pornography, and gay sex, among other things, were struck down by federal courts. Traditional families consisting of a married man and woman and their children declined. In opposition to these trends, Latter-day Saint leaders made traditional families and the old morality central to their preaching. Utah conducted a series of political quarrels as Latter-day Saints struggled unsuccessfully to save legal support for the old morality. Latter-day Saints turned Republican as the party stood more for the old morality and more against the expansion of federal power. In some surveys Latter-day Saints are the most Republican group in America. As the majority of Utah voters, they made Utah a Republican state. Most non-Mormons vote Democratic, and Utah has the most religiously divided electorate of any state.

For four decades now, Utahns have divided by religion, and the Latter-day Saint majority has elected Republicans, but it was not always so. From statehood in 1896 until the mid-1970s, Utah was politically ordinary, voting with national majorities, showing vigorous two-party competition, and alternating state power as voters swung with national parties in national elections. Utah entered into the American political mainstream just before statehood when Latter-day Saints gave up polygamy. As long as plural marriage was church doctrine, the territory had a religious-political division similar to the religious division that dominates Utah politics today. After the Church[2] renounced polygamy, Latter-day Saints embraced the same Victorian family morals that were predominant in America, and for eighty years until the sexual revolution Latter-day Saints and Americans broadly agreed on both families and politics.

Family and moral differences affect aspects of Utah beyond politics. Though the old morality lost legal force, many Utahns, especially Latter-day Saints, continued to adhere to it. Utah is the most married

---

2. I use "Church" (capitalized) as short for the Church of Jesus Christ of Latter-day Saints.

state, the state where a child is most likely to live with two married parents, and the state with the lowest rate of children born out of wedlock. Those family patterns affect demography. Utah has the highest birth rate, the largest proportion of children, and the youngest population. That, in turn, influences incomes and poverty. Lone-mother families are disproportionately poor. With fewer lone-mother families, Utah has a lower poverty rate, especially for children, than the nation. Partly because of less poverty, Utah incomes are among the most equal of any state, and Utah is a bastion of the middle class. Utah has fewer social troubles, less violent crime, incarceration, and homelessness than America. Chapters 4, 5, and 6 show more specifically how Utah differs in demographics, economics, and public order, and traces some of those differences to family patterns.

Most of Utah is arid, empty, and federally owned, and those characteristics affect the continuing issues of defense, water, and federal land. All three issues changed in ways that reinforced Utah Republicanism. Utahns once welcomed federal defense projects. But in recent decades, they have regarded defense proposals with suspicion. Federal water projects once seemed chief hope for Utah's future, but now seem unimportant and disappointing. Beginning in the 1960s, the federal government tightened its management of federal land, and national environmental groups gained influence at the expense of locals who live near the land. With so much federal land in the state, many rural Utahns feel bullied by their landlord. Chapters 7–10 present a history of the changes and how they pushed Utah rightward.

Utah's opposition to the federal government grew as federal power grew. From 1960 to 2000, the federal budget expanded from 17 to 23 percent of national GDP, and new laws extended federal influence over civil rights, voting rights, workplace regulations, criminal law, the environment, and other issues.[3] Federal land actions dispossessed

3. "Total Government Expenditures as Percentages of GDP: 1948–2017," *Office of Management and Budget*, www.whitehouse.gov/omb.

rural Utahns. The state was most affected as federal courts took control of public morality and decided issues contrary to Latter-day Saint preferences. The federal government became the agent and symbol of changes Latter-day Saints opposed. Republicans won Utah elections by opposing federal power, but their state successes did not halt moral change or federal activism. Latter-day Saint Republicans found themselves in a long retreat, continually adjusting to unwelcome change and unwanted federal initiatives. Utah reaction is a strand in the national reaction that brought Barry Goldwater, Ronald Reagan, the Tea Party, and Donald Trump. Utahns, however, are not angry, aggrieved, or left behind, as people sometimes are who lose political battles on defining issues. Utahns have remained optimistic and cheerful. As of this writing, the state prospers.[4]

The last six chapters describe Utah government and recount stories from institutional history, which holds some surprises. Take three examples: (1) Before they became the aggressive agent of the Latter-day-Saint-Republican majority, Utah lawmakers were weak and complained of how they were put upon by the other branches. (2) Though Utah now conducts exemplary public administration, Chapter 13 tells how the government used to run on spoils, disorganization, and private profit at public expense. And (3) Republicans tried to reform schools, but educators resisted, and outsmarted the politicians at every turn but one: the politicians beat educators when it came to keeping school budgets low.

Previous Utah political histories stop in the 1990s,[5] and this book brings the story up to date. More importantly, a central thesis here is that Utah politics changed in the 1970s and became Republican,

---

4. A monthly survey of consumer confidence places Utah higher than the US average 96 percent of the time. Other surveys have placed Utah first, second, or fourth in happiness and well being. The US Bureau of Economic Analysis it among the top states for growth (GDP, personal income, personal spending). "Utahns' Strong Confidence," www.zionsbank.com; Adam McCann, "Happiest States in America," wallethub.com; "Gallup and Sharecare," wellbeingindex.sharecare.com; "U.S. Economy at a Glance," www.bea.gov.

5. E.g. Alexander, *Utah: The Right Place*, 1995. Allen's *Still the Right Place* appeared in 2017 but was written earlier and extends only to 2000.

conservative, and religiously divided, and contemporary Utah politics still follow that pattern. But the duration and significance of that change were not apparent until after the 1990s. This book, therefore, has an advantage over predecessors from a longer view that shows important developments that were not seen before. From the present vantage, the whole of Utah history looks different. Until now, historians have seen the story of Utah as assimilation. In pioneer times, Utah society was different from America, but the federal government forced Utahns to give up polygamy and theocracy and conform to national ways. After statehood, Utah continued to become more like America because the national economy offered the best opportunity to make money. "After World War II the integration of Utah and the United Sates became virtually complete," wrote historian Richard D. Poll.[6] That was true into the 1970s, but then Utah became different again. The new changes showed most in politics and demography, but they ramify throughout Utah society. Although economics had driven assimilation, religion and morals drove the new differences, as religion and polygamy had driven political differences in territorial times. The contemporary differences are much less important than the quarrels of Utah territory; nonetheless, they partly explain the past four decades of Utah politics. Religion, morals, and families have played a larger role in Utah history and politics than scholars have seen before.

Because this book is about Utah politics, it focuses on Latter-day Saint Republicans who determine political outcomes. Other groups get less attention than they would deserve in a more comprehensive account, and I apologize for scanting them.

---

6. Poll, *Utah's History*, 678.

1

THE FOUNDING

Two years after their arrival in the Salt Lake Valley, Latter-day Saints petitioned Congress for statehood. They sent the *Constitution of the State of Deseret with the Journal of the Convention Which Formed It and The Proceedings of the Legislature Consequent Thereon* to President Zachary Taylor and members of Congress. The documents told how citizens had assembled in convention and drafted a constitution like the United States Constitution. Brigham Young was elected governor, and the new legislature voted unanimously for statehood. Members of the Church of Jesus Christ of Latter-day Saints (they called themselves "Saints") followed prescribed procedures and acted in traditions of American self-government, according to the documents.

It was, however, all a fraud. There had been no convention, no election, and no legislature. Church leaders decided privately to apply for statehood shortly before Congress was to meet, so they had no time for democratic folderol. But to appear properly American, they fabricated public proceedings and sent false documents to Washington. The Saints supported their leaders: No one told. Congress was fooled. Until recently, historians were fooled too. Even so, Congress did not grant statehood to "Deseret," but instead created the Territory of Utah as a small part of the Compromise of 1850, enacted to avoid civil war.[1]

---

1. Crawley, "Constitution of the State of Deseret," especially 9–12; Quinn, *Extensions of Power*, 237.

The Saints schemed for statehood because they hoped it would preserve local political control and shield them from national forces as they built a "Kingdom of God," different from America in politics, economics, individual rights, and families. But Congress denied Utah statehood, and instead forced Saints to conform to American ways. Statehood was granted only after the Saints changed to accept national norms and institutions. The Utah changes were sincere and enduring. Historians say that over the first fifty years after statehood, Utahns became indistinguishable from other Americans.[2] In recent decades, however, Utah changed direction again, and differences with America revive. Republican politicians now win elections in Utah defending the new differences, and scheme, like Church leaders in territorial times, to fend off national power and preserve local control. The new differences resemble old territorial issues, but they are more civil and less important. This chapter looks briefly at Utah Territory, when conflicts were fresh and sharp, and people fought and suffered for them.

In politics and government, pioneer Utah differed from America in both ideal and everyday practice. In America citizens debated issues, and then elected officials made decisions in public government proceedings. In contrast, pioneer government followed the leadership of the Church of Jesus Christ of Latter-day Saints. Utah Saints sustained government decisions made in private by leaders of their Church. For every important election until the 1890s, Church leaders privately selected a single list of candidates. People called it the "regular ticket." One study showed regular-ticket candidates received 96 percent of 96,107 votes cast from 1852 to 1870. Church leaders became government officials. Brigham Young was governor, and his counselors and the Church's apostles occupied high offices and legislative seats. Bishops were elected local magistrates. Officers elected on the regular ticket consulted with Church leaders and followed Church policies. Votes in the Territorial Legislature were

---

2. Poll, "American Commonwealth," 678.

usually unanimous. Lawmakers boasted of one session that was held "without the occurrence of any negative vote on any question or action."[3] While Americans believed in separation of church and state and limited government, Saints believed their Church was divinely inspired, and by following Church leaders in all things they could live in harmony with their religious brothers and sisters and in accord with the will of God.

In contrast to American economic individualism, pioneers co-operated in digging irrigation ditches, building forts, grading roads, and fencing common ground, usually not for pay but as a shared task. Towns were planned with uniform grids, property lots of standard size, and building regulations. In a few communities, people held property in common. Towns where property remained private had a cooperative store where people shopped partly to show support for their Church and community. The Church launched big projects (many of which failed) to produce coal, iron, lead, cotton and woolen cloth, paper, pottery, sugar, and companies that hauled freight, ran railroads, and operated telegraph lines. Brigham Young directed the economy toward growth, self-sufficiency, and building a powerful Latter-day Saint community and government.[4]

While Americans were proudly free to pursue happiness as they chose, Saints believed they should do what church leaders asked of them. Brigham Young directed the settlement of more than 300 communities across the West, calling church members to leave their homes and livelihoods and pioneer inhospitable places. Others were called on proselyting missions or to work for church projects. George Goddard's call to gather rags for the Church paper factory was "a

---

3. Jack, "Utah Territorial Politics," 84; Ivins, *Moses Thatcher Case*, 3; Campbell, *Establishing Zion*, 209. Quinn, *Extensions of Power*, 265–69, shows that almost all legislative votes were unanimous before 1884.

4. Leone, *Roots of Modern Mormonism*, 21, on town planning; Stegner, *Mormon Country*, 108–28, on property in common; Arrington, *Great Basin Kingdom*, for coal, 275; communal power, 203; cotton, 216; freight, 159; iron, 345; lead, 127; paper and pottery, 114; railroads, 399; sugar, 116; telegraph, 228; wool, 121.

severe blow to my native pride." But on reflection, he wrote he had come "to these valleys … for the purpose of doing the will of my Heavenly Father," and so for three years he gathered rags.[5] Like Goddard, most members obeyed Church requests and believed the needs of Church and community came before their individual interests.

American morality was Victorian, while Latter-day Saints were notoriously polygamous. Church founder Joseph Smith initiated polygamy within a decade of founding the Church, saying it would help Saints reach the highest degree of glory in the next life. Not all Saints were polygamous, but the most influential were. Nearly all the highest leaders (general authorities) had more than one wife, as did most bishops and stake presidents. Men were sometimes asked to take a second wife before they were called to leadership. Wealthy men were likely to have many wives. Sister-wives were preferred for leadership positions in the Women's Relief Society, Young Women's Association, and other Church and women's organizations. One study showed 20 percent of male householders in Davis County, and 30 percent in St. George, had plural wives. By choosing polygamy in violation of American morality, men committed themselves to the Church, and formed a corps of male leadership by marrying each other's half-sisters or daughters.[6] Polygamy shocked and repulsed most Americans, who refused to support statehood or accept Latter-day Saints until the Church renounced plural marriage.

Starting from their founding in upstate New York in 1830, the Saints had experienced trouble with neighbors. Opposition pushed them from New York to Ohio, then to Missouri, where they fought "The 1838 Mormon War" with Missourians; both sides raised militias, made threats, destroyed property, and suffered casualties. Saints fled to Illinois, where six year later, vigilantes murdered Joseph Smith.

---

5. *Great Basin Kingdom*, 115.
6. Bennion, "Incidence of Mormon Polygamy," 36; Logue, "Time of Marriage," 9–10; Quinn, *Extensions of Power*, 178–93; Arrington and Bitton, *Mormon Experience*, 178–205.

Taken in about 1885, this photograph from the Prints and Photographs Division of the US Library of Congress is titled "A Latter-day Saint with his six wives, posed on porch."

Church leaders pleaded for federal protection from violence and restitution of their property, without success. In 1846, they abandoned their city of Nauvoo, left United States territory, and sought refuge in western wilderness.[7]

In Utah, Latter-day Saints hoped for Christian peace, but understood that political power grows out of the barrel of a gun. They reinstituted the Nauvoo Legion militia and enforced peace with cannon when necessary. Non-Mormons who tried to settle areas near Great Salt Lake City said they were threatened, sometimes beaten, and driven off. Saints sought to avoid violence with Native Americans but still fought repeatedly and seized their land.[8] In early Utah, the Kingdom of God deployed superior force.

On their arrival, the Saints were in a region that was still part

---

7. Hill, *Quest for Refuge*, 78, 93, 137. See also LeSueur, *Mormon War in Missouri*.

8. Howard, "Men, Motives, and Misunderstandings," 126–27, for the Morrisite War; Bigler, *Forgotten Kingdom*, 247–54, on non-Mormons; Christy, "Open Hand and Mailed Fist," 220–23, on Native Americans.

of Mexico, though Mexico City was too distant to exercise any real governance. After the Mexican War in 1848, the region became part of the United States and the Saints were again under American rule. At first they hoped for quasi-autonomy within the union. They asked for a state the size of Texas, including today's Utah and Nevada and parts of Arizona, Colorado, Idaho, New Mexico, Oregon, Southern California, and Wyoming. Congress rejected the petition, but President Fillmore appointed Brigham Young governor of a new territory. Other officials appointed to Utah were all non-Mormons from the East. Some of them made the arduous journey, assumed their duties, quarreled with Saints, and returned home with tales of polygamy, theocracy, and treason.[9]

The Saints chafed under officials appointed from Washington. Six times the settlers petitioned for statehood and were turned down. By the 1860s, Utah had 60,000 residents, the usual number required for statehood. By 1880, with 145,000 residents, the population of Utah was "far beyond any territory in the history of the United States," Governor Eli Murray noted.[10] During the years they rejected Utah, Congress admitted thirteen states, all with fewer citizens.[11] Instead of granting statehood, Congress reduced the size of Utah six times, and conducted a punitive campaign to force Latter-day Saint conformity to American ways.

To begin the process of Americanization, President James Buchanan sent an army in 1857 with a new governor to replace Brigham Young. In the face of 2,500 troops, Church leaders negotiated an agreement: Brigham Young would step down in favor of the new governor and the troops would march through Great

---

9. MacKinnon, "Like Splitting a Man Up His Backbone," 102, 119; Alexander, *Utah: The Right Place*, 119–124.

10. Ellsworth, "Utah's Struggle for Statehood," 60–61; Murray, *Report of the Governor*, 62.

11. Minnesota and Oregon (1850s); Kansas, Nebraska, Nevada, West Virginia (1860s); Colorado (1876); Montana, North Dakota, Washington (1880s); Idaho, Wyoming (1890).

Salt Lake City to make camp forty miles away in the desert. In addition, President Buchanan agreed to pardon the Saints for sedition and treason, which they denied they had committed. When the Civil War began, and the soldiers marched away; President Abraham Lincoln sent a smaller force, the California Volunteers, who built Camp Douglas on the eastern hills, where their artillery could reach Great Salt Lake City.[12] Federal control of early Utah required military force.

Even after federal troops arrived, non-Mormons feared violence. They suspected secret Danite bands, bound by blood oaths, were ready to strike on orders from Church leaders. Non-Mormons blamed unsolved murders on such groups. Some of those stories were obviously false, while others were plausible but unproved.[13] One infamous incident, the Mountain Meadows Massacre, showed the settlers were capable of murder. When news came in 1857 that a federal army was marching on Utah, Latter-day Saints from Cedar City set upon a wagon train bound for California and murdered about one-hundred-twenty men, women and children, and stole their property. Twenty years later John D. Lee became the only perpetrator to be tried, convicted, and executed for the crime. Word of the massacre soon reached the East, where it contributed to an evil reputation for the Church, and increasingly stern measures against the Saints in Utah.[14]

Through all the troubles, Utah continued to grow. Besides Saints, non-Mormons, who were called "Gentiles," came to Utah, as federal

---

12. Bigler, "Lion in the Path"; Alexander, *Utah: The Right Place*, 134–37. Long, *Saints and the Union*, 94–124, discusses the California Volunteers.

13. For example, the murder of non-Mormon doctor John K. Robinson; murder of six gamblers called the Aiken Group; and murder of apostate William Parrish, his son, and their acquaintance, in Baskin, *Reminiscences*, 13–16; Bigler, *Forgotten Kingdom*, 247–58; "Aiken Party Executions," 457, 475–76; Aird, "Nasty Apostates," 173, 191; Parshall, "Pursue, Retake & Punish," 64–65, 85–86. For an LDS view, see Roberts, *Comprehensive History of the Church*, 5:194–215.

14. Four books with different perspectives are Bagley, *Blood of the Prophets*; Brooks, *Mountain Meadows Massacre*; Denton, *American Massacre*; and Walker, *Massacre at Mountain Meadows*.

Cannon shot could reach Great Salt Lake City from Camp Douglas, here on the eastern hill overlooking the city. For several years, relations were tense between the 1,500 soldiers and city residents. *Photograph ca. 1864, Classified Photograph Collection, Utah State Historical Society*

officials, camp followers, merchants, miners, and railroad workers. After the transcontinental railroad was completed in 1869, people could ride to Utah, and they did, Saints always in greater numbers than Gentiles. Converts in the eastern states, Canada, Europe, and the Pacific Islands were urged to "come to Zion." The Church loaned money for their journey from a "Perpetual Emigration Fund" that converts promised to repay after they arrived in Utah and found work, and the repayments were loaned to other converts.[15]

Saints and Gentiles came on the same trains but formed separate and contentious societies once they arrived. Shut out of political decisions, non-Mormons formed the Liberal Party in 1870 to compete in elections. In response, Saints formed the People's Party, which beat the Liberals in almost every election until the late 1880s when non-Mormons rose in numbers and Liberals won city elections in Ogden and Salt Lake City.[16] Non-Mormon political strength lay in their agreement with appointed territorial governors, judges, attorneys, and marshals, all of whom were Gentiles, often exasperated at local recalcitrance. While Saints wanted statehood, non-Mormons did not. The outsiders feared that if things were left to majority governance without federal troops and marshals, the minority would be ignored at best and maybe driven out. As the Utah legislature repeatedly sent delegates to Washington to plead for statehood, non-Mormons sent emissaries of their own, at their own expense, to argue against statehood, plead for stronger laws against polygamy, and ask for more zealous appointees to enforce those laws.[17]

The two groups rarely worked together. "Agricultural pursuits here are carried on almost exclusively by Mormons, and ... the mining enterprises of the Territory almost entirely conducted

---

15. Peterson, *Utah: A History*, 31–36.

16. Erickson, "Liberal Party of Utah." Non-Mormons prevailed in the "Republic of Tooele" election in 1874 (Stout, *History of Utah*, 1:55), and the Liberal Party won elections in Ogden in 1889 and Salt Lake City in 1890 (Lyman, *Political Deliverance*, 110–19).

17. Larson, "Government, Politics, and Conflict," 247–48; Maxwell, *Robert Newton Baskin*, 179–88.

by anti-Mormons," territorial governor George Emery reported to Washington in 1878. A few non-Mormons made mining fortunes and became Utah's richest men. Non-Mormon merchants were often more successful, until Brigham Young declared a boycott of Gentile shopkeepers in 1866, an act that further widened the gulf between the two communities.

As the Church of Jesus Christ sent missionaries to other states and nations, Christian churches did the same in reverse by sending missionaries to Utah. They were as shocked as the federal officials had been by local practices. Some missionaries later went on lecture tours to denounce the evils of polygamy. Others sent condemning letters to be read from pulpits.[18] Within Utah, sermons in both churches and ward houses criticized the opposing camp.

Schools were established at first in Latter-day Saint meeting houses, where children were taught basic skills alongside Church doctrine. The territorial legislature voted small subsidies to these ward-house schools, though tuition was still charged. Gentiles complained of being taxed for schools that taught Latter-day Saint doctrine. Their own children did not attend the Church schools, but went to private missionary establishments. The Gentile schools were better academically, and missionaries offered scholarships to lure Latter-day Saint children to non-Mormon classrooms and teach them the errors of their parents' religion. The Saints did not trust any schools not controlled by their Church. In 1884, Salt Lake City voters rejected a ballot proposal for free public education by a four-to-one majority. The Church-owned *Deseret News* said it was "because institutions supported by general taxes cannot be conducted on a religious basis."[19] Free schools did not come to Utah until 1890.

Responding to clamor from press, pulpit, and non-Mormons

---

18. Emery, *Report of the Governor*; Goodman, "Jews in Zion," 195–97; Dwyer, *Gentile Comes to Utah*, 151–89.

19. Becky Bartholomew, "Methodist Women Missionaries," *History Blazer*, Oct. 1996; Ivins, "Free Schools Come to Utah," 322–36; "The District Schools Are Secular," *Deseret News*, Nov. 26, 1884.

in Utah, the federal government began "the Raid," a progressively stronger attack on polygamy, the Church, and its people. Congress passed three statutes, each one harsher than the last, aimed at Utah.[20] The laws made polygamy a crime in the territories, then made cohabitation a crime because it was easier to prove in court. Federal judges applied the laws punitively against marriages contracted before the laws were passed and against men who no longer lived or slept with polygamous wives but lived near them, gave them money, or helped raise their children. Federal law disinherited the children. Judges jailed wives who refused to testify against their husbands. Sarah Barringer Gordon found that of 2,500 federal prosecutions in Utah from 1871 to 1896, 95 percent were for polygamy, cohabitation, fornication, or adultery—almost all of these charges related to polygamy. "This level of enforcement far exceeds anything historians have found elsewhere in the country," she wrote.[21]

The federal government attacked the Church as an institution by disincorporating it, disbanding the territorial militia, and seizing the *Deseret News*, Deseret Telegraph, Perpetual Emigration Fund, Salt Lake Street Railway, utilities, and cooperative stores.[22]

Congress excluded Latter-day Saints from politics and government. Federal law required voters to swear they were not polygamists. Congress nullified territorial laws that "establish, support, maintain, shield or countenance" polygamy. Local courts were barred from hearing cases which were diverted to federal courts instead. Territorial attorneys and marshals were abolished in favor of federal marshals and attorneys, whose jurisdiction was enlarged. Saints were excluded

---

20. The 1862 Morrill Act, 1882 Edmunds Act, and 1887 Edmunds–Tucker Act. See Linford, "Mormons and the Law," 314–28; Arrington, *Great Basin Kingdom*, 353–79; Firmage and Mangrum, *Zion in the Courts*, 160–260.

21. *Chapman v. Handley*, 151 U.S. 443 (1894); *Ex Parte Harris*, 5 Utah Terr. 120 (1884); "Mormons and the Law," 586, 557; *Zion in the Courts*, 205–09; Gordon, *Mormon Question*, 155–56.

22. The Morrill Act repealed the church's incorporation; the Edmunds–Tucker Act disincorporated it again for good measure. See also Arrington, *Great Basin Kingdom*, 371.

from juries in polygamy cases.[23] Twelve years after Utah gave women the vote, Congress took it away because most Utah women were voting for Latter-day Saint candidates.[24] Congress vacated Utah elected offices and put all future elections under the direction of a federal commission, which soon disfranchised 12,000 Latter-day Saint voters. In Idaho the territorial legislature required voters to swear they were not members of any organization that supported polygamy, so no Latter-day Saint could vote, hold office, or sit on a jury.[25] Congress was considering a similar oath for Utah.

Caught in an ever-tightening federal vice, the Church surrendered. At a general conference in 1890, President Wilford Woodruff announced a "Manifesto": He said he would obey laws against polygamy and he urged all Church members to do the same. Latter-day Saints gave up their peculiar institutions. They disbanded the People's Party and divided their votes between Democrats and Republicans. Because Republican congresses had passed the anti-polygamy laws and Republican presidents had led enforcement of those laws, Latter-day Saints had favored Democrats, who since the Civil War had advocated states' rights and local control. Church leaders feared that the members would become Democrats and that the non-Mormons would become Republicans, and the same political division by religion would continue under new names. They asked some of the Saints to become Republicans so that both parties would include Saints and non-Mormons.[26] Latter-day Saints

---

23. Firmage and Mangrum, *Zion in the Courts*, 231. An oath was introduced in 1884, successfully challenged in *Murphy v. Ramsey*, 114 U.S. 15 (1885), then re-imposed by the Edmunds–Tucker Act (reinforced by *Miles v. United States*, 103 U.S. 304 [1880]). See Firmage and Mangrum, *Zion in the Courts*, 148–49, for the Poland Act.

24. Larson, *Americanization of Utah*, 69–70, explains that Wyoming passed women's suffrage first in 1869, followed by Utah two months later, but that Utah women voted first in February 1870. Congress took away their right in 1882.

25. *Davis v. Beason*, 133 U.S. 333 (1890); Firmage and Mangrum, *Zion in the Courts*, 231; Gordon, *Mormon Question*, 161–181

26. Anderson, *Deseret Saints*, 327; Lyman, *Political Deliverance*, 135–140, 296–97; Moyle, *Mormon Democrat*, 149–60; Poll, "Political Reconstruction of Utah Territory," 124; Williams, "Separation of Church and State," 37.

had never divided their votes before. In Utah they had voted for the People's Party and the "regular ticket"; in Illinois and Missouri their bloc-voting had given them power, while also angering their non-Mormon neighbors. Years later, Church president David O. McKay recalled that his family in Huntsville had reluctantly become Republican at Church request. "How ashamed we were to be Republicans in that day," he remembered. In the past, the only Republican in the area was the town drunk.[27]

The Church helped elect some Gentiles to public office, while informally Church leaders said they would not "interfere in politics." When the Church was allowed to own property and engage in commerce again, it continued to invest in businesses but gave up its role as an economic arbiter and advised its members to patronize Gentiles institutions. Utah's economy fell under control of absentee corporations, like other Western states.[28] Public schools were established. After Latter-day Saint capitulation became clear, Congress in 1894 passed an enabling act inviting Utah to become a state. Utahns held a convention, drafted a constitution, and approved it at a referendum. In January 1896, Utah joined the United States and all Utahns celebrated.

REMARKS

Like states that seceded prior to the Civil War, Utah is a reconstructed state. The United States forced the people to change their social order to conform to American principles. Note, Utah and the confederacy differed from each other as much as either differed from the dominant American society. Not slavery and race, but polygamy and theocracy were Utah's quarrels, and the Utah issues proved easier to overcome in the aftermath.

Though non-Mormons lost the elections in early Utah, they often

---

27. *Deseret: Bicentennial History*, 200; Arrington and Bitton, *Mormon Experience*, 50–53.

28. Arrington, *Great Basin Kingdom*, 406–12.

got their way because they shared the views of the majority of Americans, and they allied with appointed territorial officials and national government to defeat Latter-day Saint majorities in Utah. Nowadays, on public morals and federal lands, a minority of Utahns, who are unable to win state elections, still prevail over Utah majorities at times through federal courts or because they agree with national policy. As it turns out, Utah majorities are Latter-day Saints and the minorities are mostly non-Mormon in a pale reenactment of territorial ways.

When Latter-day Saints held power in pioneer times, they opted for a communitarian model for the economy. Brigham Young directed the use of Utah's resources toward economic independence and the power of the community. Nowadays most Latter-day Saints believe in free markets. But Church tradition allows for central planning as well as *laissez-faire*, and no religious teaching mandates the markets.

Utah pioneers denounced the United States and talked of leaving it. But Latter-day Saints became patriotic. A 1981 study polled a national sample on "civil religion" and asked whether respondents agreed with statements such as, "America is God's chosen nation"; "To me, the flag of the United States is sacred"; and "Human rights come from God, not merely from laws." Latter-day Saints agreed with those statements more than members of any other religion in the survey.[29]

In early Utah, Latter-day Saints built a democratic façade to cover a theocracy. Over 120 years since statehood, Church leaders have reduced their participation in Utah politics. But they still wield influence, sometimes with fanfare, other times quietly. Some Utahns still suspect that state government is sometimes a façade hiding Church control. Utah politics are marked by continual questions and suspicions over Church actions and influence.[30]

---

29. Wimberly and Christensen, "Civil Religion," 91–100.

30. Compare two *Salt Lake Tribune* articles from different centuries: "Wells Says It's False," Apr. 14, 1896, and Lee Davidson, "Former Utah Senator Criticizes 'Secretive Puppet-String Lobbying,'" Aug. 14, 2017.

As the Latter-day Saints built a succession of frontier communities and quarreled with their non-Mormon neighbors, they always had the option of moving on. But by the time they were subjected to non-Mormon power in Utah, the frontier was closing. The Saints offered resistance but stayed, eventually giving in to national force. Utah political history is partly the story of contention and accommodation between Latter-day Saints and non-Mormons. They live in amity, but retain a capacity for difference. In the 1970s, after eighty years of assimilation, there was a second separation between Utah Latter-day Saints and non-Mormons. That story is told in the next chapter.

2

THE REPUBLICAN ASCENDANCY

Utah politics differ from politics elsewhere in America because Utah voters choose differently. They divide by religion: Latter-day Saints tend to vote Republican, and non-LDS tend to vote Democratic. The religious split is the proverbial elephant in the room. It is the most important fact about Utah politics but is rarely mentioned. Utah politicians debate mostly the same issues as politicians elsewhere, and Utah campaigns sound like campaigns in other states. There seems to be little reason to bring up religion, it may even be impolite to do so. But though religion has little place in political discourse, it determines political outcomes. Polls and elections both show its underlying power. Though non-Mormons vote Democratic, and Latter-day Saint voters make Utah a one-party-dominant Republican state.[1]

Table 1 shows the Utah vote in the past eleven presidential elections. Beginning with Gerald Ford in 1976, Utah had the highest Republican vote percentage of any state in seven of those eleven elections. Besides Gerald Ford, Utah voted most Republican twice for Reagan, once for the first Bush, Bob Dole, once for the second Bush, and for Mitt Romney. When Utah was not the most

---

1. Political scientist Austin Ranney developed an index for state party competition and control. Two scholars updated the index for 2007 to 2011 and ranked Utah second (behind Idaho) for Republican control and lack of party competition. Holbrook and La Raja, "Parties and Elections," 87–88.

TABLE I. Utah percentages for GOP candidates, 1976–2016

year	candidate	percent	state GOP rank
1976	Gerald Ford	62.4	1
1980	Ronald Reagan	72.8	1
1984	"	74.5	1
1988	G.H.W. Bush	66.2	1
1992	"	43.4	6
1996	Bob Dole	54.4	1
2000	George W. Bush	66.8	3
2004	"	71.5	1
2008	John McCain	63.2	3
2012	Mitt Romney	72.6	1
2016	Donald Trump	46.5	29

From the *Statistical Abstract of the United States*.

Republican, it was among the most Republican in every election except in 2016 when Donald Trump barely carried the state. (The Trump election is discussed below.) In the ten elections from 1976 to 2012, Utah was overall the most Republican state.

While Table 1 shows election returns, Table 2 divides Utah voters into LDS and non-LDS. Information for that table comes from exit polls of voters leaving polling locations, conducted by the Center for the Study of Elections and Democracy at Brigham Young University, and includes presidential elections beginning in 1984. Note that the summary at the bottom shows the average of nine elections. Latter-day Saint Utahns gave 73 percent of their votes to Republicans and only 16 percent to Democrats. In contrast, non-LDS cast 56 percent of their ballots for Democratic candidates and only 34 percent for Republicans. The rightmost column in Table 2 shows where Utah would have ranked among Democratic states if only non-Mormons had voted. Compare the non-Mormon results shown in that column with

TABLE 2. Utah presidential voting by religion

year	candidate	party	non-LDS	LDS	rank*
2016	Hillary Clinton	D	57%	14%	5
	Donald Trump	R	27	47	
	Evan McMullin	I	5	32	
2012	Barack Obama	D	66	9	2
	Mitt Romney	R	34	89	
2008	Barack Obama	D	70	19	2
	John McCain	R	30	75	
2004	John Kerry	D	57	12	3
	George W. Bush	R	39	86	
2000	Al Gore	D	61	13	1
	George W. Bush	R	30	83	
1996	Bill Clinton	D	61	26	1
	Bob Dole	R	25	62	
1992	Bill Clinton	D	44	16	2
	George H.W. Bush	R	17	53	
	Ross Perot	I	31	26	
1988	Michael Dukakis	D	58	20	1
	George H.W. Bush	R	39	77	
1984	Walter Mondale	D	44	16	12
	Ronald Reagan	R	57	82	

	non-LDS	LDS
average voting for Democrats	56%	16%
average voting for Republicans	34%	73%

Source: BYU Center for the Study of Elections and Democracy exit polls.
*This column ranks Utah's non-Mormon vote for Democratic candidates against the percentage vote for Democratic candidates in other states.

overall state results shown in Table 1. For example, in 2012, instead of being the most Republican state for Mitt Romney, Utah would have been the second-most Democratic state for Barack Obama. Instead of being the state with the highest percentage vote for George H. W. Bush in 1988, Utah would have been the state with the highest percentage vote for his Democratic opponent, Michael Dukakis. In 2016, Utah would have been the fifth strongest state for Democrat Hillary Clinton. Republican presidential candidates won every Utah election shown in Table 2. But if only non-Mormons had voted, Ronald Reagan still would have won in 1984, and the Democratic candidate would have won every other Utah presidential election beginning in 1988.[2]

Over those eight elections, Utah would have been the most Democratic state three times, and the second most Democratic state three times. Utah non-Mormons are mostly Democrats, but Latter-day Saints are more numerous, more likely to vote, and more partisan, and thus put Utah among the reddest states. Religion determines voting in Utah more than any other state. Utah is "extremely polarized by religion," writes political scientist Patrick Fisher, "the religion gap in Utah is larger than anywhere else in the country."[3]

The 2016 election of Republican Donald Trump was an exception that showed a moral component of LDS voting. Trump won only 46.5 percent of Utah's Republican vote, and Utah was the twenty-ninth state in backing him, with the lowest percentage in any state Trump won. Donald Trump offended Latter-day Saints. He finished third of three candidates in the state nominating caucuses. In the final campaign, the Church's *Deseret News* said he should resign his candidacy, editorializing that his boasts of adultery and sexual assault made him unfit to be president.[4] It was

---

2. CSED exit polls didn't begin for presidential elections until 1984, so there is no direct evidence of the split in presidential voting along religious lines before that year.

3. Fisher, *Demographic Gaps*, 58.

4. Robert Gehrke and Lee Davidson, "Ted Cruz Swamps Donald Trump," *Salt Lake Tribune*, Mar. 23, 2016; "Donald Trump Should Resign His Candidacy," *Deseret News*, Oct. 8, 2016.

the first time in eighty years the *Deseret News* had taken sides in a presidential election. (The editors said they spoke for themselves, not for Church leaders, an important distinction for Latter-day Saints.) So in contrast to the 76 percent average Latter-day Saints gave to eight Republican candidates before Trump, he received only 46 percent of their vote. But disaffected Latter-day Saints did not vote for Democrat Hillary Clinton. Rather, 32 percent of them chose Evan McMullin, a fellow Church member who had never run for political office before. McMullin won a slender 5 percent of the state's non-Mormon vote, 7 percent of the vote in Idaho, and negligible votes anywhere else.[5] Most of the Latter-day Saints who voted against Trump returned and voted in their usual Republican percentages for senator, governor, and other offices. For example, Republican governor Gary Herbert received 80 percent of the Latter-day Saint vote, a little more than the votes of Donald Trump and Evan McMullin combined.[6]

Religious-based Republicanism trickles down through Utah politics. The last Democrat elected governor in Utah was Scott Matheson in 1980. Utahns have chosen only Republican governors in the ten elections since then. Exit-poll numbers from BYU show non-Mormons voted Democratic in eight of those ten elections. Governors Mike Leavitt and Jon Huntsman each received a majority of non-Mormon votes in one reelection race, but in every other gubernatorial race non-Mormons voted Democrat. On the other side, Latter-day Saints never chose a Democrat for governor in any of the ten elections. Table 3 shows a summary of gubernatorial voting since 1984. Latter-day Saints on average gave 71 percent of their votes to Republican candidates, while non-Mormons on average voted 60 to 34 percent for Democrats. (Results of each election can be seen in table 4.) In addition, Utah's legislature is among the most Republican in the nation, as

---

5. Katie McKellar, "Evan McMullin," *Deseret News*, Oct. 30, 2016; CSED exit poll, Nov. 8, 2016; "Idaho Presidential Election Results," Politico, Dec. 13, 2016, www.politico.com.
6. Utah Colleges Exit Poll, Nov. 8, 2016.

TABLE 3. Utah gubernatorial voting by religion

	LDS	non–LDS
average voting for Republicans	71%	34%
average voting for Democrats	22%	60%

Source: CSED Exit Polls

is its US Congressional delegation.[7] The last Utah Democrat elected to the United States Senate was Frank Moss in 1970.

Faced with an enduring religious–political majority, non-Mormons joined an informal coalition against Latter-day Saint Republicanism. In some other states, Catholics, for example, may vote differently from people who have no religious preference, called "nones." But in Utah, Catholics, nones, Protestants, Jews, and people of other religious affiliations usually vote together in one bloc for Democrats. Moreover, Utah non-Mormons vote more strongly Democratic than their national co-religionists. A survey by the Pew Research Foundation showed 44 percent of American Catholics identified themselves as Democrats.[8] But Utah College Exit Polls show 61 percent of Utah Catholics voted Democratic in presidential elections. The Pew Survey showed 54 percent of nones identifying as Democrats. But 64 percent of Utah nones chose Democratic candidates for president.[9] Latter-day Saints are more politically unified than non-Mormons. In the Pew Survey, 70 percent of them claimed the Republican Party. They were more Republican than any other group, more than the rich or the old, and slightly more than evangelical Christians. Though they lose to Republicans statewide, where

---

7. Democrats last controlled both houses of the Utah legislature in 1975, after President Nixon's Watergate scandal. Utah's Congressional delegation of two senators and four representatives was all Republican from 2015 to 2019. Democrat Ben McAdams won in 2018 to become the lone Democrat.

8. "Deep Dive into Party Affiliation," Apr. 7, 2015, *Pew Research Center*, www.people-press.org.

9. My comparison of the Pew Research Center poll and CSED exit polls. Utah Protestants voted Republican in presidential elections from 2004 to 2012.

TABLE 4. Utah gubernatorial voting by religion

year	candidate	party	LDS	non–LDS
2016	Gary Herbert	R	80%	31%
	Mike Weinholtz	D	14	59
2012	Gary Herbert	R	81	36
	Peter Cooke	D	14	64
2010	Gary Herbert	R	80	29
	Peter Corroon	D	20	71
2008	Jon Huntsman Jr.	R	77	62
	Bob Springmeyer	D	18	38
2004	Jon Hunstman Jr.	R	70	32
	Scott Matheson Jr.	D	29	68
2000	Mike Leavitt	R	69	27
	Bill Orton	D	28	73
1996	Mike Leavitt	R	87	54
	Jim Bradley	D	11	46
1992	Mike Leavitt	R	52	16
	Stewart Hanson	D	13	59
	Merrill Cook	I	33	34
1988	Norman Bangerter	R	50	18
	Ted Wilson	D	29	61
	Merrill Cook	I	19	21
1984	Norman Bangerter	R	64	34
	Wayne Owens	D	35	65

Source: CSED Exit Polls

non-Mormons are in a majority they elect Democrats, for instance in Salt Lake City, which has a tradition of Democratic mayors.[10]

---

10. Salt Lake City has had Democratic mayors since 1976, none of them Mormon, some quite progressive. After his 2000–08 term, Rocky Anderson ran for US president with the Peace and Freedom Party. Mayor Jackie Biskupski (2016–) is the first openly gay mayor in Utah.

The religious division and Republican dominance that now characterize Utah politics did not begin until the 1970s. From statehood until 1976, Utahns voted about the same as other Americans. In twenty presidential elections from statehood in 1896 through 1972, Utah voted with American majorities—that is, for the winner—seventeen times. Only three states voted for the winner more often than Utah in those twenty elections.[11] Utah voted in the minority for Democrat William Jennings Bryan in 1896, Republican William Howard Taft in 1912, and Republican Richard Nixon in 1960. In this mainstream period, Utah voted for winning Democrats Woodrow Wilson, Franklin D. Roosevelt, Harry S. Truman, and Lyndon Baines Johnson.[12] Of all the Democratic presidents elected before 1976, only John F. Kennedy failed to get Utah's vote. Differences between Latter-day Saint and non-Mormon voters cannot be directly detected before 1984 because there were no exit polls. But political science estimates indicate all the winning Democrats had substantial support from Latter-day Saints, and some won majorities.[13]

In its mainstream period, Utah had strong two-party competition because voters did not divide by religion. One political science study found that from 1914 to 1929, Utah was the most competitive two-party state. From 1930 to 1945, Utah ranked twenty-eighth in party competition (Utah was Democratic in those years) and fourth from 1946 to 1963 when the study ended.[14] In the twenty elections from statehood to 1972, Utah elected a Democratic governor ten times and a Republican governor ten times. Republicans controlled twenty

---

11. Fourteen states matched Utah's record. New Mexico, Arizona, Oklahoma, Alaska and Hawaii became states after Utah and therefore had fewer elections to match Utah's seventeen winning votes.

12. Utahns only voted for Woodrow Wilson in his 1916 reelection race. In 1912, Utah voted against Wilson and for Republican president William Howard Taft.

13. Unpublished study by David E. Campbell, John C. Green, and J. Quin Monson, referenced in Campbell, *Seeking the Promised Land*, 80–84.

14. Dawson, "Social Development," 216, measures competitiveness by how close the vote is for governor and the number of legislative seats for each party.

legislatures, while Democrats controlled eighteen and, in three, each party controlled one house.

Utah voters—specifically Latter-day Saints—changed in the mid-1970s and brought the Republicans to continuous power. In the national election of 1976, Americans chose Democrat Jimmy Carter as president and the Democrats held both houses of Congress. But Utah abandoned its tradition of voting mostly for the presidential winner and voted more decisively than any other state for the loser, Republican Gerald Ford. Utah's Democratic senator Frank Moss lost, as did Democratic congressman Allan Howe.[15] Up to this writing, Utah has never again voted for a Democrat for president or US senator. Before 1976, Utah had never been first among states in percentage vote for any presidential candidate. Beginning in 1976 it became the most strongly Republican state through four consecutive presidential election, and Republicans gradually took over and kept almost all major Utah offices.[16]

The shift can be seen in Graph 1. Political scientist Richard C. Fording used votes of state congressional delegations and partisan makeup of legislatures and the governor's office to measure each state's "policy mood."[17] Utah's mood from 1960 to 2010 can be seen compared to the average state's mood. Until 1974, Utah was close to average, but then it turned more conservative. Over the fifty years shown in the graph, Utah had the most conservative mood of any state. In a different measure, a team of political scientists, including some from Brigham Young University, analyzed election

15. Moss lost to Republican Orrin Hatch. Howe, the subject of a sex scandal, lost to Republican Dan Marriott. Representative Gunn McKay was Utah's only remaining Democrat, and he lost in 1980.

16. All governors since 1984 and all senators since 1980 have been Republican. Five Democrats have served in Congress since 1976: Wayne Owens, 1987–93; Bill Orton, 1991–97; Karen Shepherd, 1993–95; Jim Matheson, 2001–2015; and Ben McAdams, elected in 2018 and currently serving. Two Democrats served as Attorney General: Paul Van Dam, 1989–93, and Jan Graham, 1993–2001.

17. Fording drew from models pioneered by William D. Berry, "Measuring Citizen and Government Ideology," 329–32, and applied it to the states in data reproduced on his website, "State Ideology Data," rcfording.wordpress.com.

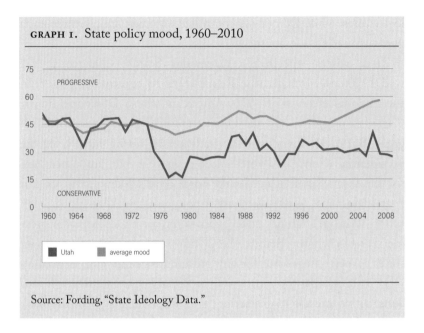

GRAPH I. State policy mood, 1960–2010

Source: Fording, "State Ideology Data."

returns geographically to estimate Latter-day Saint vote percentages back to statehood and found that members of the Church became steadily more Republican after World War II. Though the BYU researchers saw the change developing more gradually than shown on the policy-mood graph, they agreed that in the 1970s Latter-day Saint voters changed more and changed Utah politics.[18]

Church leaders did not direct the change in Latter-day Saint voting. Latter-day Saints follow their leaders, and their leaders are mostly Republicans. But Church leaders have not advocated Republicanism or any partisan positions. Surveys show that LDS say they hear less political talk from their pulpits than members of any other denomination.[19] In the twentieth century, Church leaders did sometimes tell their followers how to vote. In 1912,

18. Campbell, *Promised Land*, 85, fig. 4.4, showing the shift in the 1970s.
19. Campbell and Monson, "Dry Kindling." The two studies of what people hear in church are the "Faith Matters Survey," in Putnam and Campbell; *American Grace*, 424, 440, and "Peculiar People Survey," discussed in Campbell, *Seeking the Promised Land*, 98–100.

President Joseph F. Smith told members they should vote for Republican William Howard Taft, and Taft carried Utah. In 1936 the Church-owned *Deseret News* endorsed Republican Alf Landon in a front-page editorial, clear counsel from leadership. But Utah went 60 percent for Roosevelt. The last overt endorsement was in 1960 when Church president David O. McKay told Republican candidate Richard Nixon, "We hope you win" (Utah voted for Nixon that year).[20] But nowadays Church leaders urge people to vote, but are quick to say they are not endorsing any politician or party.[21]

Latter-day Saints became Republican because they opposed the American sexual revolution (discussed in the next four chapters). Beginning after World War II, Americans changed their views on sex and families, while Latter-day Saints continued to believe in the old morality, which said that sex should be confined to marriage, and that society should favor traditional families. Federal courts followed American sexual and family change and struck down state laws that had aimed to enforce traditional morality. Latter-day Saints disagreed with many of those changes, became Republican as the Republican Party remained more attached to old morality, and became more opposed to federal power, which was seen as supporting the new morality.[22]

The Latter-day Saint change was part of a national religious realignment. Provoked, in part, by the increase in pornography, the women's rights movement, sexual freedom, and especially abortion, strongly religious people became more politically conservative. By 2014 political scientist Patrick Fisher could say that "the more often one worships, the more likely one is to vote Republican."

---

20. Joseph F. Smith, "Coming Election," *Improvement Era*, Oct. 1912; "The Constitution," *Deseret News*, Oct. 31, 1936; Cannon, "Mormons and New Deal," 10–11; James B. Allen, "American Presidency and Mormons," *Ensign*, Oct. 1972. In the 1964 election, the Church seemed to endorse Republican Barry Goldwater, although without explicitly naming him (Williams, "Separation of Church and State," 43n36).

21. See "Political Participation," www.mormonnewsroom.org, for a letter read to all US wards, posted Oct. 5, 2016. A similar letter is read every election year.

22. Campbell and Monson, "Dry Kindling," 14.

"We hope you win," LDS President David O. McKay told Republican candidate Richard M. Nixon in 1960. Nixon lost to John F. Kennedy, but Utahns voted for the Republican, shown here with McKay in 1966. *Salt Lake Tribune Negative Collection, Utah Division of State History*

A Pew Foundation survey found Utah was the most church-going state, consistent with Utah's Republicanism.[23] Most notable in this change of political loyalties, evangelical Christians became Republicans. Until the mid-1970s, evangelicals had been less politically active, and they became strongly Republican at the same time Latter-day Saints did, and for similar reasons.[24] The effects of the Latter-day Saint change were concentrated in Utah. Across America evangelicals and Latter-day Saints together make up only

23. Fisher, *Demographic Gaps*, 59. My discussion largely follows Fisher's conclusions. For the survey, see Michael Lipka and Benjamin Wormald, "How Religious Is Your State?" *Pew Research Center*, Feb. 29, 2016, www.pewresearch.org.

24. Brooks, "Religious Influence," 195; Brint and Abrutyn, "Who's Right about the Right?" 3335n8; Olson and Green, "Religion Gap," 456–57.

UTAH POLITICS

about 25 percent of the electorate, while in Utah Latter-day Saint voters constitute almost two-thirds of all voters.[25] The religious realignment, which altered American politics generally, transformed Utah politics and continues to determine Utah's voter preferences and election outcomes.

Utah politics have always been influenced by whether Latter-day Saints agreed or disagreed with national views on sex and families. In Utah Territory, Americans and Latter-day Saints disagreed over polygamy. In their respective times, both polygamy and the contemporary disagreement over family morality affected Utah politics. Both disagreements put Latter-day Saints at odds with the federal government, and both divided Latter-day Saints from non-Mormons within the state. In both periods Utah had a mostly Latter-day Saint political party and a mostly non-Mormon party. Latter-day Saints won most elections and made most decisions, except the federal government frequently invoked its supremacy and overruled Utah majorities. But between those two periods of disagreement came eighty years when Latter-day Saints and Americans agreed on family morality. After Latter-day Saints gave up polygamy, both they and their fellow Americans believed in limiting sex to marriage and favoring traditional families. Utah then voted with the national majorities, welcomed federal programs, and was friendly toward Washington, DC. Latter-day Saints and non-Mormons shared political parties and had two-party competition.[26] Utah's political history divides into the territory, 1850–96; mainstream, from statehood in 1896 to 1976; and a Republican ascendancy after 1976. The

---

25. Latter-day Saints made up 66.4 percent of the CSED sample in presidential elections from 1984 to 2012, but only 58.5 percent of the sample in 2016 when Latter-day Saints did not like the choice of candidates.

26. Campbell et al., "Politically Peculiar People," shows Mormons moving into and out of the American mainstream, although they differ with me on exactly when and why. Later chapters discuss Utah friendliness to Washington's programs, including the New Deal, and especially highways, reclamation, and defense projects. See Williams, "Separation of Church and State," 30–54.

politics of each period depended on whether Latter-day Saints and Americans agreed about sex and families.

Graph 2 shows the partisan division of Utah's House of Representatives since statehood. On the left side, the party that won Utah's presidential vote is indicated by a dark (Republican) or lightly shaded (Democratic) R and D. On the right, the party that won the governorship is indicated in the same way. A marker shows 1976 when the Republican ascendancy began. Above the marker is Utah's mainstream period, and below is the era of Republican dominance. The graph shows the volatility of Utah politics in early statehood. Voters awarded big majorities now to one party, then suddenly to the other. With support from Church leadership and a national tariff policy favorable to the state, Republicans were Utah's default majority. Nonetheless, Democrats came to power three times (labeled 1, 2, and 3 on the graph) before World War II. Each of those local wins happened in a presidential election, when Utah voters followed a presidential candidate advocating national issues. In 1896, Utahns supported Democrat William Jennings Bryan and silver coinage. In 1916, Democrats won again with Woodrow Wilson, who "kept us out of war." In 1932, Utahns followed Franklin D. Roosevelt. Democrats kept power during the Depression, New Deal, and World War II. (These shifts are discussed in chapters 5 and 7.) After World War II, until 1976, victories were less complete, majorities less decisive, and power more divided. But Utahns continued to vote in the American mainstream, choosing six of seven winning presidential candidates from 1948 to 1972. And state political power often flowed from the effects of national elections.[27] (Number 4 on the graph shows 1964, when Democrat Lyndon Baines Johnson won the presidency and Democrat Cal Rampton became governor with a Democratic

---

27. Utahns sometimes split tickets. Democrat George Dern was elected governor in 1924, although the state voted Republican. J. Bracken Lee became governor in 1948, though Utah went Democratic. Democrat Cal Rampton won re-election in 1968, despite Utah going Republican, and Democrat Scott Matheson won two terms early in Utah's Republican ascendancy.

GRAPH 2. Utah House majorities, 1896–2016

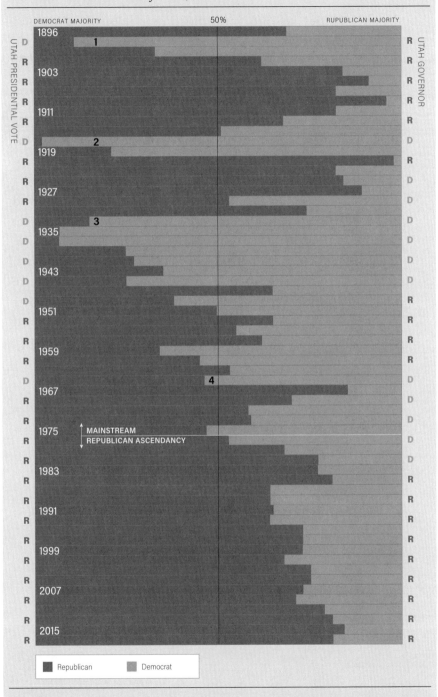

Note: The trend in political composition of the Utah Senate almost exactly parallels that of the Utah House of Representatives. The arrows indicate when Utah's voting habits turned solidly Republican (minor parties are counted with Democrats).

legislature.) But in 1976, Utah broke its connection to national politics, swung Republican, and never returned. In the mainstream period, national victories usually brought state victories. Republican presidential victories brought Republican state government to Utah, while Democratic presidents Wilson, Roosevelt, Truman, and Johnson won Utah victories and brought Democratic state government with them. But after the Republican ascendancy, Presidents Carter, Clinton, and Obama were unable to lead Utah in a Democratic direction, and seemed rather to provoke reaction and increased Republican power. Before 1976 the longest one political party had power in Utah government was during the Democratic control that lasted from 1932 to 1946. As of this writing, Republicans have won the governor's chair and both houses of the legislature for 34 years, the longest current streak of one-party control of any state, and there is no end in sight.[28] Since statehood, Utah politics moved from being a part of American politics to being a separate, religiously determined politics, largely unresponsive to national trends.

---

28. Kennedy Elliott and Dan Balz, "Party Control by State," *Washington Post*, Dec. 28, 2013.

3

PUBLIC MORALITY

Latter-day Saints and non-Mormons act out religious differences in arguments over public morality. Latter-day Saints believe sex should be limited to marriage and public policy should favor traditional families, and they hold traditional beliefs on many other moral questions. Though once the dominant morality of the West, that old morality has lost its grip in most places and now rouses laughter. As this book is written, *The Book of Mormon*, a musical making fun of Latter-day Saints, fills theaters in both Broadway and London, while *Saturday's Voyeur*, another musical that mocks Latter-day Saints, has just completed its fortieth season in Salt Lake City. Latter-day Saint adherence to the old morality supplies jokes for both shows. Offstage, however, moral differences between Latter-day Saints and non-Mormons provoke continuous quarrels over how people ought to live and what, if anything, government should do about it. Latter-day Saints quarreled with neighbors over polygamy before they came west, and the disputes resumed as soon as gentiles arrived in the territory. Utahns have argued over polygamy, liquor, tobacco, gambling, Sunday closing, school prayer, pornography, birth control for teens, abortion, the Equal Rights Amendment, cable TV censorship, gay marriage, and gay rights. Beginning with abortion in the 1970s, the issues changed from internal Utah disputes to decisions by federal courts with which Latter-day Saints ineffectually disagreed. New rights, enforced by federal judges dismantled the legal support for the old morality. In reaction, Latter-day Saints left the American political mainstream, and Utah politics became divided once again by religion.

POLYGAMY

Officially the Church of Jesus Christ of Latter-day Saints stopped performing polygamous marriages in 1890. Nonetheless, many men continued to live with their plural wives, some new marriages were performed, and a few Church leaders themselves secretly took additional wives. Gentiles suspected the violations and said Church leaders had promised to end polygamy as a condition of statehood, then broke faith.[1] When Utahns elected polygamous Church leader B. H. Roberts to Congress in 1898, a national outcry persuaded the House of Representatives to refuse him a seat. When the Utah Legislature elected apostle Reed Smoot to the US Senate in 1903, gentiles said the choice violated separation of church and state and accused Smoot of polygamy. A four-year senate investigation found Smoot had only one wife and the senate let him keep his seat. But Church officials, including President Joseph F. Smith, testified before the investigating senate committee and were embarrassed by disclosures of ongoing polygamy.[2] Only gradually, as the last polygamous generation died, did plural marriage die as a political issue.

A century later federal judge Clark Waddoups ruled in 2013 that Utah's criminal laws against polygamy were unconstitutional. The Tenth Circuit Court of Appeals overruled Waddoups saying anti-polygamy laws were not properly an issue before him,[3] so he could not rule them unconstitutional. But the appeals court seemed

1. Quinn, "LDS Church Authority," 13–15, 103–05; Hardy, "That 'Same Old Question,'" 221–22; Baskin, *Reminiscences of Early Utah*, 234–35.

2. Bitton, "B. H. Roberts Case," 46; Flake, *Politics of American Religious Identity*, 75–76; Jorgensen and Hardy, "Taylor–Cowley Affair," 22.

3. *Brown v. Buhman*, 947 F. Supp. 2d 1170 (D. Utah 2013); *Brown v. Buhman*, 822 F. 3d 1151 (10th Cir. 2016); cert. denied, 137 S. Ct. 828 (2017).

to indicate that if Utah attempted to enforce criminal laws against polygamy, they might be struck down.

LIQUOR

Liquor provoked Utah's longest-lasting moral controversy and set patterns that affected other disputes. The liquor battle had three phases: (1) from 1895 to 1917 Utahns argued over Prohibition, (2) then until 1933 over repeal of Prohibition, (3) and after 1933 over liquor regulation. Prohibition was urged on Utah's constitutional convention by Protestant clergy and some Latter-day Saints. But both Latter-day Saint and non-Mormon delegates rejected a constitutional ban.[4] Anti-alcohol forces gained strength, however, and their issue dominated the 1909, 1911, 1915, and 1917 legislative sessions. Unlike other moral controversies, Prohibition crossed religious lines. Protestants first advocated Prohibition, and Latter-day Saints joined later as their Church strengthened its teachings against alcohol and tobacco. Even so, for a time Latter-day Saint machine politics militated against Prohibition. The Utah machine, was called the "Federal Bunch" and was led by senator–apostle Reed Smoot. The Federal Bunch gave federal jobs to Republican Party workers who kept working for the party as they worked for the government. In addition, Church president Joseph F. Smith secretly gave Church funds to the Federal Bunch to support its newspaper.[5] Smoot believed Republicans needed non-Mormon votes to win, but non-Mormons would desert the party if it backed Prohibition, so he spoke for temperance: that is, for individual decisions not to drink, but against Prohibition, a general law prohibiting liquor. In 1904, Smoot quietly ordered Utah Governor John C. Cutler not to seek a second term partly

---

4. White, *Charter for Statehood*, 80–82.
5. Nelson, "Utah Goes Dry," 341; Alexander, "Word of Wisdom," 80; Shipps, "Utah Comes of Age," 103–04; Merrill, *Reed Smoot*, 194. Stauffer, "Utah Politics," 104–06, which discusses the Smoot political machine; Callister, "Edward Henry Callister," 69, showing church money subsidizing the *Intermountain Republican* newspaper.

because of his support for Prohibition. Cutler did as he was told, and Smoot picked federal marshal William Spry as the Republican nominee to replace him.[6]

Although Smoot commanded governors, he could not persuade his apostolic brethren. The Church taught abstinence and the apostles fought the evils of drink. Apostle Heber J. Grant introduced a Prohibition resolution at the 1908 general conference and received a supporting show of hands from the congregation. At the next legislature, Grant and other Church leaders urged Prohibition, and Federal Bunch lobbyists—who were also Latter-day Saints—fought it. Caught in the middle, President Joseph F. Smith declared the Church neutral and left for vacation in Hawaii. Federal Bunch governor William Spry vetoed the weak compromise legislators passed. When the legislature met again in 1911, Latter-day Saints again led both sides of the Prohibition fight. This time Governor Spry signed a bill giving each local government power to choose wet or dry. Most small towns prohibited liquor, but in the big cities people continued to drink. In the 1916 election, Utah Democrats routed Republicans from office by promising prohibition. The new Democratic legislature passed a "bone dry" bill, and for good measure legislators proposed a constitutional amendment to outlaw liquor, which was ratified by a vote of the people.[7]

Church leaders saw public disagreement among apostles did not serve Latter-day Saint interests and changed their practice. After Reed Smoot, no apostle has run for elective office.[8] Church policy

---

6. John C. Cutler to Reed Smoot, Nov. 30, 1908, cited in Shipps, "Utah Comes of Age," 98; Roper and Arrington, *William Spry*, 2, 70–71.

7. Aydelotte, "Political Thought," 34, 50; Dyer, "Adoption of Prohibition," 21, 38–39. See also Kenneth G. Stauffer, "Utah Elections," 100–10; Peterson and Cannon, *Awkward State of Utah*, 35–49. Democrats benefited from the popularity of President Woodrow Wilson, who "kept us out of war."

8. Apostle Ezra Taft Benson was appointed US Secretary of Agriculture by President Dwight D. Eisenhower. When he returned from Washington, he argued with other apostles over politics. Quinn, *Extensions of Power*, 66–115; Campbell and Monson, "Following the Leader?" 617.

said leaders would speak in politics only on "moral issues," where they believed they had a special responsibility. After Prohibition, Church leaders spoke on moral issues with one voice.

Like most of America, Utah found no peace in Prohibition. Bootleggers flourished. State Democratic and Republican platforms deplored the flouted liquor law and blamed each other. In the poverty of the Depression, Utahns were ready to believe President Franklin D. Roosevelt's promise that a repeal of Prohibition would help restore prosperity. Over Church objection, legislators ordered the election of delegates to a convention to decide whether Utah would ratify the Twenty-First Amendment to the US Constitution repealing Prohibition. Though Church leaders campaigned against repeal, the wets won by 60 percent, and Utah helped bring back liquor. Within two years, the state prohibition law and constitutional amendment also fell.[9]

Liquor continued to rouse Utah voters. In 1944, Democratic Governor Herbert Maw sought a second term, and was opposed by Republican J. Bracken Lee, who had been mayor of the non-Mormon coal-mining town of Price. He had allowed drinking, gambling, and prostitution. Just before the election, a pamphlet entitled *Morals and the Mayor* described violations of state law in Price and implied that Lee might not enforce state laws. Maw won by less than one percent. Lee's backers blamed the pamphlet. When Maw ran for a third term in 1948, Lee opposed him again, this time going on the offensive. He pointed to a state liquor enforcement officer who was convicted of taking a bribe and charged that the state liquor administration was corrupt, and Maw was part of the corruption. "The major issue of the current campaign is liquor," the *New York Times* reported from Utah. Lee was the only Republican who won statewide that year. One of his first acts was to disband

---

9. Peterson and Cannon, *Awkward State of Utah*, 255–57; Papanikolas, "Bootlegging in Zion," 274, 288; Skyles, "Repeal of Prohibition," 1–2.

the state liquor enforcement agency and leave enforcement to local government, thereby cutting state costs, he said.[10]

Legislators responded to repeal with strict regulations. Only weak beer with a legally limited alcohol content could be sold in stores or taverns. To buy wine or liquor, an individual had to obtain a personal state liquor license, go to a state-owned liquor store, fill out a form, and wait while a clerk fetched a bottle from the storeroom. To imbibe in a bar or restaurant, a drinker had to bring his own bottle, out of sight in a brown paper bag, order a mixer, and pour his own drink. Drinkers repeatedly asked legislators to mitigate the law's inconvenience, but with small success. In the legislature in 1937, 1947, 1955, 1959, and 1965 liquor reforms that were introduced were vigorously debated and voted down. The *Wall Street Journal* described the pattern in a story on the 1965 mini-bottle bill: "At first the Church stood silent as the so-called 'mini-bill' gathered momentum and public support. Then the Church-owned *Deseret News* opened fire editorially, and the bill died a quick death."[11]

Utahns found a pattern for moral issues in liquor controversies as Church leaders met privately, adopted a position, and presented a unanimous front. Their voice usually decided the question in the legislature. Because liquor was a moral issue, it was less subject to legislative give and take. Avoiding political maneuvers and deals was, after all, part of the reason Church leaders made special provision for moral issues. Some non-Mormons believed liquor policy made by Church leaders was a façade for Church control, as in early territorial Utah. "The LDS Church and its people possess many fine and admirable qualities, but non-Mormons are blinded to these by their anger over the political, economic and social

---

10. Lythgoe, *Let 'Em Holler*, 33–50; "The Political Picture," *New York Times*, Oct. 31, 1948; Allen, *Still the Right Place*, 56–68. See also Russell, *J. Bracken Lee*, 33–35.

11. O. N. Malmquist, "Utah Liquor Law History," *Salt Lake Tribune*, Jan. 9, 1968; "Utah and the Mormons," *Wall Street Journal*, Aug. 10, 1965.

control exercised by the Church in Utah," one writer to the *Salt Lake Tribune* said.[12]

Drinkers gathered enough signatures on petitions to force a vote of the people in 1968 on "liquor by the drink" to allow bars, hotels, and clubs to sell drinks as they did in other states. Both sides described the fight as bitter. Memory of the repeal of Prohibition gave drinkers hope that in the secrecy of the voting booth, people would again defy Church leaders as they had in 1933 and vote for freer alcohol. Church leaders offered peace to gentiles, saying that they had come to understand how angry the non-Mormons were, and if Utah rejected the referendum the Church would agree to gradual changes in the liquor laws. Non-Mormons disbelieved the offer and predicted that if the referendum failed, liquor-law reform would languish for decades. In the election, voters defeated the referendum by 65-to-35 percent.[13]

Despite skepticism by non-Mormons, Church leaders did as they said. In their next session, legislators passed a "mini-bottle bill" resembling the one the Church had opposed before the referendum. A new pattern formed in the legislature. Liquor proposals were sent to Church lawyers, who sometimes suggested changes. If Church leaders found a bill acceptable, they would publicly state that the Church took no position, and the bill would likely pass.[14] Utah liquor law gradually became freer in small steps over many years.

In 2009, Governor Jon Huntsman held a bill-signing ceremony in the New Yorker Club in Salt Lake City before a crowd who filled every chair and bar stool and stood in the aisles. The

---

12. Joseph L. Taylor, Public Forum, *Salt Lake Tribune*, June 7, 1968.

13. Gordon B. Hinckley, "Liquor by the Drink," *Improvement Era*, Oct. 1968, 4–7; O. N. Malmquist, "Liquor Proposal's Tough," *Salt Lake Tribune*, May 29, 1968; Emenhiser, "1968 Election in Utah," 532.

14. For instance, Charles Seldin, "Senate, Church," Dan Bates, "LDS Stand to Determine New Liquor Bill's Course," Dave Jonsson, "Liquor Bill Receives Big Boost," *Salt Lake Tribune*, Jan. 29, 1985; Nov. 18, 21, 1987.

New Yorker was one of the "private clubs" the state allowed to sell alcoholic drinks, similar to a bar in most other states. Drinkers who did not belong to the club had to fill out a form and pay $4 for a temporary membership. Television comedian Jay Leno said, "Guy walks into a bar in Utah ... and walks back out." The BBC called Utah laws "weird," the *Washington Times* said they were "arcane," and the *New York Times* labeled them "old world." The law Huntsman signed allowed bars, restaurants, and hotels to serve alcoholic drinks. It resembled the "liquor-by-the-drink" proposal the Church opposed forty-four years before. Latter-day Saint lobbyists had negotiated with sponsors of the new law and won provisions to "reduce underage drinking, over consumption, and drunk driving." Still, the Church surprised people by consenting to changes it had earlier opposed. "This is an important new day in our state," Governor Huntsman said. Spectators applauded (but raised no toasts).[15] Even after the new law, Utah remained restrictive, just less so. It still has liquor controversies, but they no longer drive state politics.

TOBACCO

In 1919 when hopes for Prohibition were fresh, Church leaders wanted to prohibit tobacco as well as alcohol. "This should not mean undue publicity," they cautioned, counseling followers to seize the advantage of surprise. Articles appeared in Church publications attacking smoking, sermons denounced cigarettes, but without mention of any contemplated legislation. Church members quietly formed committees and drafted a bill, and stake presidents privately spoke with legislators to solicit their support. Early in the 1921 legislature, the Church struck. The Sunday schools had gathered 127,000 signatures calling for cigarette prohibition. A full-page ad

---

15. Lee Benson, "'Arcane' Liquor Laws," Lisa Riley Roche, "Huntsman Signs Bill," *Deseret News*, Apr. 1, Mar. 31, 2009; Robert Gehrke and Dawn House, "Huntsman Signs Landmark Liquor Bill," Gehrke, "Did New LDS Leaders Quietly Back Alcohol Reform?" *Salt Lake Tribune*, Mar. 30, Apr. 1, 2009.

in the *Deseret News*, paid for by the Young Men's and Young Women's Mutual Improvement Associations, said a smoker is "a physical, mental and moral defective." Urged on by Latter-day Saints, lawmakers agreed to prohibit the sale and advertising of tobacco and smoking in public places, one of fourteen states to do so. At first, neither smokers nor police paid any attention. Then Church president Heber J. Grant said Latter-day Saints should vote for officials who enforced the law, and suddenly officials saw the need to act. One evening at the Vienna Café, the manager of the *Salt Lake Tribune*, Utah's Republican National Committeeman, and the director of the American Smelting and Refining Company were smoking cigars after dinner. Police came into the cafe, arrested them, and marched them to the police station. They were booked into jail and then released on a promise to appear in court. "Utah is without the pale of the United States, and itself a stench in the nostrils of the free people of America," the *Salt Lake Tribune* editorialized. The Salt Lake Chamber of Commerce held a meeting in the Orpheum Theater packed with angry smokers and businessmen who feared the effect on the tourist trade and the state's national reputation if this continued. In the next legislative session, the law was quietly changed, so tobacco was allowed, but taxed.[16]

HORSE RACING

In Utah picking fast horses is a skill. The state constitution in article 6, section 28, bans gambling on games of chance "under any pretense or for any purpose." However, some of the drafters of the constitution wanted to continue betting on horses, so they held a colloquy, a formal conversation on the record to show their intent. "Will this prohibit horse racing? I am very fond of horse racing. I never bet much on it, but I am fond of it," asked one delegate. "No

16. Smith, "Cigarette Prohibition," 41; Peterson and Cannon, *Awkward State of Utah*, 257–59. The smokers were Ambrose N. McKay (1868–1924), Ernest Bamberger (1877–1958), and Edgar L. Newhouse Jr. (1890–1975).

it will not," said the sponsor of the language.[17] Legislators neverthe-less banned such bets in 1913 because, they said, betting attracted criminals. In 1925 they restored wagers by establishing a racing commission to oversee pari-mutuel betting, to keep the sport hon-est.[18] When the new betting law was challenged, the Utah Supreme Court cited the colloquy and ruled that betting on horses was a con-stitutionally protected exercise of skill. Even so, lawmakers banned it again in 1927, amid (unproven) charges of bribery.

Three decades later in 1958, Utah horsemen gathered enough signatures to force a vote of the people on reviving pari-mutuel bet-ting. Opponents scrutinized the signatures and charged that a good many of them were forgeries or duplications—and the *Deseret News* implied that this was just what one might expect from people who bet on horses. Utah's Supreme Court allowed the referendum to go forward, but it went down in defeat by more than 60 percent of the vote.[19] The horsemen persisted and tried six times to persuade the legislature to reinstate betting without success. In 1992 racing fans gathered enough signatures again to force another vote of the peo-ple on pari-mutuel betting. Latter-day Saint leaders declared betting a "moral evil." Closed-door meetings of local Church leaders were held to rally them against the pari-mutuel plan.[20] In public, betting opponents warned that if Utah allowed pari-mutuel wagers, Native Americans could open casinos on reservations, an insinuation the Ute Tribe found "offensive and degrading."[21] When it came time to

---

17. *Official Report of the Proceedings and Debates*, 1: 938.

18. See Westergren, "Utah's Gamble," 4–21, for horse betting up to 1928; Peterson and Cannon, *Awkward State of Utah*, 252.

19. *Utah State Fair Association v. Green*, 68 Utah 251, 249 P. 1016 (1926); *Cope v. Toronto*, 8 Utah 2d 255, 332 P. 2d 977 (1958); Peterson and Cannon, *Awkward State of Utah*, 252. See Edwin O. Haroldsen articles in the *Deseret News*, Oct. 15, 21, Nov. 4, 1958, and *DN* editorial, Oct. 15, 1958.

20. Amy Donaldson, "Supporters Will Change Tactics," Bob Bernick Jr., "LDS Leaders Attack Pari-Mutuel Betting," *Deseret News*, Dec. 1, 1991, June 1, 1992.

21. "Backers Say Pari-mutuel Foes Promote Phony Issues," Marjorie Cortez, "Pari-Mutuel Foes Surge Past Backers," *Deseret News*, Apr. 2, Oct. 28, 1992.

TABLE I. Horseracing by religion

	Protestant	Catholic	LDS	other	none	total
percent pro-betting	70	83	21	77	82	37
percent anti-betting	30	17	79	23	18	63
number of respondents	426	426	4,263	329	637	6,081

Source: BYU CSED exit poll, 1992

vote, Utahns defeated betting by 63 percent. Table 1 shows the results of an exit poll. Members of every religion except the Church of Jesus Christ of Latter-day Saints favored betting by large majorities.

SUNDAY CLOSING

In 1943, Utah's Supreme Court struck down an 1898 law requiring some businesses to close on Sunday.[22] Gradually Church leaders came to see that unless people were restrained by law, competition would force stores to stay open on Sundays, even when owners and workers would rather close. That would burden families, they said, and joined with stores that already closed on the sabbath to ask for a new Sunday-closing law. Utah's legislature accommodated the request in 1953, but Governor J. Bracken Lee believed the bill was unfair to small businesses and religious minorities. He took a call from J. Reuben Clark, a counselor in the Latter-day Saint First Presidency, urging him to sign the bill. Lee was a non-Mormon, but as a Utah politician he wanted the Church's friendship. Nonetheless,

---

22. *Broadbent v. Gibson et al.*, 105 Utah 53, 140 P. 2d 939 (1943). The decision overturned *State v. Sopher*, 25 Utah 318, 71 P. 482 (1903), and ruled for Broadbent's fruit market in Carbon County that had to close while gas stations that stayed open sold fruit. The court also ruled against Sunday closings in *Gronlund v. Salt Lake City*, 113 Utah 284, 194 P. 2d 464 (1948).

he vetoed the bill, inciting statewide furor. The *Deseret News* called for the legislature to override the veto. By contrast, the *Salt Lake Tribune* praised Lee and editorialized against Sunday-closing laws. The veto survived by one vote in the senate. In 1959, Utah lawmakers passed another Sunday-closing law that went to Lee's successor, Governor George Dewey Clyde. A devout Latter-day Saint, Clyde nevertheless vetoed the legislation for the same reasons Lee cited. Moreover, he taunted that the bill would "keep open beer taverns while shutting groceries."[23]

The controversy drew national attention. Locally the *Deseret News* called it "a bitter disappointment to the people." Legislators passed yet another bill in 1967 and sent it to Governor Calvin L. Rampton. Before vetoing it, he received more than 25,000 letters or phone calls. One comment from "old-time barber" Ralph K. Peterson read: "Utah ain't like the rest of the nation because of the LDS Church. The non-Mormons are always on guard because they think the church is trying to make its religion law. It's because of this division that we got some funny laws." In 1970 lawmakers tried again, and this time Rampton let the bill become law without his signature. But Utah's Supreme Court said the law was so vague, and the exceptions so many, that businessmen could not tell who could stay open, or what could be sold, and again declared a Sunday-closing law unconstitutional, a final defeat for the issue.[24]

Note that over decades, the Utah Supreme Court struck down three Sunday-closing laws but never referred to the state's constitutional provisions banning the establishment of religion or domination of the state by any church. To the court, Sunday-closing seemed a due-process and equal-protection issue, rather than a

---

23. Quinn, *Extensions of Power*, 362; Clark, *Diaries of J. Reuben Clark*, 198 (Jan. 30, 1953); Lythgoe, *Let 'Em Holler*, 98–99; *Salt Lake Tribune* editorial, Feb. 12, 1963.

24. "One Mormon's Revolt," *Time*, Mar. 2, 1959; Dave Jonsson, "Rampton Vetoes Controversial Sunday Closing," *Salt Lake Tribune*, Mar. 17, 1967; Bill Marling, "The War for the Holy Day," *Daily Utah Chronicle*, Mar. 2, 1967; Rampton, *As I Recall*, 175–76; *Skaggs Drug Centers Inc. v. Raedel E. Ashley*, 26 Utah 2d 38, 484 P.2d 723 (1971).

The police confiscating a poker table in 1956 from a women's organization called the Variety Club, which sponsored luncheon speakers and fund-raisers featuring bingo and canasta. *Salt Lake Tribune Negative Collection*

religious matter. Though they were defeated politically, Church leaders were proven right in their fears. In the absence of legal restraint, stores opened on Sunday and shoppers flocked to them. A *Deseret News* survey in 1953 showed 16 percent of the state's grocery stores were open on Sundays. A 2005 survey found 84 percent of all types of retail establishments stayed open and 87 percent of Utahns shopped on Sundays, at least occasionally.[25]

SCHOOL PRAYER

When the United States Supreme Court ruled in 1962 that a New York school prayer violated the First Amendment, Utah barely

---

25. Lee Davidson, "Open Sunday?" *Deseret News,* Jan. 23, 2005.

noticed. "The specific decision as such should not do religion any great harm," the *Deseret News* editorialized. The New York State Board of Regents had written the prayer in question as part of school policy. In Utah there was no written prayer for public schools, and no prayer policy. Many Utah schools had prayers, but they received scant official attention. The Salt Lake City School District had "an implied policy discouraging prayer in the classroom." In the Granite School District, prayers were "permitted but not required." Jordan District left the decision to principals and teachers, so some schools had morning prayer, just "like the legislature," the superintendent explained. Some school administrators may have quietly adjusted prayer policies. If so, hardly anyone noticed. A clip file at the *Deseret News* covered school-prayer demonstrations across the country for twenty-five years, but showed none in Utah.[26]

Then in 1989 a Rhode Island man sued over prayer at his daughter's middle-school graduation. Word of that case incited Utahns to a flurry of litigation. The Utah chapter of the American Civil Liberties Union sued both Alpine and Granite school districts to stop prayers at graduation. The Society of Separationists sued Jordan District to stop Christian prayer and sued Utah's attorney general, the state school superintendent, and Alpine District officials. The Washington District School Board voted to end graduation prayers, prompting three citizens to sue for the right to pray.[27] Some districts settled, but no Utah suit for or against prayer prevailed in court.

Though prayers were not said in classes, prayer pervaded Utah schools. In the Cache School District, a student pointed to prayers by

---

26. *Engel v. Vitale*, 370 U.S. 421. "Utahns Show Concern," "One Nation under God," *Deseret News*, June 26, 28, 1962; "S. L. Reaction," "Not against Prayer" editorial, *Salt Lake Tribune*, June 26, 28, 1962.

27. *Weisman v. Lee*, 728 F. Supp. 68 (D. RI 1990); *Albright v. Board of Educ. of Granite School Dist.*, 765 F. Supp., 682 (D. Utah 1991); *Society of Separationists v. Taggart*, 862 P. 2d 1339 (Utah 1993); Sillitoe, *Friendly Fire*, 108–15; Twila Van Leer, "Jordan District Bans Graduation Prayer," Marianne Funk, "Suit against Van Dam," Jim Rayburn, "Alpine District Faces Suit," AP, "Three Seek to Protect School Prayer," *Deseret News*, Sept. 27, 1989, June 5, 1993, Oct. 2, 27, 1991.

athletic teams, honor societies, choirs, and bands. which the school board members said they had not been aware of. News reports found prayers at pep rallies and cast parties. "We know it's going on, and they need to cut it out immediately," said Michelle Parish–Pixler of the American Civil Liberties Union.[28]

The Supreme Court ruled against the Rhode Island graduation prayer, and with that, Utah schools complied.[29] Despite the Jordan School District's ban, student body president Josh Peterson prayed at the Bingham High School graduation in 1991 and the crowd stood and clapped. The school withheld his diploma, briefly. "They told me not to say a prayer, but that's a crock," Peterson said. Outlaw prayers drew applause at three Davis School District graduations in 1993.[30] But defiance did not last. Students soon subsided into silence.

At first, Utahns had remained placid after the banning of school prayer by the Supreme Court. By contrast, twenty-seven years later Supreme Court consideration of graduation prayer provoked half a dozen Utah lawsuits and public uproar. The 1962 prayer decision seemed like an isolated action. By 1989 all Americans, Utahns included, could see federal courts had seized control of moral and religious issues, and would impose national rights, often over Utah disagreement. Federal court intervention meant another issue would be decided. Non-Mormons in Utah rallied at the opportunity for victory. Latter-day Saints rallied in defense. But the controversy soon subsided. Latter-day Saints complained, a few schoolboys broke the rules in protest, and then things quieted down. Prayer did not provoke the enduring conflict of later court decisions that

---

28. AP, "Cache Board Adopts Policy," Sheila Sanchez, "ACLU Seeks Prayer Ban," *Deseret News*, Aug. 13, May 31, 1990; "News: Graduation Prayers Ignite Church/School Debate," *Sunstone*, Oct. 1990.

29. *Lee v. Weisman*, 505 U.S. 577 (1992).

30. Patty Henetz, "Bingham Student Defies Ban," Twila Van Leer, "Opinion Says All Prayer Illegal," Karl Cates, "Students Defy Ban," *Deseret News*, June 8, 1991, June 3, 6, 1993.

touched religion less directly but offended Latter-day Saint family morality more directly.

TEEN BIRTH CONTROL

When Planned Parenthood tried to open a clinic in Bountiful in 1972, Mayor Morris Swapp said it must be stopped "at all costs" because these clinics gave birth control information and devices to unmarried teenagers without informing their parents. "This will encourage promiscuity and the break-up of families," he predicted. About five hundred citizens packed a city council meeting to encourage the council to deny Planned Parenthood a business license. Planned Parenthood also tried to open a clinic in the neighboring suburb of Clearfield, which sued to bar the clinic and won a restraining order. The state then diverted federal grant money to an alternative birth-control clinic sponsored by Davis County, one that required parental consent before a teen could get birth control. But only five clients came to that clinic in its first three months of operation.[31]

As teen pregnancy rose in America, Congress voted money for birth control. Planned Parenthood Association of Utah won federal grants and opened three clinics serving mostly poor women, about 20 percent teenagers, in Salt Lake County.[32] But when they expanded into the suburbs, conservative groups opposed them, saying parents should help teens decide whether to have sex and use birth control. In a series of legislative controversies and court cases, Utah state and local government took the conservative side. Planned Parenthood went to federal court and judges struck down state laws, so clinics served teens and didn't tell their parents.

Planned Parenthood first tried to overturn state restrictions in state court. The judges said family planning was "not intended to

31. Steve Wayda, "Lawsuit Closes Clinic," "Davis County to Open Its Own Planning Clinic," *Salt Lake Tribune*, Mar. 21, Apr. 27, 1972; "License Denied Planned Parenthood Unit," "Family Planning Used in Davis?" *Deseret News*, Jan. 27, Sept. 5, 1972.

32. Carol Sisco, "Student Founded Utah's Planned Parenthood," *Salt Lake Tribune*, Oct. 6, 1988.

make strumpets or streetwalkers out of minor girls" and ruled for the state. Planned Parenthood went to federal court where Judge David Lewis took note of federal law that said birth control could be provided to sexually active teens who asked for it. He ruled Congress had intended those to be the only conditions, and states could not add other requirements such as parental consent. No judge had said that before, but others followed Lewis nationwide. Parental consent requirements were banned by judicial interpretation of the federal statute.[33]

Unable to impose parental consent, Utah tried to intercept federal grant money going to Planned Parenthood. In 1979 the legislature directed the Utah Department of Health to contract only with public agencies, thereby excluding Planned Parenthood. Utah's Department of Health negotiated with the Reagan administration, promising to serve all teens, including those without parental consent. Reagan officials awarded family-planning money to the state with that promise. In Washington, DC, Planned Parenthood sued and lost. The appeals court pointed to Utah's promise, and said as long as all teens were served, Reagan officials could award the money as they chose. Utah legislators again passed a law in 1980 requiring parental consent for teen birth control. Planned Parenthood sued again, noting that Utah had not kept its promise. The judge agreed, and the Reagan administration then took family-planning funds from the state and awarded them back to Planned Parenthood.[34]

Utah and the Reagan administration tried another tactic. In 1981, Utah lawmakers required anyone who supplied birth control to a minor to notify the parents. "Parents have a right to know what's going on with their children," the bill's sponsor, Kevin Cromar, said. In Washington, DC, the same notification rule was adopted. Planned

---

33. *Doe v. Planned Parenthood Association of Utah*, 29 Utah 2d 510 P. 2d 75 (1973); *T H v. Jones*, 425 F. Supp. 873 (D. Utah 1975); Chitwood, "Publicly Funded Contraceptive Services," 283–86.

34. *Planned Parenthood Association of Utah et al. v. Schweiker*, 700 F. 2d 710 (D.C. Cir. 1983); *Jane Does v. State of Utah Dept. of Health*, 776 F. 2d 253 (10th Cir. 1985).

Parenthood called it a "squeal rule" and challenged it in both Utah and Washington. Both courts struck down the squeal rule.

In the Utah case, a boy called John Doe testified he was having sex and using condoms from Planned Parenthood. But if Planned Parenthood threatened to tell his parents, he would not stop having sex but would just stop using condoms. Federal judges believed him, deciding that parental involvement in birth control decisions might result in unprotected sex. One national survey showed about half of the teens using birth control told their parents, including about two-thirds of girls fifteen and younger. The judges said a fifteen-year-old should have help in making sex and birth-control decisions, but added that "mature and trained adults" at Planned Parenthood could help.[35] Parents might only make things worse.

Near the end of a special legislative session in 1985, Governor Norman Bangerter asked for a bill to require parental consent for all non-emergency medical care for children, including birth control. Lawmakers rushed the measure through during the last two hours of the session. Then doctors raised an alarm, because, for example, a doctor would need consent from a parent suspected of abusing a child before the child could be examined. An embarrassed Governor Bangerter vetoed his own bill the next morning.[36] This was Utah's last attempt to force parents into teenage birth-control decisions.

PORNOGRAPHY

When pornographic movies came to Utah theaters in 1974, police made arrests, but in Salt Lake City juries acquitted the first two defendants. When a third case was brought, deputy attorney general Robert B. Hansen obtained a list of prospective jurors, phoned their

---

35. Joe Costanzo, "House Debate Next," *Deseret News*, Feb. 19, 1983; *Planned Parenthood Association of Utah v. Matheson*, 582 F. Supp. 1001 (D. Utah 1983); *Planned Parenthood Federation of America, Inc. et al. v. Heckler*, 712 F.2d 650 (D.C. Cir. 1983). See also Weed and Olsen, "Effects of Family Planning," cited in Lynn D. Wardle, "Parents Rights v. Minors Rights," *Nebraska Law Review*, 68, no. 1 (1989): 216.

36. Douglas Parker and Dan Bates, "Governor Vetoes Parental Consent," *Salt Lake Tribune*, July 17, 1985.

local Latter-day Saint bishops, and asked whether the candidate jurors were church-going people of reliable morals. Prosecutors used this information to pick a favorable jury. Hansen, who was running for attorney general at the time, boasted on KUTV news of having helped prosecutors, saying that based on their Church leaders' opinions, five jurors favored conviction. Jurors learned of Hansen's inquiries during the trial and told the judge about it. Even though he voiced concern, he allowed the trial to proceed. When defense attorneys appealed the conviction to Utah's supreme court, arguing jurors were improperly influenced, Chief Justice A. H. Ellett wrote, "This is a smart move and a practice of all good lawyers." A smart defense lawyer would have inquired among "pimps, prostitutes [and] homosexuals" to find jurors favorable to pornography.[37] Pleased with Hansen's zeal for decency, Utahns awarded him the highest vote percentage of any candidate who had ever run for Utah attorney general.

After the United States Supreme Court granted constitutional protection to explicit speech and pictures, adult movie houses and magazine stores took over whole commercial districts in many American cities. Utah pornographers found Church and state united against them, with scant protection from the courts. Leaders of the Church of Jesus Christ of Latter-day Saints denounced pornography, produced anti-pornography films and literature, and recruited members to picket adult theaters. The demonstrations were quietly organized by the Church Public Communications Office and local bishops. Latter-day Saint leaders helped organize both Latter-day Saints and non-Mormons into several anti-pornography citizen groups.[38]

Law enforcement showed little regard for legal technicalities in

---

37. Edwin O. Haroldsen, "The Porn Plague," *Mountain West*, Oct. 31, 1978; Rod Decker, "A Tainted Porn Jury?" *Deseret News*, July 2, 1976; *Salt Lake City v. James Piepenburg*, 571 P. 2d 1299 (Utah 1977).

38. "The Porno Plague," *Time*, Apr. 5, 1976; "First Presidency Issues Statement," *LDS Church News*, Oct. 28, 1984; Dave Jonsson, "LDS Leaders Approve of Volunteer[s]," *Salt Lake Tribune*, May 22, 1976; also Leith, "Regulation and Trial of Obscenity."

attacking pornographers. Utah judges, especially the supreme court justices, abandoned normal rules and manners. In writing for the court, Justice Ellett said the opinion of the federal Supreme Court "ought only to be advanced by depraved, mentally deficient, mind-warped queers." When US justices ruled that pornography could be punished only if it lacked socially redeeming content, Ellett said this was "reminiscent of a dog that returns to his vomit looking for some morsel in the filth redeeming to its own taste."[39]

Ten pornography cases came to the Utah Supreme Court from 1975 to 1983, resulting in ten losses for the pornographers. When they claimed First Amendment protection, the justices said the First Amendment did not apply to the state of Utah. Legal scholars worried that the Utah Supreme Court had abandoned the rule of law. In another trial a judge instructed jurors they should find material obscene if it offended community standards for the "average adult or average minor" even though no minor had seen the material. The justices conceded that the instruction was wrong but upheld the conviction anyway.[40]

After years of fighting, one adult theater was bought by the Salt Lake City Redevelopment Agency. Two others closed as part of a plea bargain in a federal income-tax case. In Ogden an adult bookstore closed after its landlord said he had been harassed by the community. Pornography on the internet made adult bookstores and movie theaters obsolete. Utah made an attempt to regulate material available to minors on the internet, but without success.[41] Years later,

---

39. *Salt Lake City v. Piepenburg;* see Ellett, *Redneck Judge.*

40. *State of Utah v. Phillips,* 540 P. 2d 936 (Utah 1975); *Ogden City v. Eagle Books* 586 P. 2d 436 (Utah 1978); *State of Utah v. International Amusements,* 565 P. 2d 1112 (Utah 1977). The ten cases, besides those already cited, included *West Gallery Corporation v. Salt Lake City* 586 P2d 436; *State v. Amicone,* 689 P2d 436; *State v. Haig* 578 P 2d 837; *State v. Peirren* 583 P 2d 69; and *State of Utah v. International Amusements* 565 P2d 436. See also Firmage, "Utah Supreme Court," 593.

41. Jeff Hunt, "Tax Evasion Plea Bargain," *Deseret News,* Dec. 29, 1986; Timothy Egan, "Erotica Inc.," *New York Times,* May 16, 2008; *King's English v. Shurtleff,* memorandum decision, case no. 2:05–CV–485 (D. Utah 2008).

after new justices were appointed, Utah's supreme court quietly "disavowed" its earlier language and violation of US constitutional law in pornography cases.[42]

ABORTION

Until the United States Supreme Court struck down state laws in *Roe v. Wade*, Utah allowed abortion only to save a mother's life. Abortionists were punished by up to ten years in prison. From statehood to *Roe*, appellate records show twelve cases against abortionists: eight criminal prosecutions and four license-revocation proceedings. The defendants included ten men, seven of whom were doctors, and two women. There are no appellate court records for any woman charged with ending her pregnancy, although that was a felony too.[43] In a few cases, worse things happened. Nineteen-year-old Evelyn Bonnett took the train from Provo to Salt Lake City in 1896 for Dr. William McCoy to perform an abortion, which killed her. At trial a witness said another woman, a Mrs. Stansfield, had also died on McCoy's table. He was sentenced to eight years in prison.[44]

After *Roe v. Wade* in 1973, Utah abortions climbed steeply to a peak in 1989 and then declined, as graph 1 shows. Utah's trend roughly paralleled the nation's but averaged less than a third the national rates. Twice when Utah legislators tried to stop most abortions, they were defeated in federal court. Soon after *Roe*, legislators passed a law that was backed by Democratic governor Cal Rampton requiring a woman to obtain permission for an abortion from her husband or the baby's father, or from her parents if she were underage, and from a judge. Federal Judge Willis Ritter struck down that law "in its entirety."[45]

---

42. *State v. Taylor*, 664 P.2d 439 (1983) p. 448, n4.

43. *State of Utah v. Cragun*, 85 Utah 149, 38 P. 2d 1071 (1934) explains Utah abortion law at the time. Criminal cases include *State v. Crook* 51 P 1090 (1898); *State v. Davis* 75 P 785 (1904); *State v. Wells* 100 P 681 (1909); *State v. McCurtain* 172 P 481 (1918); *State v. Schreiber* 245 P2d 222 (1952); *State v. Clark* 284 P2d (1955), in addition to others named in this section.

44. *State of Utah v. McCoy*, 15 Utah 136, 49 P. 420 (1897).

45. *Doe v. Rampton*, 366 F. Supp. 189 (D. Utah 1973).

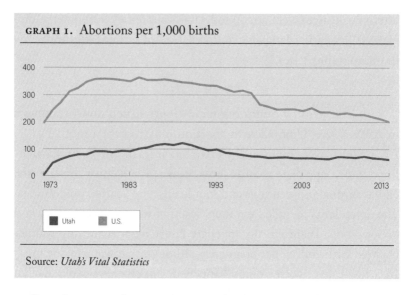

GRAPH I. Abortions per 1,000 births

1973	1983	1993	2003	2013

Utah   U.S.

Source: *Utah's Vital Statistics*

Legislators tried again in 1989 after the Supreme Court said in *Webster v. Reproductive Services* that states could refuse public money or facilities for abortions. Legislators took the decision as a signal that the Supreme Court was changing its mind and might uphold more restrictive laws. They passed a bill outlawing abortion except to save the life or health of the mother or in cases of rape, incest, or fetal defect.[46] Lawyer Janet Benshoof of the Reproductive Law and Policy Center in New York challenged Utah's law in court and said she would mount "a political show trial," predicting that "the Mormons will just die" from bad publicity. She composed the text for a full-page ad in the *New York Times* that was headlined, "In Utah they know how to punish a woman who has an abortion: shoot her."[47] The Utah chapter of the National Organization for Women resisted Utah policy by teaching women how to abort themselves

---

46. *Webster v. Reproductive Health Services*, 492 US 490 (1989); Allen, *Still the Right Place*, 337–40; Lisa Riley Roche, "Utah Legislature Passes Toughest U.S. Abortion Bill," *Deseret News*, Jan. 25, 1991.

47. *Legal Times*, Dec. 2, 1991; JoAnn Jacobsen–Wells, "ACLU Demands Utah Officials Apologize," Dawn House, "State Accuses the ACLU," *Salt Lake Tribune*, Mar. 25, 1991, Jan. 7, 1992. In court, Benshoof said she had been misquoted.

with a syringe, plastic tubing, and a canning jar. After years of litigation, federal courts struck down Utah's law.[48]

One public-opinion study showed that Utahns were more opposed to abortion than residents of any other state.[49] Legislators followed the public by debating anti-abortion measures almost every year. They required notification of parents of a minor girl before an abortion and of the baby's father, and those restrictions were sometimes approved and sometimes struck down in federal court. Utah imposed a twenty-four-hour waiting period and denied public funds for abortion. Fetal experimentation was banned, as were wrongful life suits, abortion counseling by phone, and partial birth abortions. Legislators asked the US Congress to pass anti-abortion measures and called for a convention to change the US Constitution. They debated but rejected bans on abortion in defiance of *Roe*. Though Utahns debated, demonstrated and litigated, there was no violence against clinics or abortionists as there had been in some other states.[50]

Latter-day Saint leaders denounced abortion, but did not politic as energetically as they did against pornography, same-sex marriage, or the Equal Rights Amendment. The court decisions left little opportunity for politics. Instead, the Church launched a program to help women have their babies and put them up for adoption. In Utah about as many babies were adopted as aborted. In 2014, however, the Church closed its agency because fewer teens were getting pregnant and fewer mothers were willing to give up their babies.[51]

---

48. Nancy Hobbs, "Utah Women Learn How," *Salt Lake Tribune*, Jan. 11, 1992; *Jane L v. Bangerter*, 102 F. 3d 1112 (10th Cir. 1996); cert. denied 520 U.S. 1274 (1996).

49. Brace et al., "Public Opinion," 176.

50. E.g. *H. L. v. Matheson*, 604 P2d 907 (1979), 504 US 137; *H. B. v. Wilkinson*, 690 Scup. 952 (1986); *D. R. v. Mitchell*, 456 F. Supp. 609 (1978); *Utah Women's Clinic v. Graham*, 892 F. Supp1379 (1997).

51. Douglas Palmer, "LDS Offer Abortion Alternatives," *Deseret News*, May 12, 1976; Keller, "Gender and Spirit," 175–79; Ryan Morgenegg, "LDS Family Services," *LDS Church News*, June 27, 2014. See also *Adoption Factbook* from the National Council for Adoption.

Political scientists say *Roe v. Wade* caused a long-term change in American political parties. Before the court acted, Republicans were more pro-choice and Democrats more pro-life because more Catholics were Democrats. The membership was divided on the issue in both parties, and neither party had a clear position. After the court's decision, however, representatives in Congress led the way in sorting out each party's stance, as they faced a succession of roll-call votes responding to *Roe*. Advocacy groups also chose sides, and some voters changed parties. More religious people tended Republican, and less religious people went with the Democrats.[52]

Utah followed that national pattern. Before *Roe*, party positions were unclear. In the 1972 gubernatorial election (the election directly before *Roe*), Democrat Cal Rampton said he would veto any liberalization of Utah's abortion law, while Republican Nick Strike favored more freedom to choose.[53] The issue attracted little attention. After *Roe*, Governor Rampton fought abortion but was defeated in federal court. Utah parties then followed national parties, and as positions clarified, Utah voters became more Republican. After *Roe*, Utahns never voted for another Democrat for president or senator, up to this writing.

EQUAL RIGHTS AMENDMENT

When Utah legislators considered ratification of the Equal Rights Amendment in 1973, a group of mostly Latter-day Saint women from Utah County and rural areas organized an opposition group called HOT DOGS (Humanitarians Opposed To Degrading Our Girls) and wore plastic frankfurter pins as they lobbied legislators. Professional women, academics, and journalists supported the amendment but lacked the energy and numbers of the HOT DOGS. The Church of Jesus Christ of Latter-day Saints took no

---

52. Adams, "Abortion," 718, 735; also Carmines et al., "How Abortion Became a Partisan Issue," 1135–58.

53. "Rampton [and] Strike," *Salt Lake Tribune*, Sept. 20, 1972.

position. The amendment, which reads, "Equality of rights under the law shall not be denied or abridged by the United States or by any state on account of sex," was decisively defeated in the House.[54]

Even so, forces behind ratification gained strength as Utah's Democrats made it a part of their 1974 platform. Aided by the Watergate scandal, they won both houses that year, for the last time up to this writing. A public opinion poll in Utah showed 60 percent approval for ratification. Then just before the 1974 legislative vote, an editorial in the LDS Church News argued against ratification. Representative Byron Fisher, co-sponsor of the amendment, changed his mind. "It is my church," he said, "and as a bishop, I'm not going to vote against its wishes." He was one of many lawmakers who changed their position, and ratification failed again.[55] Debate continued until 1982 when Congress said time had run out, and the amendment died.

Latter-day Saint women clashed again with feminists in 1977, this time at the state-level International Women's Year conferences. The United Nations had dedicated the year to women, and a US national committee created by Congress adopted resolutions—including passage of the Equal Rights Amendment and the right to an abortion—and invited women across the country to participate in conferences held in every state. Latter-day Saint leaders asked the women's Relief Society to recruit at least ten members from each ward to attend the Utah conference. More than 14,000 women attended, ten times the sponsors' expectations, and more than attended in any other state. The women jammed meetings and hallways, shouted down chairpersons, voted down every national resolution,

---

54. Reed Madsen, "Utah Group Fights Rights Amendment," DeAnn Evans, "Utah House Defeats Equal Rights," *Deseret News*, Jan. 4, 25, 1973.

55. "Utah Eyes New Bid," "ERA Effort Fails," *Salt Lake Tribune*, Jan. 12, 22, 1973; Hal Knight and Dan Jones, "Most Favor Full Rights," DeAnn Evans, "Utah House Defeats Equal Rights 54–21," *Deseret News*, Nov. 15, 1974, Feb. 19, 1975; "Equal Rights Amendment" editorial, *LDS Church News*, Jan. 12, 1975; Quinn, "Campaign against the ERA," 103.

The Equal Rights Amendment briefly drew majority support from Utahns until 1973 when the Church opposed it as a threat to the traditional family. After the Church weighed in, support in the legislature plummeted. Pictured here is a pro-ERA demonstration at the state capitol in 1975. *Utah State Historical Society*

and elected a delegation of eighteen Latter-day Saints and one Catholic to attend the national conference in Houston.[56]

Partly in response to the strong feelings expressed by women members, leaders of the Church of Jesus Christ of Latter-day Saints launched a nationwide campaign against ratification. They said the Equal Rights Amendment was a moral issue because it threatened families. With Church approval, Latter-day Saint activists organized campaigns against the ERA in sixteen states, and were successful in most of them.[57]

---

56. Bradley, "Mormon Relief Society," 114, 127, 135; also Brim, "IWY Conference in Utah"; Decker, "LDS Church and Utah Politics," 114–18.

57. Quinn, "Campaign against the ERA," 123–35; "First Presidency Statement," *LDS Church News*, Aug. 26, 1978; also Quinn, "Exporting Utah's Theocracy," 132–40.

CABLE TELEVISION

Utah tried harder than any other state to censor erotic movies on cable television. During the 1970s, companies used new cable technology to bring unedited films, as shown in theaters, into the homes of paying customers, along with soft pornography. In 1981 the Utah Legislature banned all nudity on cable television. That was quickly struck down in federal court. In 1982 lawmakers debated but failed to pass another cable-censorship bill. Legislative inaction spurred citizens to organize pro-decency groups that gathered signatures for a referendum on censorship, and to ask local governments to censor cable television. Roy City enacted criminal penalties for indecency on cable TV. In response, Community Television of Utah deleted all movie channels for Roy subscribers. Angry movie lovers filled the next city council meeting and demanded their films back. The council first repealed and then reinstated the censorship ordinance. Community Television sued in federal court, where a judge agreed that the ordinance was unconstitutional.[58]

Cable television bills roused more public interest than any other issue when the legislature passed two censorship bills in 1983. Governor Scott Matheson said he received more calls and mail than for any other issue in his six years as governor. In vetoing both of them, he said the bills infringed on rights and probably violated the constitution. Lawmakers convened a veto-override session. While senators caucused, a pro-censorship group showed scenes from *Young Lady Chatterley*, *The Bitch*, and other cable TV movies in the senate chamber. Only lawmakers were invited to the show. After seeing the movies the legislature overrode one of the two vetoes, voting similar restrictions

---

58. For non-Utah efforts, see *Cruz v. Ferre*, 571 F. Supp. 125 (Florida, 1983); *Capitol Cities Cable Inc. v. Crisp*, 467 US 691 (Oklahoma, 1984); *US v. Playboy Entertainment Group*, 529 US 801 (2000). For Utah, see *Home Box Office, Inc. v. Wilkinson*, 531 F. Supp. 987 (D. Utah 1982); *Community Television of Utah, Inc. v. Roy City*, 555 F. Supp. 1164 (D. Utah 1982); also "[Lloyd] Selleneit Lowers His Profile," *Utah Holiday*, June 1, 1982; "Three Movie Channels Restored," "Groups Begin Petition Drive," *Salt Lake Tribune*, July 27, Sept. 17, 1982.

TABLE 2. Cable TV censorship

	Protestant	Catholic	LDS	Jewish	other	none	total
percent for	12.7	14.6	46.6	0	14.2	4.5	38.2
percent against	82.2	84.1	49.8	100	86.6	94.5	61.8
number of respondents	118	82	1,042	5	49	109	1,405

Source: CSED exit poll, 1984

on cable TV as the Federal Communications Commission had for broadcast television. Cable companies again sued in federal court. Pro-decency groups had simultaneously gathered enough signatures to force a vote of the people in 1984 on a stricter censorship measure. LDS Church leaders gave an endorsement to cable-TV censorship in principle but without mentioning the legislative act or referendum.[59] Utahns voted the referendum down by 62-to-38 percent. As Table 2 shows, even Latter-day Saints narrowly rejected censorship, the only time since repeal of Prohibition that they voted against their leaders' advice on a moral issue. While Latter-day Saints barely rejected censorship, 86.5 percent of non-Mormons voted against it, a 37-percent difference in the two groups' preferences.

A federal court struck down the legislature's censorship law. Utah attorney general David Wilkinson appealed to the Tenth Circuit and lost.[60] Wilkinson then appealed to the US Supreme Court—a

---

59. Diane Cole, "PTA Delegates Seek Curbs," "Matheson Says Concern on Cable TV Bill High," Con Psarras, "Matheson Vetoes Cable TV Bills," George Raine, "Stag Films Key to Veto Override," *Salt Lake Tribune*, May 9, 1982, Mar. 9, 31, Apr. 22, 1983; Barbara Bernstein, "Roy Anti-Porn Group," Bob Bernick Jr., "Cable TV Initiative," *Deseret News*, Aug. 13, 1982, Apr. 8, 1983; "Seeds of Sinister Sex" editorial, *Church News*, Oct. 7, 1984; Michelle MacFarlane, "Cable TV and the Mormon Vote," *Sunstone*, Jan. 1985.

60. *Community Television of Utah, Inc. v. Wilkinson*, 611 F. Supp. 1099 (D. Utah 1985); *Jones v. Wilkinson*, 800 F. 2d 989 (10th Cir. 1986); Levine, "Utah's Cable Decency Act," 410–11.

controversial move in light of how overwhelmingly Utahns had already voted against censorship in their referendum. The court declined to hear the appeal and the Tenth Circuit decision stood. When Wilkinson ran for reelection in 1988, he was the only Republican in the state, running for a major office, who was defeated. He said his tenacity on the cable television issue was the chief reason for his defeat.

LOTTERY

Utahns wanted a state lottery. But legislators, supported by the Church of Jesus Christ of Latter-day Saints, would not let them have one. For decades games of chance were not an issue. For instance, a 1975 poll showed 70 percent of Utahns opposed to a lottery. But then forty-four states began lotteries and made money. Neighboring Idaho had a lottery, and Utah's "Lotto-day Saints" drove to border towns to bet. By one estimate, Utahns gambled $10.5 million a year, placing almost 20 percent of all Idaho bets. In each of the six Utah public opinion polls published from 1985 through 1988, majorities (on average 55 percent) favored a lottery.[61]

Every year from 1985 to 1995, Democrats introduced pro-lottery legislation. Gambling is forbidden by Utah's constitution, so lottery advocates knew the constitution would have to be amended by the legislature and ratified by the people. Lottery advocates said, "Let the people decide." Three published polls from 1986 through 1988 showed an average of 70 percent of Utahns wanted a popular vote. But legislators defied their constituents. In 1986 when 73 percent of poll respondents wanted a vote, the enabling resolution failed in the House 54-to-12.[62] Other years committees defeated

---

61. See articles by Roy J. Bardsley in the *Salt Lake Tribune* for Dec. 21, 1975, June 2, 1985, Oct. 26, 1986, May 10, 1987, Apr. 28, 1988, and by Lee Davidson for Apr. 7, 2012; Bob Bernick, "51% of 645 Utahns Polled," "Most Want Lottery Issue Placed on Ballot," Peter Tourney, "Idaho Lottery Thanks Utah," *Deseret News*, Oct. 22, 1986, Jan. 23, 1987, July 10, 1990. See also Dunstan, *Gambling in California*.

62. Joseph Bauman, "Legislator Wants Utahns to Vote," "House Members Quash Resolution," *Deseret News*, Nov. 29, 1985, Feb. 25, 1986. For the polls, see the *Salt Lake Tribune*, Oct. 26, 1986, Apr. 24, 1988; *Deseret News*, Jan. 23, 1987.

lottery resolutions with no floor vote. To explain why, pollster Dan Jones said, "Until the predominant church in the state makes a statement in favor of a lottery, there is little chance that one will ever be established, preliminary public opinion to the contrary."[63] Church leaders declared the lottery a moral issue and opposed gambling. Still, public opinion remained pro-lottery, just not strongly enough to move legislators. After a while, newspapers stopped polling, and the matter slipped out of public discussion, making it a victory for the Church and the republican institutions over public opinion.

SAME-SEX MARRIAGE

Beginning in 1994, Utahns argued over gay rights. The Church of Jesus Christ of Latter-day Saints declared same-sex marriage a moral issue and fought its legalization but did not fight other gay issues that raised similar controversies in Utah. The Church first campaigned against same-sex marriage in other states, and it helped bring the controversy to Utah. Beginning in the 1990s, judges in several states had ruled that state constitutions required recognition of same-sex marriage. Latter-day Saint leaders said such recognition threatened traditional families and rose in opposition. They hired lawyers, lobbyists, and public relations firms and gave money to oppose gay marriage. Most effectively, Church members were asked to campaign in referenda. Though not numerous outside Utah, they were organized and energetic. Joining with Catholics and Evangelical Christians, they won anti-gay-marriage initiatives in Hawaii, California, Alaska, Nevada, and Nebraska. As an institution, the Church politicked quietly. Members were told not to say they were Latter-day Saints when

---

63. Douglas L. Parker, "Committee Dispatches Lottery Vote," Tony Semerand, "Will Utah Ever Have a Lottery?" *Salt Lake Tribune,* Jan. 24, 1987, Mar. 15, 1992; "'Lucky 7th' Try for Lottery Fails," *Deseret News,* Feb. 23, 1991; "Straw Poll Shows Support," *Daily Herald,* Dec. 12, 1985. See also the 1988 LDS pamphlet, *Concerning Gambling,* and "LDS Business College Public Opinion Survey," *Deseret News,* Nov. 20, 1989.

TABLE 3.	Amendment against gay marriage					
	Protestant	*Catholic*	*LDS*	*other*	*none*	*total*
percent for	45.8	31.1	77.8	30.4	16.7	61.9
percent against	54.2	68.9	22.2	69.6	83.3	38.1
number of respondents	216	241	2,884	229	492	4,264

Source: CSED poll, 2004

they campaigned, and spokesmen often declined to discuss the Church's involvement.[64]

No Utah state court ever threatened to legitimate same-sex marriage, but Utah reacted to threats in other states. After Hawaii's supreme court ruled for gay marriage, the First Presidency asked members to advocate for legislation upholding traditional marriage. Utah legislators passed the nation's first Defense of Marriage Act denying recognition to gay marriages performed legally in other states. When the Massachusetts Supreme Court ruled for gay marriage, Utah passed another law defining marriage as a union of one man and one woman. To leave nothing undone, the state also amended its constitution to bar legal recognition of same-sex marriage, and in addition to bar other civil unions or any marriage-like arrangement for homosexuals.[65] As table 3 shows, all religious groups except Latter-day Saints opposed the amendment, but strong Latter-day Saint support carried it by a large majority.

64. "LDS First Presidency Opposes Legalization," *Deseret News*, Feb. 14, 1994; Patty Henetz, "LDS Cash Carries Gay Marriage Fight," *Salt Lake Tribune*, Oct. 26, 1998; Richley H. Crapo, "Chronology of Mormon/LDS Involvement," *Mormon Social Science Association*, Jan. 4, 2008, www.mormonsocialscience.org; Quinn, "Exporting Utah's Theocracy," 143–44; Quinn, "National 'Defense of Marriage' Campaign," 10–11n26, 12–13n29.
65. *Baehr v. Lewin*, 852 P. 2d 44 (Haw. 1993); "Lawmakers Pass Late Measure," *Deseret News*, Mar. 2, 1995; *Goodridge v. Department of Public Health*, 798 N.E. 2d 941 (Mass. 2003).

Smaller disputes over gay rights proliferated. Salt Lake City and the University of Utah extended health insurance and other benefits to same-sex partners of employees. After months of wrangling, Salt Lake City broadened its policy to allow benefits for any "adult designee" who lived with the employee, thus avoiding the appearance of recognizing same-sex couples. Salt Lake County and Utah State University both considered extending benefits but retreated after Utahns passed the anti-gay-marriage amendment. Salt Lake County changed its mind once again four years later and extended benefits anyway.[66] Salt Lake City began a domestic partner registry the legislature forced it to reword as a "Committed Couple Registry" so it would seem less like condoning same-sex marriage.

Federal courts decided the issue just before Christmas 2013 when judge Robert Shelby struck down Utah's rule against gay marriage. Shelby noted that almost two-thirds of Utah voters had approved the anti-gay-marriage amendment in 2004 but said, "The state's current laws deny its gay and lesbian citizens their fundamental right to marry and, in so doing, demean the dignity of these same-sex couples for no rational reason." He ruled that the constitutional amendment and both Utah statutes were unconstitutional. He called the same-sex couples who had sued by their first names, which is unusual in judicial writing, and seemed moved as he recounted their stories of meeting, falling in love, and suffering hardship because they were gay.[67] Shelby was the first federal judge to overturn a state law against gay marriage because it violated the United States Constitution.

The state asked Shelby to stay the ruling during appeal. Shelby refused, and so did the Tenth Circuit Court of appeals. Utah finally

66. Arrin Brunson, "USU Same-Sex Benefits Proposal," Derek P. Jensen, "Partner Benefits," Jeremiah Stettler, "Wilson's Benefits Push," *Salt Lake Tribune*, Mar. 29, July 13, 2005, Feb. 19, 2009; Deborah Bulkeley, "Senate Kills Bill," *Deseret News*, Feb. 2, 2005.

67. *Kitchen et al. v. Herbert*, 961 F. Supp. 2d 1118 (D. Utah 2013).

obtained a stay from the US Supreme Court sixteen days after the initial ruling, but not before 1,362 gay couples had rushed to county clerks to marry while they could. "When we heard the news, we screamed, and we danced and we ran out of the house. I didn't even put on makeup. We loaded the baby in the car and rushed to the courthouse. We wanted to get married as soon as we possibly could," one lesbian newlywed said on television. About a dozen clergy and Salt Lake City mayor Ralph Becker came to the Salt Lake County Government Center to perform ceremonies in the jammed hallways. Hundreds of people waiting in line cheered as couples vowed, kissed, and displayed marriage licenses. Many couples brought their children. Seth Anderson married Michael Ferguson then tweeted wedding pictures. "Me and my new husband!!" he wrote. "My polygamous Mormon great grandparents would be so proud!"[68]

"Judicial tyranny," said the *Deseret News* in a front-page editorial. "Marriage should be between a man and a woman," Church leaders echoed in a statement. However, the Tenth Circuit Court of Appeals upheld Judge Shelby's ruling, and the US Supreme Court declined to hear the case. Same-sex marriage had come to Utah to stay. Though the Church of Jesus Christ of Latter-day Saints continued to oppose gay marriage, many members changed their views after the court decision. Surveys by the Public Religion Research Institute showed that in 2014 68 percent of Latter-day Saints opposed gay marriage, but by 2017 the number had declined to 53 percent. In contrast to Latter-day Saints, Americans generally had come to favor gay marriage two-to-one.[69]

---

68. Ralph Becker, "This Mayor Will Never Forget," *Salt Lake Tribune*, Feb. 12, 2014; KUTV Channel 2, Dec. 20, 2013; Erik Eckholm, "Federal Judge Rules," *New York Times*, Dec. 21, 2013.

69. "In Our Opinion: Judicial Tyranny," *Deseret News*, Dec. 20, 2013; "Church Statement on Court Ruling," *Newsroom*, Dec. 20, 2013, www.mormonnewsroom.org; *Kitchen v. Herbert*, 755 F. 3d 1193 (10th Cir. 2014); Alex Vandermaas–Peeler et al., "Emerging Consensus," *Public Religion Research Institute*, May 2018, www.prri.org.

HATE CRIME LAWS

Utah legislators refused to pass hate-crime legislation that protected gays. In 1992 Democrats proposed a bill to increase penalties for crimes committed from hatred of race, religion, sex, disability, ethnic group, or gender preference. They said Utah was the only state without some sort of hate-crime law. But Representative Merrill Jensen said, "Once we include the term 'sexual preference,'... we grant special recognition and status, we recognize, we legitimate homosexuality under Utah law." Legislators wrote out mention of sexual preference or other special classes and instead imposed stricter penalties on crimes intended to "terrorize or intimidate" anybody. The bill passed, but prosecutors said it was unenforceable. Another provision required police to keep count of hate crimes but excluded gays from the list.[70]

Every legislative session for seven years beginning in 1999, Democrats unsuccessfully introduced a hate-crimes bill. In 2003, Latter-day Saint spokesman Dale Bills said the Church had no objection: "The Church's well known opposition to attempts to legalize same-gender marriage should never be interpreted as justification for hatred, intolerance or abuse of those who profess homosexual tendencies." Nonetheless, legislators voted down each new bill. "If this is giving special protection to the gay community, then I'm opposing it," said Senator Chris Buttars. Finally in 2006, sponsors deleted mention of sexual orientation and other classes of people and substituted extra punishment for crimes that "incited community unrest," among other things. That bill passed, and legislators congratulated each other on their statesmanlike willingness to compromise.[71]

---

70. Bob Bernick Jr., "Hate-Crime Bill," "Hate Crime Measures," Amy Joi Bryson, "Utah Lawmakers," Derek Jensen, "Gay-Bashing Defendants," *Deseret News*, Jan. 29, Feb. 12, 1992, Feb. 5, 1999, Mar. 6, 2000; *Utah Code Annotated* 76–3–203.3(2)(a) (2007); 53–5–203.

71. Jennifer Dobner, "LDS Won't Oppose," Deborah Bulkeley, "New Hate-Crime Bill," Bulkeley, "House Passes Hate-Crimes Measure," *Deseret News*, Feb. 21, 2003, Nov. 14, 2005, Mar. 22, 2008.

A pro-gay demonstration at the Utah capitol in January 2014, three weeks after Judge Robert J. Shelby ruled in favor of gay marriage. Among those in attendance, newlyweds Jason Walker (center) and Greg Jones (right) had taken advantage of Shelby's ruling and tied the knot, along with 1,361 other couples.

GAY STUDENT CLUBS

Republican senators met secretly during the 1996 legislative session to discuss gay student clubs. Three students had asked to form a "gay/straight alliance" at East High School in Salt Lake City, and senators feared gay clubs would recruit young people into homosexuality. In their meeting, Senator Charles Stewart showed video pictures of gays dancing and kissing as they marched on Washington. He called gay relations "bestial." After the video, the senators invited the commissioner of higher education and superintendent of schools into the room and accused them of allowing schools to advocate homosexuality. One senator charged speakers at a University of Utah symposium with having favored gay rights, while an unnamed professor had advocated homosexuality in a class entitled Gender Equity. Another senator displayed a training booklet for elementary teachers that explicitly described homosexual acts. The discussion became heated and everyone was cautioned to keep the meeting secret.[72]

KCPX reporter, Chris Vanocur, broadcast news of the meeting that evening and the *Salt Lake Tribune* published an account the next morning. When questioned, senate leaders admitted their secrecy was a technical violation of Utah's Open Meetings Act, and the American Civil Liberties Union sued them. After a year of legal maneuvers, a judge ruled that the case could go to trial. Senators then admitted their fault and paid $10,000 in legal fees to settle the case.[73]

Three weeks after the secret meeting, the Salt Lake City Board of Education met to decide whether to allow the East High gay/straight alliance. More than five hundred people attended and more than a hundred spoke. The board's legal counsel explained that the Equal Access Act allowed them to ban all non-curriculum-related clubs or permit all of them, but they could not selectively remove clubs based on content and receive federal money. Congress had passed the act in 1984 to keep schools from ousting Bible clubs. Utah senator Orrin Hatch was a cosponsor. After five hours of debate, the board voted four-to-three to ban all clubs. Students and parents who wanted gay clubs wept. Among others, the board's decision ousted the Hispanic, Lacrosse, Students against Drunk Driving, and Bible Clubs.[74]

Although there were many students who opposed gay clubs, almost

---

72. Jerry Spangler and Marjorie Cortez, "Forty-four Percent Favor," *Deseret News*, Feb. 2, 1996.

73. Tony Semerand, "Utah Senators Hold Secret Anti-Gay Meet," Dan Harrie and Judy Fahys, "Lawmakers Admit Being Lawbreakers," *Salt Lake Tribune*, Feb. 1, Dec. 20, 1996; Jerry Spangler, "Beattie Defends Closure," Howard Stephenson, "Caucus Was Not for 'Gay Bashing,'" Brent Israelsen, "Suit Says Senators Violated Law," "Justices Refuse to Hear," Chip Parkinson, "Answer to Meetings Issue," *Deseret News*, Feb. 3, 8, 16, Dec. 10, 23, 1996.

74. Joe Costanzo, "Legal Blessing Likely," Marjorie Cortez, "Board Votes to Ban," Ruth Ann Mitchell, "Ironic Twist," *Deseret News*, Dec. 22, 1995, Feb. 21, 23, 1996.

all of them wanted some non-curriculum-related clubs. Two days after the board decision, hundreds of students left class to march on the capitol. On the way a fourteen-year-old girl was run over and hurt, but the march went on. At the statehouse Highway Patrol troopers barred marchers from entering the building, so the students stood on the capitol steps and chanted, "Save our clubs, save our clubs." Coincidentally Senator Orrin Hatch was visiting legislators inside and could faintly hear the students shouting. He said using the Equal Access Act to allow gay clubs was "crazy."[75]

In the midst of the controversy, the Gay and Lesbian Utah Democrats were asked by party leaders to change their name because association with gays hurt the party. Gay Democrats said they would rebrand if Democratic legislators would introduce a bill to decriminalize sodomy. The meeting ended with ill feeling and no agreement.[76]

Utah's school-club dispute drew national attention, but lawmakers were not sure what they could do that would pass federal-court scrutiny. They passed a bill forbidding teachers from "encouraging, supporting, or condoning" illegal conduct, even in their private lives. It was an attempt to prevent gay teachers from disclosing their sexual orientation. As the bill neared final passage, Clayton Vetter, the Skyline High debate coach, declared at a news conference that he was gay. The Granite School District received calls saying he should be fired, but he kept his job and Governor Mike Leavitt vetoed the bill.[77]

Leavitt asked two prominent lawyers to draft a bill that would survive a challenge in the courts and keep gay clubs out of schools. The resulting bill banned any club that advocated illegal conduct,

75. Marjorie Cortez, "S. L. Students Walk Out," *Deseret News*, Feb. 23, 1996; Dan Harrie, "Leavitt, Hatch Say Schools Have Right," *Salt Lake Tribune*, Feb. 7, 10, 1996.
76. Dan Harrie, "Demos Ask Gays to Lower Profile," *Salt Lake Tribune*, Feb. 7, 1996.
77. Marjorie Cortez, "Teacher Says Silence Would Be Hypocritical," "Legislative Top Ten," *Deseret News*, Feb. 28, 29, 1996; Dan Harrie and Samuel Autman, "Leavitt Vetoes Bill," *Salt Lake Tribune*, Mar. 20, 1996. See Louis Sahagun, "Utah Board Bans All School Clubs," *Los Angeles Times*, Feb. 22, 1996; James Brooke, "To Be Young, Gay, and Going to High School in Utah," *New York Times*, Feb. 28, 1996.

or bigotry, or involved human sexuality. Governor Leavitt called a special session, legislators passed the bill, and Utah became the first state to outlaw gay student clubs. Seventeen other states considered similar legislation the following year.

The East High gay/straight alliance obtained help from the ACLU, went to court, and argued that the school board had banned all clubs as a ruse just to get rid of gay clubs. Judge Bruce Jenkins said the school board's motives were irrelevant and ruled for the state. The lawyers sued a second time, arguing that the rule was arbitrarily applied. Jenkins said no, it looked fair to him. After students reorganized their club, lawyers brought a third case to court and argued that the club was, in fact, curriculum related studying history and society from gay and straight perspectives. Judge Teena Campbell ruled in the students' favor.[78] With that, the Salt Lake School Board changed its policy once again to allow all student clubs, and gay/straight alliances sprang up intermittently in about a dozen Utah high schools. Judge Campbell ignored the state law against clubs that involved sexuality, and after her decision neither courts nor schools paid it any mind.

GAY ADOPTIONS

Utah imposed the most comprehensive state ban on gay couples adopting children or being foster parents. Lay members of the Board of Child and Family Services overrode the professional staff in 1999 and banned adoption or foster care by gays for children in state custody. The Utah Division of Child and Family Services and the National Association of Social Workers denounced the ban, and the division's lawyer opined that it was illegal. In the middle of this, Utah legislators sided with the board and put the ban into law. Utah would place children preferably with married couples, rarely with single individuals, and never with cohabiting couples. Unmarried

---

78. Burrington, "Public Square," 107–13; *East High Gay/Straight Alliance v. Salt Lake City Board of Education*, 81 F. Supp. 2d 1199 (D. Utah Jan. 1999), 1166 (D. Utah Oct. 1999); *East High School Prism Club v. Seidel*, 95 F. Supp. 2d 1239 (D. Utah 2000); also Goldsmith, "Limitations regarding Student Clubs"; Parkinson, "Utah Senate Bill 1003."

couples could not even adopt children related to them. Although the statute did not mention the term "homosexual," that was the underlying issue driving both the board and legislative actions. As in other states, Utah had a shortage of foster parents and many children whom no one would adopt. Even with its ban, however, it did better than other states at finding children homes. Florida's ban on gay adoption was upheld in federal court, so Utah's ban may have been constitutional.[79] It became irrelevant when federal courts struck down Utah's same-sex-marriage ban in 2014, and married gays became eligible and began adopting children.

REMARKS

Utah battles over moral matters rise decade after decade like recurring family quarrels. The sides remain mostly Latter-day Saint versus non-LDS. Each side carries principles and its own vocabulary from issue to issue.

Utahns fight over morals because they want to. Latter-day Saints want to act together for the good of their community, follow their leaders, be true to their tradition. Non-Mormons want to stand for their rights as Americans against foolish, religion-directed attempts to legislate morality. Each group reaffirms its own tradition and its continuing identity different from the other.

Each side sees itself as a besieged minority. Non-LDS fear Latter-day Saint power and willingness to use government to impose their morality. Latter-day Saints are a minority in America, fighting a rearguard action against moral change they have been unable to stop.

For non-Mormons, Utah moral issues mean Latter-day Saint power over non-Mormons who want liberty, equality, and secularity but talk mostly about money. They despair of agreement with Latter-day Saints on values other than prosperity. Advocates of

---

79. Gina Holland, "Gay Adoption Issue," *Deseret News*, Jan. 11, 2005; *Utah Code Annotated* § 78-30-9(3)(a) (2005); *Lofton et al. v. Secretary of Department of Child and Family Services*, 358 F. 3d 804 (11th Cir. 2004). See also Clark, "Married Persons Favored," 203, and "Utah Prefers Married Couples," 215–26.

drinking and gambling say freer rules would bring tourists and keep Utah money home. Advocates for abortion, the ERA, and gay rights say moralistic laws put off outsiders and make the state appear weird and backward. If Utah would become more like the rest of America, Americans would visit, invest, and buy. Utah would prosper.[80]

Latter-day Saints talk about families even more than non-LDS talk about economics. Traditional families became more important in Church teachings as they became more beleaguered in America. Sociologists Gordon and Gary Shepherd analyzed Church leaders' speeches at twice-annual general conferences. They found that from 1950 to 1979, "family" was the eighth most important topic. But from 1990 to 2009, "family" was the second most important topic. Only Jesus was more prominent. In 1995, LDS leaders issued "The Family: A Proclamation to the World," asserting that traditional families are integral to Latter-day Saint belief, important to individual happiness, and "the fundamental unit of society." Many Latter-day Saints hang framed copies of the proclamation on their kitchen or living-room walls.[81]

The meaning of family changed for Latter-day Saints. In Utah Territory, Latter-day Saints were polygamous. They challenged nineteenth-century American Protestant morality, and lost.[82] Latter-day Saints then modified their teachings to become more like nineteenth-century American Protestants. The Church made teachings against alcohol stricter and became more like Protestants who advocated temperance. Latter-day Saints changed their families from polygamous to monogamous. Now when Saints talk of "family," they mean the traditional family of a married man and woman and their children. After the Saints adopted traditional family morals, Utah

80. Carrie Moore, "Farley Advises NOW Members," *Deseret News*, Oct. 22, 1989.

81. Shepherd and Shepherd, *Kingdom Transformed*, 76, 205; Dallin Oaks, "Priesthood Authority," Oct. 2005, www.lds.org/general–conference; "The Family: A Proclamation to the World," *Ensign*, Nov. 1995; Tad Walch, "Unique LDS Family Doctrine," *Deseret News*, Sept. 29, 2015.

82. See Gordon, *Mormon Question*, 221–38.

spent eighty years in the American political mainstream. Utah's mainstream period rested on broad moral agreement between the Saints and America. Both supported versions of the nineteenth-century Protestant belief that government should uphold traditional morals and favor traditional families.

Beginning after World War II, American morality and sexual behavior changed (discussed in the next chapter), and the changes eventually came to courts. Federal judges ruled for freedom, equality, and secularity, and struck down old laws supporting traditional morality. The "Rights Revolution" in federal courts brought law more in line with behavior, which had already changed, and helped Americans accommodate the new morality. Latter-day Saints, however, did not accommodate. They became the rearguard of the nineteenth-century Protestant morality once invoked to condemn and imprison their polygamous forebears.

Federal court decisions on public morality did not force anyone to change. Federal judges limited the power of state and local governments to regulate morality. Individuals could choose a traditional family, an abortion, or same-sex marriage, among other options. But federal court actions changed moral battles from disagreements among Utahns to futile Latter-day Saint complaints against new rules. Judicial decisions made America's new morality a Utah political issue, and Utahns again divided between Latter-day Saint and non-LDS. Latter-day Saints voted Republican as the more socially conservative party. Many non-Mormons, in contrast, disliked church-imposed public morality and approved the courts' new freedoms. Utah non-Mormons face a Latter-day Saint Republican juggernaut, a permanent religious majority that dominates state elections and opposes moral change. Utah non-Mormons became Democrats. Sex and family issues came one after another: abortion, pornography, birth control for teens, and gay marriage. Each new sex-and-family issue refreshed both Latter-day Saint disagreement with the federal government and religious division within Utah.

In Utah's mainstream period (1896–1976), Latter-day Saints and non-Mormons argued over liquor, tobacco, horse racing, and Sunday closing. None of those issues directly affected families. In contrast, in both Utah Territory and the Republican ascendancy, the federal government imposed public morality measures affecting sex and families over Latter-day Saint objections. When Saints agreed with American family public morality, Utah was politically like other states. When Americans chose a family morality opposed by Latter-day Saints, they and non-LDS in Utah separated, and Utah became politically different from other states.

4

DEMOGRAPHY: FAMILIES AND CHILDREN

Latter-day Saints believe in traditional families, and Utahns are more likely to live in them than other Americans. The last two chapters covered the effects on Utah politics of pro-family beliefs. This chapter and the next discuss the effect on Utah society of traditional family life. Utahns are more likely than people in other states to live and raise their children in two-parent homes. They are less likely to cohabit or have children out of wedlock. Traditional family behavior affects Utah's demography. Utahns are younger, have more children, and their families are larger than in the rest of the country. Though Latter-day Saints advocate traditional families partly from religious belief, social science has found they are good for people who live in them, especially for children.

Utah families became unusual because American families and morals changed while Utah changed less. Beginning after World War II, birth control improved and the consequences of sex changed, and soon opinions changed too. In 1969, 70 percent of Americans thought sex out of marriage was wrong, but by 1974 the percentage had sunk to below half, and opinions of young people changed more than their elders. Most college students wanted more sexual freedom, endorsed legal abortion, and accepted gay sex. Pollster Daniel Yankelovich called the change "revolutionary." Behavior changed as well. Of American women born in 1942, 30 percent had had sex outside of marriage before they were twenty-one, but that share rose to 72 percent for women born in 1955.[1]

Changes in birth control and beliefs about sex changed families. Beginning about 1960, people began marrying less, had more sex outside marriage, and cohabited more. They produced more out-of-wedlock births, as well as fewer children overall, often fewer than would replace the population. All Western countries were affected. And though families had changed before, this change was bigger and faster. Sociologist Frank Furstenburg said, "The American, and more broadly the Western, family changed more dramatically in the last half of the twentieth century than in any comparable span of time in our history." Utah followed the international trends, but partly because of Latter-day Saint beliefs, Utah resisted the family changes. So Utah followed slowly, and Utah families diverged from American families.[2]

More Americans chose not to live in traditional families. In 1960, 72 percent of American adults were married; by 2010, the married share had shrunk to 51 percent. Marriage remained more popular in Utah, however. Both the 2000 and the 2010 censuses showed that more Utahns lived in households headed by a married couple than the residents of any other state; 61 percent of Utahns lived in husband–wife households, compared to 48.4 percent nationally. Latter-day Saints made Utah the most-married state in the country. A Pew Foundation Research Report showed 66 percent of all Latter-day Saint adults were married. Utah households were also more likely to have children than households elsewhere. In both the married and married-with-children categories, Utah was an outlier, with a gap separating it from other states.[3]

---

1. Goldin and Katz, "Power of the Pill," 736. See also Yankelovich, *New Morality*.
2. Furstenburg, "Recent Transformation," 192–93; Lesthaeghe, "Second Demographic Transition," 17.
3. Michael Lipka, "Mormons More Likely to Marry," *Pew Research Center*, May 22, 2015; Tavia Simmons and Grace O'Niell, "Households and Families: 2000," and

Utahns were more often married in part because they marry younger than other Americans. Utah in recent years has had the youngest median age at first marriage of any state. For example, in 2016 an average Utah groom was 26.3 years of age, compared to 29.9 nationally. A Utah bride was 24.7, compared to the national average of 27.9. Couples who marry young also divorce more often. From 1960 to 1980, divorce rose from 9 to almost 23 per thousand married women in America, then declined slightly. Divorce rose in Utah, and Utah has always had more divorces per 1,000 residents than the national average. But the Current Population Survey counted marriages each year and kept track of when any of those marriages ended in divorce. By that measure, Utah's divorce rate was lower than the national rate for marriages made every year after 1959. Utah marriages seem to last even though Utahns marry young.[4]

Partly because they marry younger, Utahns have more children than other Americans. (Fertility delayed is fertility denied, say demographers.) Utahns have had higher fertility than the national average for decades. In 1984 the *Wall Street Journal* noted that Utah's birthrate was about twice the national rate. "Its baby-boom is perennial, in effect giving the U.S. a third-world enclave," the headline read. At the time, the birthrate in Utah was between that of Djibouti and Nepal. Since then, it has fallen to only about half again as large as the national rate, but still higher than any other state's and higher than Mexico's but lower than Fiji's. An average Utah woman has 2.33 children in her life, compared to 1.86 for the average American woman. Utah, with so many children, is consequently the youngest state with a median age of 30.5 compared to 37.7 for all Americans.

Daphne Lofquist et al., "Households and Families: 2010," *Census Briefs*, Sept. 2001, Apr. 2012; also Heaton et al., "In Search of a Peculiar People," 87–118; Pamela S. Perlich, "Coming to Our Census," *Department of Workforce Services*, jobs.utah.gov.

4. US Census Bureau, "American Community Survey State Rankings," tables 1203, 1204, www.census.gov (Utah has usually had the lowest age at first marriage but was second or third lowest in 2005, 2006, and 2009); *Statistical Abstract of the United States*, 2001, 87 (table 117); Kang Fu and Wolfinger, "Marriage and Divorce in Utah," 39.

High fertility has given Utah the largest families in the country, as well as the largest households.[5]

As marriage declined in America, cohabiting rose. Cohabitation shows how family change sneaked up on social scientists. It was not predicted, and in fact was not seen clearly until decades after it began. Before the 1960s, cohabiting couples were so rare that the census had no name for them. Census workers coined the term "Persons of Opposite Sex Sharing Living Quarters," POSSLQ, as in Charles Osgood's

> There is nothing I wouldn't do
> If you would be my POSSLQ

In 1990 "cohabiting couples" replaced POSSLQ as the official name. The census showed 440,000 POSSLQs in 1960. By the 2010 census, 6.8 million couples were cohabiting, representing a fifteen-fold increase. In the 2010 census, Utah had the lowest percentage of cohabiting households of any state, 3.9 percent, one of only two states with a rate of less than 5 percent.[6]

Extramarital births show the decline of marriage and the rise of non-traditional families. As graph 1 shows, about one in twenty American births was extra-marital in 1960, but that rose to eight in twenty by 2010, and seems to have leveled off. In Utah the out-of-marriage rate rose ten-fold, but Utah still had the lowest percentage of extramarital births of any state for every year shown in the graph, and the difference between Utah and the nation steadily increased.

As the number of children born out of marriage and living with lone mothers grew, social scientists studied the new lone-mother

---

5. Ken Wall, "As the Nation Ages, Utah Gets Younger," *Wall Street Journal*, Nov. 7, 1984; *Utah Demographics Fact Sheet*, Jan. 2016, gardner.utah.edu. In 2014, Utah families had 3.65 members, American families 3.26. For all households, the numbers were 3.16 and 2.65.

6. Furstenberg, "Fifty Years of Family Change," 13, 18; Lynne M. Casper, Philip N. Cohen, and Tavia Simmons, "How Does POSSLQ Measure Up?" US Census working paper, www.census.gov; Daphne Lofquist et al., "Households and Families: 2010," *Census Briefs*, Apr. 2012, 15, 16.

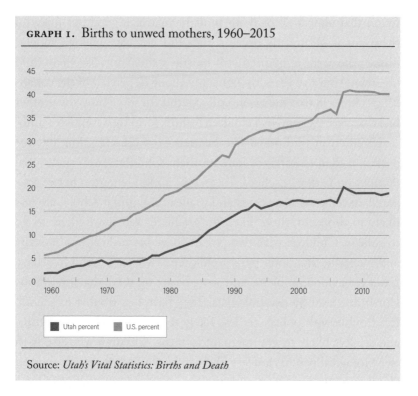

GRAPH 1. Births to unwed mothers, 1960–2015

Utah percent   U.S. percent

Source: *Utah's Vital Statistics: Births and Death*

families, compared them to traditional families, and found that traditional families seemed better for children. Children who live with both parents are less likely to be poor. Lone mothers, Adam Thomas and Isabel Sawhill found, earn 37 percent of an average married couple's income (cohabiting parents earn 61 percent). A child living with one parent is more than four times more likely to be poor than a child living with married parents. More than half of all poor children in America live with a lone parent.[7]

In addition, family stability seems to help children, and non-marriage relationships are less stable. Most children born out of marriage are born to cohabiting parents. Sara McLanahan and colleagues interviewed thousands of new parents, many of them not married, and

7. Thomas and Sawhill, "For Love and Money?" 62–66; Page and Stevens, "Economic Consequences of Absent Parents," 81, 100; Brown, "Marriage and Child Well-Being," 13, 18.

found that almost all of them thought marriage good but many of them put it off, mostly because they did not have enough money. Those who were unmarried still mostly wanted to raise their child together. After five years, though, only about 20 percent of the cohabiting couples in the study were still together. In some cases the mother had a new partner and had children by him, forming a complex family.

Children in traditional families receive more attention and supervision than children of lone mothers. Children from traditional families do better in school. They come to kindergarten better prepared, have better test scores and grades throughout school, are less likely to drop out, more likely to graduate, and more likely to go to college. Children with two parents have better health, physically and mentally, than lone-parent children. Two-parent children have fewer behavioral problems and score better on the Behavioral Problem Index used by psychologists. They have less trouble in school, less trouble with police, are less likely to be incarcerated as youths, and are less likely to get pregnant as teens. Children who live with two biological parents are less likely to be abused; one study showed children under five living with their mother and her boyfriend were fifty times more likely to be fatally harmed than children living with two biological parents.[8]

Children in traditional families do better but maybe not because of the structure of their families. Richer, more educated people tend to marry and have children in marriage, while poorer less educated people are more likely to have their children out of marriage. Social scientists use a college degree as a convenient dividing line. "The people with more education tend to have stable family structures

8. McLanahan, "Family Instability," 111–12; Musick and Michelmore, "Change in Stability," 16; Jason M. Fields et al., "A Child's Day: 1994," *Current Population Reports*, Feb. 2001, 19, 23, 25; Kalil et al., "Time Investment in Children," 151, 153–54; Artis, "Maternal Cohabitation," 224; Harper and McLanahan, "Father Absence and Youth Incarceration," 389; Bumpass and Lu, "Trends in Cohabitation," 39; Schnitzer and Ewigman, "Child Deaths," 253–56; also Carlson and Corcoran, "Family Structure," 779–92; Manning and Lamb, "Adolescent Wellbeing," 876–93; Ziol–Guest and Dunifon, "Complex Living Arrangements," 424–37.

with committed involved fathers," said Sara McLanahan. "The people with less education are more likely to have complex, unstable situations involving men who come and go." Maybe children in traditional families do better, not because their parents are married, but because their parents are richer, better schooled, and better behaved. In McLanahan's study of new parents, married couples were older and less likely to be minorities. Of married mothers, 36 percent were college graduates, compared to 1.4 percent of single mothers. Married fathers earned $40,000, single fathers $16,000, and single fathers were more likely to use drugs, drink heavily, hit their partners, and to have been jailed. Social scientists disagree on the importance of marriage. Some say marriage improves behavior and is important for children and society, and others say marriage scarcely matters, and the troubles that beset poor, lone-mother families come from dysfunctional American institutions.[9]

Family scholar Samuel H. Preston noted different ways people have responded to family change. Consider five of them:[10]

1. American college-educated young people marry late, after completing education and establishing careers. Before they get married, they have relationships and may cohabit. But they put off having children until they marry and have fewer children than they otherwise might have. (College-educated young people rein in their selfish genes.)[11]

2. American poor and working young people put off marriage but are less likely to postpone children. Where middle-class women postpone children for education, career, and wealth, these goals may seem unattainable to young working or poor women and offer little incentive to put off childbirth. One study of unwed mothers showed that most were young adults who had children out of love for their

---

9. McLanahan, "Fragile Families," 111–31; Stephanie Coontz, "Marriage," *American Prospect*, Mar. 2002, online at www.prospect.org.; Akerlof et al., "Analysis of Out-of-Wedlock Childbearing," 313–14; Wilson, *Marriage Problem*, 1–11.

10. Preston, "Value of Children," 263–66.

11. See Cahn and Carbone, *Red Families v. Blue Families*, 37–41.

boyfriend, a belief that they would be good mothers, and a hope that a child would make them happy.[12]

3. Swedes, Danes, and the French, among others, have more children out of marriage than Americans, but their governments offer generous benefits, so they have fewer poor families and poor children than America has.[13]

4. Greeks and Spaniards put off marriage, have few children out of marriage, and have fewer children overall. Their fertility is too low to replace their populations. If Americans had only the children born in marriage, their fertility would resemble Greek and Spanish fertility. But with the additional 40 percent of all American births that occur out of marriage, American fertility is closer to replacement.

5. Utahns marry young, have most of their children in marriage, and have more than enough children to replace the population. (Scholars debate whether a growing or declining population is better.)

Traditional families have brought higher fertility and population growth to Utah. Since white settlement, every census has shown Utah growing faster than the nation as a whole. The increase has been mostly homegrown. Demographers calculate that 78 percent of Utah's growth since 1940 has been due to natural increase, the excess of births over deaths. More people have moved in than out, but migration depends on the strength of the economy compared to other parts of America, which historically has been less reliable than Utah fertility. In its first five decades of statehood, Utah lost migrants, as it did in the 1960s and 1980s; it has had a net in-migration in the other five decades.[14] The 2010 Census showed 2,763,885 people living in Utah, just less than one percent of all Americans.

Utah also has fewer minorities than America, only about 2 percent of the population until the 1960s when the percentage tripled and has

---

12. Edin and Kefalas, *Promises I Can Keep*, 9.
13. Rainwater and Smeeding, "Single-Parent Poverty." 96–115.
14. Pamela S. Perlich and John C. Downen, "Census 2010: A First Look," *Utah Economic and Business Review*, 2011, 3–4; Poll, *Utah's History*, 690; *Economic Report to the Governor 2018*, 5.

continued to rise since then to 19.6 percent in the 2010 census, about half the national percentage. Currently about two-thirds of Utah's minority population is Hispanic, with smaller percentages of African Americans, Asians, Pacific Islanders, and Native Americans. Some differences between Utah and the United States may be due to differences in minority populations. For example, I attribute differences in child poverty to differences in families, but minorities may play a role, as they more often struggle financially. Fewer minorities in Utah may contribute to the lower rate of child poverty.

REMARKS

Utahns marry more and cohabit less than other Americans. They have the highest birthrate, highest fertility, and the lowest share of extramarital babies. A Utah child is more likely to live with two parents than a child in any other state.[15] Utahns marry youngest, and young marriage forestalls extramarital birth and promotes fertility.

Utah differs partly because most Utahns are Latter-day Saints who marry young because many of them will not have sex until marriage.[16] Church leaders preach against extramarital sex, and Latter-day Saint parents reinforce those teachings. In studying teens and sex, Mark Regnerus found that Latter-day Saint parents were the second-most likely to talk to their children about sex as a moral issue and the least likely of any religious group to talk about birth control. Latter-day Saint teens were most likely to say they wanted to put off sex until marriage, and most agreed that if they had sex it would "upset your mother." Despite teachings of home and church, surveys show young Latter-day Saints have sex in numbers that would dismay some of

---

15. "Child Population by Household Type," *Kids Count Data Center*, kidscount.org. The data comes from the US Census Bureau's American Community Survey. In 2016, 82 percent of Utah children lived in married-couple households, compared to 66 percent nationwide.

16. Lipka, "Mormons More Likely to Marry," *Pew Research Center*; Heaton et al., "In Search of a Peculiar People," 87–118, who from the National Survey of Families and Households determined that Mormons are more likely to be married and have a favorable view of marriage but not a higher rate of marital satisfaction.

their mothers, although still less than the average young American.[17] Latter-day Saint youth follow the teachings of Church and parents enough to make Utah demographically unusual.

Better birth control and changed attitudes enabled young people to have sex as they chose and to put off babies for education and careers. Birth control helped women to gain an education and careers and to escape dependence on men. A few scholars said, "Good riddance to The Family." But the decline of traditional families and the increase in out-of-marriage children seemed entangled with poverty, crime, child abuse, and other social troubles that worried politicians and engaged social scientists. Governments made gestures to restore marriage. The 1996 welfare reform act that was signed by President Bill Clinton contained measures to promote marriage, especially among poor women. President George W. Bush sponsored an initiative that advertised marriage and provided classroom instruction on marital success. Louisiana, Arkansas and Arizona enacted Covenant Marriage to allow couples to make divorce more difficult. US Senator Mike Lee from Utah proposed a tax advantage to married couples and their families, although his idea was not enacted. None of this seemed to slow the decline in marriage. It may be that government lacks capacity for matchmaking.[18]

Most social scientists who study families believe that marriage is the wrong point of attack. Discussions of marriage decline, such as this one, inescapably stigmatize lone mothers and their children (which I regret), when many of them raise successful children and do not deserve criticism. Moreover, family decisions are private, and perhaps government should not meddle in them; government may do best to take families as they come and offer help where needed.

17. Regnerus, *Forbidden Fruit*, 65, 87, 104, drawing from the National Survey of Youth and Religion to show that 12.6 percent of LDS teens had sexual intercourse, the lowest of any religious group. The National Study of Adolescent Health showed 21.7 percent of LDS teens having sex, the second lowest percentage. See also Heaton et al., *Statistical Profile of Mormons*, 89–90.

18. Stacey, "Good Riddance to 'The Family,'" 545–47; also Haskins and Sawhill, "Decline of the American Family," 8–34.

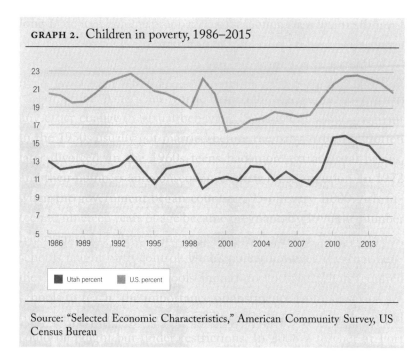

GRAPH 2. Children in poverty, 1986–2015

Source: "Selected Economic Characteristics," American Community Survey, US Census Bureau

Most family social scientists say the right point of attack is poverty. They point to Sweden and Iceland as proof that even as families change, government programs reduce poverty, in contrast to the government's ineffectiveness in promoting marriage. Government money could assure all or almost all children sufficiency. Scholars prescribe more welfare and offer reasoned hope that reduced child poverty might reduce other social troubles.[19]

Utah, however, has followed a different strategy. Conservative politics make for stingy social programs. Poor children in Utah receive less government help overall than in other states. But Utah is an outlier for the lowest percentage of children living with a single parent, at just one half the national rate, and so, as graph 2 shows, Utah has had a lower percentage of poor children than the nation every year since government began reporting child poverty by state.

---

19. E.g., Kenworthy, *Social Democratic America*, 15, 179.

Over the thirty years annual state data are available, Utah child poverty has averaged 62 percent of national rates.

While social scientists disagree on the effects of marriage, they find that poverty harms children. Poor children have lower birth weights, higher infant mortality, delayed language development, more chronic illness, and are more prone to injury. Children who are poor at nine years of age are more likely at seventeen to be smokers or obese. Their brain development may lag, and they are less likely to graduate high school.[20] Though Utah government acts with less energy to curb poverty, Utah children fare better because they live in traditional families.

Utah became different from America because the two change at different rates, but both Utah and America change in the same demographic direction: marriage and fertility decline, cohabitation and out-of-marriage births rise; family and household size decrease; and the population ages. Utahns resist family change, but their families change anyway. Though lagging behind, Utah moves steadily in the American direction in families and demography.

20. "Child Population by Household Type," "Children in Single-Parent Families," *Kids Count Data Center*, Council on Community Pediatrics, "Poverty and Child Health," 1–2; Lacour and Tissington, "Effects of Poverty," 523–25; also Evans and Kutcher, "Loosening the Link," 3–7; Hair et al., "Association of Child Poverty," 822–29.

5

ECONOMY

When Utah governor Herbert Maw met President Franklin D. Roosevelt, he asked, "You know I'm the only governor who is both a ma and a pa?" Maw had come to the White House to state his case for locating a defense plant in Utah. The president seemed puzzled. Maw explained, "You see, my name is *Maw*, but I'm the *Pa* of five children."

How the president laughed! That joke put the New York aristocrat at ease, and he listened attentively and agreed that Utah would be a good place for the plant. Then as Maw was leaving, the president turned to an aide and asked, "Isn't there something more we can do for my friend here from Utah?" On the spot, President Roosevelt gave Utah additional war-related work Maw had not even asked for. All his life, Maw loved to tell the story of how his Utah wit made the president laugh and won jobs for folks back home.[1]

Utahns want prosperity, and governors try to deliver. Maw founded a Department of Publicity and Industrial Development to plan Utah's economy and recruit federal-government work. All gubernatorial candidates promise economic growth, and economic performance affects gubernatorial popularity. Incumbent Governor Gary Herbert says he focuses "laser-like" on the economy. During his terms, Utah has prospered, and he boasts of the state's success.

---

1. Clark Lobb, "Governor's Joke," *Salt Lake Tribune*, Apr. 14, 1975. Peterson and Cannon tell a more complicated version in *Awkward State of Utah*, 339–40.

His formula differs from Maw's: "I keep government out of your wallet and off your back," he says.[2]

Political scientists often see politics as a struggle for economic interest. They believe economics explain political outcomes. In the state's history, economics have sometimes explained political outcomes, but not always, particularly not in the contemporary period of the Republican ascendancy. This chapter reviews Utah's economic history with an eye to how economics has affected politics, and looks at how scholarly theories of economics, politics, and families apply in Utah.

Economic historian Leonard Arrington divided Utah history into four economic phases, and after his writing the state entered a fifth. In the first phase, from settlement in 1847 until completion of the transcontinental railroad in 1869, Latter-day Saints built a centrally directed, cooperative economy based on irrigated agriculture. Brigham Young made political decisions, and directed Utah's economy toward communal self-sufficiency, developing the ability to meet local needs. The census of 1850 showed 85 different occupations in Utah, compared to California, where 75 percent of workers mined gold.[3] Most western settlements attracted people by economic opportunity. Latter-day Saint settlements brought in people through religious proselytizing and organized immigration. Early Utah flourished on faith.

Utah's second economic phase lasted from the completion of the railroad until statehood. Utah needed rails to move goods. Elsewhere in the world, most goods moved on water, and most cities were located near navigable waterways. Land-locked Salt Lake City had 40,000 people who needed to have merchandise brought in 1,500 miles overland by wagon. A teamster could make only one trip each summer from Salt Lake City to Independence,

---

2. Anderson, "History of Reorganization"; Gary R. Herbert, "Executing Fundamentals," *Deseret News*, Apr. 17, 2014; Robert Gehrke, "Herbert Says Utah Economy Is Best," *Salt Lake Tribune*, Mar. 14, 2012.
3. Arrington, *From Wilderness to Empire*, 7, 11–12.

Missouri, and back, and freight costs kept prices high. No mine was able to succeed before the railroad arrived. After rails could haul ore, a mining industry run by non-Mormons grew up next to the Latter-day Saint-run agriculture.[4] The two fit together: Latter-day Saints sold goods to miners, who sold metals outside the territory. But other issues—conflict over polygamy and government—divided them.

From statehood to World War II, Utah's third economic period, Latter-day Saints and non-Mormons unified their separate economies. Gentile ways prevailed, and Utah exported commodities to meet national demand instead of making different goods to meet community needs. Though the Church continued to own businesses, eastern banks and corporations began making big economic decisions. Latter-day Saints forsook aspirations for a self-directed, self-sufficient economy. Utah came to rely on outsiders for capital, goods, and markets.[5]

Utah produced sugar, wool, silver, lead, and copper. Politics followed those commodities, which required federal tariffs. Sheep men needed protection from Australian wool, and sugar companies needed a tariff on Cuban cane. Utah supplied 13 percent of American lead because cheaper foreign lead bore a duty. Utah prosperity could rise no higher than the tariff walls. Utah Republicans trumpeted tariffs every election: "Sugar, Lead, Wool, Vote the Republican Ticket," read one campaign ad. The chief protectionist, Senator Reed Smoot, was known as the "Apostle of Protection" from 1903 to 1933, and author of the Smoot–Hawley Tariff.[6] He was the boss of Utah politics.

Democrats in Utah could not compete on tariffs. Privately they complained that national Democratic tariff policies favored the South and harmed Utah. But they won brief victories with silver.

---

4. Nelson, *Utah's Economic Patterns*, 243; Arrington, *Great Basin Kingdom*, 293–322.
5. Arrington, "Commercialization of Utah's Economy," 3–7.
6. Poll, "Political Reconstruction," 124–25; Allen, "Great Protectionist," 340; also Stauffer, "Utah Politics, 1912–1918," 28–32.

In the national depression of 1896, Democrats called for minting silver coins. "You shall not crucify mankind on a cross of gold," said Democratic presidential candidate William Jennings Bryan. Utahns were debtors who wanted easy money, and they produced 13 percent of the nation's silver. Utahns cast 83 percent of their votes for Bryan's losing campaign, the largest share they ever awarded a presidential candidate. Bryan's silver tongue helped Democrats win control of the legislature in 1896 and 1898. Democrats elected a US senator and a congressman as well. Then the economy improved, silver lost political luster, and Utah returned to the Republicans in 1900.[7]

Commodity men became the political leaders. Senator Thomas Kearns (R, in office 1899–1903) wrested a fortune from Park City silver. Congressman James Mays (Progressive, 1915–21) made money in coal. Governor Simon Bamberger (D, 1917–21) earned his fortune in coal and railroads. Governor George Dern (D, 1925–33) invented a new silver extraction process for the Mercur mines. Governor John Cutler (R, 1905–09) built sugar mills. Senator Reed Smoot (R, 1903–33) directed the Provo Woolen Mills. Of these politicians, the ones who made money in wool and sugar were Latter-day Saints; those who made their money in mining (and were richer) were non-Mormons.[8]

Utah did not compete well nationally, and over forty years, slipped behind. Per capita income fell from 90 percent of the national average in 1900 to 80 percent in 1929 and rose only to 82 percent by 1940. Development spread from the East but skipped Utah in favor of California. The population grew, but only because Utahns had more children than other Americans. Utah could not support its

---

7. Moyle, *Mormon Democrat*, 262–63; "Bryan's 'Cross of Gold' Speech," *History Matters*, historymatters.gmu.edu; Griffiths, "Far Western Populism," 398 (Senator Joseph L. Rawlins and Congressman William H. King were elected); also White, "Utah State Elections," 111–13.

8. For more, see master's theses by Larsen, "Life of Thomas Kearns," and Morn, "Simon Bamberger"; Bringhurst, "George H. Dern," and Murphy, "John Christopher Cutler," *Utah History Encyclopedia*; Merrill, *Reed Smoot*.

progeny, and every decade from 1890 through 1940 more people moved out than moved in. Utah was the only Western state with net outmigration. Good times came but did not last. The First World War boosted prices for metals and crops, so money flowed into Utah. But in 1920 postwar depression struck nationwide. America quickly recovered and turned the twenties into the prosperity decade, but prices for Utah's commodities remained low, so the twenties never roared in Utah.[9]

The state bumped ever farther down a slope and eventually seemed to fall off a cliff into the Great Depression. Utah fared worse than other states. Per capita income, $537 in 1929, fell to $275 by 1933, when 36 percent of Utah's labor force was out of work. The New Deal offered help, and by 1935 one-third of all Utahns were on government relief. In 1936, 30,000 Utahns did government make-work, almost 20 percent of all workers who had jobs.[10] Governor Henry Blood and other officials spent weeks in Washington trooping from agency to agency, waiting in anterooms, pleading for money. Men in national government remembered Utahns as especially importunate. In reward for supporting Roosevelt, and out of greater need and continual pleading, Utah got more than its share of federal help.[11]

When the economy failed, Utah politics and government changed. The Church of Jesus Christ of Latter-day Saints lost its political influence. Church leaders urged their members not to become dependent on government and began their own welfare program to keep Mormons from federal welfare; nevertheless, church members took more federal welfare than other Americans. Church leaders politicked for conservatism, and met defeat. Utahns rejected Senator Reed Smoot when he sought a sixth term in 1932, even though he was an apostle endorsed by the Church president.

---

9. Poll et al., *Utah's History*, 713; Huntsman, "Historical Study," 3, 65–66, 82–83; Peterson and Cannon, *Awkward State of Utah*, 234–35; also Alexander, "Economic Consequences," 57–91.

10. Bluth and Hinton, "Great Depression," 481–96.

11. Quinn, "Governorship of Henry H. Blood," 82.

Voters elected New Dealer Elbert Thomas instead and voted with President Roosevelt to end Prohibition, defeating the Church campaign to keep liquor illegal. Seventy percent of Utahns ignored the front-page editorial in the Church-owned *Deseret News* in 1936 endorsing Republican Alf Landon and voted to reelect Roosevelt.[12] In moving away from Church influence, Utahns became Democratic. The legislature, which had been Republican since 1920, swung Democratic in 1932, and by 1937 only one Republican sat in the state senate. Utah's governors were Democratic, and from 1932 to 1946, Utah sent only Democrats to Congress.[13] The political changes were temporary. Eventually the Church regained political influence and Republicans came back to power. But in government institutions, the Depression brought changes that still endure. Welfare became a large permanent program. Sales tax, income tax, and corporate taxes, all began in the Depression, and grew to bring in the bulk of state revenues. Progressive Democrats introduced primary elections to Utah's electoral process.

In the state's fourth economic phase, from World War II to the early 1960s, federal defense spending transformed Utah's economy. War brought boom times. The military built or expanded ten major bases and a hospital in Utah, as well as factories to repair airplanes and make ammunition. More than 50,000 Utahns found jobs in war work. The 10 percent unemployment of 1940 shrank to below 5 percent, never rising higher until 1947. Partly because factories were safer from enemy attack far from the coast, the government chose Utah for the Geneva Steel mill, an oil refinery, and plants for

---

12. Darowski, "WPA versus Utah Church," 167–85; also Kearnes, "Utah Electoral Politics," 82–111, 197–99; Decker, "LDS Church and Utah Politics," 107–09.

13. US Senator William King, elected in 1916, was replaced in 1940 by another Democrat, Congressman Abe Murdock, who served until 1946. King's fellow Democratic senator Elbert Thomas was elected in 1932 and stayed in office until 1952. In 1932 Democrats Abe Murdock and J. Will Robinson had both beaten Republican incumbents to go to Congress. The Democratic governors were George Dern, Henry Blood and Herbert Maw.

vanadium, tungsten, alunite, chemicals, and electronics. Spoils of war fell to Utah throughout the conflict.[14]

When the war ended, troops came home and unemployment rose, but unlike the malaise that followed World War I, Utah's economy continued to grow after World War II. The big difference was California. From its vast new prosperity, California bought almost as many exports from Utah as all other markets combined. Utah's economic face turned from east to west. Factories and bases built for war survived peace. The Geneva Steel mill was sold cheaply to United States Steel, and the furnaces never cooled. Utoco bought the government's oil refinery, an alunite plant became a uranium mill, and a chemical plant began producing fertilizer. Developers built a new town on the streets, plumbing, and wiring of the surplus Kearns Air Force Base.[15]

In the mid-1950s, Cold War missiles delivered another defense-spending payload. Hill Air Force Base, the biggest base in Utah, repaired planes and missiles. Missile-making companies moved near Hill and took advantage of Utah's cheap land and cheap, educated labor. Sperry, Marquardt, Thiokol, Hercules, Boeing and Litton all opened plants in Utah and hired tens-of-thousands of workers to build missiles on defense contracts. By 1962, Utah had the largest defense sector, compared to the size of its economy, of any state. Scholars and politicians noted defense had transformed Utah's economy, but they feared the state might suffer when defense work declined.[16]

From the end of World War II to the mid-1980s, Utah Republicans grew from holding almost no Utah offices to holding almost all of them. They did not gain because of state economic issues. In

---

14. Alexander, "Utah War Industry," 73–74, 79–80, 84; Christensen, "Impact of World War II," 497–514.

15. Arrington, "Wilderness to Empire," 18; Alexander, "Brief Histories," 126.

16. Arrington and Jensen, "Defense Industry," 10–13, 28–30; cf. Clayton, "Unhallowed Gathering," 241.

One of the companies in the defense industry that established a manufacturing plant in Utah in the 1950s was Thiokol of New Jersey, here testing a
solid-fuel engine for a Minuteman rocket near Brigham City. *Utah State Historical Society*

Washington both Utah parties sought defense contracts, highway
money, water projects, and other federal favors. These peculiar economic interests did not dominate elections as they had when tariffs
reigned. Neither military people nor defense-company executives
held high public office.

Rocketry reached its apogee as an economic booster in 1961. Thereafter the economy entered a long period of growth and diversification,

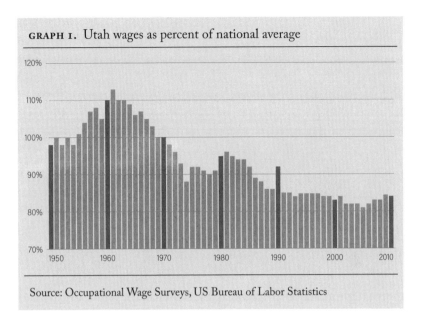

GRAPH 1. Utah wages as percent of national average

Source: Occupational Wage Surveys, US Bureau of Labor Statistics

but lost its best-paying jobs. From 1961 to 2010, the manufacturing share of state jobs fell from 18 to 9 percent, in keeping with a national manufacturing decline. Utah also lost jobs in mining, which had paid the highest wages. From 1961 to 2010, mining fell from 5 percent of all Utah jobs to less than 1 percent. Many jobs disappeared because miners had become more productive. Utah produced more coal and copper (the state's chief mining products) with fewer miners. In addition, the federal government changed its policy and refused to permit new mines on federal land, resulting in fewer Utah miners.[17] As graph 1 shows, from 1961 to 2011, Utah average wages declined from 113 percent to only 84 percent of the national average.

State and national changes left Utah's economic structure closely aligned with the nation's. Economists invented the Hachman Index to measure how closely a state resembles national job distribution, and Utah's resemblance is close. In 2011, Utah's Hachman Index was

---

17. *Economic Report to the Governor*, respective years; Lawrence and Edwards, "Deindustrialization," 3; Perlich et al., "Structure and Impact," 5; Isaacson, "Structural Changes," 1.

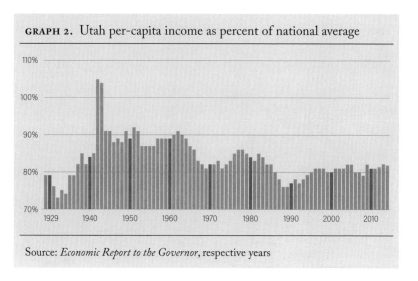

GRAPH 2. Utah per-capita income as percent of national average

Source: *Economic Report to the Governor*, respective years

fourth highest, and in 2015 and 2016, Utah had the highest Hachman Index of any state. That means the percentage of Utahns doing each kind of work was nearly the same as the percentage of Americans. Utah had a higher percentage of miners, construction workers, and teachers, but lower percentages in health-care, finance, and business services. None of the differences was large. Utah politics and demography differed from America's, but its economic structure was similar.[18]

The relative decline in wages partly caused a corresponding decline in per capita income, as shown in graph 2. Both income and wages lost ground against the national average after 1962. But while Utah had periods of higher-than-national wages, per capita income has been chronically lower, averaging less than 84 percent of the nation's since 1929 when the federal government began keeping data. Utah exceeded the national figure in only two years, both during World War II, and a look at the graph rouses suspicion those may have been mismeasured. In current dollars, Utah's per capita income grew more than ten-fold from 1962 to 2014 but still failed to keep pace with national prosperity.

---

18. Mark Knold, "Industrial Diversity," *Utah Insights*, 3; Jeff Edwards, "Which State Economy Is Most Economically Diverse?" *UtahPolicy.com*, Mar. 28, 2016.

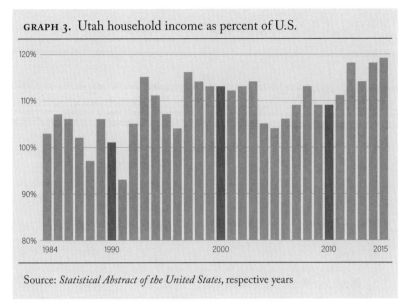

GRAPH 3. Utah household income as percent of U.S.

Source: *Statistical Abstract of the United States*, respective years

Utah economists say demographics distort those numbers and make Utah appear poorer than it is. Per capita income is low because Utahns have more children to divide incomes. Wages are lower because Utah workers are younger and workers typically earn less early in their careers. In addition, a woman is more likely to work part time in Utah than in any other state so as to leave time to take care of her children.[19] The picture looks different if incomes are divided by household, as in graph 3, rather than by individual. Utah exceeded the national average household income in twenty-nine of the thirty-one years from 1984 to 2015. But demographics skew that comparison too. Utah households are the largest in the nation, 3.1 people on average compared to 2.58, and so they are more likely to have multiple earners.

Though their wages and incomes are lower, Utahns are more likely

19. Laura Summers, "Is Utah *Really* a Low-Wage State?" research brief, June 5, 2008, www.utahfoundation.org., drawing from the US Current Population Survey to show Utah full-time male workers earn 98 percent of the national average. Utah women are more likely to work part-time (most say because of family responsibilities), lowering the average.

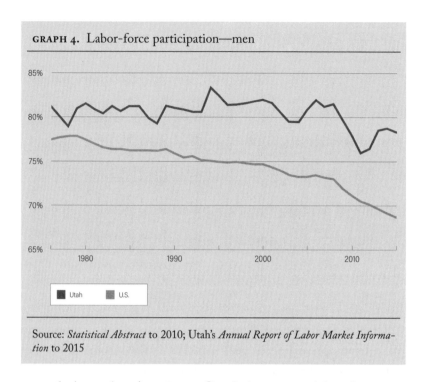

GRAPH 4. Labor-force participation—men

85%

80%

75%

70%

65%

1980   1990   2000   2010

Utah   U.S.

Source: *Statistical Abstract* to 2010; Utah's *Annual Report of Labor Market Information* to 2015

to work than other Americans. Graph 4 compares labor-force participation of Utah and American men. To "participate in the labor force," a man must either be working or actively looking for work (those looking are "unemployed"). The percentage of American men participating in the labor force fell from 78 percent in 1978 to 68 percent in 2015, and this was part of a longer fall beginning in the mid-1950s when male labor-force participation nationally was above 85 percent. Although unemployment draws more attention, more men—sometimes three times as many—are out of the labor force at any given time as are unemployed. Since the federal government began releasing labor-participation rates for the states in 1976, Utah's rate has fallen from 81 to 79 percent, about one-fifth the national fall. Utah participation has been higher than the national rate every year. For a few years, Utah had the highest rate of any state. The gap between Utah and American men averaged more than 6

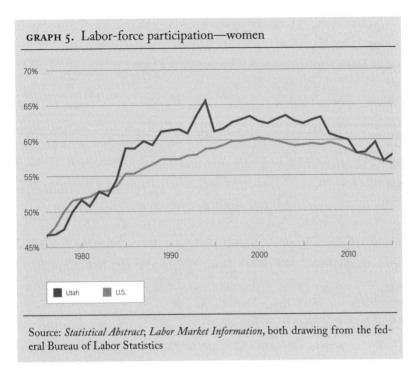

GRAPH 5. Labor-force participation—women

Source: *Statistical Abstract*, *Labor Market Information*, both drawing from the federal Bureau of Labor Statistics

percent over the thirty-eight years shown in the graph and rose to 11 percent in recent years.

Utah women are also more likely to work than their national counterparts, as graph 5 shows, although the average difference from 1976 to 2015 was only 3 percent. Note that until 1985, Utah women were no more likely to be in the labor force than other women. In fact, the graph shows the end of a long-term change in the work habits of Utah women. In 1950 only 24 percent of Utah women had jobs outside the home, the ninth lowest percentage of all states. More American women, compared to Utahns, worked outside the home since at least 1900. But from 1940 to the 1980s, women generally went to work, and Utah female labor-force participation rose from less than one-fourth to more than 60 percent, and from below the national average to above it.[20]

20. Lecia Parks Langston, "Hard @ Work: Utah Women," *Department of Workforce Services*, https://jobs.utah.gov.

Notoriously, in Utah women are paid less than men. A 2018 study showed that Utah had the second largest pay gap of any state. An average Utah woman earned 70 percent of a man's wage, compared to 80 percent nationwide. The gap reflected a difference in education. The number of Utah men with college degrees was six percent higher than the percentage of Utah women with degrees, the largest such difference in any state. Utahns with college degrees were 4 percent above the national average for men and 2 percent below the national average for women.[21] In other words, Utah women are less educated, work more, and earn less than their counterparts nationally.

Not only are Utahns more likely to look for work, they are more likely to find it. From 1976 to 2011, Utah's unemployment was lower than the national rate every year, and on average, national unemployment was 25 percent higher than the Utah jobless rate. Utahns' proclivity for work helps keep them out of poverty. Graph 6 shows Utah and national poverty rates from 1979 when the Health and Human Services Department began reporting by state. The national rates have been, on average, one-third higher than Utah's, and Utah's poverty was lower than the national average every year.

Utah may have more economic mobility than other states. A team of researchers compared outcomes for children who grew up in America's fifty largest "commuter zones" and found that Salt Lake City had the highest overall score in what they called "absolute upward mobility," meaning that a Salt Lake City child whose parents ranked in the 25th income percentile was more likely to rise higher than a similar child in any other city. Salt Lake City also ranked sixth highest in "relative mobility," that is, how likely is a child born in the bottom one-fifth to rise to the top one-fifth in income. The authors also looked at counties and found that all Utah counties were in the top or next-to-top category for income mobility.

---

21. "The Simple Truth," *Economic Justice*, Apr. 2018, www.aauw.org/research, with data from state labor economist Lecia Parks Langston.

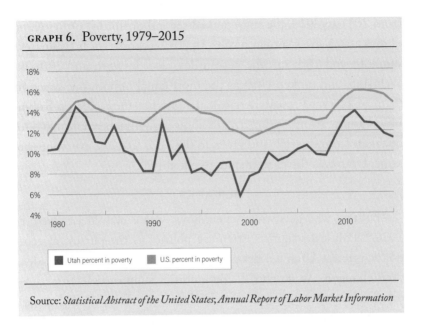

GRAPH 6. Poverty, 1979–2015

Utah percent in poverty
U.S. percent in poverty

Source: *Statistical Abstract of the United States; Annual Report of Labor Market Information*

Utah is America's middle-class state.[22] The Brookings Institute measured the size of the middle class in the hundred largest metropolitan areas in the United States and ranked Ogden, Provo, and Salt Lake City as the top three cities. They had a larger percentage of people with incomes between three-quarters and twice the national median than anywhere else. The middle-class declines in America because incomes are becoming less equal, but Utah's robust middle shows the state is among the most equal in household income.[23] Economists usually use the Gini coefficient to measure inequality. Two calculations by the American Community Survey showed Utah had the lowest Gini coefficient; that is, it was the most nearly equal state in 2010 and 2015, and that in other years

22. Chetty et al., "Where Is the Land of Opportunity?" 3, 24, 26, 53, 70.
23. Richard V. Reeves and Edward Rodrigue, "American Middle-Class," *The Avenue*, Mar. 6, 2016, www.brookings.edu/blog ("middle class" meaning 66 to 200% of median income); "American Middle Class," *Pew Research Center*, Dec. 9, 2015, www.pewsocialtrends.org.

from 2011 to 2016, the state ranked second or third.[24] Other ways of measuring show similar results. In 2011 a census study compared the 90th and 10th income percentiles, also the 95th and 20th, in each state and ranked Utah as the most equal in both measures. A team of Harvard researchers calculated what they called a Robin Hood Index twenty years ago to show how much would have to be taken from the rich and given to the poor to make everyone the same. Utah was the closest state to equality.[25]

REMARKS

"Politics, who gets what, when, how," wrote Harold Lasswell in 1936.[26] Political scientists often see politics as the pursuit of economic interest. Utah politics pursued economic interest for decades, then changed. At statehood, commodities supported Utah's economy and dominated its politics. Utahns voted Republican because Republican tariffs protected Utah commodities. Commodity men won high office. For a few years of economic depression, silver coinage surpassed tariffs in the state's economic interest, and Utahns switched to Democrats, then switched back when the economy recovered and silver seemed less important. When the economy failed in the Great Depression and Utah became dependent on the federal government, Utahns switched again. They voted for Democrats as the party better able to deliver federal help. From statehood through World War II, Utah politics followed economic interests, and political changes followed economic changes.

But when Utah politics changed in the 1970s, from a mainstream

24. Jennifer Burnett, "State-by-State: Income Inequality," *Council of State Governments*, http://knowledgecenter.csg.org; Kirby G. Posey, "Household Income: 2015," www.census.gov; also Alemayehu Bishaw and Jessica Semega, "Income, Earnings, and Poverty Data," US Census Bureau report, Aug. 2008.

25. "Historical Income Tables: Households," *US Census Bureau*, www.census.gov; Dominique Hansen, "Income Inequality," *Voices for Utah Children*, https://utahchildren.org; Daniel H. Weinberg, "US Neighborhood Income Inequality," *American Community Survey Reports*, Oct. 2011, www2.census.gov.

26. Lasswell, *Politics: Who Gets What*.

UTAH POLITICS

state to a one-party-dominant Republican state, economic change was not apparent. [27] Utah politics became different from America's, though Utah's economy showed a close resemblance to America's, at least by some measures. Utah Latter-day Saints and non-LDS people split in politics, though their economic interests remained similar. Economics explain early Utah state politics, but Utah's Republican ascendancy resulted not from economics but from religious and moral differences between Latter-day Saints and other Americans.

Just as they look to economics to explain politics, many social scientists look to economics to explain family change. Sociologist Andrew Cherlin, for example, recounts how American economic change undermined working families. After World War II, high-school-educated men worked high-paying jobs in manufacturing, married, and had families. But starting in the mid-1960s, many American industries lost to foreign competition, to automation, or to jobs being sent abroad. Income went up for owners, managers, and technicians, but jobs disappeared for less-educated workers. Young men without a college degree often had difficulty supporting a family. Women would not marry them and instead sometimes had children out of marriage. When asked why they did not marry, these women usually said they and their baby's father did not have enough money. In contrast, marriage slightly increased among the college-educated. They waited to establish careers, and when economically established, they began traditional families. Cherlin notes that poor and working people, whose incomes as a class declined, changed their family behavior, while college-educated Americans, whose incomes increased, continued to live in traditional families. But he adds that for most of the time before World War II, especially during the Depression, poor and working people had less money, but they still married and raised children in traditional families. Economics may provide part of the reason American families changed, but cannot be the whole

27. Alexander, "Emergence of a Republican Majority," argues that a change in business ownership helped Utah Republicans.

explanation. Like America's economy, Utah's economy lost good jobs for non-college men. Starting in the 1960s, Utah lost high-paying manufacturing and mining jobs, and in official statistics the average Utah wage fell almost one-third in comparison to the average American wage. Though Utah's economy changed as the American economy changed, Utah families changed less than American families. Economic differences contributed to family changes in America, but religious and moral factors slowed family change in Utah.

Many economists say the loss of jobs for working men also explains the decline in male labor-force participation. Concerned about the number of non-working men, President Barack Obama's White House ordered a study which noted that educated men are more likely to be in the labor force and concluded that the decline of good jobs for non-college men likely caused much of their decline in labor-force participation.[28] As in the case of family change, Utah's economy is similar to the American economy but with different outcomes. Utah's higher male labor-force participation is partly due to Utah's family differences. Studies show that marriage and work go together for men. Married men—especially if they live with their children—are more likely to work than non-married men, especially those who never married.[29] Utah men are more likely married and living with their children, which accounts in part for their greater labor-force participation.

Utah religion and morals affect Utah families, which affect Utah demography, which affects the economic indicators. Utah per capita income is low partly because Utahns have more children (who divide adult incomes). Utah wages are low partly because Utah's labor force is young, men are more likely to work part time while going to school, and women are more likely to work part time to care for children. But because Utahns live in larger families and households, often with multiple earners, Utah household income is higher than American

---

28. "Long-Term Decline," June 2016, https://obamawhitehouse.archives.gov.
29. Eberstadt, *Men without Work*, 63–66.

household income. Utahns are less likely to live in single-mother households and thus less likely to be at high risk for poverty. Because of their traditional family living and proclivity for work, Utahns—especially Utah children—are less likely to be poor than other Americans.

As traditional families linger in Utah, so does the traditional division of work between men and women. Partly because they marry young, Utah women are less likely to finish college. They have more children than American women, and children reduce their mothers' earnings. Michelle Budig and Paula England estimated a "mother penalty" on earnings of seven percent for each child, though they found no such parent penalty for men. In addition, Utah women begin families when they are younger, and the babies born to young mothers have an even larger effect on incomes than babies born after a woman has established her career. Surveys show many Utah mothers choose to work part time so they can take care of families; part-time workers are counted in some wage statistics and reduce average female wages. Utah women choose younger marriage, earlier motherhood, and more children, and the outcomes support feminists who say traditional families bring women lower earnings and greater inequality compared to men.[30]

Though Utah does poorly with respect to gender pay equality, it fares better in household income equality. In recent decades, the American rich have won an ever-larger portion and left less for poor and working people. Many progressives see maldistribution as the root of American trouble, associated with educational failure, violent crime, ill health, and other problems, some of which are discussed in the next chapter. They want government redistribution to protect democracy and advance justice and happiness. President Obama called his policies "middle-class economics."[31] Utah may be the most

---

30. Budig and England, "Wage Penalty," 204; also Summers, "Low-Wage State?" www.utahfoundation.org; Stacey, "Good Riddance," 545–47.

31. Wilkinson and Pickett, *Spirit Level*, 49–145. showing social troubles resulting from income inequality; also Payne, *Broken Ladder*; Hacker and Pierson, *Winner-Take-All*; Stiglitz, *Price of Inequality*; Obama, "Remarks by the President."

middle-class state, and Utah incomes are among the most equal. Utah equality, however, results from neither income redistribution by government nor other progressive policies. Rather, its middle-class living seems to come from what Alfred P. Doolittle called "middle class morality"–that is, Utahns live more in traditional families and are more likely to work.[32]

---

32. G. B. Shaw, *Pygmalion*, 1913

6

THE TIME OF DISORDER

Social disorder beset America in the last four decades of the twentieth century. Utahns were most concerned with crime, drugs, child abuse, homelessness, welfare dependency, and teen pregnancy. Each of these issues worried citizens, made news, and roused political debates. Lawmakers dealt with issues of disorder every legislative session. Police, social workers, courts, bureaucrats and teachers all struggled with rising troubles. Violent crime enthralled local television news, and in Utah the politics of disorder were news-story-driven. That is, sensational, easily-understood-and-remembered news stories of crime, gang violence, kidnapped children, and drug tragedies changed and focused public opinion, which in turn influenced politicians who changed policies, partly in response to the news stories. Social conservatives believed that the troubles came as the result of changes in families and public morality, mixed with bad federal policy. They especially blamed federal judicial decisions that strengthened the rights of accused criminals and may have reduced police effectiveness. The troubles provided a political weapon for conservatives across America and helped fasten conservative politics on Utah.

CRIME

As graph 1 shows, the number of violent crimes per 100,000 Americans rose almost five-fold from 1960 to a peak in 1991. In Utah the rate increased even faster, rising from one-third to a rate just less

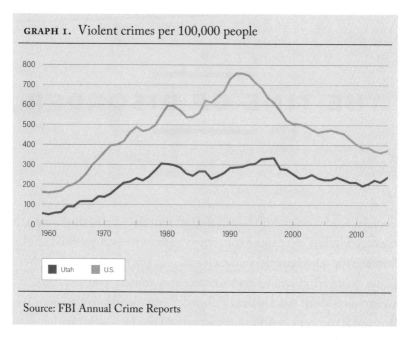

GRAPH 1. Violent crimes per 100,000 people

Source: FBI Annual Crime Reports

than half the rate nationally over the fifty-five years depicted. Utah always had less murder, robbery, and aggravated assault than the nation, but rapes doubled from 1987 to 1991 and stayed higher than the national rate.[1]

Graph 2 shows the rise of property crime. Utah had nineteen property crimes for each violent crime, exceeding the national rate by eight percent from 1960 to 2015. Though Utah had more property crime than the nation, it still beat expectations. Young men commit most crimes, and Utah had the first or second highest percentage of young men in its population. If Utah's young men offended as often as their national counterparts, violent crime in Utah would triple. To respond to more crime, Americans built more prisons and locked up more criminals. Seven times as many Americans were in prison

---

1. "Uniform Crime Reporting Statistics," *US Department of Justice*, www.ucrdata-tool.gov. Utah reported 365 rapes in 1987, 808 in 1991, and 926 in 2013, and then the FBI changed the definition of rape. Utah's number was revised that year to 1,522, a 60 percent jump.

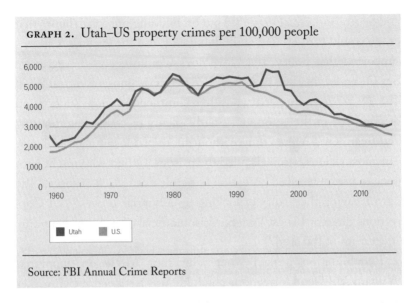

GRAPH 2. Utah–US property crimes per 100,000 people

Utah   U.S.

Source: FBI Annual Crime Reports

in 2004 as in 1970. Imprisonment also rose in Utah. In 1960, Utah had 525 inmates in state prison; by 2010 the state had 6,692. Prisons were the state's primary response to crime. Local governments (with some help from federal grants) mostly determined the number of police. Legislators could pass stricter laws, but federal courts limited prison crowding and ordered inmates released if a prison exceeded the limit. Utah prisons were full or nearly full since 1960. "If you build it, they will come," prison officials said. Even so, Utah imposed less punishment than the nation, with an incarceration rate less than half the national average.[2]

Before they built new prisons, both Utahns and Americans changed their minds. Through the 1950s and 60s, they believed treatment and education could rehabilitate criminals. As Utah crime rose through the 1970s, Democratic governors Cal Rampton (1965–77)

2. Lynch, *Big Prisons, Big Dreams,* 50–51; "Utah Prison Population Reaches Highest Point," *Salt Lake Tribune,* June 11, 1961; "Average Yearly Incarcerated Population," State Department of Corrections slide presentation, Jan. 6, 2012; "Incarceration Rate: U.S., Western States, and Utah: 1982–2015," in *Data Analysis for Utah Sentencing Commission,* April 2017.

and Scott Matheson (1977–85) put off building prisons in hopes that crime would turn around and Utah could save the expense. Citizens supported that policy. The Governor's Commission on Aggressive Sex Offenders in 1962 recommended better diagnosis and treatment. The *Deseret News* agreed when it recommended more supervision of criminals in the community, with "plenty of counseling, training and treatment." More crime without more prisons implied leniency. The most vicious criminals filled the prisons. Others who might have gone to prison received probation or parole due to lack of space. "The day of having the luxury of locking up a burglar is over," said Corrections director Ernest Wright. Prison officials joked they kept only "the cream of the crud."[3]

Rehabilitation peaked when Governor Matheson appointed William Milliken Corrections chief. He was a trained social worker who said that just locking men up was "barbaric." Prisons should rehabilitate. Even better, criminals should be rehabilitated in the community to save money and teach them to live successfully outside prison.[4] Then publicized crimes changed beliefs and policy. One policy-changing crime occurred just after Christmas 1983. As eighteen-year-old LaDawn Prue walked to her car from work, a strange man pointed a gun at her, forced her into his car, shot her in the neck, pushed her into the snow, then got out of his car, and shot her again. Afterwards, Ms. Prue sued the state, won a settlement, and became Miss Wheelchair Utah. Her assailant, Kenny Roberts, had been sent to prison for rape but was furloughed by Corrections officials who stretched the rules to let him out for Christmas. The crime and its aftermath led Utah news for months. Chief Milliken sued KCPX Channel 4 for libel, but his case was dismissed. After an investigation, Governor Matheson demanded resignations from

3. "Utah's Criminal Control," *Salt Lake Tribune*, Mar. 8, 1962; "Why Utah Should Test Iowa's Rehabilitation Plan" editorial, *Deseret News*, Mar. 22, 1974; "Utah's Cost of Crime," *Deseret News*, Sept. 26, 1975.

4. Douglas D. Palmer, "Director to Stress Community Corrections," *Deseret News*, Jun. 10, 1977.

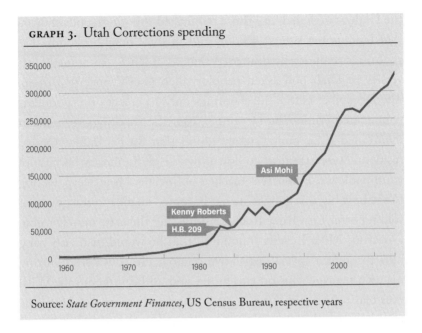

GRAPH 3. Utah Corrections spending

Source: *State Government Finances*, US Census Bureau, respective years

Milliken and his boss, the director of Social Services, and changed policy. He asked the legislature to take Corrections out of the Department of Social Services and create a new, sterner Corrections Department. He asked for money to enlarge prisons. Republican legislators refused Matheson's request in an election year. But after Republican Norman Bangerter became governor in 1985, the legislature created the new department and appropriated more money for prisons.[5] Graph 3 shows the Corrections budget from 1960 through 2010. Note the increase after Kenny Roberts.

Corrections spending rose again after the West High School football captain, Asi Mohi, shot and killed fellow teenager Aaron Mitchell outside a rock concert in 1993. Mitchell was evidently wearing the wrong gang colors. Another gang shooting a few days later wounded a young man as he stepped off the ferris wheel at

5. Bob Bernick and Roger Pusey, "Milliken, Gallegos Resign," Roger Pusey, "Paralyzed Victim," Brett Del Porto, "Settlement Pleases Prue," *Deseret News*, June 1, 1983, Nov. 25, 1986; Allen, *Still the Right Place*, 340–42.

the Utah State Fair. Until those publicized shootings, polls showed that Utahns felt safe at schools and in their neighborhoods. The shootings temporarily destroyed that confidence. An annual University of Utah poll asked people which issues concerned them. The December before the shootings only 1 percent of respondents volunteered crime. The December after the shootings, 40 percent mentioned it. A police survey found that 80 percent of Ogden residents were afraid to go downtown at night, mostly because of youth violence. Public fear reached politicians. "It is overpowering to me how big this gang issue has become," an aide to the governor told reporter Lisa Riley Roche. Addressing the state on television, Governor Mike Leavitt announced that he would rush anti-gang bills through a special legislative session. He considered putting his own teenage sons on curfew, he said, to keep them safe. With eyes tearing, he said, "This is crazy. This is where we live." He proposed more lock-ups, a juvenile work camp, and a law to try violent youths as adults.[6] A poll showed that public support ranged from 80 to 95 percent for each measure. Lawmakers passed anti-gang bills almost unanimously.

After crime statistics rose for three decades, they fell in the 1990s, as graphs 1 and 2 show. Social scientists offered conflicting explanations:

Politics. In the 1960s and 70s, young people challenged authority over civil rights, the Vietnam War, and American inequality. They said America and its laws were immoral and those attitudes may have fostered crime.

Demographics. Baby boomers entered their crime-prone years as crime rose. Then, as they aged, the percentage of young men in the population fell, and crime fell as well.

Abortion. Some social scientists say abortion changed demographics. The US Supreme Court ruling in *Roe v. Wade* resulted in fewer young men of criminal age when, fifteen years later, crime rates fell.

---

6. See news coverage and Dan Jones polls in *Deseret News*, Dec. 14, 1992, Apr. 11, May 27, Sept. 13, Oct. 10, Dec. 11, 1993, Dec. 12, 1995; *Salt Lake Tribune*, Feb. 11, Sept. 13 and 16, 1993.

Furthermore, these studies say, babies who were most likely to grow up to be criminals were the ones most likely aborted.

Economics. Entry-level wages declined as crime rose. Work was sometimes scarce. Crime may have paid young men better than work. Then in the 1990s entry-level wages rose and crime decreased.

Police. Federal-court decisions restricted police interrogations and searches and may have let crime flourish. In the 1990s police numbers rose. For example, President Bill Clinton signed the Violent Crime Control and Law Enforcement Act in 1994 that paid for 100,000 more police nationwide, and may have contributed to the fall in crime.

Drugs. The use of illegal drugs increased as crime rose. Addicts stole to support their habits, and some dealers shot rivals and debtors. Scholars say drug use was like an epidemic: it spread by personal contact but eventually subsided. Changes in drug habits may have reduced crime.

Prisons. Imprisoning ever more criminals may have reduced crime.[7]

Franklin Zimring and Gordon Hawkins say that social scientists do not know the causes of crime. Crime increased in America and then went down. Scholars make plausible guesses but do not know why crime increased or which policies, if any, caused it to fall.[8] Note that social conservatives say crime rose as traditional families declined, but crime fell starting about 1992, while traditional families continued to decline. So the arc in crime does not support the social conservative explanation.

Though crime fell, incarceration continued to rise. America had the highest rate of imprisonment of any developed country. Utah prisons continued at near capacity, and legislators sought money to build more. Minority men suffered. At times in Utah, African-American men were ten times more often imprisoned than in the population.[9] In 2015, Utah lawmakers passed the Justice Reinvestment Initiative

---

7. James Allen Fox, "Demographics," 288; Donahue and Levitt, "Impact of Legalized Abortion," 3, 8, 13; Grogger, "Economic Model," 226; Johnson et al., "Rise and Decline," 164.

8. See, e.g., Zimring and Hawkins, *Crime Is Not the Problem.*

9. Oldroyd and Haddon, *Report to Utah*, 25.

to reduce prison populations and offer more treatment to drug-addicted criminals. Utah's prison population fell 11 percent over the next three years.

CHILD ABUSE

While the federal government imprisoned men for drugs, Utah imprisoned men for sex. At times drug convicts constituted more than 60 percent of federal inmates. Utah had fewer drug inmates, usually less than 20 percent (rising to above 40 percent a few years surrounding 2005). In contrast, sometimes more than 30 percent of Utah's inmates were sentenced for sex crimes, among the highest percentages for any state. Utah passed strict sex-offender laws in 1983 after a plague of child kidnappings and murders. Starting in 1979, five little boys disappeared over five years. In 1982 three-year-old Rachel Runyon was taken from a playground and murdered. These publicized crimes changed state policy, the same as the LaDawn Prue and Asi Mohi shootings had. US Attorney for Utah Brent Ward and Utah Attorney General David Wilkinson campaigned for stricter laws against child molesters, who, they said, often avoided prison. Ward disparaged treatment for sex offenders as "30 days in the outpatient clinic." He said that few child molesters changed, and most molested again.[10]

In March 1983 legislators passed HB 209 that added mandatory sentences and no parole for child molesters. Sponsor Lyle Hillyard said that his bill was "the most stringent in the United States." It was not tough enough for some legislators. Representative Frances Hatch Merrill proposed capital punishment for kidnapping and erecting billboards at the state's boarder reading, "Kidnapping in Utah is punishable by death." Her bill was narrowly defeated. Pundits said passage of HB 209 showed "the public's mistrust of the courts." It also flouted Utah's tradition of allowing parole boards to release prisoners partly

---

10. Mumola and Karberg, *Drug Use and Dependence*, 4; "Child Molestation," Sheena McFarland, "Utah Locking Up More Sex Offenders," *Salt Lake Tribune*, Feb. 13, 1983, Dec. 30, 2011.

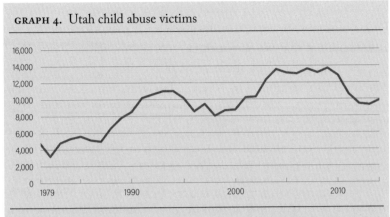

GRAPH 4. Utah child abuse victims

Source: Utah Central Register for Child Abuse and Neglect; Incidence Studies of Child Abuse and Neglect, US Division of Child and Family Development

on their conduct and progress. The new laws did increase punishment. Sex offenders released from prison in 1984 had served thirty-six months on average; by 1994 the average time served was eighty-seven months. Soon after HB 209 became law, Arthur Gary Bishop, a former honors student, Eagle Scout, and LDS missionary, confessed to kidnapping, molesting, and murdering five little boys. He led police to the boys' graves in the desert, pleaded guilty, asked for death, and was executed.[11] Little Rachel Runyon's killer was never caught.

Despite the harsh penalties, sex abuse proliferated. In 1982, the year before the change, Utah had 264 cases. By 1992 the state had 2,444. Scholars and officials said sex abuse had gone unreported until publicity and the state's willingness to act induced victims and those who cared for them to come forward, although little evidence was presented to support that view. Other kinds of abuse and child neglect increased as well, as shown in graph 4. Beginning in 1999 the federal government gathered state reports and computed rates. For

---

11. Joe Costanzo, "Child Abuse Bill," Brett Del Porto, "HB 209 Expresses Rage," Jerry Spangler, "Bishop's Unwitting," *Deseret News*, Mar. 4, Apr. 10, June 9, 1988; Carol Sisco, "House Panel," *Salt Lake Tribune*, Feb. 12, 1983; also Oldroyd et al., *Analysis of Utah's Child Kidnapping Law*.

the sixteen years to 2014 federal reports showed seven to thirteen Utah children had been killed by abuse each year, a fatality rate per 1,000 children that was about three-quarters the national rate. And yet, the national rate of abuse per 1,000 children was three-quarters the Utah number. Dr. Navinia Forsythe, who kept numbers for Utah's Division of Child and Family Services, noted that states have different definitions of child abuse. For example, Utah enacted domestic-violence-related abuse legislation in 1997 making it abuse to see one adult family member hit another. Domestic-violence cases swelled Utah's abuse number, but were not legally counted as abuse in other states. True comparisons between Utah and the nation may not be possible, given the available data.[12]

In the final hour on the final night of the 1995 legislature, senate president Lane Beattie gave up the gavel and spoke from the floor to introduce a bill repealing mandatory minimum sentences for sex abuse. Beattie said Utah should return to indeterminate sentences and trust the parole board, the same as for other crimes. He had kept his bill secret until the end, he said, to avoid committee hearings and emotional testimony that would have made his bill difficult to pass. Legislators approved it. "There was no one in that room who knew what they were voting on," one lawmaker said. Police, prosecutors, victims, and families urged Governor Leavitt to veto the bill. Leavitt said he "philosophically agreed" with Beattie and called for a special session to put Beattie's bill on hold for a year, while a committee studied it. At subsequent public hearings, most citizens spoke for mandatory minimum sentences, but despite public opinion, the commission recommended that the parole board should determine time served, as it did for other crimes. Lawmakers passed that recommendation. Nonetheless, Utah sex-offenders continued to serve

---

12. Oldroyd and Haddon, *Report to Utah on Crime*, 75; Table 3–2, "Statistics and Research," *US Department of Health and Human Services: Children's Bureau*, www.acf.hhs.gov; Navinia Forsythe to author, Feb. 10, 2014. As Utah has a high number of incidents and a low number of resulting deaths, it indicates different definitions across jurisdictions.

long sentences, and the proportion of sex-offenders remained almost one-third of prison inmates.[13]

TEEN PREGNANCY

For a time, Americans worried more about teen pregnancy than any other change in sexual behavior. Teens who became pregnant in the 1950s usually got married before the baby arrived but often later divorced. In the 1960s teens had more extramarital babies, and their numbers and consequences drew more attention. In 1972 when the government began counting, 95 of every 1,000 girls fifteen to nineteen years of age became pregnant. By 1990 the number had risen to 117. Americans argued over what to do. In many states, schools taught birth control. Utah's policy, however, was that families should teach and schools should do no harm. Utah required schools to teach "the importance of abstinence from all sexual activity before marriage, and of fidelity after marriage." Birth control could be taught but under restrictions. In 2008 a teacher at Fort Herriman Middle School answered students' questions about sex and birth control, some parents complained, and the teacher was fired.[14] Utah legislators imposed restrictions on schools so as not to blur the message delivered in homes and churches against sex outside marriage.

The policy provoked controversy. Social scientists said abstinence education does not work. Teens have sex despite what teachers say, and have unprotected sex if they are not taught about birth control. The *Salt Lake Tribune* editorialized that "Utah, a state where the Church of Jesus Christ of Latter-day Saints doctrine

---

13. Tony Semerand, "Beattie's Bombshell," *Salt Lake Tribune*, Mar. 3, 1995; "Citizens Strongly Support Minimum–Mandatory Terms," Jerry Spangler and Amy Donaldson, "Same Idea, New Approach," *Deseret News*, July 7, 1995, Jan. 7, 1996; "Corrections Announces Changes," Department of Corrections news release, Apr. 3, 2017, https://corrections.utah.gov.

14. Coontz, *Way We Never Were*, 82–84; Kost and Henshaw, *U.S. Teenage Pregnancies*, 10; *Utah Code Annotated* 53G–10–402.2(b); "Sex-ed Flap Spurs Ouster of Teacher," *Deseret News*, June 29, 2008; also Luker, *When Sex Goes to School*, 35–89.

and conservative beliefs about abstinence-only education prevail, is an example of the failure of 'just say no' as a way to protect teens." Yet, in fact, Utah teens got pregnant at only half the national rate and also had lower rates of sexually transmitted diseases. The teen birth rate rose to three-quarters the national average because pregnant Utah teens were less likely to abort. In both Utah and the country as a whole, teen pregnancy rose for three decades and then declined. By 2008 the rates were lower than any other year since the counting began. One study said girls seventeen to nineteen were having as much sex as ever but using more birth control, while younger girls had fewer pregnancies partly because they were less likely to begin sex than previously.[15] Despite flouting social-science advice and national best practices, Utah had better outcomes in teen pregnancy than did most places that followed the experts.

DRUGS

Though drug troubles elsewhere had made news for years, Utahns were shocked by stories of high-school pot parties in the canyons. "It's just like cancer," said Tooele mayor Robert Swan, "we can't keep up with it." In 1968, Governor Calvin L. Rampton, hearing that 30 percent of Utah high school students were using marijuana, convened a citizen's advisory council to investigate. The committee found that 12 percent of students had tried marijuana and 4 percent used it regularly. Rampton still worried. "It's getting worse," he said. Graph 5 shows the results of periodic surveys of high school students. Teen marijuana use fell and remained about half the national rate. The surveys also asked about cocaine, heroin, and other drugs. Few Utah young people admitted using these, and use was less than

---

15. "Broken Promises" editorial, *Salt Lake Tribune*, Jan. 4, 2009; "Utah Adolescent Reproductive Health," *U.S. Department of Health & Human Services*, www.hhs.gov; "Complete Health Indicator," https://ibis.health.utah.gov. See also Trenholm, *Impacts*; Kohler, "Abstinence-Only," 344–51; Underhill, "Sexual Abstinence," 248; Kost and Henshaw, *U.S. Teenage Pregnancies*"; "Utah and U.S. Teen Pregnancy Data Reference Sheet," Utah Department of Health, June 2011.

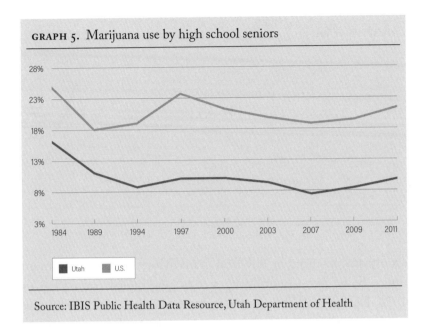

GRAPH 5. Marijuana use by high school seniors

28%

23%

18%

13%

8%

3%

1984   1989   1994   1997   2000   2003   2007   2009   2011

■ Utah   ■ U.S.

Source: IBIS Public Health Data Resource, Utah Department of Health

in the nation. Utah teens also used less alcohol and tobacco, some years less than teens in any other state.[16]

Rampton nevertheless persuaded legislators to create a new state division of drugs in 1970 expecting two-thirds of the funding to come from federal grants.[17] He called a lawyers' committee, chaired by C. M. Gilmour, to update drug law. Schools hurried to teach the evils of drugs. The state was coming late to the drug wars. Congress had passed the Drug Abuse Control Act in 1965, and President Richard Nixon declared a war on drugs in 1971. Utah had drug problems but was partly lured into the drug war by federal money. In 1967 the Salt Lake County Sheriff had one deputy enforcing drug laws. By 1970 the sheriff had a task force of

16. "Tooele Seeks Aid in Drug Battle," *Deseret News*, Nov 20, 1970; "Reports and Rumors Prompt Governor's Drug Response," *Utah Daily Chronicle*, Nov. 21, 1969; *Advisory Committee Report on Drug Abuse*, State of Utah, Sept. 1969, 66; "Data and Dissemination," *Substance Abuse and Mental Health Services Administration*, www.samhsa. gov/data; "Utah Teens Have Lowest Alcohol," *Deseret News*, Nov. 22, 2010.

17. Calvin Rampton "Message to the Legislature," *Utah Senate Journal*, 18.

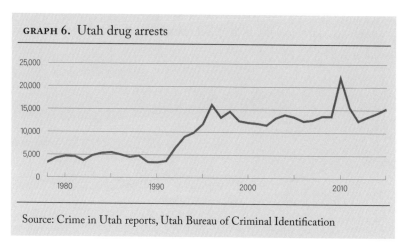

GRAPH 6. Utah drug arrests

Source: Crime in Utah reports, Utah Bureau of Criminal Identification

six officers, financed by a federal grant. More officers found more drugs. Salt Lake County drug arrests quadrupled from 1969 to 1970. Davis and Weber counties obtained grants and formed task forces as well. Graph 6 shows the increase in drug arrests from 1978, when statewide data were first published, until 2015. The number of arrests rose six-fold; moreover, officers began seizing harder drugs. Marijuana occasioned 82 percent of drug arrests in 1982 but only 48 percent in 2015.[18]

Treatment for drug addiction drew federal money too. In the early 1970s, one or more clinics treating people addicted to illegal drugs opened every year in Utah, many relying on federal money. Statewide numbers showed that 15,000 Utahns went to drug or alcohol treatment in 2016, but state officials said surveys showed 146,000 people in the state needed treatment. Many clients were sent to treatment by the courts, and government paid a large share of treatment costs.[19]

---

18. George A. Sorensen, "Workshop Sifts Drug Safety," Max B. Knudson Jr., "County Drug Arrests Rise," Charlotte Hoe, "Task Force Steps Up," *Salt Lake Tribune*, Sept. 29, 1967, Jan. 7, Nov. 14, 1971; "Utah Crime Statistics," *Criminal Identification*, https://bci.utah.gov/.

19. Barbara Springer, "Centers Develop," *Salt Lake Tribune*, Aug. 8, 1978; "Mental Health," *Substance Abuse and Mental Health*, http://hs.utah.gov.

Besides receiving money from the federal government, Utah took money from dealers and users, and that money influenced lawmen and politicians. The 1988 legislature passed a tax requiring purchase of a stamp for every gram of illegal drugs. Buying a stamp did not exempt anyone from criminal law, so drug dealers and users did not buy them. But when officials found drugs, they levied the stamp tax and doubled it as a penalty for tax evasion. Tax levies did not require conviction. Lawmen could get a court order to confiscate whatever a drug possessor owned. "They're pretty shocked when we come in and start seizing all their assets," said Richard Strong, director of collections; "it wipes them out financially." Tax-stamp levies totaled $228 million by the end of 1991, most of it uncollectable. But police seized cars, boats, planes, furniture, and other property to satisfy the debts. In Millard County sheriff's deputies gave a jail inmate six pounds of marijuana and sent him to the home of a family suspected of dealing. Deputies then arrested Coreena Callahan and seized the family house. A judge dismissed the case as entrapment, but Millard County kept the house without a court order for two years. Other states had similar laws. When Montana seized a ranch to pay taxes on a marijuana crop, the owner appealed to the US Supreme Court, which ruled that such taxes were a disguised second punishment unconstitutionally imposed without due process. [20] That ended the stamp tax, but Utah lawmen found other ways to take money from the trade.

Utah Highway Patrol troopers earned fame interdicting drug shipments along "Cocaine Lane," a stretch of I-15 through central Utah that carried drugs from Mexico and Los Angeles to eastern markets. They won a national award for making the most successful drug stops, and some of them travelled the country telling other lawmen how to catch drug runners on freeways. Law agencies kept any cash they found, along with drug runners' cars. In 1988, Sevier County received

---

20. Jerry Spangler, "Tax Agency Wild," "Judge Rejects Utah's Drug Stamp," *Deseret News*, July 26, 1988, May 19, 1999; Bill Gephardt, "Get Gephardt," KUTV News, Nov 10, 1999; *Department of Revenue of Montana v. Kurth Ranch et al.*, 511 U.S. 767 (1994).

$890,000 from drug seizures, 21 percent of its budget. Police could spend drug money with less political control. For example, in 1997 the Utah Department of Public Safety asked the legislature for a helicopter but was turned down. In 1998 the Department received $1 million in drug-forfeiture money and used it to buy a helicopter and two airplanes prior to legislative approval. Courts were skeptical of so many arrests and seizures. Some judges excluded evidence and freed drug runners because they had been stopped and searched without legal cause. Troopers had stopped cars for traffic violations, such as improper lane changes. Judges said such stops were just a pretext. In reality, judges said, suspects were stopped who were black or brown or had long hair. The US Supreme Court, however, ruled that the troopers were right. If a driver broke a traffic law, the trooper could stop him, and any ulterior motive did not matter.[21]

Three wealthy men from outside Utah mounted a campaign to change drug laws. They spent $650,000 to gather signatures for a referendum in 2000 to require a jury verdict before drug property could be seized. Worse still, from a law-enforcement perspective, seized property would go to public schools, not to law enforcement, so that drug money would not tempt lawmen to abuse, petition backers said. An investigation by the legislative auditor general uncovered no large forfeiture abuses. Governor Leavitt and Attorney General Mark Shurtleff spoke against the referendum. It still passed with a vote of 69 percent, the largest majority ever to approve a Utah initiative. Lawmen were shocked. At first, prosecutors claimed to have found a loophole so that lawmen could still keep drug money. It took three years for courts to force them to give the funds to schools. Then lawmen stopped seizing assets, saying that a jury trial was too much bother. After four years, the legislature gave in, overruled the

---

21. Ted Cliwick, "The Heat's On," Dawn House, "Drug Busts," "Collapse of Pretext Doctrine," *Salt Lake Tribune*," May 3, 4, 1992, June 19, 1996; Lisa Riley Roche, "Drug Funds," *Deseret News*, Jan. 13, 1989; *Whren v. United States*, 517 U.S. 806 (1996); Jason Bergreen, "State Troopers Scoring Big in Utah's Drug Corridors," *Salt Lake Tribune*, Apr. 4, 2009.

voters, and changed the law back so that seizures did not require a trial and police could keep the money. Lawmen resumed seizing drug assets for the benefit of their departments.[22]

Methamphetamine caused Utah particular trouble. From 2001 to 2009, more Utahns were treated for meth addiction than for any other illegal drug. It was the only street drug more used by Utah women than men; almost 40 percent of women entering treatment in 2007 had abused meth and about 60 percent were mothers with children. Governor Jon Huntsman pointed to meth moms and launched an anti-methamphetamine campaign. Criminals manufactured the drug in labs hidden in homes, motels, and trailers. Legislators passed several bills restricting the chemicals used to make the drug, but the police still found more labs: thirteen in 1994, 105 in 1997, and a peak of 272 in 1999. Utah raided more meth labs in 1998 than any other state, but Utah had only "trailer-park labs," not big commercial operations. Police and tougher laws eventually suppressed Utah labs, and only one was found in 2014.[23] But then gangs smuggled it in from Mexico.

Utah favored treatment instead of jail for minor drug offenses. With a federal grant, Utah began drug courts in 1996. In drug court, an addict who had committed a nonviolent crime could plead guilty in abeyance. If he attended drug treatment, took drug tests, and behaved for eighteen months or so, the guilty plea would be cancelled. If an addict used drugs, missed court, or broke the law, the judge could incarcerate him forthwith. Utah statistics indicated that addicts who completed drug court were less likely to return to drugs or crime than those sent to jail. A second effort to treat drug criminals

22. Dennis Romboy, "Leavitt Opposes Property Initiative," Jennifer Dobner, "Change in Law," *Deseret News*, Aug. 25, Sept. 24, 2000; *A Performance Audit of Asset Forfeiture Procedures*, Nov. 1999; AP, "Asset Seizure Law," *Ogden Standard–Examiner*, July 20, 2003; Dan Harrie, "Forfeiture Bill," *Salt Lake Tribune*, Mar. 3, 2004.

23. SAMHSA annual reports, 2008, 2010; Kirsten Stewart, "Huntsman Launches Anti-Meth Initiative," *Salt Lake Tribune*, Jan. 10, 2007; "Measure Targets Illegal-Drug Chemists," Geoffrey Fatah, "Meth Labs Busted in Utah," *Deseret News*, Jan. 24, 1989, Mar. 4, 2008.

came in 2005 when 42 percent of Utah inmates were in prison for drug crimes. Lawmakers passed the Drug Offender Rehabilitation Act and appropriated state funds to divert criminals from prison into drug treatment. An early study showed the program did not work as well as predicted, but lawmakers stuck to the policy and by 2010 only 15 percent of Utah inmates had been sentenced for drug crimes.[24]

Surveys by the federal Substance Abuse and Mental Health Administration found Utahns used illegal drugs less than other Americans, in some years, less than residents in any other state. In contrast, Utahns abused prescription drugs more than other Americans. A 1988 story on NBC's *Today Show* labeled Utah the "Ritalin capitol of America." The Drug Enforcement Administration reported that from 1986 to 1988, more Ritalin was bought in Utah than anywhere else. It was prescribed for children, mostly boys, for hyperactivity and Attention Deficit Disorder. After the publicity and resulting controversy, doctors prescribed less of it, and Utah sank to average use. More serious than Ritalin was the damage caused by opioids. Prescription drug overdose became an epidemic. In 2007, 371 Utahns died from prescription overdose—about four times as many as from street drugs and more than from automobile accidents. Opioids caused almost 90 percent of those deaths. For several years, Utah had the fourth-highest death rate for prescription drugs of any state. Lawmakers set up a state-wide data base so addicts could not forge prescriptions or get multiple prescriptions from different doctors. Prescription-drug deaths declined slightly.[25]

---

24. Utah Division of Substance Abuse, "Annual Report," Oct. 2006," https://dsamh.utah.gov; Ben Winslow, "Drug Offenders," *Deseret News*, June 22, 2006; *Performance Audit of the Drug Offender Reform Act*; Utah Department of Corrections, "Offense Type Distribution in Prison," Jan. 6, 2012.

25. Substance Abuse and Mental Health Administration Surveys, 2001–05, www.samhsa.gov. JoAnn Jacobsen-Wells, "No. 1 Ranking," *Deseret News*, June 26, 1988; Stricker and Warchol, "Law Bars Schools," *Salt Lake Tribune*, Mar. 10, 2007; "Prescription Opioid Deaths," *Utah Department of Health*, http://health.utah.gov; Tim Gurrister, "Utah Ranks 4th," *Ogden Standard Examiner*, Nov. 1, 2011.

State officials estimated (although no studies were cited) that 75 percent of state prison inmates were drug or alcohol involved and that drugs and alcohol were associates with 50 percent of rapes and domestic violence, 62 percent of assaults, and 80 percent of violence against children. In a study at the Salt Lake County Jail, urinalyses showed 58 percent of male admissions and 74 percent of females tested positive for illegal drugs. Though many inmates were not charged with drug crimes, drug users kept the jails and prisons full.[26]

HOMELESSNESS

Drugs helped bring homelessness. Though it now seems surprising, Utahns hardly saw a homeless problem until the 1980s. The annual state report, *Poverty in Utah*, did not mention it until 1983. In the 1970s the Union of the Poor demonstrated against housing demolition in Salt Lake City but did not speak of homelessness.[27] Until the 1980s, Utah newspapers referred to *homeless* people only after fires, floods, or earthquakes. Charities served *transients*, who were seen as a small, separate class of people mostly from out of state. During the Reagan recession of the early 1980s, homelessness rose in Utah cities. Shelters overflowed. Hoboes built camps called "Little Tijuana" and "The Condos." The homeless became bolder and more visible after the US Supreme Court struck down vagrancy and loitering laws. Downtown businessmen complained that homeless people begged, vomited, and defecated on the streets, driving away customers. Some winters several homeless people froze to death. Police called them *bumsicles*.[28]

---

26. SAMH annual reports, 2003; Jacqueline Cheney, "Meth News Alarming," Dennis Romboy and Lucinda Dillon Kinkead, "Meth-Using Moms," *Deseret News*, July 22, 2000, Nov. 16, 2004.

27. "Union of Poor Protests Demolition," *Deseret News*, Apr. 4, 1972. Homelessness was not a national problem before the 1980s, according to Mary Ellen Hombs, *American Homelessness*, 15–16, although Bahr and Caplow, *Old Men Drunk and Sober*, 8–11, note that many cities had a skid row, and McCormick, *Salt Lake City*, 79, mentions indigent camps during the Depression. See *Poverty in Utah*; "Housing" clip file, Marriott Library.

28. *Shuttlesworth v. City of Birmingham*, 382 U.S. 87 (1965); Rosemary Reeve, "Only Way to Stop Beggars," *Deseret News*, Oct. 9, 1987; Linda Sillitoe, "Cold Weather,"

Private citizens formed the Emergency Housing Assistance Program in Salt Lake City in 1982 and asked Governor Scott Matheson for help. He arranged to lease at no cost an empty state transportation building as a winter shelter. In the recession, families became homeless. A 1981 survey in Utah made no mention of children or families, but in the 1983 winter, 791 families came to the shelter, mostly single mothers with little children, who had been evicted for not paying rent. When the economy improved, families found homes, but bad times brought them back to the shelters. Homelessness grew partly because court decisions put mentally-ill people on the street. In 1979 a judge followed new federal decisions and ruled that Utah could not force patients to stay in mental hospitals just because they needed care. By 1984 the University of Utah psychiatric ward reported that 70 percent of all patients who came from jail led an "active transient lifestyle." Mentally-ill people sometimes refused care, became homeless, had trouble with police, went to jail, then to a psych ward for medication, were released, stopped taking their meds, and got in trouble again. A 1991 survey showed 23 percent of Utah homeless people had psychiatric problems, and the 2016 Point-in-Time Survey showed 29 percent of the homeless said they were mentally ill.[29]

Local government worsened homelessness as cities used urban renewal, redevelopment, eminent domain, and tax incentives to help knock down shabby old buildings where poor people had rented cheap rooms. In the 1950s the Beverly Hotel on Salt Lake City's State Street advertised "fill-ups" (several people to a room) for sixty-five cents a night. But the Beverly was torn down, along with the Wabash, the Boston, and other flop houses. As cities spruced up, cheap rooms disappeared and left the poor with nowhere to stay. While

"Woman, 39, Freezes," "One of Two Bodies Identified," *Salt Lake Tribune*, Nov. 5, 1982, Mar. 1, 1996, Mar. 27, 2009.

29. *Colyar v. Third Judicial Court for Salt Lake County*, 469 F. Supp. 424 (D. Utah 1979); Point in Time Report, *Utah HMIS*, 2016; also Page et al., "Homeless Families," 130–35; de Gooyer and Bate, "State of Utah."

some Utahns helped the homeless, most did not want them close. When Governor Matheson let people sleep in the empty transportation building, neighbors complained, and local politicians said that if Salt Lake provided shelter, the homeless would flock to the city. The transportation building's lease lasted only one winter, and homeless programs scrambled year after year to find a warm place when the weather turned cold. Temporary shelters opened in an empty car garage, an empty high school, a cafeteria, and an empty warehouse. Neighbors objected to almost every proposed shelter. On cold nights pastor Wayne Wilson let men sleep on the pews of his Spectacular Ministries Church. Officials cited the church because it lacked sufficient bathrooms and fire exits. Wilson defied the city, and under public criticism city officials chose not to prosecute. Cities urged people not to give to beggars. The police bulldozed homeless camps and burned homeless people's sleeping bags, clothing, and furniture.[30]

In 1986, Salt Lake City and Salt Lake County formed a Task Force for Appropriate Treatment of the Homeless, which conducted a survey that found that 78 percent of homeless were single men, mostly loners estranged from their families. More than two-thirds came from outside Utah. The task force raised $4 million, two-thirds from private donors, and built the Road Home shelter in Salt Lake City's Rio Grande neighborhood with four hundred beds, and an extra hundred beds in an emergency.[31] As the Road Home was built, the US Congress passed the McKinney-Vento Act with grants for homeless programs. Federal money took over from private action, and state bureaucrats began talking of homelessness in federal jargon and acronyms. By 2016 non-profit groups had opened thirteen homeless shelters statewide, supported in part by federal money. In addition, Utah had other federal programs: "transitional housing,"

---

30. David Schneider, "S. L. Council," Lois Collins, "Ogden Policy," *Deseret News*, Nov. 19, 1982, Oct. 4, 1988; Dan Egan, "No Charges," *Salt Lake Tribune*, May 28, 1997.

31. Mavrin and Russell, "Homelessness in Utah," 15–18; Lois M. Collins, "Safety Net," *Deseret News*, Nov. 18, 1988.

"permanent supportive housing," and "rapid rehousing"—more than 6,800 beds in all. To keep receiving federal money, Utah resumed counting homeless people. The state had each year counted the homeless from 1986 to 1997, and over those 12 years homeless had tripled to 2,051 people. In 1998, Utah stopped counting, but began again in 2004, under federal direction. One night every January when shelters report how many guests they have, volunteers walk the streets counting unsheltered homeless. From that "point-in-time," count officials estimated the number of people who were homeless at some time during the year. The estimate peaked at 16,642 in 2012 and declined to 14,516 in 2015. In the 2016 point-in-time count, Utah had about nine homeless for every 10,000 people, and America had 17. In contrast to the 1986 survey, the new counts showed most homeless people were from Utah, more than one-third were families, and most were homeless only for a short period of time.[32]

In 2004, Utah began a program called Housing First and became a national media model. Housing First settled the "chronically homeless," meaning substance-abusing, mentally-ill loners, in government apartments with almost no pre-conditions. Most stayed in the apartments; some changed their lives. The state claimed that it had reduced chronic homelessness 91 percent, to "functional zero." The national media were intrigued by such a successful program in such a conservative state. "The surprisingly simple way Utah solved chronic homelessness," read a headline in the *Washington Post*. "The state can just about declare victory," said National Public Radio.[33]

As praise mounted, problems worsened. In official numbers, both total homelessness and chronic homelessness fell. But the neighborhood around the Road Home became an "open-air drug market."

---

32. *Poverty in Utah*, 1983, 19–20, 1985, 34–35; Day et al., *Comprehensive Report on Homelessness*; Ashley Tolman powerpoint presentation to State Homeless Coordinating Committee (2012).

33. Terrence McCoy, "Surprisingly Simple Way," *Washington Post*, Apr. 17, 2015; Kelly McEvers, "Utah Reduced Chronic Homelessness," *All Things Considered*, Dec. 10, 2015, www.npr.org.

The count in 1992 showed that 39 percent of the homeless abused drugs or alcohol. In the 2016 survey, 23 percent said they had a substance-abuse problem. Addicted homeless people affected neighborhoods disproportionately. When drug dealers stopped their cars, customers flocked to them like children to a Good Humor ice-cream truck. Small-time drug dealers on foot or bicycles moved among the groups of homeless. Guards were placed at portable toilets to keep them from being taken over as drug-sales offices. At the Road Home Shelter, the count swelled to more than 1,100 guests a night. The shelter installed triple bunks, and men slept on a cafeteria floor across the street. Homeless camps dotted the streets of downtown Salt Lake City. Businesses closed or moved, unable to draw customers through the homeless crowds on sidewalks.[34]

Minor league baseball pitcher Logan Taylor came to Salt Lake City in 2017 for a July 4 game and was hit with a tire iron by a homeless man who demanded his wallet. Sports reporters told the story nationwide. Three days later Shutney Kyzer, on probation for burglary and kidnapping, drove to the Rio Grande, bought a drug called "spice," smoked it in her car, then drove into a group of homeless on the sidewalk, killing one and injuring five. "You can talk with a straight face about calling out the National Guard," said Utah Speaker of the House Greg Hughes.[35] The neighborhood must be "cleaned up," he said, and led a partial state takeover of Salt Lake City's homeless problem. Politicians held closed-door meetings, found money, marshaled law officials, and moved inmates from the Salt Lake County Jail to neighboring lockups to amass an arsenal of three hundred waiting jail beds. Then in mid-August dozens of state and local police flooded the Road Home neighborhood in Operation Rio Grande. Over the next few months, they made a total of 3,000 arrests. The police shut down homeless camps, rousted pan

---

34. Matt Canham, "Blitz Targets Drug Dealers," Paul Rolly, "It Just Keeps Getting Worse," *Salt Lake Tribune*, Sept. 29, Oct. 21, 2016; Bate, *Utah's 1992 Homeless Count*, 2016; Maria La Ganga, "Utah Says It Won," *Guardian*, Apr. 27, 2016.

35. Christopher Smart, "Escalating Violence," *Salt Lake Tribune*, July 6, 2017.

handlers, and tracked drug dealers to their homes. The legislature funded two hundred more treatment beds and money for counselors and other help. Quickly the Rio Grande neighborhood changed from squalid and threatening to cleaner and more orderly, but other neighborhoods complained that their troubles grew as the homeless fled Rio Grande. Still, the intense troubles ended at Rio Grande neighborhood and have not yet reappeared elsewhere.[36]

Officials said the concentration of homeless made an easy target for drug dealers. They planned to close the Road Home and build several smaller shelters in locations that would be harder for drug dealers to reach. State legislators appropriated $27 million for new shelters and passed a law to close the Road Home. In public meetings, those who lived near proposed shelter sites voiced fear for their children and property. They shouted at and pleaded with officials to put the facilities somewhere else. Officials picked three new sites and changed the name of the facilities from "shelters" to "resource centers." They promised the new resource centers would not ruin neighborhoods as the Road Home shelter had.[37] Homelessness, barely a problem in the 1980s, had become a scourge that no one wanted. Even with state and federal money, it seemed unclear whether Utah could deal with the troubles it brought.

WELFARE

Welfare dependency rose over the same thirty-five years as crime before it fell, and, like crime, it also caused public dismay. "Welfare" meant Aid to Families with Dependent Children, the legislation Congress enacted in 1935 that gave poor families with children cash grants. Depression-racked Utah welcomed the program. Few families

---

36. See Katie McKellar's three articles in the *Deseret News*, Oct. 18, Nov. 9, 2017, Feb. 5, 2018; Matthew Piper, "Operation Rio Grande," *Salt Lake Tribune*, Aug. 14, 2017; D. J. Bolerjack, "Operation Rio Grande," KUTV Channel 2 live news report, Sept. 7, 2017.

37. Katie McKellar, "County, City Leaders," "Space of Hope," *Deseret News*, Mar. 9, 2017, May 7, 2018; Taylor W. Anderson, "Draper Pulls Shelter Sites," "Road Home Must Work Better" editorial, "It's Not Just Outside," *Salt Lake Tribune*, Mar. 29, May 17, 2017, May 16, 2018.

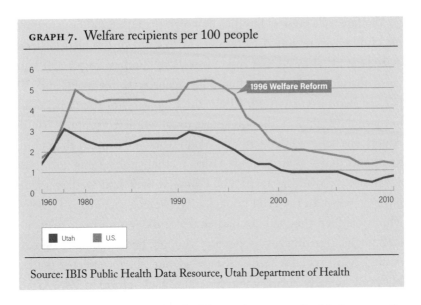

GRAPH 7. Welfare recipients per 100 people

Source: IBIS Public Health Data Resource, Utah Department of Health

qualified and most were headed by widows or a disabled parent. In 1942, 32 percent of Utah welfare families qualified because the father was dead, 34 percent because the father was incapacitated, and 29 percent because the father was estranged. When prosperity returned in the 1940s, welfare diminished as a public concern. Parsimonious governor J. Bracken Lee (1949–57) barely mentioned "welfare relief" in eight years denouncing government spending. The controversy came with accelerated growth in welfare rolls. In 1960, 12,500 Utahns were welfare recipients. By 1973, almost 46,000 Utahns were on the program. Welfare grew so unexpectedly, it caused a budget crisis in the early 1970s for Governor Calvin Rampton, who made emergency cuts in grants to keep the budget near balance.[38] Welfare cases increased even faster nationwide. Graph 7 shows the percentage of people on welfare for Utah and the nation from 1960 to 2010. Over the period of half-century, the Utah average was less than 60 percent of the national welfare rate.

38. "Dependent Child Aid," *Deseret News*, July 28, 1960; "Total Case Load, 1974," *US Department of Health and Human Services*, http://archive.acf.hhs.gov; "Welfare a Major Problem," *Salt Lake Tribune*, Jan. 10, 1971.

Welfare rolls grew as families in which the father did not support his children were added to families with dead or disabled fathers. A 1984 study showed that of Utah welfare families, 26 percent had been abandoned by the father, 33 percent were divorced, and 30 percent had never married. About three-quarters of the fathers did not pay child support, though courts usually ordered support. Many Americans believed that parents should work and support their children, and that welfare parents failed in their obligations and took advantage of working taxpayers. Conservatives said welfare made poverty worse. In his 1984 book *Losing Ground*, sociologist Charles Murray argued that welfare had enabled idleness and out-of-wedlock births, thus increasing poverty. A long, fierce scholarly debate ensued. Most social scientists disagreed, but Murray affected policy. His book helped to bring about federal welfare reform in 1996. Utah had administrative problems. In the 1970s officials estimated that as many as 15 percent of Utah welfare cases were "in error." Washington threatened to withhold money unless Utah reduced fraud. Ronald Reagan won the presidency in 1980 partly by campaigning against such welfare fraud.[39] The system was criticized by experts, politicians, and citizens alike.

Politicians planned to reduce welfare rolls and public discontent. In 1935 most mothers had stayed home and cared for children, and welfare was designed to allow poor women to do the same. By the 1960s, however, more mothers worked, so politicians sought to get welfare mothers into jobs. But many of them had little education and few skills, and some were mentally ill or abused drugs. When they found work, it was often a minimum-wage job that could not support a family and paid less than welfare and its benefits. Politicians tried to "rehabilitate" welfare mothers so they could find jobs

---

39. Douglas D. Palmer, "Welfare Fraud," LaVarr Webb, "Utahns Favor Boost," Palmer, "Study Explodes Utah Welfare Myths," *Deseret News*, Aug. 3, 1972, Jan. 15, 1984, Apr. 19, 1984; "Dwelling on Shiftless," *Salt Lake Tribune*, May 4, 1971; Murray, *Losing Ground*, 8–9, 219. The winter 1985 issue of *Focus* summed up the arguments. Reagan's January 1976 "welfare-queen" speech is at *Soundcloud.com*.

and become self-sufficient. From 1961 to 1988, Congress passed a series of measures with such names as the Work Incentive Program (WIN), Family Support Act, and Job Opportunity and Basic Skills Program (JOBS) that offered education and training, paid family medical bills, provided daycare, continued food stamps, subsidized housing, collected child support, made allowance for clothing and transportation, let a mother keep part of her grant as she earned wages, and, in addition, let a mother receive money from the Earned Income Tax Credit if her wages were low. Despite all this, welfare rolls continued to grow.[40]

Utahns believed in work, and Utah politicians were ahead of the nation in pushing welfare recipients off the rolls and into jobs. In 1974, Utah lawmakers passed the Work Experience and Training Program (WEAT) requiring men receiving welfare and women with no pre-school children to work for the government without pay three days a week to keep their grants. By 1978, 1,200 welfare recipients were working, 1,300 had left welfare, and 222 had been expelled for refusing to work. Utahns counted WEAT a success and said it should serve as a model for the nation.[41] Democratic governor Matheson announced a plan to hire 1,400 welfare mothers for state jobs. In 1978–79, only 281 were hired, but Matheson still said that the program was successful. When Republicans gained control of the Utah legislature in the Ronald Reagan victory in 1980, they ended assistance for able-bodied fathers. Partly to replace the federal grants, they offered the Emergency Work Program. Any person could take a job with the government or with a non-profit organization and work forty hours a week for less than the legal minimum wage. Eight of the work hours would be used to look for another job. About 225 people signed up each month, and the cost per case

---

40. Mangum et al., *Being Poor in Utah*, 95–139, gives a historical account of federal–state welfare interaction.

41. Ann McCreary, "Utah Plan," "Utahns on Welfare," *Deseret News*, Aug. 25, Nov. 17, 1978.

was lower than for welfare. Utahns said that their program should be a national model.[42]

Utah offered a voluntary "self-sufficiency" program in 1983. Self-sufficiency social workers helped each client make an individual plan, then Utah provided education and services to follow the plan to employment. In 1993, Utah expanded the idea into the Single Parent Employment Demonstration Program (SPED). New recipients of welfare were randomly assigned either to SPED or a control group. Those in SPED got self-sufficiency help, the control group stayed on regular welfare. Social scientists compared the two and saw that more SPED mothers found work and left welfare.[43] Welfare officials planned to apply SPED to all welfare cases, but Utah's legislature and federal welfare reform intervened.

In 1992, Democrat Bill Clinton won the presidency promising to "end welfare as we know it," and in 1996 he and a Republican Congress passed the Personal Responsibility and Work Opportunity Reconciliation Act, the toughest federal welfare law ever enacted. Assistance ceased to be an entitlement and became, instead, a grant to the states, thus increasing state power over the program. Utah politicians welcomed this new power. Since welfare began, the federal government had paid more than two-thirds of its costs and made most decisions. Utah politicians could make plans, but needed federal permission to put them into effect. For example, Utah passed the WEAT program in 1974 but then had to wait two years for the required federal waivers. Asking permission frustrated Utah politicians, but as compensation, they could blame Washington for welfare problems. In his 1995 State-of-the-State address, Governor Leavitt had 7-foot-4-inch Mark Eaton, center of the Utah Jazz basketball team, come to the podium and stand beside a stack of papers

42. "Welfare Program," *Salt Lake Tribune*, Dec. 9, 1971; also Brinton, *History of the Unemployed*; Chi, *Welfare Employment Programs*.

43. Carol Sisco, "System Is Putting Needy on Path to Independence," *Salt Lake Tribune*, May 11, 1985; Janzen and Taylor, *Evaluation of Utah's Single Parent Employment*.

almost as high as he could reach. Leavitt explained that the stack consisted of waiver requests Utah had submitted for federal permission to change welfare. Utah politicians had long believed their ideas were better than federal programs, and in the 1996 act they saw federal acceptance of ideas long advocated in Utah.

Besides giving states power, the 1996 federal welfare reform said no adult could receive assistance for more than five years in her life, and states could enact a shorter limit if they chose. Congress changed the name to Temporary Assistance to Needy Families (TANF) to emphasize the time limit. Utah legislators enacted a three-year welfare limit, one of seven states to impose a shorter time than the federal limit. [44] In 1997, Utah created a new Department of Workforce Services. Welfare was taken out of the Department of Human Services and placed in the new department with Unemployment Insurance, Job Search, and other work programs. The department, in a big new building, showed Utah welfare had changed from a human-services program to an employment program.

As graph 7 shows, the 1996 reforms reduced welfare rolls in Utah and the nation. From 1994 to 2000, Utah reduced the family count from 18,000 to 6,800. National reductions were similar. A national study five years after the reform showed 60 percent of the women who had left welfare were working. Employment rates among single mothers went up and poverty rates for their children went down. In Utah two social-work scholars, Mary Jane Taylor and Amanda Smith Barusch, studied women who had been on welfare for three years or more but left after the reform. Many had not believed welfare would ever end. When it did, their average monthly income declined by $300 and over half of them lived in poverty. Forty-five percent were depressed. About 14 percent had experienced severe domestic violence in the past year. Some 31 percent had not worked six months in the past five years. Even so, 37 percent said their lives

---

44. Vogel–Ferguson, "Developing a Profile."

were better without welfare, while 34 percent said they were worse off than before and the rest said they were about the same.[45] Welfare reform had helped many women to move to work and lead independent lives. It reduced expense and political discontent. But many women and their children remained poor and dependent, and reform made some of their lives more difficult.

After reform, welfare slipped from political controversy, but other federal programs continued to serve more poor people at increasing expense. For example, Medicaid expenditures rose from 12 percent of Utah's general fund in 1993 to 24 percent in 2013. (The federal government was senior partner in Medicaid, as it was in welfare.) The increased cost dismayed legislators and incited opposition to President Barack Obama's Affordable Care Act. But in Utah only 13 percent of Utahns received Medicaid in 2010, compared to 21 percent nationally. Utahns also used SNAP, formerly called food stamps, but less than people in other states. Nine percent of Utahns were enrolled in SNAP in 2013, compared to 15 percent of Americans. Social Security Disability Insurance burgeoned across the country. Scholars said the growth was "unsustainable" and reduced labor-force participation. One study of SSDI showed that Utah had the lowest application rate of any state. Its participation had been lower than the nation's every year since 1993. Part of the reason fewer Utahns were served by anti-poverty programs was that Utah had less poverty than America. Also, the state government held down participation in federal programs where it could. Besides limiting TANF to only three years, Utah barred able-bodied adults from Medicaid. But the state had limited influence on federal programs. Federal anti-poverty programs in Utah were mostly the same as elsewhere. Utah politicians tried to keep programs from growing, but they grew anyway. Politicians then blamed Washington and complained

---

45. Isabel Sawhill, "From Welfare to Work," *Brookings Review*, June 2001; Taylor and Barusch, *Multiple Impacts*, i–iii, v, vi, 62. America prospered in this period, and it's difficult to separate the effects of reform from those of prosperity.

of federal control. Still, Utahns depended less on government than other Americans. A 2014 study by the National Priorities Project showed that Utah received the least individual aid from the federal government of any state. The report included Medicare, Social Security, veterans' benefits, and unemployment, as well as anti-poverty programs. Utahns averaged $3,568 federal payment per resident in 2013, almost $2,000 less than the national average of $5,566.[46]

REMARKS

"Law and Order," cried conservatives, and for a time they won elections across America. Disorder, especially violent crime, alarmed people, filled local TV news, and diverted politics. Looking back on it, some political scientists saw the troubles as a reason Presidents Nixon, Reagan, and the first Bush found political success.[47] The troubles worried and angered Americans, and people tended to blame liberal policies and to favor conservative solutions.

Utah was less affected than other states. It had less violent crime, illegal drugs, homelessness, teen pregnancy, abortion, out-of-wedlock births, and welfare dependency, but more property crime and prescription-drug abuse. Child abuse eludes comparison. Overall, Utah had fewer troubles. Its incarceration rate was less than half the national average.

Social conservatives claimed that Utah experienced less disruption partly because of its family patterns, and they have some social science to support them: states with higher percentages of married parents have lower rates of violent crime. Married men get arrested less often, even controlling for age, race, economic status, and other factors. One team of researchers noted that marriage reduced the odds of arrest

46. "Average Annual Growth," *Henry J. Kaiser Family Foundation*, https://kff.org; "Food Stamp Use Rises," *Wall Street Journal*, Aug. 9, 2013; "State Smart," *National Priorities Project*, Nov. 20, 2014, www.nationalpriorities.org; Kelly Schmidt, "Latest Utah Medicaid Rules," *Salt Lake Tribune*, Sept. 23, 2017; also Autor, "Unsustainable Rise," 1; Coe et al., "What Explains State Variation?" 1–17.

47. Simon, *Governing through Crime*, 3–12; Zimring and Hawkins, *Crime Is Not the Problem*, xi–xii; Flamm, *Law and Order*, 2–11.

35 percent among men who had previous convictions. They quoted country-singer Johnny Cash, "Because you're mine, I walk the line." Most criminals start young, before adulthood. Boys from traditional families are less likely to engage in crime, become delinquent, and use drugs. Married families are less likely to become homeless.[48]

Social scientists pointed to income inequality and child poverty to explain some of the troubles, and Utah, with less inequality and poverty and fewer social troubles, fits that theory too. Some researchers blamed the troubles on the decline of good jobs for non-college men, as discussed in the last chapter. Some social scientists concede that they do not know what causes criminal behavior or why the rates of teen pregnancy and abortion rose and fell again. The troubles came and went. Social scientists offered conflicting explanations, most of which could not be proven.[49]

Progressives argue that their policies have made America better. Before the Rights Revolution in federal courts, African-American children attended segregated schools. Men without lawyers were imprisoned on confessions police might have coerced. Laws against sodomy kept gays in fear and hiding. Laws, customs, and discrimination restricted choices for women. Movies, books, and the arts were censored. Federal judges ruled that these restrictions were unconstitutional.[50] Americans became freer and more equal. The young were freer to love and the arts were freer from censorship, and minorities, gays, and women were more equal. Moreover, progressives believe that active government solves problems. Severity may have reduced crime and welfare dependency. Teen pregnancy fell partly from sex education and birth control. Patience, reasoned policy, and government energy might also address other troubles.

---

48. Price et al., *Strong Families*, 11; also Sampson, "Does Marriage Reduce Crime?"; van Schellen, "'Because You're Mine'"; Harper and McLanahan, "Father Absence and Youth Incarceration"; Haber and Toro, "Homelessness among Families."

49. Wilson, *Truly Disadvantaged*; Wilkinson and Pickett, *Spirit Level*, Zimring and Hawkins, *Crime is Not the Problem.*

50. Epp, *Rights Revolution*, 26.

Conservative Utahns saw decades of social trouble as they suffered defeats on public morality from the federal government. The defeats helped to explain the troubles; troubles kept in mind the defeats. Social conservatives blamed disorders on bad federal policies, the decline of traditional families, and a changing morality[51] Utah had a large, social-conservative majority that was inclined to believe the social-conservative explanations. They believed that Utah fared better than other states because morality and families changed less in Utah, and they voted against the federal government, its social policies, and its growing power.

---

51. Himmelfarb, *De-moralizing of Society*; Hymowitz, *Marriage and Caste*; Murray, *Losing Ground*.

7

THE
DOWNWINDERS' TALE

After World War II, when nuclear weapons seemed supreme, the United States tested atomic bombs in southern Nevada. From 1951 to 1958, the Atomic Energy Commission set off about 120 detonations. Each blast sucked tons of dirt up into its mushroom-shaped cloud. Winds blew the irradiated dust and gasses mostly eastward over sparsely settled parts of Nevada, Arizona, and Utah. Dust and gas from as many as eighty-seven explosions escaped the Nevada Test Site. As the clouds spread and cooled, radioactive debris fell on ranches, mines, and small towns.[1] People who lived in the path of the most intense fallout later called themselves downwinders. Most downwinders lived in Utah.

Utah was a patriotic, pro-defense state. Defense work had pulled Utah out of the Depression. Utah had the largest defense sector for its population of any state for a few years in the early 1960s, and Hill Air Force Base remained a big employer. The rise of defense, and the ways it changed Utah, have been chronicled by economic historians Leonard Arrington and Thomas G. Alexander, among others. This and the next chapter discuss defense decline. Utah defense faltered

---

1. Ball, *Justice Downwind*, 20–83. Nevada tests began in 1951. In 1958 a moratorium was declared. When the tests resumed in 1961, they were conducted underground. Of 244 new detonations, about a dozen of the explosions vented, meaning they spewed radioactive material into the air. Nevada nuclear testing ended in 1970.

partly because attitudes changed in the 1970s. Projects that had appeared patriotic and remunerative came to seem dirty and dangerous. Similar attitude changes occurred in other states.[2] But in Utah, the change came partly from the Downwinders' Tale, a story partly true about how nuclear fallout inflicted cancer on southern Utahns. Fallout, along with defense facilities and nuclear projects, had come to Utah because the state had empty land; the land was empty because it was arid and federally owned. Water, federal land, and defense became political issues related to Utah's geography and climate. All three changed in the 1970s, 1980s, and 1990s in ways that changed Utah from a client to critic of the federal government. The Downwinders' Tale became a weapon wielded by opponents of defense projects. While Latter-day Saints and non-Mormons divided on moral and family issues, they united in their dismay of cancer from atomic bomb testing. Repeatedly Utahns retold the downwinders' tale and opposed federal defense and nuclear initiatives. This chapter recounts the Downwinders' Tale to try to separate the true from the false and to show how it affected Utah. The next three chapters discuss the politics of defense, water, and land.

As they tested bombs, the Atomic Energy Commission (AEC) assured citizens that fallout posed no danger. "The possibility of any real danger to human health or livestock outside our proving grounds does not exist," the chairman of the AEC wrote to Utah senator Arthur V. Watkins.[3] Similar statements appeared in press releases, speeches, movies, and other government communications.

At first local citizens supported the tests and joked about houses shaking from the blasts. But as the tests continued, Utahns became more knowledgeable about the fallout, more fearful of harmful effects, and more skeptical of government assurances. Still, they were patriots who believed that the United States must stay ahead of Russia and Communist China in weapons development. Utahns

---

2. See, for instance, Hevly and Findlay, *Atomic West*.
3. Fradkin, *Fallout*, 20.

never effectively opposed open air tests. Even so, officials, scientists, and the public grew suspicious.[4] Officials ended the tests, temporarily at first, then above ground, and finally altogether. Scientists studied the effects of the fallout and asked whether it had caused cancer among downwinders. No test can tell if any specific cancer is caused by radiation. Scientists tried to determine the amount of radiation downwinders received (dosimetry) and the number of extra cancers they suffered (epidemiology). Researchers spent millions of dollars over fifty years; the results were controversial, contradictory, and inconclusive.

Scientists reconstructed dosimetry with some success. AEC officials had given radiation-detecting badges to some residents and set up stations that measured radiation. The measurements fell below what scientists at the time believed would be safe exposure levels, which is why they said the tests were safe. (Many scientists now say no measurable dose is safe.) Later when scientists had more exacting standards, it turned out there had not been enough badges and stations to calculate radiation doses precisely. Scientists made additional estimates by studying cesium 137 deposited on soil, and they looked at changes in thermoluminescence in bricks that had been exposed. They found "approximate agreement" among data from badges, survey stations, cesium, and bricks only for areas, not for individuals.[5] In the *Journal of the American Medical Association*, Walter Stevens and colleagues compared the dosimetry results to the small amounts of radiation people receive from natural background. During the seven years of open-air testing from 1952 to 1958, residents of Washington County in Utah's southwest corner received on average four times as much radiation from fallout as from background. Residents of neighboring Kane County received about twice the background

4. Ball, *Justice Downwind*

5. Miles, *Radioactive Clouds of Death*, 23. Miles is a physicist, downwinder, and chief skeptic of the downwinder tale. Beck and Krey, "Radiation Exposures," 24, show that cesium 137 samples "generally confirm the ... monitoring data." See also Lloyd et al., "Individual External Exposures," 731; Anspaugh and Church, "Historical Estimates."

Documentation of an open-air atomic explosion on May 25, 1953, at the Nevada Test Site, this one designated Upshot Knothole Grable. The image was captured by a US Army photographer. *Atomic Energy Collection, Oregon State University Libraries*

dose, and residents of all other Utah counties received less radiation from fallout than from background during those years. These are small doses, but they are averages over a large area and long time. More than three-quarters of all the radiation measured in the town of St. George, for example, came over a few days during the 1953 Upshot-Knothole Harry (nicknamed "Dirty Harry") test, and some individuals received much higher than average doses.

While agreement was found on dosimetry, epidemiologists had less agreement on cancer incidence. They divide into three camps:

early findings that fallout caused cancer was "slight or non-existent"; most studies that saw fallout as causing some cancer; and Dr. Carl Johnson, who said that fallout caused a lot of cancer. In 1984, Johnson published a study in the *Journal of the American Medical Association* showing 288 cancers in downwind populations of Latter-day Saints compared to 179 expected. In Johnson's study, leukemia occurred five times more often than expected and thyroid cancer eight times expectations. Among a "fallout effects group," who said they had suffered burns, sickness, or hair loss from fallout, the incidence of leukemia was forty-five times higher than normal, higher in fact than among the most irradiated survivors of Hiroshima and Nagasaki. Other scientists tried to replicate Johnson's results without success. Critics pointed out that he had asked people about themselves and their families decades after the events but did not check what they said against doctors' records, death certificates, or cancer registries.[6]

Other studies, based on records rather than recollections, focused mostly on thyroid cancer and childhood leukemia, called "sentinel cancers" because radiation causes them first. Early, an unpublished paper discussed the danger of people ingesting fallout in milk that could cause thyroid cancer. That radiation would not show up in monitoring stations or on badges and might escape official notice. Acting on that suspicion, the National Public Health Service funded a five-year study of 4,800 school children, about half in downwind areas of Utah and Nevada and half in Arizona as a control group from an area less subjected to fallout. A doctor checked each child's thyroid and found two cancers, both in the Arizona control group. The study concluded that fallout had not caused thyroid cancer among children. Then, fifteen and thirty-five years later, two other

---

6. Charles E. Land et al., "Childhood Leukemia," *Science*, Feb. 1984, 139–44; Johnson, "Cancer Incidence," 230–36; Johnson et al., "Leukemia in Utah," 166–68. Johnson and colleagues focused on Latter-day Saints because of their low cancer rate and good record-keeping. See also Machado, "Cancer Mortality," 44–61; Lyon and Schuman, "Radiation Fallout and Cancer."

teams conducted follow-up studies to re-examine as many of the original subjects as they could find. By the time of these studies, downwinders had developed eight thyroid cancers, zero to six of them caused by radiation, scientists estimated. These had not been detected initially, scientists believed, because the first study had been conducted too early to catch the cancers.[7]

A stronger case showed that fallout caused childhood leukemia. Of five studies (not including Carl Johnson's), three found persuasive evidence. The evidence in an earlier study did not reach statistical significance, and the fifth found no evidence. Depending on the area and time covered and whether non-fatal cases were counted, the actual number of childhood leukemias found ranged from nine to thirty-two, and some of them were probably caused by radiation.[8]

Before, during, and after atomic testing, southern Utahns had less cancer than other Americans. The Utah Cancer Registry showed that Utah had the lowest age-adjusted cancer rate of any state from 1966 through 1977. A study by Stella Machado and colleagues found Utahns in the downwind counties had even lower cancer rates, 30 percent below national averages except for childhood leukemias, which were 35 percent higher than the state average.[9]

Some epidemiologists used dosimetry studies and other information to estimate individual doses for the cancer cases they found. Others checked results against the dosimetry studies to show that the number of cancers were within the range that might be caused by the doses downwinders received. The exception was Carl Johnson's study. Health physicist John Gofman "reverse engineered" Johnson's results, taking Johnson's number of cancers and calculating how much radiation would have been required to cause so many.

---

7. Knapp, "Observed Relations"; Kerber et al., "Cohort Study of Thyroid Disease," 2076–82; Lyon et al., "Thyroid Disease," 604–16.

8. Lyon et al., "Childhood Leukemias," 397–402; Machado, "Cancer"; Stevens, "Leukemia"; Land, "Childhood."

9. Harmon et al., *Cancer in Utah.*

He found doses more than ten times higher than those found in the independent dosimetry studies.[10]

Excluding Johnson's study, epidemiology has only been able to show how fallout caused a likely increase in childhood leukemia and thyroid cancer. Machado and colleagues checked every death certificate in Washington, Iron, and Kane Counties from 1950 through 1980. They looked for excesses of all types of radiogenic cancer and found that only the incidence of childhood leukemia reached statistical significance.[11] Both Weiss and Stevens found higher-than-expected levels of leukemia in adults, but not high enough to conclude that they were caused by fallout rather than bad luck. Epidemiologists agree that fallout brought radiation to Southern Utah, where it probably caused two kinds of cancer, but if it caused other cancers, they were too few to reach the horizon of epidemiology. Actual findings are between nine and forty-one cases of leukemia or thyroid cancer and some of them were probably caused by fallout.

Besides the efforts of science, courts tried to find the truth. In 1978, 1,091 Downwinders who had cancer, or whose family members did, sued the US government in federal court in Utah. All parties agreed to try twenty-four bellwether cases first. The proceeding took thirteen weeks and produced 54,000 pages of exhibits. Judge Bruce Jenkins deliberated for seventeen months and wrote a 225-page opinion. He said the government had not properly warned citizens of the danger, so that many downwinders had not taken simple precautions such as staying indoors, wearing a hat, or showering, and they therefore suffered risk they might have easily avoided. Moreover, the government failed its duty to monitor. Instead of distributing a few film badges, the government should have given every downwinder a badge, just as all workers and visitors at nuclear facilities

---

10. Gofman was a plaintiff witness in the Allen case below.

11. Miles, *Phantom Fallout*, 21; Weiss et al., "Thyroid Nodularity," 241–49; Stevens, "Leukemia," 585–91. See also Kerber, "Cohort," 2076–82; Machado, "Cancer," 44–61.

are given badges. Any exposed person should have been tested to confirm exposure and to measure the dose. The government should have monitored milk and leafy vegetables to ensure they were not pathways of ingested radiation. Had government properly monitored fallout, the court would have known individual doses and been better able to rule in individual cases. As it was, Jenkins wrote, the government should not escape responsibility only because it failed to monitor. Moreover, Judge Jenkins rejected epidemiological standards that say probabilities must be 90 or 95 percent before scientists would conclude fallout caused cancer. Such certainty was not necessary in a civil case, Jenkins wrote. He found that ten of the twenty-four cancers were of a kind that could have been caused by radiation and were "more likely than not" due to the fallout. He ordered moderate damages. The government appealed, and the Tenth Circuit Court overturned Jenkins's decision. But the appeals judges did not question Judge Jenkins's findings of fact. Rather, they ruled testing was a policy decision, and the government could not be sued.[12]

Folklore flourished around fallout. Later accounts told how fallout had arrived in pink clouds and fell like snow. "After a bomb, there it would be, the fallout, fine like flour, kind of grayish white. We would play like that was our snow." "You know how little kids love snow. They went out and would eat fallout snow." The fallout was corrosive, according to some stories: "The bombs' ashes ... burned the paint off the hoods of trucks, leaving behind the names scrawled by children who would eat and breathe the bone-seeking radioactive isotopes," according to Carole Gallagher. Dr. Daniel Miles, himself a downwinder and a physicist, read through the *Washington County News* for the fallout years. The paper had paid close attention to the tests and local effects. The *News* reported that Upshot-Knothole Harry, the dirtiest of all tests, left debris on about a hundred cars in Nevada that were covered by a barely visible film and that the cars

---

12. *Irene H. Allen et al. v. United States*, 588 F. Supp. 247 (D. Utah 1984), 404, 416–19; *Allen v. U.S.*, 816 F2d 1418.

were washed. That incident was also described in official reports. Neither the *Washington County News* nor any contemporary document reported pink clouds or fallout-like snow that children ate, or fallout burning the paint off of anything.[13]

Downwinders tell of immediate radiation sickness: skin burns, temporary blindness, vomiting, diarrhea, and hair loss. These stories form the basis of Carl Johnson's "fallout effects group" and Goffman's "human dosimeters." Again, the *Washington County News* paid close attention to health issues, including colds and flu, and left no record of radiation sickness. No official reports tell of radiation sickness among downwinders. Fradkin told how JoAnn Taylor lost her hair, "the skin [coming] off her scalp in strips." Miles reports that Taylor had all her hair in the five pictures of her in the 1954 Dixie College yearbook.[14]

Downwinders tell of epidemic deaths. Isaac Nelson of Cedar City said: "And when the young boys and girls developed leukemia, dropping off like flies, a regular epidemic around here, nobody seemed to know. They were holding three or four funerals a week." Dr. Stella Machado and colleagues who surveyed death certificates for that period in three counties found a total of twelve childhood leukemia deaths, of which at least five were in St. George. There were not enough childhood-leukemia deaths to cause "three or four funerals a week" in Cedar City. Political science professor Howard Ball cited J. Preston Truman saying that he had eight close friends in the town of Enterprise die of cancer before they were twenty-eight. When asked, Truman said he never told such a story. He knew one child, a few years older than he, who died of leukemia but had no other friends from his youth who died from cancer. One press account said that the St. George cemetery had an unusually high number of children's graves for 1926 when there was a diphtheria epidemic and

---

13. Gallagher, *American Ground Zero*, 157, 159; Ball, *Justice Downwind*, 92; Daniel Miles, "Great Fallout-Cancer Story of 1978," *Physics and Society Newsletter*, Oct. 2005.
14. Fradkin, *Fallout*, 15.

1955 when childhood leukemia struck the town. Miles checked the graveyard and found only one child buried there in 1955, and she died in an automobile accident.[15]

Downwinders formed groups and held vigils. They lit candles, sang sad songs to guitar accompaniment, and held demonstrations to bring attention to their cause and to persuade Utahns of government wrongdoing. Downwinder complaints, backed by scientific studies, led to journalistic investigations and Congressional hearings. In 1990, after several years of debate and failed bills, Congress passed a compensation act for downwinders. Opponents noted that neither science nor the courts had produced clear proof of the cause or extent of the cancer, predicting that claims would multiply. Many would be paid who were not, in fact, harmed by fallout. Finally, though, Congress was persuaded that "someone was hurt" and voted $50,000 for each claimant who had been in one of ten Utah counties or designated counties in Nevada and Arizona during the fallout and developed any of the types of cancer that fallout could cause. Congress recognized that this was inadequate for actual victims, but thought it fair as many who would be compensated had cancer not caused by fallout. As of October 2014, a total of 18,087 downwinder claims had been paid at a total cost of about $900 million.[16]

The congressmen who passed the compensation bill assumed that fallout harm was limited to people living close to the Nevada Test Site. That assumption now seems wrong. Fallout spread in small amounts across the United States and around the globe, and some scientists now believe it may have caused cancer nationwide. An article in *American Scientist* estimated that the fallout is responsible,

---

15. Gallagher, *American Ground Zero*, 135; Ball, *Justice Downwind*, 98–99; also Machado, "Cancer," 44–61, who found that nine of twelve childhood leukemia deaths may have been due to fallout.

16. Gordon Eliot White, "Deaths High," "Fallout Levels Understated," *Deseret News*, Aug. 12, 1977, Feb. 13, 1979; "Clouds of Doubt," KUTV Channel 2, Salt Lake City, Oct. 26, 1977; "Radiation Exposure Compensation Act: Program Status," *US Government Accountability Office*, Sept. 28, 2005, www.gao.gov; "Radiation Exposure Compensation System," *US Department of Justice*, Oct. 20, 2014, www.justice.gov.

or will be, for 1,100 deaths from leukemia, 4,900 deaths from thyroid cancer, and 11,000 deaths from other cancers.[17] The deaths are spread over seven or eight decades. The authors of the article estimate that fewer than half of these deaths had occurred by the time the article was published in 2006. Fatal cancers from fallout account for less than 1 percent of total cancer deaths during that period of time. Their calculations are based on nationwide measurements of cesium137 (which show that fallout from the Nevada Test Site reached most of the nation) and on projections estimating how much cancer might result from such exposure. The authors emphasize the data can support only rough estimates. Their upper limit on the number of deaths from atomic testing is 200,000.

The Downwinders' Tale comes in two versions, oral and written. Each has its own epidemiology and dosimetry. Carl Johnson based his epidemiology on oral recollections and found hundreds of cases of radiation-caused cancer. Other epidemiologists began with documents and found forty-one or fewer documented cancer cases. For the oral story, radiation doses were found by calculating how much radiation must have been present to cause the large number of reported cases. The written story found doses from records of badges, monitoring stations, cesium137, and thermoluminescence studies. Those doses agreed with the number of documented cancers but showed only a fraction of the radiation needed to produce the cancers found in the oral studies. The oral Downwinders' Tale offers accounts of pink clouds, fallout-like-snow, radiation disease, and epidemic death. The written Downwinders' Tale finds none of those stories in contemporary documents. They seem to have grown by word of mouth decades after the events.

The Downwinders' Tale grips Utah memory. More Utahns may remember that fallout caused cancer and that "the government lied about it" than remember any other Utah historical event since statehood. Dozens of books have been written about the Downwinders'

---

17. Miles, *Radioactive Clouds*, 53–54; also Simon et al., "Fall out from Nuclear Weapons."

Tale, and it continues to draw national media attention.[18] The story changed Utah politics, but politics also changed the story. The story showed Utahns harmed by a powerful, dishonest defense bureaucracy. It furthered criticism of the military after the Vietnam War, and it fit the views of those Utahns who were increasingly opposed to the federal government. The written version of the story showed that fallout caused cancer. But journalists, writers, activists, storytellers, and others enlarged and embellished the story, creating and using the oral version. A series of controversies over defense and nuclear projects kept the Downwinders' Tale fresh in Utah politics, as is recounted in the next chapter.

---

18. See Bradley, *Learning to Glow*; Fox, *Downwind*; Fuller, *Day We Bombed Utah*; Wasserman et al., *Killing Our Own*; Miller, *Under the Cloud*. Miller also wrote a book on fallout for each state.

8

DOWNWINDER POLITICS

Beginning in 1968 defense and nuclear projects became recurring Utah issues. Empty federal land attracted dangerous projects and facilities that no one wanted nearby. Nuclear missiles, nerve gas, weaponized disease, and radioactive waste all sought homes in Utah deserts. Utahns pursued two partially conflicting goals of keeping dangerous projects out of their state while also keeping defense jobs. In most cases Utahns had little choice. They pleaded and protested, but although Utah money, health, and lives were at stake, the decisions were made by the federal government. As Utahns protested projects they did not want, they retold the Downwinders' Tale as a warning, justification, and guide. The name "Downwinder" was taken by the Utah Downwinders protest group and by other individuals who opposed defense plans. The tale reminded Utahns that they were more vulnerable than other Americans to far-away government that might harm them again.

SHEEPKILL

Snow fell on remote Skull Valley grazing lands March 13, 1968, and thousands of sheep died. "The ground looked like it was carpeted with dying sheep," a herder said. Veterinarian D. A. Osguthorpe drove to the desert the next morning to examine the animals. The surviving sheep looked as if they had been healthy but now could not hold their heads up. Some foamed at the mouth and stood on palsied legs. Doctor Osguthorpe surmised that they had been poisoned by an organophosphate. The herds died over a large area about forty miles northeast of the Dugway Proving Grounds.[1]

The army had built Dugway eighty-five miles southwest of Salt Lake City during World War II, when it became known that the Germans had poison gas and officials feared they would use it. The facility tested chemical and biological weapons, poison gas, disease-causing weapons, gas masks, flame throwers, fire bombs, and other unconventional weapons. It closed after World War II but reopened again during the Korean War. Remote and bigger than Rhode Island, Dugway flourished in the Cold War. By 1968 about 4,000 people lived on the Proving Ground.[2]

Army officers said they had not conducted any tests in the last month that could have killed sheep forty miles away. But a week later in a closed-door meeting with Governor Calvin L. Rampton, they admitted they had, in fact, tested an organophosphate nerve agent, VX, in the open air on the day of the sheepkill. It was a routine test. They had tested poison gas in the open about 1,600 times before without trouble. This time, however, a fighter plane with a spray rig flew over a target range three times. On two practice runs, the plane sprayed a non-lethal simulant. On the third pass, it sprayed tiny droplets of the nerve agent. The plane flew fast to stay ahead of the VX mist and flew only 150 feet above the ground to keep droplets in the target area. But the spray-rig nozzle failed to close and continued to dribble nerve agent as the plane climbed to 1,500 feet. Gusty winds blew the drops halfway to the cities along the Wasatch Front until a snowstorm washed the poison out of the air onto the range. Some of it fell on the sheep, and they ate contaminated snow and plants.[3] Lab tests confirmed that the carcasses contained VX. About 5,000 sheep

1. "Sheep Mystery," *Tooele Transcript–Bulletin*, Mar. 22, 1968; "Vet Wins Claim," *Deseret News*, Jan. 13, 1971.
2. Arrington and Alexander, "Sentinels on the Desert," 32, 34, 36–37.
3. "Probes Confirm Sheep Killed by Army," *Salt Lake Tribune*, Mar. 24, 1968. Molecular biologist Matthew Meselson told me the nerve gas likely would not have had

were buried in trenches, and the army paid damages to the owners. Rancher Ray Peck, who lived in the fallout zone, said the VX had sickened him and his family, but evidence was against his claim, and the official finding was that no people were hurt.[4]

In 1968 the Vietnam War made the military controversial, and the sheepkill led to national news stories and congressional hearings. Some commentators said the army had bungled the test and lied about it, but Tooele County people stood by Dugway.[5] The Chamber of Commerce passed a resolution saying there had been no negligence. Governor Rampton spoke reassuringly, saying people should not become fearful or overreact, and Congressman Sherman Lloyd defended the army.[6] But President Richard Nixon banned open-air tests of lethal chemicals, and the army, distressed by the sheepkill, the dissembling, and bad publicity, disbanded the Chemical Corps, though with no mention of the sheepkill. Seven years later the corps was reinstated.[7]

WETEYES

Ten years later Governor Scott Matheson fought against moving Weteye nerve-gas bombs to Utah. The bombs had been stored at the Rocky Mountain Arsenal near Denver. As Denver grew and Stapleton International Airport opened nearby, Coloradans asked the army to move the bombs. The Defense Department agreed and planned to move the 888 Weteye bombs to the Tooele Army Depot, forty miles southwest of Salt Lake City, where 40 percent of US chemical weapons were already stored. Tooele residents were used

---

the same fatal effect for people along the Wasatch Front because, unlike the sheep, they would not have ingested it.

4. Statement of D. A. Osguthorpe to US House of Representatives, qtd. in *Environmental Dangers* 63–66; Lee Davidson, "Nerve Gas," *Deseret News*, Dec. 22, 1994.

5. Walter Sullivan, "Deadly Peril," *New York Times*, Mar. 31, 1968; "Sheep and the Army," *Time* magazine, Apr. 5, 1968. "Chamber Votes," *Tooele Transcript–Bulletin*, Apr. 26, 1968.

6. "Rampton Refutes High Peril," *Salt Lake Tribune*, May 23, 1969; Sherman P. Lloyd to US House of Representatives, qtd. in *Environmental Dangers*, 23.

7. Al Mauroni, "U.S. Army Chemical Corps," Jan. 28, 2015, *US Army History Museum*, https://armyhistory.org.

to nerve gas and wanted more work for their depot. Experts said the plan was safe. Utah congressmen listened to Tooele residents, believed the experts, and consented to the move. Governor Matheson became the lone voice of opposition. He reminded people how winds blew from Tooele to Salt Lake City as they had blown toward St. George from the Nevada Test site and persuaded public opinion to his side. One of the Weteyes had leaked, and about a dozen had been destroyed in Colorado. All of the bombs should be destroyed, not moved, Matheson said. He sued in federal court, where evidence showed that more bombs had minute leaks and all of them might eventually leak. Leaks changed military mind, and to the dismay of Colorado leaders the move was cancelled. But Colorado senator Gary Hart quietly attached an amendment to an appropriations bill directing the military to move the bombs to Utah. Matheson was outflanked. The Weteyes were safely flown to Tooele, stored, and eventually destroyed.[8]

MX

President Jimmy Carter planned a missile project in Utah and Nevada. He said the United States had slowed building missiles, but the Soviet Union, instead of matching the slowdown, had accelerated and built more and bigger missiles until it threatened a successful surprise attack. In the Cold War, defense experts imagined elaborate scenarios backed by mathematical calculations. Such scenarios led President Carter to choose MX and led President Reagan to change the plan. In one imagined scenario, Soviets would use their missiles to wipe out American land-based missiles and bombers but would not attack American cities. Then the president would have a choice: he could fire missiles from American submarines, which could destroy Soviet cities but were not accurate enough to hit Soviet missiles. In that case, the Soviets would destroy American cities in reply.

---

8. Matheson, *Out of Balance*, 104–13; "Minute Amount of Nerve Gas Found," *New York Times*, Aug. 26, 1981; Joe Bauman, "Final Goodbye," *Deseret News*, Dec. 26, 2001.

Or the president could accept partial defeat. American and Soviet people would survive then, though American missiles and bombers had been destroyed. Military leaders wanted a third choice. They wanted a missile that would survive a surprise attack and would be accurate enough to attack Soviet missiles. The president could then reply to an attack on American missiles with retaliation on Soviet missiles, which might spare the American and Soviet peoples or, even better, deter the imagined attack in the first place.[9]

Carter proposed MX, a "survivable, second-strike, counterforce missile." Each MX would carry ten hydrogen bombs, and each bomb could be accurately aimed to hit a separate Soviet missile. To keep the missiles safe from surprise attack, Carter planned 200 elaborate bases in the West Desert of Utah and Nevada, one base for each of the 200 missiles. At each base a large covered vehicle would carry MX around an oval "racetrack" ten-to-fifteen miles in circumference. Twenty-three concrete missile shelters would adjoin each track. The MX carrier would stop at each of the twenty-three shelters and pretend to hide the missile in the shelter. Soviet satellites could watch but would not be able to tell which shelter hid the missile. So, to destroy one MX, the Soviets would have to fire forty-six warheads (theory advised two warheads for each shelter in case one missed). Carter relied on the Strategic Arms Limitation Treaty, which limited the number of missiles each side could have, to keep Soviet numbers too low to overwhelm MX.[10]

When Carter announced MX in 1979, Governor Matheson sent a telegram of support, saying it brought "no adverse environmental impacts" and "substantial economic benefits." Governor Bob List of Nevada called MX a "pot of gold." Utah senator Jake Garn led a united congressional delegation in support of the proposal; in fact, he had offered an amendment to speed development. A *Salt Lake Tribune* poll

9. Auten, *Carter's Conversion*, 40, 66.
10. See Edwards, *Superweapon*, 190–99.

in October 1979 showed 69 percent of Utahns were "not personally bothered" by the plan to locate missiles and bases in their state.[11]

Small groups of citizens formed to oppose the president's plan. They mocked its complexity and said the Air Force lied to Utahns about the dangers MX would bring. If the Soviets attacked MX, the wind would carry fallout from thousands of nuclear bombs over all of Utah, as winds had carried fallout over downwinders twenty-five years before, opponents said. This argument found a home in people's fears. By March 1980, a *Tribune* poll showed 51 percent of Utahns opposed to President Carter's plan and only 36 percent in favor. A *Deseret News* poll in April showed 60 percent opposed. An earlier *Deseret News* poll in March of 1980 had asked Utahns whether they supported MX, and 50 percent had said they favored building the missile, against 20 percent who were opposed. Then the same poll asked whether Utahns supported MX *in Utah*. Only 35 percent favored MX in Utah, while 51 percent opposed it.[12] Utahns believed MX would aid national defense but they did not want it near them.

Politicians changed their minds to agree with public opinion. Senator Garn said Utahns were "patriotic, determined, loyal" but they "should not be asked to bear an unreasonable share of the burden of national defense." He still spoke for developing the missile but against the Utah racetrack. Governor Matheson said the missiles were a military necessity but should not be based in Utah. Since it would entail America's biggest ever construction project, it would overwhelm the people's way of life. He added that MX was "the most important public policy issue" in Utah history. Like the public, politicians said MX would be good for defense but not good for Utah. Even the First Presidency of the Latter-day Saints broke their usual political silence and issued a statement saying Latter-day Saints had

---

11. Matheson, *Out of Balance*, 58; Rod Decker, "MX May Blow Up," *Deseret News*, Mar. 10, 1980. Matheson devoted two chapters to the MX proposal.

12. "Utah MX Opposition Continues," *Salt Lake Tribune*, Mar. 16, 1980; LaVarr Webb, "Utahns Favor MX—But Not Here," "Opposition to MX," *Deseret News*, Mar. 21, Apr. 18, 1980; also Glass, *Citizens against MX*, 130–32; Firmage, "MX," 13.

settled Utah hoping to build a place of peace, and it would be a cruel irony to take it for war.[13] They agreed that the MX racetrack should not be based in Utah and reinforced public political opinion against President Carter's plan.

Soon after Ronald Reagan defeated Carter in 1980, US Senators Garn of Utah and Paul Laxalt of Nevada met with the new president to explain their opposition to Carter's MX plan. They were a persuasive pair, in part because Laxalt was Reagan's personal friend and Utah had given the strongest vote for Reagan of any state. Moreover, the president was already inclined to the senators' arguments. Even before he became president, Reagan had opposed the Strategic Arms Limitation Treaty. But without that treaty, the scenario changed. The Soviets could build enough missiles to destroy every MX shelter, so MX would no longer be safe from surprise attack. Reagan said he would dump the racetracks but still build the missiles, rename them Peacekeepers, and find some other way to keep them safe. Though they tried many ideas, Reagan's military planners could not find a politically acceptable way to keep the missiles safe. Finally, they put fifty Peacekeepers in extra-strong silos near existing missile silos. That left America almost as vulnerable as it had been before the MX argument began. After the fall of the Soviet Union, the Peacekeepers were junked in 2005 as part of arms-control negotiations.[14]

ENVIROCARE

Vitro Chemical Company milled uranium ore in South Salt Lake City from 1951 to 1964 and left behind 4.3 million tons of mildly radioactive tailings. Contractors used the sandy tailings as fill in construction, and most people did not worry about them. In 1978 Congress passed the Uranium Mill Tailings Radiation Control

---

13. LaVarr Webb, "MX Puts Pressure On," *Deseret News*, Mar. 10, 1980; Edwards, *Superweapon*, 206; Matheson, *Out of Balance*, 55–86; "First Presidency Statement," *Ensign*, June 1981.

14. Author's interview with Jake Garn, Apr. 2005; Kristen Moulton, "Lethal Cold-War Symbol," *Salt Lake Tribune*, Oct. 7, 2005; also Sorrels, "Scowcroft Commission."

Act identifying uranium-mill tailings as hazardous. Utah received a $60-million grant from the Department of Energy, cleaned up the Vitro site, and turned it into a golf driving range. To dispose of the tailings, the state designated a square mile of land eighty-five miles west in the Tooele County desert, completed an environmental impact study, and built a railroad spur and power lines to the site. In 1988, after the tailings had been moved, ninety of the available 640 acres had been used.[15]

Khosrow Semnani, an urbane and charming Iranian immigrant who grew up in Utah, asked to buy the land and continue to dump slightly radioactive waste there as a commercial continuation of the Vitro-tailings operation. State attorneys said the law would not allow the sale of land, but Larry Anderson, director of the Utah State Division of Radiation Control, found a way through the obstacles. He said the United States had insufficient capacity for radioactive waste, so Semnani would be doing the state and nation a service if he opened a disposal company. Anderson arranged for Tooele County to buy the property from the state and resell it to Semnani for $339.000, less than half the price another waste company paid for land nearby that did not have the environmental study, permits, power lines, and railroad line that came with Semnani's purchase.[16] The Iranian entrepreneur named his company Envirocare.

The original permit allowed the company to accept only three types of the least radioactive subcategory of waste, but Envirocare applied to expand its permit. State radiation workers complained that Envirocare was unable to prepare the applications correctly, so Anderson directed state employees to help, which meant that they, as regulators, then approved the applications they had helped to write. Envirocare's permit expanded from three to seventy kinds of waste,

15. Dames and Moore Consultants, "Preliminary Draft Environmental Impact Statement: Remedial Actions at the Former Vitro Chemical Company Millsite," 1982; "Tailings Cleanup," *Deseret News*, July 18, 1989.

16. Dames and Moore; "Tailings Cleanup."

and the company was allowed to take mixed waste that was both radioactive and chemically hazardous. That made Envirocare the only commercial facility in the country that accepted certain kinds of contaminated material. When competitors complained that Anderson showed favoritism toward Envirocare, the state investigated and recommended changes.[17] Governor Mike Leavitt replaced Anderson as division chief, and a few years later Anderson retired.

In 1996 Anderson sued Semnani, saying the two had agreed to an unwritten consulting contract before Envirocare began. Semnani had paid him but then stopped payments, and still owed him $7 million. Such a contract violated Utah's conflict-of-interest laws, but Anderson said he had received informal advice from the attorney general's office on how to stay within the law. The attorney general's office denied giving such advice. Semnani admitted that he had paid Anderson $600,000 over eight years but said that Anderson had extorted the money by implied threats to Envirocare. "There's not a shred of evidence Larry ever did a thing for me," Semnani explained. After an FBI investigation, Semnani pleaded guilty to a federal misdemeanor, paid a $100,000 fine, and testified against Anderson. A federal jury convicted Anderson of tax cheating but acquitted him of extortion. Anderson called the verdict a "moral victory." He was sentenced to thirty months in prison, but he kept the money. A national environmental group demanded revocation of Envirocare's license, but state and federal regulators found the company's operations were safe and legal and allowed it to continue. The federal Department of Energy pressured Semnani into leaving Envirocare, but after a few years he returned and took control again.[18]

In the decades around the turn of the twenty-first century, Americans cleaned up radioactive sites and needed places to dump mildly

---

17. Legislative auditor general, *Audit of Environmental Quality*, 46–47; Jim Woolf, "Envirocare," *Salt Lake Tribune*, Jan. 7, 1997.

18. Jim Woolf, "Utah Dump," Brent Israelsen, "Envirocare," Judy Fahys, "Anderson Guilty," Israelsen, "Key Figure," *Salt Lake Tribune*, Dec. 28, 1996, Apr. 14, 1998, Sept. 6, 2001, June 17, 2003.

contaminated waste. The same impulse to cleanliness brought passionate local opposition to any dump, thus making the facilities rare and profitable.[19] For some contracts Envirocare had only two or three national competitors, and for others it had none. Long trains of covered gondola cars hauled dirt from all parts of America to Envirocare and brought payment of near-monopoly charges.

Like some rough beast chained in the desert, Envirocare fed on waste, grew large, and struggled against its regulatory shackles. The company asked permission to accept waste of higher radioactivity; to grow beyond its one-square-mile original size; to pile waste higher, up to eighty feet above the desert floor; to take waste from Italy; and to mix more potent radioactive waste with less radioactive dirt so the resulting mixture would be within Envirocare's permit.

Every proposed change provoked a political fight. Envirocare met safety standards and often won in the state regulatory bureaucracy. Radioactive waste roiled every legislature session from 1993 through 2007. Envirocare donated to political campaigns, hired lobbyists, pointed to government safety findings, and succeeded with legislators and congressmen. For example, lawmakers made Envirocare's financial data "proprietary" so that only the company knew its earnings and expenses, and legislators passed another law to relieve the company of regulatory costs.[20] But despite its safety record and legislative success, Envirocare lost public opinion. A professional environmental group, HEAL, opened an office in Salt Lake City and attacked the company. Crusading news reporters publicized nuclear dangers and Envirocare missteps. In 2002 a citizens group gathered enough signatures on a proposition to raise Envirocare's taxes to more than its gross revenues. Envirocare spent $3.8 million to defeat the referendum, but though the punitive tax measure failed, public suspicion grew. Polls showed that 84 percent of Utahns opposed letting the company

---

19. Gerrard, "Fear and Loathing," 1047.
20. Jim Woolf, "Provision Benefitted Envirocare," Judy Fahys, "Governor Allows Energy Solutions," *Salt Lake Tribune*, Sept. 5, 1997, Feb. 27, 2007.

take higher-level radioactive waste; 68 percent wanted higher taxes on the company (this was one year after 68 percent of Utahns had voted against higher taxes on the company); and 81 percent wanted the governor and legislature, not bureaucrats, to make final decisions about what the company would be allowed to do. Utah governors read the polls and loudly took the popular side. When Utah Republican congressmen and senators seemed willing to let Envirocare take higher-level radioactive waste from an Ohio project, Governor Olene Walker denounced the plan and defeated it. Governor Jon Huntsman vetoed legislative bills, invoked interstate compacts over legislators' heads, barred hotter waste, and blocked Italian waste. Utah governors rallied the public against Envirocare and beat senators, congressmen, regulatory experts, and legislators. Hoping to buy off the public, Envirocare offered to split profits on Italian waste and pay $1 billion to Utah schools. Though Italian is no more dangerous than American waste, Utah scarcely considered the offer before rejecting it.[21] Envirocare's hopes were blocked by public influence on political decisions.

Envirocare's adversaries talked more of reputation than of safety. They said radioactive waste made Utah look like the nation's toilet bowl. Outsiders would think worse of Utah. "What an embarrassment for the entire state," one letter to the editor said. "Thousands of people have worked for decades to give Utah a good reputation ... and one company destroys it all." Being "dumped on" made Utahns feel "helpless" against the "greedy company. ... They can pretty much just steamroll over the rest of us poor slobs with their toxic crap." Opponents rejected assurances that low-level radioactive waste was not very dangerous as "eerily similar to the very same claim made when the atomic bomb was tested in Nevada."[22]

---

21. See articles by Donna Kemp Spangler in the *Deseret News*, Jan. 4, 2001, Feb. 4, 2003; and Judy Fahys in the *Salt Lake Tribune*, Jan. 7, Nov. 12, 23, 2003, Nov. 11, 2005, July 14, 2010.

22. Frank Pignanelli and LaVarr Webb, "American West Isn't a Toilet," *Deseret News*, Apr. 3, 2005; letters to editor (Jeff Clap, Brad Parker, David Smith), *Salt Lake Tribune*, Oct. 19, 2003, Dec. 2, 2006, Dec. 31, 2007.

Khosrow Semnani sold Envirocare in 2004 for a reported $500 million.[23] The new owners changed the company name to Energy-Solutions, launched an ad campaign, and bought naming rights to Utah's professional basketball arena. Despite all that, they remained unpopular and hamstrung by regulation.

CHEMICAL WEAPONS

After World War II, the military loaded chemical weapons onto ships and sank them or just threw old bombs and shells into the ocean. Scientists think—or at least hope—salt water neutralized the poison as it flowed into the sea. Other chemical weapons were buried or burned in open pits. Even so, in the early 1970s, the army had about 30,000 tons of chemical weapons, and some were old and leaking. The army planned to load those weapons onto ships and sink them, as it had before. Disposal would be called Operation CHASE, or "Cut Holes And Sink 'Em." The public and politicians objected, and Congress outlawed CHASE in 1972.[24] The army convened a committee to find a new plan, and the committee said burn the weapons.

Sixty miles southwest of Salt Lake City, the Tooele Army Depot stored more than a million chemical weapons in half-buried igloos arrayed in straight military rows across the desert floor. Eight other US Army bases stored chemical weapons, but none had even one-third the tonnage of Tooele. The army built the depot in 1942 to gear up for World War II, and its main job was to repair trucks, machine guns, and other equipment. To start burning the deadly chemicals, the army built a pilot plant at Tooele in 1979 called CAMDS (pronounced Kamdess), which stood for Chemical Agent Munitions Disposal System. In the plant, remotely operated machines cut up bombs and shells, and liquid nerve and mustard agents were incinerated along

23. Patty Henetz, "Envirocare Owner Cashes Out," *Salt Lake Tribune*, Dec. 16, 2004.
24. See Hilmas et al., "History of Chemical Warfare," 53–54; "History," *Chemical Weapons Elimination*, www.cdc.gov.

with the dissected bomb fragments. Filters removed 99.99 percent of stack gasses and particles and turned them into benign salts. Utahns paid little attention. When the army held a public hearing on a larger facility, no one came. In 1993 the army built a full-scale version of the incinerator called TOCDF (pronounced Tockdiff), an acronym for Tooele Chemical Weapons Disposal Facility. As TOCDF neared completion in 1997, it was given a deadline when the United States joined sixty-four other nations and signed an agreement promising to destroy all chemical weapons by 2007.[25] The army estimated it could do the job for $1.7 billion.

Just before TOCDF was completed, activists met in Kentucky, where Blue Grass Arsenal also stored chemical weapons, and said that burning was too dangerous. Instead, the army should neutralize chemical weapons by some still-to-be-developed process that would not allow any emissions. National activists formed the Chemical Weapons Working Group, and in Utah like-minded citizens formed FAIR, Families Against Incinerator Risk. One incinerator opponent wrote, "Forty years ago we were the downwinders of the nuclear fallout. ... Must we (and especially our children) pay the price as military guinea pigs again?" Roused by activists, journalists paid closer attention to accidents at the plant, and citizens worried. A poll in 1996 showed 46 percent of Utahns wanted the incineration stopped, while 39 percent though it should continue. A poll the next year showed 44 percent saying the risk was significant. Six months later, however, the public worried less, and only 28 percent still thought the risk was high. Tooele residents lived by nerve gas and worried less. County commissioners invited the army to move all its chemical weapons to Tooele for destruction, saving the cost of building a plant at each storage location. Commissioners asked for

25. Arrington and Alexander, "They Kept 'Em Rolling," 7; "No Residents Attend," Matthew S. Brown, "Army Launches TAD," *Deseret News*, May 5, 1989, Aug. 11, 1993; *Risk Assessment and Management at Deseret Chemical Depot*, 9; NRC, *Review of Closure Plans*, 5–6; "Environmental Impact Statement: Operation of CAMDS at Tooele Army Depot," May 1976, *Hathi Trust Digital Library*, https://babel.hathitrust.org.

money for schools and a hospital in return, a proposal that brought dismay from other Utahns, ridicule from activists, and a veto from Governor Mike Leavitt.[26]

As contractors tested the completed plant, a whistleblower, Steve Jones said it was a "bomb ready to go off." He had been the plant safety boss until he was fired. Jones worked with plant opponents, held news conferences, and testified in court. He was the first of four whistleblowers who said safety reports were falsified and the plant was dangerous. Jones successfully sued to get his job back, but after he returned he said procedures had improved and the plant was "absolutely safe." His anti-burn friends accused him of selling out.[27]

As the plant started burning chemicals, things went wrong. Two days after the plant opened, it closed again because nerve agent had leaked within the plant, the first of about a dozen accidents that caused delays, shutdowns, investigations, and redesigns. Visitors from Oregon stood in a room with an empty shell that turned out to be contaminated, although no one was hurt. A worker got traces of agent on his glove and hair. A safety switch turned a furnace off, and activists charged that unburned agent escaped up the stack. The official investigation concluded that the agent had remained in the plant. In May 2000 a droplet of agent did escape, the only one in sixteen years of operation. A Center for Disease Control investigation said no one was hurt, but the plant shut down for four months and was partially rebuilt to prevent another leak. Unexpectedly, workers found arsenic and mercury in the chemical agent and had to change procedures to cope with those pollutants.[28] Activists pointed to the

26. Lori Flygare to editor, Jim Woolf, "Most Trust Tooele Depot," *Salt Lake Tribune*, Oct. 18, 1995, Oct. 3, 1999; Matthew S. Brown, "Tooele's Hopes Dashed," Zack Van Eyck, "Many Lack Fervor," *Deseret News*, Aug. 9, 1993, Aug. 25, 1996; James Brooke, "So Far, So Good," *New York Times*, Apr. 13, 1997; Ward, *Canaries on the Rim*, 80–84.

27. Joseph Bauman, "Ex-Worker Slams Incinerator," *Deseret News*, June 27, 1997; Jim Woolf, "Is Arms Burner Unsafe?" Woolf, "Whistle-Blower," *Salt Lake Tribune*, Jan. 12, Feb. 19, 2000.

28. "Destroy Nerve Gas" editorial, Brooke Adams, "No Big Glitch," Joseph Bauman, "Nerve Agent," Lee Davidson, "Army Admits Foul-Ups," Bauman, "Nerve-Agent

troubles and said nerve gas might escape and be carried downwind to Utah cities, threatening catastrophe.

Anti-burn lawyers contested the depot's permit in state court and brought seven cases or appeals before federal judges in Utah or Washington, DC. They lost every case. In all, fourteen judges ruled on the plant, and all of them ruled for continued burning.[29] Activists went to Congress, which also declined to close the plant. In Kentucky and three other states, governors and legislatures outlawed burning, so the army agreed to use a non-burning process in those states. But the Tooele plant was built and destroying agents when the other processes were yet to be invented.[30]

The strongest argument for burning came from the Stockpile Committee composed of senior members of the National Academy of Science. They noted hundreds of chemical-weapon leaks, of which 73 percent were at the Tooele Army Depot. Many of the leakers put more agent into the environment than ever escaped from the burn plant. After one mustard-agent leak, the army said that any unprotected person could have been harmed up to 900 meters from the puddle. Moreover, some rocket propellant became volatile as it aged, and the committee feared that a rocket might go off by itself in an igloo full of chemical weapons. "Cumulative risk," said the committee, "is dominated by storage rather than disposal," meaning that it was more dangerous to store than to dispose of the chemicals, so any delay would come "at the expense of increased risk." Activists called storage fears "Chicken Little." But judges and congressmen believed

Exposure," Steve Fidel, "Depot Prepares," *Deseret News*, June 11, 1989, Aug. 24, 1997, Jan. 12, May 1, 1999, Oct. 10, 2002, Mar. 31, 2008; Glen Warchol, "Run of Errors," *Salt Lake Tribune*, June 25, 2000.

29. The Sierra Club and others sued the US Army (1996), US Department of Agriculture (1997), Utah Solid and Hazardous Waste Control Board (1998), US Environmental Protection Agency (1999), and US Department of Defense (2009).

30. R. Jeffrey Smith, "Army Poison," *Washington Post*, Jan. 22, 1989; Dylan Lovan, "Chemical Weapons," *Washington Times*, Oct. 27, 2015; Keith Schneider, "U.S. Plan to Burn Chemical Weapons," *New York Times*, Apr. 29, 1991.

the committee, and Utah governors helped persuade citizens that burning was safer than storing.[31]

Tooele completed its chemical-weapons destruction in 2012, five years after the original deadline, but on time because signatories had agreed to delay. Officials in Tooele were proud that no employee had missed a day of work because of job injury, and only one drop of agent had escaped the plant. The Blue Grass Army Depot in Kentucky, in comparison, with its non-burn disposal method, still hopes to begin destroying weapons in 2020 and to finish by 2023.[32]

BIOLOGICAL WARFARE

Rolland Bivens volunteered for a Q fever test in 1955 because he was a Seventh-day Adventist and it was against his religion to fight. Soldiers led him and twenty-nine other volunteers into the desert at Dugway Proving Ground. It was night, but they could see cages holding monkeys and guinea pigs, also part of the test. They could hear the generators that emitted an aerosol containing Q fever germs, which the wind carried over the volunteers. "It was invisible, though," Bivens told reporter Lee Davidson. "All we saw was clear air." The volunteers were flown to a hospital. Some of them got Q fever, with flu-like symptoms, but recovered.[33]

Besides testing nerve gas and other chemical weapons, Dugway Proving Ground tested biological weapons and defenses against them. After the 1968 sheepkill, open-air testing ended and Dugway fell into neglect. The United States and Soviet Union joined twenty other nations in 1972 to sign a treaty banning biological weapons. But the Reagan administration suspected that the Soviets were cheating and responded by renovating Dugway. As part of the renovation, the army planned a new $1.4 million lab with "maximum containment" that could work with "bio-level 4" diseases. Until then

---

31. Lee Davidson, "Nation's Leakers," *Deseret News*, Mar. 21, 1993; NRC, *Recommendations* 130; Ward, *Canaries on the Rim,* 175–88.
32. Becca Schimmel, "Chemical Weapons," *WKYU–FM,* Bowling Green, Apr. 10, 2017.
33. Lee Davidson, "Pacifist Volunteers," *Deseret News*, Dec. 22, 1994.

A 1960 orientation class in CBR (chemical, biological, radiological) weapons at the Dugway Proving Ground, a facility the size of Rhode Island. *Classified Photo Collection, Utah State Historical Society*

Dugway had worked with anthrax, botulism, tularemia, plague, and Q fever, all less dangerous bio-level 3 diseases. Bio-level 4 bugs did not yet exist but might be created by genetic engineering. The biological-weapons treaty permitted work on defense against germ warfare, and the army said the lab would continue bio-level-3 work unless Soviets developed new diseases, and then the lab would be ready for research on detectors, masks, and decontaminants to protect troops against the new, human-created pathogens.[34]

Activist groups and university professors led the opposition. They said the United States had no evidence of Soviet cheating and was "using allegations" to heighten funding. Jeremy Rifkin of the

---

34. Joseph T. Liddell, "Dugway Targeted," Lee Davidson, "Did Dugway Conduct Tests?" *Deseret News*, Dec. 4, 1984, Apr. 10, 1994; also Department of the Army, "Final Environmental Impact Statement: Life Sciences Test Facility," Mar. 1992; R. J. Smith, "New Army Biowarfare Lab," *Science*, Dec. 1984, 1176–78.

Foundation for Economic Trends said the United States was planning to break the treaty itself. "Their whole reason for building this facility is to have the capability to do long-range experimentation with gene-spliced novel genetically engineered viruses," he said. If the new pathogens escaped, Utahns downwind would be imperiled. "Genetically engineered weapons could rival nuclear bombs in their ability to extinguish life on this planet," Rifkin said.[35] Opponents argued that the United States should stop work on a new lab and instead negotiate a stronger treaty.

Rifkin and the Union of Concerned Scientists sued in federal court for an environmental impact study. Democratic governor Scott Matheson wanted Utah to join the suit, but Rifkin asked him not to because army lawyers might try to move the suit to Utah and Rifkin wanted the more liberal court in Washington, DC. Matheson then wanted the state to file a brief in support of Rifkin's suit. But Utah's Republican attorney general David Wilkinson refused to act.[36] In any case, Judge Joyce Green ruled for Rifkin and ordered an environmental impact statement.

Many Utahns shared Matheson's dislike of the project. At the University of Utah, fifty-six professors of medicine or biology signed a petition saying they feared the germs might escape and be blown to Utah cities. They suggested the army use simulants that would act like pathogens but did not kill people. About 350 Utahns came to an army hearing in Salt Lake City, and all of them opposed the lab. "We beat you on MX, and we will beat you here," law professor Edwin B. Firmage told army officers.[37] Utah congressmen divided on party lines. Democratic Representative Wayne Owens sponsored an amendment to deny funding for the lab, sponsored a bill to take germ research away from the army,

---

35. Guy Boulton, "Proposed Lab," Boulton, "Utah Facility," *Salt Lake Tribune*, Mar. 13, 1985, Feb. 7, 1988, quoting biologist Jonathan King.

36. "Suit Stirs Second Thoughts," *Salt Lake Tribune*, Dec. 21, 1984.

37. Mike Gorrell, "U Scientists Sign Petition," Guy Boulton, "Dugway Test Facility's Opponents," *Salt Lake Tribune*, Mar. 7, 23, 1988.

and said assurances of safety "could be taken as an insult" after the deaths of sheep and downwinders. In contrast, Republican senator Jake Garn worked for the lab.[38]

Governor Norman Bangerter found a compromise. "If they are only going to test Bio-Level 3, they should build Bio-Level 3 and not Bio-Level 4," he said. At his suggestion, the army agreed to build a bio-level 3 lab capable of handling only the level of danger Dugway had worked with before. In September 1988, Bangerter was in a re-election campaign and wanted public credit for the agreement. But Dugway was too far away to lure TV cameras, so he stood in the gate of the Tooele Army Depot for dramatic effect to announce that the army had accepted his terms.[39] The army completed its bio-level 3 lab in 1997 at a cost of $23 million.

After the fall of the Soviet Union, Russian officials revealed a secret plant had produced anthrax spores for weapons, in violation of the treaty. Premier Boris Yeltsin confirmed that a leak in 1979 had killed at least sixty-eight people in the town of Sverdlovsk. The anthrax had been genetically altered to resist antibiotics.[40]

SPENT FUEL

Spent fuel from nuclear power reactors remains deadly for thousands of years and will kill any unshielded person nearby. In 1982 the federal government promised to take spent fuel and bury it. But after fifteen years of failure to keep that promise, a group of utilities formed Private Fuel Storage and offered to pay any Native American tribe to store the fuel temporarily on its reservation while the government dithered. "It might as well be us," said Leon Bear, chairman of the Skull Valley band of Goshutes. The Goshutes leased 820

---

38. "Germ Research," *Deseret News*, Aug. 21, 1988; "Garn Votes," *Salt Lake Tribune*, Dec. 15, 1984.

39. Brett Del Porto, "Bangerter Says No," Lee Davidson, "Army Won't Build," *Deseret News*, Mar. 14, Sept. 20, 1988.

40. Keim et al., "Time to Worry about Anthrax," 71–75; also Guillemin, *Anthrax*.

acres of their 18,000-acre reservation in Utah's west desert to Private Fuel Storage for an amount kept secret.[41]

Private Fuel Storage planned for utilities to seal ten tons of spent fuel in a steel cylinder, insert each cylinder into a 150-ton transportation cask, and ship it by train to the reservation. There the cylinder would be put into a 180-ton storage cask and placed on a cement slab like a parking lot. Four-hundred casks would sit there for forty years, or until the government took the fuel. Goshutes would work at the facility. Fewer than forty of the 130 tribal members lived on the reservation, partly because the tribe was the only employer there.[42] Nuclear waste might enable them to move back to their land, earn a living, govern their own community, and survive as a people.

Governor Mike Leavitt (1993–2003) grew up in Cedar City and retained in his mind's eye a childhood image of his grandmother hanging out laundry in a pink cloud he later heard was fallout. He said Utah had been sacrificed once before and should not be sacrificed again. Opposition to spent fuel became the most deeply felt position of his administration. "It's an over-my-dead-body issue," he said. Public opinion backed him. "Don't Waste Utah" became a popular bumper sticker. The Church of Jesus Christ of Latter-day Saints issued a statement against bringing spent fuel to the state. Four published opinion polls showed 65 to 84 percent opposition to the plan. In contrast, Tooele County, where the project would be located, made a deal with Private Fuel Storage to make payments to the county as if it were off the reservation and paying taxes, and then the county supported the project. "We're looking at economic advantages for Tooele County," said Commissioner Teryl Hunsaker.[43]

41. Erickson et al., "Monitored Retrievable Storage," 97–98, 101–02; Judy Fahys, "Tribal Vote," *Salt Lake Tribune*, Nov. 14, 2005.

42. Matthew L. Wald, "Tribe in Utah Fights," *New York Times*, Apr. 18, 1999; *Skull Valley Band of Goshute Indians v. Davis*, 728 F. Supp. 2d 1287 (D. Utah 2010).

43. Jerry Spangler, "Sovereign Quest," Robert Gehrke, "Tooele Rips Governor's Plan," Spangler, "In Harm's Way," Joe Bauman, "Utahns Favor a Tax," *Deseret News*, July 8, 1993, Dec. 4, 1997, Apr. 28, 2002, Nov. 29, 2005; William Claiborne, "Utah

At first legislators had no interest in fighting the fuel project. But as public opinion swung behind Govenor Leavitt, lawmakers soon agreed with voters. The legislature passed laws requiring a $5 million application fee and a $2 billion cash bond for spent fuel projects, but federal courts ruled those laws unconstitutional. Utah's congressional delegation, usually opposed to wilderness, persuaded Congress to create a 100,000-acre wilderness area to block a proposed rail line, and Leavitt seized the only paved road into the reservation and closed it to waste shipments. But Private Fuel Storage still found a way around the interference. Leavitt had Utah pay legal fees for dissident Goshutes who challenged the tribe's decisions in court. He created an Office of High Level Nuclear-waste Opposition, with an acronym of "o-HELL-NO."[44]

Nonetheless, the federal Nuclear Regulatory Commission issued the Goshute facility a license over Utah's objections. The project also needed approval from the federal Department of Interior. Interior's environmental study found "no significant adverse impacts" and "significant economic benefits for the Skull Valley Band." Utah senators Hatch and Bennett lobbied Dirk Kempthorne, Interior Secretary in the George W. Bush administration, and in a 2006 surprise Kempthorne disapproved the plan. The project is "stone-cold dead," exulted Senator Hatch.[45]

Private Fuel Storage sued to overturn Kempthorne's decision. Governor Jon Huntsman and Attorney General Mark Shurtleff were so confident of the outcome, they did not even bother to participate. "It's a done deal," Huntsman said; "It's over." But in a bigger 2010 surprise, federal judge David Ebel ruled for Private Fuel Storage and

Resisting Tribe," *Washington Post*, Mar. 2, 1999; Dan Harrie, "Officials Covet N-Waste," Judy Fahys, "LDS Joins N-Storage Foes," *Salt Lake Tribune*, Sept. 22, 2002, May 5, 2006.

44. Judy Fahys, "Leavitt Creates Office," Robert Gehrke, "Utah Gains Ally," *Salt Lake Tribune*, Dec. 8, 2000, Dec. 18, 2005; *Skull Valley Band of Goshute Indians v. Dianne K. Nielson et al.*, 376 F. 3d 1223 (10th Cir. 2004).

45. Joe Bauman and Elaine Jarvik, "Goshute Plant," *Deseret News*, Feb. 25, 2005; James E. Cason, "Record of Decision for the Construction and Operation of an Independent Spent Fuel Storage Installation, Sept. 7, 2006.

the project was revived. Ebel noted that the politicians had killed the project against the findings of the environmental impact statement. Though he did not say so, he seemed to suspect that Republican Kempthorne might have done a political favor for Republican Utah. Worse yet, by the time of Ebel's decision, Barack Obama had become president and Ken Salazar Secretary of the Interior. Neither owed Utah any favors and declined to appeal Ebel's decision. Had Utah joined the suit, the state could have appealed with some chance of success. As it was, Private Fuel Storage had the needed permits and Utah had little means left to resist.[46]

Then, in a final surprise, Private Fuel Storage gave up and gave back its permits. Utilities saw they could keep the fuel in storage casks on their own property more cheaply than they could ship it to the Goshute reservation.[47] Utahns were relieved. The Goshutes said they would look for another project to enable them to live on their reservation.

SKIRMISHES

Electronic Battlefield

Besides big downwinder battles, Utah fought a series of smaller, similar military issues. The Air Force asked to have 396 acres of Utah's West Desert in 1988 to build an Electronic Battlefield. The Air Force planned to scatter 100 trailers over 28,000 acres. Planes would fly over the electronic battlefield to test different kinds of radar, homing devices, jamming, and evasion. No bullets would be fired, no bombs dropped; sheep and cattle would continue to graze. The Air Force hoped to start using the range in 1991, and continue to build in stages until 2000, at a total cost of maybe $4 billion. Proponents said the battlefield would bring high-tech growth to Utah. Downwinders opposed the project. They said the Air Force deceived Utahns and eventually would take tens or hundreds of thousands of

---

46. Robert Gehrke, Judy Fahys, Thomas Burr, "Interior Dumps N-Waste Plan," Fahys, "Interior Won't Fight Ruling," *Salt Lake Tribune*, Sept. 8, 2006, Sept. 27, 2010; Baker, "What Does It Mean to Comply?" 241.

47. Judy Fahys, "Money, Politics," *Salt Lake Tribune*, Jan. 7, 2013

acres. Opponents sponsored an "Air Force Blues Tour" beginning in Trout Creek in the West Desert and ending at Westminster College, where about fifty people heard how the "old anti-MX coalition" would revive against the battlefield. The Soviet Union fell; military budgets were cut; President George H. W. Bush declined to fund the battlefield; and the Air Force gave up on it in 1990.[48]

Green River Missiles

Starting in 1964, the army had tested Pershing and Athena missiles in Green River, named after the river that runs through it. "They sounded like a whistle going through the air," Mayor Rey Lloyd Hatt recalled of the old missiles. With army jobs, Green River had prospered. But after the tests ended in 1975, Green River fell from 1,400 residents to 850, as jobs fled with the army. In the First Gulf War, Iraqis fired Russian-made Scud missiles at American soldiers, and the army wanted to be able to shoot down such missiles. In 1993 the army said it would come back to Green River, fire missiles 450 miles to White Sands Proving Ground in New Mexico, where other missiles would shoot them out of the air. At a hearing in Green River, all but one of the resident speakers welcomed the army. "Anything we can do to get them back," said Mayor Hatt. "They are good for our town." On their way to New Mexico, the missiles would drop a booster in the desert. The army said they could limit the drop zone to about five square miles, but environmentalists, the Navajo Tribe, and tourist businesses objected. Democratic congresswoman Karen Shepherd persuaded Congress to stop such tests for a year and introduced a bill to stop them permanently. The army gave up in 1995. Green River stayed poor.[49]

---

48. Lee Davidson, "A. F. Revives Its Plans," Marianne Funk, "Formidable-Sounding Site," Joe Costanzo, "Dispute Over A. F. Battlefield," Davidson and Joe Bauman, "It's No Rumor," *Deseret News*, Oct. 6, Nov. 29, 1988, Jan. 7, Mar. 9, 1990.

49. Alexander, "Brief Histories," 132; Christopher Smart, "Rebirth of Missile Complex," Laurie Sullivan, "Army Shoots Down Utah," *Salt Lake Tribune*, Apr. 14, 1993, Mar. 23, 1995; Jerry Spangler, "Missile Opponents," Lee Davidson and Spangler, "Shepherd Shoots at Army," *Deseret News*, May 13, 1993, July 5, 1993.

Hurricane Fling

The army feared Scud missiles tipped with chemical weapons and wanted to know how far a missile could spread poison gas. They planned tests at Hurricane Mesa Test Track in southern Utah. In 1953 the air force had built a 12,000-foot rail to test pilot-ejection devices. They shot dummies and apes down the track on a rocket-powered sled and launched them over the mesa rim, where parachutes opened. The army wanted to fling loads of triethyl phosphate over the cliff and watch the "aeroballistic effects," which, they believed, would mimic nerve gas. Though not lethal, triethyl phosphate is used in cleaning agents and is classified as hazardous. Five miles from the mesa lies the town of Virgin, where residents worried. Mayor Joy Henderlider hoped they would not run the tests up there, "not even soap water." Environmentalists joined with the townspeople in opposition. Utah Congressman Jim Hansen, a member of the Armed Services Committee and friend of the military, told the army the plan "fails the rationality test." The army reconsidered and gave up the idea.[50]

Ground Waves

A nuclear attack would produce an electromagnetic pulse that would disable electronic communications. To prepare, military planners designed a Ground Wave Emergency Network that would still work after an attack. They planned to build 83 towers, two of them in Utah. In Kane County the military quietly bought five acres of land and hired a contractor to erect a tower. When the contractor applied for a building permit, he was told to follow the normal planning process. Captain Roy Gardner phoned Commissioner Ray Lopeman and said, "We are the federal government, and federal agencies do not need local permits." Lopeman replied, "This is Kane County, and Kane County law says they will go through the planning process like everybody else." Before the argument went very far,

---

50. Alexander, "Brief Histories," 127; Matthew S. Brown, "Army Proposes to Fling Simulants," "Mayor-Elect of Virgin Vows to Fight Tests," Lee Davidson, "Army Cancels Plans," *Deseret News*, Sept. 26, Dec. 19, 1993, Feb. 3, 1994.

Congress decided that since the Cold War had ended, a complete ground-wave network was not needed. No tower was built in Utah.[51]

More Testing

The 1992 moratorium on nuclear testing in Nevada proved precarious. Military planners wanted to make sure old bombs were still reliable. President George W. Bush wanted a new bunker-buster bomb. In 2007 the military planned Divine Strake, a big underground conventional explosion to see what it would take to penetrate a bunker. That test was stopped by public and congressional opposition, but President Bush obtained funds to renovate the test site to be ready for future explosions. Utah Democratic congressman Jim Matheson fought more testing. He said the military misled Utahns about fallout from new tests, and in every Congress, he unsuccessfully introduced a bill to prevent resumption of testing.[52]

BASE CLOSINGS

Even as they fought against missiles, waste, biological weapons, and nerve gas, Utahns struggled to keep military bases. Bases bring jobs, so politicians oppose local base closures. In 1988, Congress enacted a plan to overcome pro-job politics with a Base Realignment and Closure Commission to hear military recommendations and then make a "hit list" of unneeded facilities. Either Congress or the President could reject the whole list, but neither could change it. From 1989 to 2005, five commissions met, compiled lists, and closed bases. All of them caused Utah anxiety.

The first commission closed Fort Douglas, founded in Salt Lake City in 1863 to watch the Latter-day Saints and protect stage

---

51. Matthew S. Brown, "A. F. Decides to Build," *Deseret News*, Aug. 28, 1993; Laurie Sullivan, "Air Force Efforts," Sullivan, "Air Force Tower Won't Go Up," *Salt Lake Tribune*, Sept. 27, Nov. 16, 1993.

52. Warren Bates, "Test Site Explosion," *Las Vegas Review–Journal*, July 3, 1997; Jerry Spangler, "Matheson Moves to Block Nevada N-Tests," Joe Bauman, "Divine Strake," *Deseret News*, Mar. 10, 2005, Feb. 23, 2007; Christopher Smith, "Funding Sought," *Salt Lake Tribune*, Mar. 19, 2004.

This tank rebuilding shop at the Tooele Army Depot was closed in 1993, but the half-buried igloos and the deadly chemical weapons stored in them remained. *Classified Photo Collection, Utah State Historical Society*

coaches. Utahns congratulated themselves on the grown-up way they accepted the loss of 185 jobs, then quickly acquired Fort Douglas land for the University of Utah.[53]

In 1993 another commission closed a truck-repair plant at Tooele Army Depot. That ended 1,900 jobs, one-third of all jobs in Tooele County, making it the American county most affected by closure. To add insult, the army continued to store and destroy chemical weapons at Tooele. "We lose the cream and keep the crap," said Congressman Jim Hansen. Governor Mike Leavitt sent an angry letter to the Pentagon saying that if they moved truck repair, they should move nerve gas too, but no one in Washington paid any attention.[54]

When a third commission convened in 1995, Utahns feared for

53. "Closing Obsolete Bases," Gordon Eliot White, "Fort Douglas Targeted," *Deseret News*, July 16, Dec. 29, 1988.

54. Matthew S. Brown, "Hansen, Leavitt," Lee Davidson, "Utah Stands to Lose," Davidson, "Tooele Tops List," *Deseret News*, Mar. 12, 17, 1993.

Hill Air Force base and its 17,000 jobs. The air force had five bases, including Hill that repaired planes and missiles. All five operated at about 50 percent of capacity. The commission planned to close two bases and send their work to the surviving three. After months of worry, politicking, and analysis, Hill survived. One base was closed in Texas and another in California, the state that had already lost the most bases and jobs. President Bill Clinton needed California for reelection, and said that closing another base exceeded California's fair share. He pounded his fist on the Rose Garden podium and seemed even angrier than Governor Leavitt had been over closure of the Tooele truck shop. But the president did not want to reject all closures, so he proposed bringing private contractors onto the California base who would hire the same workers to do the same work. Utahns and others cried political interference. If work was not moved to Hill, it would remain at 50 percent capacity in a "death spiral" awaiting closure by the next commission. To carry out the president's plan, Congress had to change a law passed earlier by a Democratic congress that restricted privatization of defense work. Utah Republican Jim Hansen, who might normally have favored privatization, helped to lead the successful defense of the Democratic law against Democratic assault.[55] Clinton won California and reelection anyway.

The army recommended closing the Dugway Proving Ground. Once marked for closure, few bases escaped. But disbelieving Utahns asked the army to look again at that decision. It turned out that, yes, weapons could be tested more cheaply elsewhere, but it might be impossible to get a state permit anywhere else. Moreover, Dugway had been contaminated by chemicals and germs and might cost more to clean up than would be saved by moving. On second thought, the army decided, it would be best to stay. Dugway was too dirty to die.[56]

55. Laurie Sullivan Maddox, "Hansen Claims Victory," *Salt Lake Tribune*, July 31, 1996; Lee Davidson, "Hill Could Suffer," *Deseret News*, Nov. 21, 1996.

56. Lee Davidson, "Army Retreats," *Deseret News*, Mar. 24, 1995.

A 1997 commission closed the Defense Depot Ogden and eliminated another 1,100 Utah jobs. Private firms invited to move into the abandoned Ogden and Tooele facilities brought only half as many jobs. Even so, the base closures proved to be less damaging than had been feared. Ogden and Tooele both fared well in the prosperity of the 1990s. Utahns most feared the possible loss of Hill Air Force Base, maybe the state's biggest employer. When the last base-closure commission up to this writing met in 2005, Ogden citizens raised $600,000 to lobby for Hill and the state legislature pitched in $5 million. A busload of workers cheering and waving signs traveled to Phoenix to attend a commission hearing, and Utah congressmen and senators joined them in pleading for Hill.[57] The base was spared again.

REMARKS

Utah Democrats and people on the left led most of the downwinder issues. They won their biggest victory against MX. Downwinders raised public fears, changed public opinion, dragged politicians along, and helped expel the project from Utah. They tried to follow the same strategy for other downwinder campaigns against burning chemical weapons, against the bio-level 4 lab, against the resumption of nuclear testing, and against Envirocare receiving hotter radioactive waste, foreign waste, or a bigger dump, and they influenced some of those issues as well. In Congress, Utah's Democrats voiced downwinder concerns. Democrat Wayne Owens fought the MX, electronic battlefield, and bio-level 4 lab. Democrat Karen Shepherd opposed missiles in Green River. Democrat Jim Matheson sought to block hotter waste for Envirocare and the resumption of nuclear testing. After Utah turned to the right in the 1970s, almost the only issues Utah Democrats won came when Democratic national administrations or federal courts overruled Utah public opinion. Almost

---

57. "Army Retreats."

alone on the left, downwinders could take issues to Utahns and win by persuading popular opinion to their side.[58]

Governors proved to be the most effective persuaders, and downwinder politics changed the office of Utah governor. Utah's attitude toward defense changed in 1976 when Democrat Scott Matheson succeeded Democrat Calvin Rampton. Rampton handled the 1968 sheepkill quietly. He met privately with army officers, and said nerve gas should not alarm Utahns. After the army paid damages, he stopped talking about it. He did not mention the sheepkill in his memoirs. Democrat Scott Matheson did not come to office looking to fight the federal government, but found his stride with downwinder and other anti-Washington issues. His 1980 reelection slogan was "Matheson stands up for Utah," meaning he was standing up against the federal government. He entitled his memoirs *Out of Balance,* meaning Washington had too much power and the states too little. The book is mostly a history of Matheson's arguments with the federal government.

When Matheson opposed the Weteye nerve-gas bombs, he found Utahns eager for leadership against this kind of project. Where Rampton had been quiet, Matheson was loud. He made speeches and issued press statements to array public opinion against moving the Weteyes to Utah. Later he was not the first to speak against MX, but he became Utah's leading voice in that controversy. (In the end, Republican senator Jake Garn may have had the most influence with his access to President Reagan.) Matheson set a pattern for governors that was followed by his successors: Raise Utah health and safety concerns, charge federal officials with not taking proper care, point to the downwinders' tale to show that Washington cannot be trusted, make public and dramatic speeches and gestures, and lead the state against the project. Later governors followed that pattern by

---

58. The chief exception was school vouchers discussed in chapter 16. In 2018 as this book went to press, Utah progressives won three referendum victories on medical marijuana, Medicaid, and redistricting. That might indicate that changes are coming.

speaking and acting publicly against defense and nuclear proposals. They found they could beat the legislature and congressional delegation on downwinder issues, as for example when Governor Leavitt turned the legislature against spent fuel, Governor Walker beat the congressional delegation on hotter waste, and Walker and Huntsman out-maneuvered legislators on Envirocare issues. The governors were also effective when they favored projects. Governor Leavitt persuaded Utahns to allow nerve gas to be burned rather than to store it. Governor Bangerter found a compromise on a new Dugway lab.

Though downwinder issues were Democratic issues, Democrats hardly benefitted. Democrat Wayne Owens won a congressional seat in 1978, partly by stressing the danger of nuclear attack on MX. Democrat Jim Matheson habitually won narrowly, and his opposition to nuclear waste and testing may have assisted some of his narrow victories. But during the decades Democrats successfully led downwinder fights, they started with little influence in Utah and lost much of what they had. For one thing, downwinders organized in ad hoc citizen groups, or professional environmental organizations, rather than through political parties: MX Information Center, HEAL, FAIR, Utahns Against Spent Fuel, and Utah Downwinders. Downwinders sought support from both parties, and though Republicans were slow and unenthusiastic, they read polls and came around in time to avoid political damage. Moreover, the downwinder message resembled the Latter-day Saint Republican message: Don't trust the federal government. Democrats distinguished between military and other issues. But many Utahns seemed simply to have added downwinder issues to their list of grievances against Washington.

Utahns wanted to keep military bases as much as they wanted to stop dangerous new projects. If bases closed, some Utahns would lose their jobs, while the people who might eventually be hired on future projects were not yet organized or motivated. Tooele County showed the power of economic interest. Jobs there depended on defense, so county commissioners welcomed Weteye bombs, chemical weapons, and spent nuclear fuel. The town of Green River similarly sought economic interest in projects downwinders opposed. State government overrode Tooele, the way the federal government could override Utah. Utah was like other states in wanting to keep its military bases. But Utah was unusual in its succession of downwinder controversies and in the way Utahns retold the Downwinders' Tale to help guide themselves through those controversies. Since the beginning of World War II, Utah moved from being dependent on defense work and solicitous of more to being ambivalent about defense work and distrustful of the federal government. The change on defense became part of Utah's general estrangement from Washington.

9

WATER

Water flows through stories told in arid lands. In Israel, a dry land, the Spirit of God hovered over water before he called for light, and Amos said, "Let justice roll down like waters," comparing two good things. Utah is a dry place, and Utahns tell water stories to remember their past, explain how people fit in nature, and guide their politics.

The stories do not explain Utah's current use of water or its management of the environment. Utah is the second driest state, receiving on average only thirteen inches of rain or snow per year. Yet according to the United States Geological Survey, Utahns use more culinary water than residents of all but one other state, and more than half of that culinary water is used to water lawns. All water used in homes, landscaping, and industry together accounts for only 19 percent of water use; 80 percent irrigates crops or waters cattle, even though agriculture now accounts for less than 1 percent of Utah's gross state product.[1]

Though Utah is dry, water is cheap partly because Utahns crowd together in the "Wasatch Front oasis," 5 percent of Utah land that is watered by streams from the Wasatch and Uinta Mountains, where an abundant sixty inches of precipitation fall in a normal year. In

---

1. "Cost of Water," "Municipal and Industrial Water," and "Utah's Water Resources," *Utah Division of Water Resources*, www.water.utah.gov. See also Molly A. Maupin et al., *Estimated Use of Water in the United States in 2010* (Washington, DC: US Geological Survey, 2014).

addition, local water agencies collect property tax and receive grants from a state sales tax earmarked for water. Taxes keep water bills low, thus enabling people to use more than they would if they had to pay more for it. In 2000 the state conducted a study of how much water people used and then began a campaign asking them to use less. For fifteen years water officials claimed their campaign was working, but then the Legislative Auditor General looked at the numbers and found they were partly fictitious. Utahns did not know how much water they used in 2000 or how much they currently used, so claims of water savings were largely wishful.[2] The state started over with a new conservation program based on better accounting.

Generations of Utah schoolchildren have been told stories of how the pioneers irrigated desert land. Famously on their first day in the Salt Lake Valley, Latter-day Saints diverted City Creek to water potatoes and buckwheat. Over the next three decades, Brigham Young sent some 350 companies to found new settlements every-where they could find water meeting arable land, usually where a stream flowed out of a canyon into a valley. Working cooperatively, the pioneers then dug a ditch to bring water from the stream to their fields. "They were all working together, and all had the same ideals," Dr. Levi Edgar Young informed school children who read his 1923 Utah history text.[3]

At first the Church controlled water directly, so each bishop directed ditch digging and decided when each family would take its turn—sometimes in the middle of the night—diverting water from the ditch to their fields. In 1852 the territorial legislature gave control of water to county courts composed of a judge and select-men. The judge was often the bishop and the selectmen were elected after being nominated to the regular ticket by church leaders. "It maintained the democratic spirit ... kept up the spirit of mutual

---

2. "Municipal and Industrial Water"; Legislative Auditor General, "Performance Audit of Projections of Utah's Water Needs," May 2015, online at water.utah.gov.
3. Young, *Founding of Utah*, 165.

helpfulness," Dr. John Henry Evans wrote of water governance in his 1933 school textbook. With a series of laws, the territorial legislature provided for water associations, with each farmer–irrigator a voting member who was obliged to share maintenance work and costs for the water works. Though nominally secular, water associations often met at the ward house, opened with prayer, and if a brother lagged cleaning his stretch of the ditch the bishop might threaten to disfellowship him. "One of the most important factors was the *effective Mormon Church Organization*," Dr. S. George Ellsworth emphasized in his 1972 text book. When the federal government seized Church property in the 1880s, the territorial legislature made water a market commodity, hoping to elude federal control.[4] In the same decade, private corporations built irrigation works as business ventures all over the West, including Utah. School text books skip those parts.

Latter-day Saint pioneers are to Utah what the pilgrims and founding fathers are to America. Like Thanksgiving, irrigation is a symbol that stands for the sum of the pioneering achievement. Utahns claim they were the first to irrigate on a large scale in North America, the first to build an irrigation reservoir, and the first to generate hydroelectric power from an irrigation dam. Utahns teach their children that the "miracle of water" flows through Utah's founding. Through "wise leadership, industry, cooperative effort, brotherly love, and through living the principles of their religion, a great Mormon Empire rose in the arid West," wrote Dr. Milton R. Hunter in his book for school children.[5] The second most famous phrase in Utah history says the pioneers made "the desert blossom as the rose."

Pioneer irrigation gave way to much bigger federal works with the Strawberry Project in 1905. The US Bureau of Reclamation let contracts to dam the Strawberry River that flowed into the Duchesne

---

4. Evans, *Story of Utah*, 78; May and Arrington, "Different Mode," 17–18; Ellsworth, *Utah's Heritage*, 158; Thomas, *Development of Institutions*, 53–56. Governor Charles R. Mabey has a poetic account of family irrigating in *Our Father's House*, 161.

5. Thomas, 13–14; Arrington and Anderson, "First Irrigation Reservoir," 208; Alexander, "Investment in Progress," 296; Hunter, *Utah in Her Western Setting*, 120.

River, the Green, the Colorado, and ultimately the Pacific Ocean. Workers drilled a tunnel through the Wasatch Mountains to divert water to Wasatch Front farms and orchards and eventually into the Great Salt Lake. The water from the Strawberry River brought prosperity. From the completion of the project in 1911 to 1920, the assessed value of southern Utah County, where the water flowed, rose from $6 million to $30 million.[6]

More federal projects came after Strawberry. The number peaked in the 1930s when reclamation combined with make-work to provide employment in the Great Depression. Federal water projects brought large subsidies. The law said locals had to pay back the costs, but in fact most costs were not charged to them, and the local share could be paid back over as much as fifty years at low interest. Some of the twenty-five dams the Bureau of Reclamation eventually built in Utah were located where local water associations had built before, but the federal dams held more water and did not wash out.[7] The federal government brought capital and competence. Pioneers had often failed as they struggled with mule teams and shovels to dam streams and build canals. Professional engineers with more money and better tools were able to build projects that surpassed pioneer aspirations.

Federal projects brought water but not home rule. Utahns gave up control as federal money paid for the work and decisions were made in Washington. Local water governance became closed, professional, and managerial. Historian Thomas G. Alexander showed that in the nineteenth century, farmers attended water-association meetings, understood the issues, debated even technical decisions, voted their interests, and controlled local irrigation. By the 1920s farmers no longer attended meetings. They left business to directors unless they had a specific complaint. An interlocking directorate of

---

6. Bingham, "Reclamation and the Colorado," 236–37.
7. Freeman, "Six Federal Reclamation Projects," 319; "Projects and Facilities," *Reclamation: Managing Water in the West*, www.usbr.gov; Peterson and Cannon, *Awkward State*, 210–14; also Arrington and Anderson, "First Irrigation Reservoir," 207–23.

engineers, lawyers, politicians, and successful citizens with time for public service came to govern a confusing array of water conservancy districts, metropolitan water districts, canal companies, irrigation companies, drainage associations and water users' associations. (I call members of this interlocking directorate water people, but their detractors call them water buffaloes.) In 1983, Tim Ralph Miller studied the Central Utah Water Conservancy District, Utah's premier water organization. He found the twenty directors on the board also sat as directors of thirty-six other water organizations, many of which did business with the Central Utah district. An investigation by the legislative auditor in 1999 found three Central Utah board members had contracts for consulting or construction with agencies that took water or money from the district. Critics cried conflict of interest, but water people said such relationships were known and accepted in the water community.[8]

Westerners soon saw that federal reclamation could control the Colorado River if Congress would pay the costs. The Colorado is not large but drains the driest part of America, and more water is taken from the Colorado River Basin than from any other in America. Often the river did not reach the Pacific Ocean because all of the water was used up along the way.[9] California, with its rich farmland and growing population, led river development. The Imperial Valley on the river's delta needed irrigation and flood control. Farmers demanded an "all-American" canal built entirely within the United States so they would not have to share water with Mexico. The federal Bureau of Reclamation had even bigger plans: instead of just a canal, it wanted to build a panoply of dams, canals, siphons, levees,

---

8. Alexander, "Interdependence and Change," 307–08; Frankel, "Chicken Little's New Career," 109; Miller, "Politics of the Carter Administration," 226–46; Osterstock, "Performance Audit," 26–37; Donna Kemp, "Lawmakers Satisfied," *Deseret News*, July 16, 1999.

9. Fradkin, *River No More*, 16.

dikes, and pipelines to subdue the river. California votes and Reclamation plans assailed Congress together to demand those projects.[10]

Upstream states feared the water law of the West: First in time, first in right. That meant that the person who first diverted water and put it to "beneficial use" owned that much water and had a right to it every year forever. Later users got no water until the earlier users had taken their full share. If projects were built downstream, California would use the water first, and by the law of the West it would own that water. The other states—Utah, Colorado, Wyoming, Arizona, Nevada, and New Mexico—could divide only the water remaining, and California might use the whole river.[11] Upstream states said the water came from snow that fell on their mountains and that they deserved a share. They kept Congress from authorizing California projects until the states negotiated to divide the water. In the 1922 Colorado River Compact, states agreed that nearly half the water would go to the Upper Basin states of Wyoming, Utah, Colorado, and New Mexico, and the rest to the Lower Basin states of Arizona, Nevada and California. A later agreement divided the Upper Basin water, and Utah's share was 23 percent, about 1.7 million acre feet a year.[12]

The Colorado River does not flow conveniently. Most of the yearly flow rushes down canyons in April, May, and June when winter snows melt and farmers do not need water. The water is needed in July and August. A dam can hold back the high spring flows so farmers have water when they need it. River flows vary from year to year, and a series of dams can catch high flows during wet years and save it against drought. After the Western states shared the water, Congress appropriated money for Hoover, Parker, and Davis Dams and for the All-American Canal, bringing water, power, and prosperity to Southern California.[13] Upstream states saw the benefits and demanded their

10. Hundley, *Water and the West*, 17–52.
11. Hundley, "West against Itself," 9–42; Allen, "Governor George H. Dern," 37.
12. Fuller et al., *Water, Agriculture*, 65–106, chap. 4; Clyde, "Institutional Response," 109–34.
13. Hundley, *Dividing the Waters*, 218.

own projects. In 1950 the Bureau of Reclamation proposed the Colorado River Storage Project with big dams on the Colorado and Green Rivers. One of them would be Echo Park Dam on the Green River in northern Utah, inside Dinosaur National Monument.

The monument had begun its way toward preservation in 1900 when steel magnate Andrew Carnegie saw a picture of a Brontosaurus skeleton in a newspaper and wanted one for his museum. The directors of the museum sent field scientist Earl Douglass to find a dinosaur, and he discovered a large fossil deposit on government land in Utah's Uintah Basin. Over the course of fifteen years, workmen dug up 700,000 pounds of bones and shipped them to the Carnegie Museum in Pittsburgh. The directors would not share bones, even with the Smithsonian Institution. To gain position for bargaining, the Smithsonian director talked President Woodrow Wilson into declaring the fifteen-acre quarry a national monument. The Vernal Commercial Club asked the National Park Service to save one dinosaur for them as a tourist attraction, but the Park Service refused. In 1938, President Franklin D. Roosevelt enlarged Dinosaur National Monument to include the confluence of the Yampa and Green Rivers, while reserving the right to build a dam there. Locals supported this expansion in the futile hope that the Park Service might build roads and a visitors center. By 1950 the only way to see Echo Park was to float down the river. Only thirty people boated through the monument in 1945, and in 1950 there were still only 106. Locals liked to tell scary stories about the dangers of the trip.[14]

Echo Park dam was "the key to all the dreams" of the Uintah Basin. Citizens foresaw a construction boom, farm prosperity, tourists flocking to the reservoir, and a future as "Utah's second largest industrial area" built with cheap electricity from the dam. But as soon as Reclamation proposed the dam, the Park Service objected. "Like a dog in the manger," locals said. The Park Service had let Carnegie carry off the bones, refused pleas for improvements, and

14. Hundley, *Water and the West*; Harvey, *Utah*, 243; Neal, "Echo Park," 34.

now, as one resident wrote, there was "a chance to have a big dam and make things hum around here," and "again the damn Park says NO." Citizens launched a "dampaign" and formed the "aqualantes," volunteers who wore star-shaped badges and raised money to bring Western justice against schemes to keep Utah from its rightful share of water. Utah Senator Arthur Watkins warned Utah "hysteria" might offend Washington decision makers.[15]

The Echo Park dam proposal also united American conservationists to fight for the sanctity of parks and monuments. The National Park Association, Sierra Club, Wilderness Society, Audubon Society, Izaak Walton League, and others joined forces for the first time. Famous writers and former Utahns Bernard DeVoto and Wallace Stegner wrote books and articles denouncing the dam. The *New York Times* publisher John Oakes floated through Echo Park with the Sierra Club and then led the outcry against the dam.[16] Environmentalists published picture books, made movies, and honed techniques they have used in subsequent campaigns.

From 1950 to 1955, Congress refused to pass the Upper Colorado River bill. Californians opposed diverting water that otherwise flowed to them. Farm states opposed a plan to raise farm production when farmers already suffered low prices from overproduction. The bill finally passed after Upper Basin congressmen agreed to take Echo Park Dam out of the plan, and, in return, environmentalists ceased their opposition. Some latter-day environmentalists have denounced the deal that resulted in the Glen Canyon dam and other upstream development, but others celebrate it as the greatest conservationist victory to that time.[17] Conservationists tried to upgrade Dinosaur to a national park, but Utahns blocked the attempt in the vain hope of reviving the dam. The Park Service finally made a dinosaur exhibit at the quarry.

---

15. Neel, "Echo Park," 41, 43–46; Terrell, *War for the Colorado*, 171–98; "Clyde: Key to Resources," *Deseret News*, Oct. 30, 1964; M. Bomis, "Chamber History: Watering the Desert," *Salt Lake Chamber*, Feb. 2016, https://slchamber.com.

16. See, for instance, Stegner, *This is Dinosaur*, v–vi, 5–17.

17. Harvey, *Symbol of Wilderness*, 287.

In the twentieth century, the Colorado River and its Central Utah Project dominated Utah relations, first with neighboring states, then with the federal government. At the start of the century, Utahns built and benefitted from the Strawberry Project. Governor Charles Mabey (1921–25) negotiated the Colorado River Compact, and the next nine governors devoted time, faced crises, and lead cheers for Colorado River water. Securing water projects became important business for Utah senators and congressmen, who sought seats on interior committees where the issues were decided.[18] Only Republican governor J. Bracken Lee (1949–57) failed to share the enthusiasm. He believed that water projects, even Utah water projects, exceeded proper limits of federal action. Lee knew most Utahns disagreed with him, and he said little publicly, but Utahns lobbying for water resented his lack of zest. When Lee sought a third term in 1956, George Dewey Clyde opposed him in the Republican Party. Clyde had taught hydrological engineering at Utah State Agricultural College, served in federal conservation programs under President Eisenhower, sat on a series of water boards, and led Utah's fight for Echo Park Dam and the Colorado River Storage Project. He brought to his gubernatorial campaign people who had worked with him on water issues and ran as the man who had won passage that year of the Colorado River Storage Act. He and his water team beat Lee in a Republican primary and then won a three-man final election. Water helped float Clyde into the governor's chair (1957–65).[19]

Four beliefs underlay Utah's pursuit of federal projects: (1) water brings prosperity; (2) water supplies are finite and set the limits of

18. Fuller et al., *Water, Agriculture,* 37–62, 135–37; Matheson, *Out of Balance,* 146–64; also Allen, "Governor George H. Dern," 37, 75. Utah Congressmembers on the Interior Committee included Reva Beck Bosone, William Dawson, and Wayne Owens; on the Senate committee were Frank Moss, Abe Murdock, and Arthur Watkins; and Congressman Don B. Colton was on the Irrigation and Reclamation Committee, Senator Jake Garn on the Appropriations Interior Committee.

19. Jonas, "1956 Election," 151, 156. Clyde's water team included former Vernal mayor and state senator Briant H. Stringham, advertising mogul David Evans, and *Deseret News* editor John R. Talmage, who was later Clyde's press secretary.

Utah growth; (3) without projects, water will soon run out; and (4) only the federal government was big enough to build the needed projects. Chief advocate for this view was Utah Democratic senator Frank Moss (1957–75). In his book *The Water Crisis*, he called for federal action to slake American thirst. "Vast amounts of water are now flowing unused into the northern seas," he wrote. He proposed pumping that unused water from Alaska and the Canadian Yukon over Canadian mountains and building new dams to form a 500-mile-long Rocky Mountain Trench Reservoir astride the US–Canada border, holding as much water as Lake Erie. From the Trench Reservoir, the water would separate into two branches, one augmenting the Colorado River and the other flowing across Utah, irrigating farms along the way, to the Rocky Mountains, where pumps would lift water to the sources of the Rio Grande River to flow to Texas and Mexico. The plan also called for a canal connecting the Trench Reservoir to the Great Lakes, so ships could float from the Atlantic to the Pacific Ocean. In addition, a boat could travel up the Mississippi, through the Great Lakes, and on to Alaska. Moss reveled in the "grandeur and potential of such continental-scale thinking." In the mid-twentieth century, Utahns believed, along with Senator Moss (and against Governor Lee) in the New Deal, the Great Society, and the transformational power of energetic government to improve nature and the nation.[20]

Though Moss's grandest ideas were never implemented, he did help win the Central Utah Project, an ambitious plan to tie together and enlarge two former successes: the Strawberry Project and the Provo River Project. The Strawberry Project had taken water from a Uintah Basin stream through a tunnel in the mountains. The Central Utah Project would take more water from many streams through a bigger tunnel. An array of projects would replace water taken from the Ute Tribe and basin residents. On the Provo River, another dam

---

20. Clyde, "History of Irrigation," 26–29; Moss, *Water Crisis*, 242–54; Espeland, *Struggle for Water*, 43–73.

UTAH POLITICS

would be built to provide cities with drinking water that otherwise flowed unused into the Great Salt Lake. Utahns envisioned federal money pouring into Utah, more water to enable more prosperity, and a vindication of Utah rights against guzzling Californians. Without a big project, the state might never get its share of the Colorado River, and Utah's future would flow away with the water. For decades copious news coverage on the project read like sports reports on Utah teams against out-of-state rivals. In 1965, Utahns voted by a 93 percent majority to tax themselves for their share of project costs.[21]

Troubles, delays, lawsuits, and mounting costs plagued the Central Utah Project. Two dams leaked and required years to repair, two pipelines leaked or caved in, two giant tunnel-boring machines became stuck—one took four years to extricate and the other was abandoned, along with a mile of tunnel it had already dug. Parsimonious congressional appropriations meant that work went slowly, and the Bureau of Reclamation took a disproportionate share of the meager funds for administration. A Utah legislative audit found that 56 percent of all project spending went to administration in 1985, as did 30 percent over the decade of the 1980s. The project was designed before passage of environmental laws, and the original plans would have dried streams and killed fish. Courts held up the project while environmentalists argued that the new conservation laws should be applied to the ongoing project, but the environmentalists eventually lost.[22]

As the project dawdled, Utah changed. Water from the Strawberry Project that came through the mountains in 1911 irrigated sugar beets, fruit, and grain, crops that supported sugar factories, canneries, mills, and meat packers. When agriculture flourished, Utah prospered. The mission of the Bureau of Reclamation was to supply water to family farms, and the Central Utah Project was designed

---

21. Fuller et al., *Water, Agriculture*, 143; Adam R. Eastman, "Central Utah Project: Bonneville Unit," *Reclamation*, www.usbr.gov/projects; Vedder, "Water Development," 58. See also the Central Utah Project clip files, Special Collections, Marriott Library.

22. See Eastman, "Central Utah Project," 23–70, for construction history; also *Sierra Club et al. v. Gilbert Stamm*, 507 F. 2d 788 (10th Cir. 1974).

to further that mission. Over decades of delay, subdivisions replaced farms, and farm-dependent industries closed. New irrigation meant little more than an extra cutting of alfalfa, barely affecting the economy. The government was spending more to bring water to farms than the crops were worth. Farmers could afford the water only because electrical power generated by big dams paid up to 96 percent of the water costs. Moreover, as suburbs replaced farms, old irrigation water flowed to the Great Salt Lake. Central Utah managers bought some of the unused irrigation water for less than 5 percent of the cost of bringing water through the mountains. More still flowed unused down old irrigation canals through new neighborhoods.

Delays inflated costs, and the project ran out of money. Congress would have to authorize more spending, and Utahns would have to pay their share. In 1985, Utahns voted by 73 percent to increase their project debt from $150 million to $550 million. However, for three straight years beginning in 1986, Congressional committees refused to authorize more funds. Congressmen shared the concerns environmentalists had raised in their losing law suits. Finally project backers made a deal with environmentalists to save the project as water people had made a deal with environmentalists to save the original 1956 bill. The Central Utah Project Completion Act of 1992 reduced the amount of water coming through the tunnel by almost one-third and the rest was left in streams so that the project would kill fewer fish. The Ute tribe was paid for its water. Other Basin residents were not paid, and some of them felt badly used. Terms were made harder for irrigators, and two rural counties withdrew from the project. Democratic representative Wayne Owens, who sponsored the compromise, said that he had expected irrigators to withdraw from the completion act, and the project would be better without irrigation. In a series of decisions over the next ten years, almost all irrigation—the original purpose of the project—was eliminated.[23]

---

23. Fuller et al., *Water, Agriculture*, 283–318; Reed L. Madsen, "Two Utah Counties," Matthew S. Brown, "Deletion Will Help CUP," Dennis Romboy, "Controversial

No one knows the cost of the Central Utah Project, but an accepted rough estimate is $3 billion. That means project water would cost $12,570 per acre foot, "among the most expensive water ever developed by the Bureau of Reclamation." Most of the expense was to bring the water through the mountains, where now it flows into Utah Lake and becomes polluted before continuing on to the Great Salt Lake. In Utah Lake, the water is traded for old, unused irrigation water, which is upgraded for drinking. But, as noted above, old irrigation water was purchased and more could have been bought for a fraction of the cost of the project. As Utah cities grow, they may eventually need more water. But for now the use does not justify the expense. No one knows when the project will be completed. It is almost finished, but project managers say inadequate appropriations limit their work. In 2018, Congress spent $6 million on construction. At that rate, the work might drag on another decade. In comparison, Utahns paid $50 million in property taxes to the water conservancy district, and the district earned $16 million from water sales.[24]

Utahns see that federal water projects have dried up, and they need new policies. Some water people want the state to build the kind of big projects the federal government used to sponsor. In particular they want a $1.8 billion pipeline from the Colorado River to St. George in Utah's southwest corner. St. George became one of the nation's fastest growing cities by luring tourists and retirees to golf courses in the desert, but now needs more water if it is to continue that kind of growth. Utah has a right to the water and says St. George can have it. But environmentalists say climate change may reduce flows, and Utah should not take the water, even if it owns it. St. George uses twice as much water per person as Denver or Albuquerque. Environmentalists

Part of CUP," Amy Joi O'Donoghue, "Water Woes," Donoghue, "Duchesne County," *Deseret News*, June 27, Sept. 4, 1993, Oct. 17, 1998, Jan. 12, July 14, 2015; also Eastman, "From Cadillac to Chevy," 359.

24. Author's interviews with Central Utah Water Conservancy District general and assistant managers Gene Shawcross, Richard L. Tullis, Mar. 29, 2018; Eastman, 359, relying on estimates by US Rep. Howard Nielson (R–Utah, 1983–91).

say instead of building an expensive pipeline, residents could use less water. City and state governments seem committed to the pipeline, but they need federal permission, and may not get it.[25]

REMARKS

Utah pioneers overcame a desert, and a thirsty mindset has persisted in the state. Through the twentieth century, Utahns told themselves that water limited their growth. Their politics proceeded from fear of future shortages more than from any present lack of water. To fulfill the state's destiny, they believed, the state must have big federal water projects to deliver Colorado River water. Like defense, water bound Utah to Washington by ties of economic dependence. Utahns got what they asked for. The federal government built a big project to deliver Colorado River water. But nearing completion, the project disappoints. It seems irrelevant to Utah's growth, and most of the water is not used for drinking or for irrigation. Most Utahns now scarcely know what the Central Utah Project is.

Utah Democrats were affected more than Republicans by the decline of federal projects. They used to win elections, partly by promising water projects. The last Democrat elected US senator was Frank Moss of grandiose water dreams. The last two Democratic governors were Cal Rampton, an "aqualante," and Scott Matheson, who saved the Central Utah Project from President Jimmy Carter's "hit list."[26] Democrats have changed. They lead environmentalists both nationally and in Utah, and they say the state should avoid reclamation projects, use less water, and prepare for a drier future. Eventually they may prove right, but in Utah they lose elections with that message now.

---

25. Deborah Bulkeley, "St. George Growth," *Deseret News*, Sept. 22, 2005; David DeMille, "St. George among Fastest," *Spectrum*, Mar. 23, 2017; Frankel, "Chicken Little's New Career," 99, citing Utah Rivers Council figures for St. George at 328 gallons per person per day, Albuquerque at 150, and Denver at 168; also *Lake Powell Pipeline*, https://lpputah.org.; McGivney, "Return of Glen Canyon," 160–74.

26. Matheson, *Out of Balance*, 146–64.

10

FEDERAL LAND

On a little desk set on the rim of the Grand Canyon in 1996, President Bill Clinton proclaimed the Grand Staircase–Escalante National Monument. About 2,000 selected government workers, environmentalists, and political people cheered. The monument was in Utah, but President Clinton was in Arizona. He knew Utahns disliked the monument—America's biggest monument, almost as big as Delaware and Rhode Island combined—and Utahns felt slighted by the way he made it. For months White House staffers had worked secretly to prepare the "Utah event," taking special care to hide it from Utah senators and congressmen. Clinton staffers had consulted movie star Robert Redford, but other Utahns found out only when the administration anonymously leaked details to the press eleven days before the event. Inquiries from Utah senators were met by equivocation. "No final decision establishing a monument has been made," Interior Secretary Bruce Babbitt wrote to Utah senator Bob Bennett five days before the announcement.[1]

Utahns had grazed cattle on the land and had driven across it, sometimes for fun in off-road vehicles. The monument covered coal beds Utahns had hoped to mine. President Clinton's declaration restricted

---

1. Rasband, "Utah's Grand Staircase," 484n5; also *Behind Closed Doors*. President Jimmy Carter proclaimed fifty-six million acres of national monuments in Alaska in 1978, and two years later Congress changed them to wildlife preserves or parks, leaving the Grand Staircase the largest from 1996 to 2017 when Donald Trump reduced its size.

local use. "The mother of all land grabs," fulminated Senator Orrin Hatch. But law professor Charles Wilkinson pronounced the designation among "the grandest, most electrifying moments in American conservation history," and environmentalists rejoiced.[2] To designate the monument, President Clinton used the 1906 Antiquities Act that said when an "historic landmark" or "object of scientific interest" is in danger on federal property, the president may proclaim a national monument to protect the landmark. By 1998 presidents had used the law 102 times. Many lawsuits had asserted that a president had exceeded his authority, but every court had upheld the president. Utah counties filed federal suit nine months after the event, and in more than a dozen overlapping cases the monument spent more than twenty years in federal court.[3] Then in December of 2017, President Donald Trump reduced the size of several national monuments, including cutting Grand Staircase–Escalante by almost half. Native Americans and environmentalists filed federal lawsuits to overturn the reduction, so more years of monument litigation lie ahead.

Clinton proclaimed the monument as he campaigned for reelection. In his memoirs published after he left office, Interior Secretary Bruce Babbitt told how the monument fit into the campaign.

> Dick Morris, [the president's] shadowy backstage political consultant, ran a poll that showed a surge of interest in environmental issues. Morris, who had no discernible outdoor experience beyond a well-publicized tryst on the balcony of the Jefferson Hotel, nonetheless came up with a big idea—the President should stage a September surprise with a dramatic environmental initiative. Soon the search was on for an appropriate subject, and before long southern Utah came into focus.[4]

---

2. "Utah's Grand Staircase"; Laurie Maddox, "Taking Swipes at Clinton," *Salt Lake Tribune*, Sep. 19, 1996; Fredrick Turner, "Oh, Wilderness," *Outside Magazine*, Apr. 1997.

3. See *Utah Association of Counties v. Clinton*, 255 F. 3d 1246 (10th Cir. 2001); *Wilderness Alliance v. Bureau of Land Management*, 425 F. 3d 735 (10th Cir. 2005); *Utah Association of Counties v. Bush*, 455 F. 3d 1094 (10th Cir. 2006); *Stewart v. US Dept. of Interior*, 554 F. 3d 1236 (10th Cir. 2009); *Wilderness Society v. Kane County*, 581 F. 3d 1198 (10th Cir. 2009); and others involving Kane County, Secretary Salazar, and SUWA.

4. Babbitt, *Cities in the Wilderness*, 163.

Environmental adviser Kathleen McGinty explained why Utah was chosen in a confidential memo to President Clinton that set out the "political purpose of the monument." She warned that the monument might anger Utahns but added that opponents "are unlikely to support the Administration under any circumstances."[5] McGinty said the designation would win environmental votes in other Western states and the president would lose nothing by angering Utahns. They would vote Republican regardless of administrative actions. Morris and McGinty proved correct. In the 1996 election, Utah voted the most strongly against Clinton of any state, and voter anger spilled over to defeat Bill Orton, Utah's only Democrat in Congress. But Clinton carried six western states, more than any Democrat since Lyndon Johnson.

Land ownership gives the federal government extra power over Utah. Most Utahns live in a long urban strip at the western base of the Wasatch Mountains where streams supply water and the federal government does not own the land. The 2010 census showed 90.4 percent of Utahns living on 1.1 percent of the state's land. Utah ranks eighth highest among states in the percentage of urban population but only forty-first in the percentage of urban land. Most of Utah is empty, and most of the empty land is owned by the federal government. In all, Washington owns two-thirds of all Utah land, the second-highest percentage of any state.[6] President Clinton's monument showed how federal land brings shocks, surprises, and difficulties. Since statehood, Utahns have seen federal land as a barrier to prosperity and a shackle on self-government. They struggled to benefit from federal land and to govern themselves around federal impositions. Since the late 1960s, Democratic administrations have seen Utah as a place for federal-land gestures such as the monument, which distressed Utahns but pleased environmentalists nationwide. As Kathleen McGinty told

---

5. *Behind Closed Doors*, 7.

6. *Utah 2010*, tables 2, 7; Wendell Cox, "America's Most Urban States," *New Geography*, Mar. 2016, www.newgeography.com; Gorte et al, *Federal Land Ownership*, 5

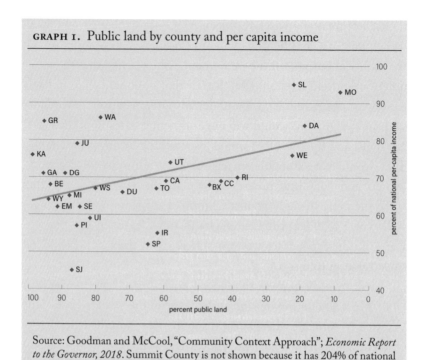

GRAPH 1. Public land by county and per capita income

Source: Goodman and McCool, "Community Context Approach"; *Economic Report to the Governor, 2018*. Summit County is not shown because it has 204% of national per capita income, too great an outlier.

President Clinton, Utah is so Republican, a Democratic administration loses nothing by angering voters there.

Federal land imposes economic costs. Graph 1 shows that the more government land a Utah county has, the lower its per capita income is likely to be. In the nineteen Utah counties where the federal government owns more than half the land, average per capita income in 2016 was $32,785. In the other ten Utah counties, average income was $47,009. A child in a federal-land county was more likely to be poor and 38 percent more likely to qualify for subsidized federal lunch than a child living in a county with less-than-half federal land. Federal land reduces money for Utah schools. A legislative study showed that if the federal government paid the same royalty from oil and gas wells as the state received from wells on private land and paid taxes for undeveloped land, Utah schools would receive hundreds of million dollars more each year. Scenic parts of federal land draw tourists, and some economists say tourism is the state's future. But tourist-industry wages average one-fifth those of miners and roughnecks.[7] Much of Utah's tourist economy is a minimum-wage economy.

Utah agreed at statehood to large federal holdings. The state constitution promised to "forever disclaim all right and title to unappropriated public lands." But Utahns have always complained, beginning with the first governor Heber Wells. When President Theodore Roosevelt planned to set aside forest reserves, Wells said that "great hardship and great evil will result," but the president reserved the land anyway. In 1929, President Herbert Hoover offered to give most federal land to the states, though the federal government would keep mineral rights. Utah Governor George Dern feared a land gift would bring reductions in federal highway and reclamation money, so he used his position as chair of the Western States Governors Association to stave it off. Harold Ickes, Interior Secretary to Franklin D. Roosevelt, proposed an enormous Escalante National Monument on the Colorado River through Utah but the idea died when World War II began.[8]

In his last ninety minutes of power in 1969, President Lyndon Baines Johnson doubled the size of Arches National Monument and enlarged Capitol Reef National Monument six-fold. Johnson timidly followed the advice of Interior Secretary Stuart Udall, who had secretly cajoled Johnson to sequester eight million acres across the West as a "parting gift" to future generations. Johnson feared taking so much and designated only 384,000 acres, all of it in Utah. Afterward Udall would brood on the dismembered grandeur of his

---

7. Muñoz, *Annual Report on Poverty*, 2016, 40, 46–76; "The APPLE (Action Plan for Public Lands and Education) Initiative" slide presentation, Utah State Legislature, 2006, https://le.utah.gov; *Economic Report to the Governor, 2009*, 75; Chamberlain, "Plan of Action," 256, 261; Power, "Wildland Preservation," 122n19.

8. Utah Constitution, article III; "Governor's Message," *Utah Senate Journal, 1903*, 20; Wells Jr., "Political Biography," 95–96; Richardson "Federal Park Policy," 109–40.

dream and almost weep. In Utah the town of Boulder, located near the monuments, changed its name to Johnson's Folly. City council members said the president doomed their town, and they wished to preserve the memory of its heyday and die as Johnson's Folly. Utah's attorney general ruled the name change illegal. Boulder still lives with about 200 residents.[9]

During the Jimmy Carter administration in the 1970s, Utah enlisted in the Sagebrush Rebellion. Legislators voted by large majorities to join other Western states in demanding ownership of federal land. Utah senators Orrin Hatch and Jake Garn introduced bills to "return" the "rightful title" of public lands to states. The Reagan administration calmed the outburst and rebellion subsided. In 2011, Utah legislators declared their own second rebellion threatening suit unless given control of federal land.[10] They invited other states to join in, but up to this writing none has. So far Utah legislators have blustered for seven years but failed to file a lawsuit.

At statehood, the federal government gave Utah 9,000 specific square-mile sections of federal land, and Utah was also granted the right to choose an additional 1.9 million acres from federal domain. In all, 14 percent of Utah became a state trust mostly for public schools. Every new state received a gift of school land upon entering the union, and Utah got a larger share than older states because, as some congressmen said, Utah land was worth less. Utah squandered much of its land. The first legislature enacted a State Land Board, and any citizen could choose a parcel of federal land by filing papers at the land office. Utah would then select that land as part of its federal grant and sell it to the citizen for $2.00 an acre, more or less. In every year from 1897 to 1907, Utah selected and sold more than 100,000 acres. When Utah Democrats came to power in 1917,

---

9. Gordon Elliott White, "Parting Gift Spurned," *Deseret News*, Mar. 17, 1969; "LBJ Proclamations," *Salt Lake Tribune*, Jan. 21, 1969; *Richfield Reaper*, Jan. 30, 1969.

10. Rogers, "Landgrabbers," 2, 29, 39; Robert Gehrke, "Utah Fires Up New Sagebrush Rebellion," *Salt Lake Tribune*, Mar. 4, 2012; also Rogers, "Volatile Sagebrush Rebellion," 367–81; Francis, "Environmental Values," 29–45.

they investigated the land board and found it had sold property with known coal deposits for the price of grazing land to buyers serving as fronts for coal companies. Moreover, money from land sales was deposited at no interest in banks friendly to politicians. As a result, by 1912 Utah had sold 4 million acres, and income from the resulting trust could not pay for a single day of school each year. In their defense, Utah politicians pointed to the federal Homestead Act and grants to railroads, universities, and other interests that transferred 816 million acres of federal land into private hands. Early Utah land sales increased private land by more than 10 percent, they said, and private land helps the economy and pays taxes, unlike government land. Utahns were generally careless of land. Up to the 1930s, both public and private lands were overgrazed, eroded, and invaded by foreign weeds. Studies showed the damage. Floods roared off denuded hillsides. And many ranchers and other Utahns joined the cry for better federal management, which was answered with the Taylor Grazing Act in 1934.[11]

Even after all the cheap sales, Utah retained 3.2 million acres, about 6 percent of the state, mostly in one-square-mile sections scattered across the map "like a blue rash," as land experts joked.[12] The state could do little with these sections, like islands in a sea of federal land, and they contributed little to schools. Utahns schemed, sued, and swapped to squeeze benefit out of the state lands.

Indemnity land roused conflict first. The federal government took back some of the land given to Utah for military bases, national parks, Native American reservations, or other uses, and federal law promised indemnity for what had been taken. Utah hoped it would be able to choose its indemnity land and in 1965 filed a claim for 157,000 acres containing oil and oil shale. Federal officials refused,

---

11. Reimann, "Federal Land Grants," 63–65; Peterson and Cannon, *Awkward State*, 59, 203–205; *Governor's Special Investigation*, 23–93; Mahoney, "Utah."

12. Vincent et al., *Federal Land Ownership*, 2; "What Are Trust Lands?" *Trust Lands Administration*, https://trustlands.utah.gov.

MAP 1. Land ownership

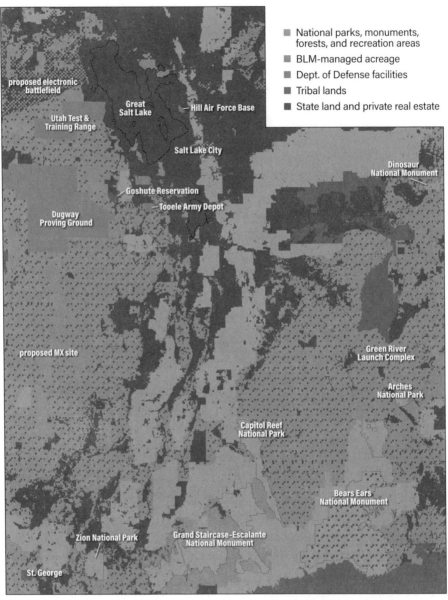

- National parks, monuments, forests, and recreation areas
- BLM-managed acreage
- Dept. of Defense facilities
- Tribal lands
- State land and private real estate

proposed electronic battlefield

Great Salt Lake

Hill Air Force Base

Utah Test & Training Range

Salt Lake City

Dinosaur National Monument

Goshute Reservation

Tooele Army Depot

Dugway Proving Ground

proposed MX site

Green River Launch Complex

Arches National Park

Capitol Reef National Park

Bears Ears National Monument

Zion National Park

Grand Staircase-Escalante National Monument

St. George

Source: Utah Division of Natural Resources. *Based on maps created by Paul Heath.*

saying they would repay only with land of equal value. By five votes to four, the US Supreme Court agreed with the federal government.[13]

After losing in court, Democratic governor Scott Matheson tried to exchange and consolidate isolated parcels into forty-seven larger and more manageable blocks. He called the plan Project Bold, saying it was a bold solution to a complicated problem. The federal Bureau of Land Management (BLM) had often stalled previous proposed exchanges, but Interior secretaries liked Project Bold and advised the BLM to cooperate. Bold required congressional approval, but just as the hearings began, Matheson left office. His successor, Republican Norman Bangerter, abandoned Project Bold because rural county commissioners believed Utah could use scattered holdings as leverage to influence federal land decisions. In an attempt to use that leverage, the State Land Board threatened in 1989 to sell sections of land it owned within national parks unless the federal government agreed to trade property in the Glen Canyon National Recreation Area to Utah. That land could then host marinas, motels, gas stations, and convenience stores on the shores of Lake Powell. Environmentalists ridiculed the plan as "Golden Arches National Park," at the imagined prospect of a McDonald's restaurant with its golden arches in Arches National Park. They filled a hearing and shouted at land board members, who dropped their threats.[14]

When President Clinton created the Grand Staircase–Escalante Monument, he promised to protect the Utah school trust fund that owned land within its boundaries. Interior Secretary Bruce Babbitt and Governor Mike Leavitt then worked out a trade of 357,000 acres of state land, mostly within the monument and national parks, for 200,000 federal acres, some containing coal, oil, or minerals.[15] It was the largest and most successful land swap in Utah history. The

---

13. *State of Utah v. Andrus*, 486 F. Supp. 995 (D. Utah 1979).

14. Matheson and Becker, "Improving Public Land Management," 11–41; Joseph Bauman, "Bangerter Supports Selective Land Swaps," *Deseret News*, May 20, 1988; Evans, "Revisiting the Utah School," 347.

15. Keith, "1998 Utah Schools," 337–38.

school fund made money, and Utahns joked that they had benefitted because Babbitt had a guilty conscience at the way Utah had been treated over the monument.

Federal land fights intensified in the late 1960s over attempts to mine coal and build power plants. America's largest undeveloped coal deposit, sixty-two billion tons, lies under federal land in Southern Utah. California's demand for electricity brought plans to use that coal. First came the Kaiparowits Project: a consortium of utilities planned to build a new power plant on the Kaiparowits Plateau near the mouth of a new coal mine, dig and burn a billion tons of coal over fifty years, and transmit power to California cities on high-tension lines. The plant would have generated enough electricity for 3.5 million homes, raised the assessed valuation of Kane County fifty times, and provided 2,000 jobs. It would also have increased American coal consumption more than 2 percent, with resulting climate change (though people did not know about climate change then).[16]

Utahns liked the proposal. Governor Calvin L. Rampton worked for it, as did the entire congressional delegation. Senator Frank Moss, an environmentally minded Democrat, said his mail ran thirty-to-one in favor. Congressman Sherman Lloyd sent questions to voters and said 80 percent of his constituents favored the plant. But Kaiparowits was the first big coal-fired proposal after the National Environmental Policy Act passed in 1970. Environmentalists had offered little resistance to other big coal plants in the Southwest, but they used the new law to stall Kaiparowits. After eleven years of futile attempts to get federal permits, the consortium gave up. "We would have had money like we never, never dreamed," Kanab mayor Claude Galzier said in epitaph.[17]

As the Kaiparowits proposal struggled, other California utilities planned the Intermountain Power Project, with another mine and power plant on another part of the Kaiparowits Plateau. To stop

16. Bishop, "Paper Power Plant," 26.
17. Sproul, "Environmentalism," 361–62, 370.

it, the Jimmy Carter administration strengthened clean-air requirements in neighboring Capitol Reef National Park so the plant could not be built. The utilities then moved the plant to Lynndyl in central Utah and burned coal brought by rail from existing mines. Two other projects sought to mine Kaiparowits but ship the coal away to burn it so they would not pollute the air around the national parks. A utility consortium planned an open-pit mine and slurry line to pipe coal to a Nevada power plant. The mine was close to Bryce Canyon National Park, and the federal government would not issue permits. Finally Andalex, a Dutch firm, asked to mine coal underground and truck it to the West Coast to sell abroad.[18] President Clinton created the Grand Staircase–Escalante National Monument partly to stop Andalex and put an end to Kaiparowits coal plans.

Federal land fights intensified again over wilderness. The Wilderness Act of 1964 said that Congress may designate wilderness on federal land parcels larger than 5,000 acres that have no structures, are mostly unchanged by humans, and possess "outstanding opportunities for recreation or solitude." Within wilderness, riding a bicycle or motorized transport are forbidden. No one may mine, drill, farm, log, or build. But ranchers retain vested grazing rights and people could hike, camp, fish, or hunt. Wilderness differs from other conservation. The Forest Service and BLM sought sustained yield from well-managed land. National parks, monuments, and recreation areas built facilities and invited visitors. In contrast, wilderness excluded most people. Wallace Stegner, the bard of Utah wilderness, said its value was that few people would ever visit, use, or see it.[19]

First the federal Forest Service selected wilderness land, and in that round, Utahns negotiated and agreed. The Utah Wilderness Association, which believed in a voice for local people, led the

18. Hinton, *Utah*, 156; Lyman and Newell, *History of Millard County*, 377–98; Lee Davidson, "House Panel OKs Bill," *Deseret News*, Apr. 4, 1990. See also Ganzel, "Regulatory Management," 268–76

19. Wilderness Act of 1964, 15 U.S.C. § 113; Stegner, *Sound of Mountain Water*, 153.

environmentalist side. "It is essential to find common ground with local officials and residents," said founder Dick Carter. "It is ignorant to ignore them." Environmentalists and Utah politicians agreed on 775,000 acres of National Forest wilderness, and Congress protected that land in 1984. But Utah had the second smallest amount of Forest Service wilderness of any federal-land state.[20] Disappointed, environmentalists blamed the Wilderness Association, which lost support and eventually died.

Environmental leadership passed to the Southern Utah Wilderness Alliance (SUWA, pronounced Soowa), ardent, uncompromising, and effective. SUWA organized against the Utah Forest Service agreement: "The memory of the 1984 compromise was woven into the fabric of our founding," SUWA leader Mike Matz wrote. He said environmentalists would not make such a compromise again. SUWA started as rag-tag but prospered through local energy and a national strategy. Utah's five national parks and (at the time) seven monuments lacked the stature of Yellowstone, the Grand Canyon, or Alaska, but were famous enough to raise national support and money and to make Utah wilderness a national issue. As one SUWA leader explained, Utahns should no more decide what to do with Utah wilderness than Kentuckians should so as they pleased with the gold in Fort Knox. As for local agreement, SUWA said, "Asking a Utah county commissioner to plan for wilderness seems a bit like asking Dr. Kevorkian to implement an intensive care program." (Dr. Kevorkian went to prison for helping people to kill themselves.) At times SUWA had as many as 24,000 members, maybe half of them from Utah. With the Utah Sierra Club and Wilderness Society, SUWA led the Utah Wilderness Coalition, sometimes backed by several hundred national environmental groups who acted together in lawsuits and in lobbying Congress. Professionals led SUWA with a staff of lawyers and Washington lobbyists. The organization raised money from foundations and rich people outside of Utah, had

---

20. Brennan, "Grassroots of the Desert"; Warrick, "Year of Utah Wilderness."

MAP 2. Population density

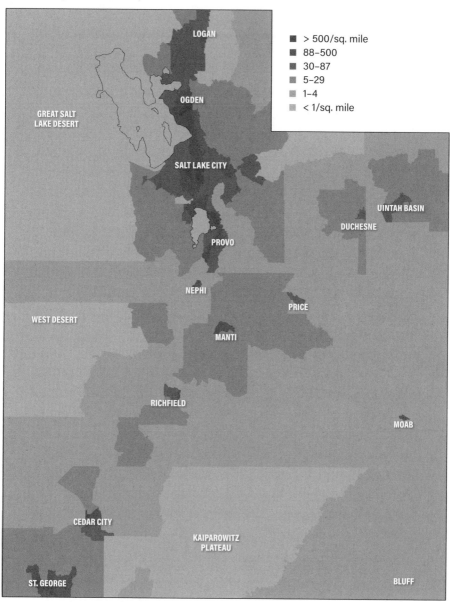

> 500/sq. mile
88–500
30–87
5–29
1–4
< 1/sq. mile

LOGAN

OGDEN

GREAT SALT
LAKE DESERT

SALT LAKE CITY

UINTAH BASIN

DUCHESNE

PROVO

NEPHI

PRICE

WEST DESERT

MANTI

RICHFIELD

MOAB

CEDAR CITY

KAIPAROWITZ
PLATEAU

ST. GEORGE

BLUFF

Source: US census 2010; Lee Davidson, "Urbanites," *Salt Lake Tribune*, Mar. 27, 2012. *Based on maps created by Paul Heath.*

annual budgets in the millions, and bank accounts that drew the envy of other environmentalists.[21]

Advocating wilderness is like selling real estate. Like real-estate agents, wilderness advocates display photos of the property in its best light and describe it in stock phrases such as "breathtakingly beautiful" or "iconic wilderness." But also as part of their sales pitch, Utah environmentalists deployed eloquence. Preservation was the chief theme of Utah literature. Edward Abbey, bad boy of green letters, set *The Monkey Wrench Gang* in southern Utah, where Sheriff Dudley J. Love, an LDS bishop, galumphs over red rocks in search of environmentalist saboteurs. Terry Tempest Williams wrote, "The simple truth is that there are too many of us." She chose not to have children and poured love into praise of the desert. Wallace Stegner wrote for SUWA. The American character was formed against wilderness, he said. "Something will have gone out of us as a people if we allow the last remaining wilderness to be destroyed."[22]

Many Utahns wanted to preserve the land. At times support for wilderness was the most common sentiment on urban bumper stickers. *The Salt Lake Tribune* printed knowledgeable opinions by citizen environmentalists. Green-leaning citizens attended public hearings where they often outnumbered their opponents. But while some people cared deeply, most Utahns seemed scarcely aware of public land. It never ranked high in polls that asked people what they most cared about. Taken as a whole, polls on how much wilderness should be set aside showed confusion. For example, in 1995, Utah congressmen sponsored a bill calling for 2.2 million acres of wilderness. The *Salt Lake Tribune* reported a poll showing that two-thirds of Utahns believed it was enough and supported their congressmen. Three days later the *Tribune* published another poll showing that two-thirds

---

21. Mike Matz, "Landscape Finds Its Voice," *SUWA Bulletin*, spring 1998; conversation with Scott Groene, executive director, July 2013; Jim Stiles, "SUWA's Rainy Day Fund," *Salt Lake Tribune*, Apr. 10, 2006; SUWA's 501(c)3 report, 2014.

22. Williams, *Red*, 93–94, 158; Stegner, *Sound of Mountain Water*, 146.

of Utahns wanted more acreage and opposed their congressmen. Lucas Smart and Amber Ayers found ten wilderness acreage polls, and SUWA later sponsored another. In one poll, Utahns wanted zero wilderness; in another 9.5 million acres; and the average of the polls was 3.9 million acres.[23]

Though polls were confused and contradictory, elections were clear and decisive. Almost every elected Utahn opposed SUWA. Since the beginning of the fight over Bureau of Land Management (BLM) wilderness in 1976, every Utah governor and senator and every Utah congressman but one has opposed the environmentalist position. The state legislature voted repeatedly for development over preservation. SUWA won support from one Salt Lake City mayor, and perhaps half a dozen politicians spoke in vague sympathy with environmentalists. A few elected officials endorsed SUWA after they left office.[24] Otherwise mayors, legislators, commissioners, council members, county and state attorneys, governors, congressmen, and senators alike opposed wilderness.

SUWA led in the second wilderness round over land owned by the Bureau of Land Management (BLM). The Forest Service owned eight million acres of Utah, the BLM 23 million acres, 40 percent of the state. It owned the land left over after private interests, national parks, national forests, national recreation areas, and fish and wildlife reserves had taken what they wanted. BLM lands were excluded from the original 1964 Wilderness Act as "not worthy of wilderness designation."[25]

Congress later mandated BLM wilderness in the Federal Land Policy Management Act of 1976. The law provided a three-step

23. Bob Bernick Jr., "Crime, Education," Amy Joi O'Donoghue, "Poll Shows Utahns Support Wilderness," *Deseret News*, Jan. 15, 1995, Sept. 29, 2009; Jim Woolf, "This Poll Says," *Salt Lake Tribune*, May 19, 1995; "Utah Priorities," 2004, 2008, 2012, 2016, *Utah Foundation*, www.utahfoundation.org; Smart and Ayres, "Don't Cry Out," 83.

24. Salt Lake mayor Rocky Anderson endorsed SUWA wilderness proposals. Salt Lake County councilman Jim Bradley and attorney general Paul Van Dam supported wilderness but not SUWA. Salt Lake mayor Ted Wilson and state representative Bryson Garbett (the only Republican) endorsed SUWA proposals after leaving office.

25. Kevin Walker, "Better Late Than Never," *Redrock Wilderness*, winter 1999/2000.

process: (1) The BLM would inventory its lands and select some areas to be protected as if they were wilderness until Congress could make a final decision. (2) The BLM would investigate the Wilderness Study Areas and recommend some to the president, who would make recommendations to Congress. (3) Congress would enact a law designating the land as wilderness. The Utah BLM completed the first two steps, and President George W. Bush made a BLM-backed wilderness recommendation to Congress, but Congress failed to act.

Environmentalists said Utah had the worst BLM wilderness inventory of any state. Utah had a "minimalist" inventory, academic theses said, and told stories of slapdash work, BLM bosses improperly overruling field workers, and indifference to wilderness values. Environmentalists filed the biggest appeal the Board of Land Appeals had ever seen. The appeals board mostly agreed with environmentalists and added 600,000 acres to the inventory. In all, the BLM put 3.2 million acres into wilderness study. Environmentalists still said Utah had a minimalist inventory, and that charge influenced federal lands policy toward Utah in both the Clinton and Obama administrations. But the charge was false. The BLM took 6 percent of all Utah land for wilderness study, the third highest percentage of any state. Across the West, the BLM put 9 percent of its own land into Wilderness Study Areas, but 14 percent of its Utah land. Of all the land in twelve federal-land states, the BLM chose about 2 percent for wilderness study, but three times that percentage in Utah.[26] Far from minimalist, Utah's survey chose more potential wilderness than was selected in most other states.

Even so, to correct the "minimalist" BLM survey, SUWA conducted its own citizens' survey. Volunteers tramped the state and found 5 million acres of wilderness. The BLM in its survey rejected land that was non-scenic, "hammered" by human use, or near roads

---

26. Torrey, "Public Lands"; Torrey, "Wilderness Inventory"; Wheeler, "BLM Wilderness Review"; "List of Wilderness," *Federal Register*, Dec. 27, 1983; "National Landscape Conservation System: Wilderness Study Areas," www.blm.gov.

or buildings. Then, as the act required, it chose only land possessing "outstanding opportunity for outdoor recreation or solitude." SUWA volunteers judged differently and chose more land. They mapped and described their proposals and put them in a book documenting their findings. The citizens' survey did not stop there, however. Volunteers continued to walk the countryside looking for more possible wilderness and have now suggested 9.7 million acres, more than the total of BLM wilderness in all other Western states combined.

After completing the legal process, the BLM and President George W. Bush recommended that Congress designate 1.9 million acres in Utah as wilderness and release the rest for commercial, recreational, and other uses. But before the president's recommendation arrived in Congress, Utah Democratic congressman Wayne Owens introduced "America's Redrock Wilderness Act" designating the five million acres of wilderness in the SUWA citizens' survey at the time.[27] Since Owens left Congress in 1993, congressmen and senators from other states have regularly re-introduced the bill, adding more acreage from the continuing SUWA survey each time so that the bill now calls for preservation of 9.7 million acres in Utah.

The US Constitution gives Congress power over federal land. Congress may designate wilderness as it chooses. It has traditionally hesitated to override a state delegation on matters within its own state. So Utah senators and congressmen have been able to prevent SUWA's Redrock Wilderness Act from receiving a floor vote up to this writing. But environmental groups also have power to block legislation. Utah environmental groups could recruit environmentalists from every state, so senators and representatives from other states are lobbied by knowledgeable activists from their home states or districts.

---

27. Thomas H. Gorey, "Differences," Jim Woolf, "BLM Closes Book," Woolf, "The Ins, Outs," *Salt Lake Tribune*, Mar. 1, 1989, Dec. 11, 1990, Mar. 19, 1995; "What Little Wilderness Remains," McIntosh and Groene, "County Wilderness Negotiations," *Redrock Wilderness*, winter 1999/2000, winter 2010; Evensen and Bauman, "Bangerter Angry," *Deseret News*, Aug. 20, 1988. See also Wheeler, *Wilderness at the Edge*, 34–40; McCormick and Osiek, "Weighted in the Balance," 35–65.

Even on exclusively Utah issues, federal lawmakers often sided with their local environmentalists against their Utah colleagues. The clearest demonstration of Utah environmentalist power was the defeat of Utah Public Lands Management Act, backed by Utah's elected senators and representatives in the 1995 Republican-controlled Congress. Utah's delegation proposed 2.2 million acres of wilderness, more than the official recommendation but less than environmentalists wanted, and the bill had other provisions environmentalists opposed. Some 200 environmental organizations denounced the bill and the national press took the environmentalist side. President Clinton threatened a veto. To slip past the president, Utah senators added their proposal to a national parks bill. Democratic senator Bill Bradley of New Jersey threatened to kill the whole parks bill with a filibuster rather than accept stingy Utah wilderness. Utah's congressional delegation failed to get a wilderness bill. "They once told us we couldn't beat a united Utah delegation," SUWA leader Scott Groene said later. "We've done that a dozen times now," he said.[28]

Governor Mike Leavitt saw that Utah could not carry Congress over environmentalist opposition and sought compromise. He suggested choosing wilderness one section at a time. He and Interior Secretary Bruce Babbitt had already made a successful post-monument land swap. They negotiated a potential wilderness compromise, jointly proposing 1.1 million acres in Utah's West Desert. That was more than twice as much land in the west desert as the BLM had designated as Wilderness Study Areas and more than SUWA had included in its original Redrock Wilderness bill. But SUWA, with its ongoing citizens' survey, had since tripled the amount of West Desert land, and led an environmentalist coalition that blocked the Babbitt-Leavitt proposal in Congress.[29]

---

28. US Constitution, article IV, §3; John H. Cushman Jr., "Bradley Leads Filibuster," *New York Times*, Mar. 26, 1996; Helen Dewar, "Senate Passes Parklands Bill," *Washington Post*, May 3, 1996; Scott Groene and Justin Allegro, "Utah's Zion," *Redrock Wilderness*, spring 2009, 5–6.

29. Brent Israelsen, "Leavitt, Babbitt," "SUWA's Petulant Walkout," Christopher Smith, "Wilds Bill," *Salt Lake Tribune*, Feb. 3, Aug. 14, 1999, Oct. 20, 1999.

A second attempt at compromise involved the San Rafael Swell, a million-acre oval that had been pushed up by underground salt deposits and eroded into picturesque rock formations.[30] The land was federal, so no one lived there. Preservation seemed inevitable. "Control your destiny, or someone else will," Emery County leaders said. They worked with environmentalists and proposed to Congress a National Conservation Area that would ban mining and drilling but leave wilderness designation for a future decision. Utah congressmen and the Clinton administration supported the plan, but SUWA dubbed it the "not-so-Swell" bill and rallied environmental groups to defeat it.

Emery County tried again. They worked with the Department of Interior under Babbitt, who demanded conservation but took pride in helping local citizens tailor preservation plans to fit local needs. He helped the county to craft a plan that was like arrangements already made in Arizona, Colorado, and Nevada to keep out motorized vehicles, protect big horn sheep, designate some wilderness, and close off some "areas of critical environmental concern." SUWA said the resulting National Conservation Area bill lacked enough wilderness and did too little to limit motorized recreation. The association rallied other groups and defeated the legislation again. Utah's congressmen were surprised at how easily SUWA and its allies beat Secretary Babbitt. "The Administration didn't deliver a single Democratic vote for us," Representative Chris Cannon said, "not one."[31]

Emery County leaders tried to slide around SUWA's congressional blocking power by asking for a presidentially designated national monument, a plan that astonished many Utahns. Governor Mike Leavitt announced the proposal at his 2002 State-of-the-State address. County officials hoped to write rules similar to those voted down in Congress, then ask President George W. Bush to designate the monument without congressional involvement. But

---

30. I rely here on Durrant, *Struggle over Utah's San Rafael Swell.*
31. Jim Woolf, "Cannon Gives Up," *Salt Lake Tribune,* July 7, 2000.

monuments had a bad reputation in rural Utah since the Grand Staircase–Escalante. "The people who have been involved with other monuments have said, 'Don't do it. Run for your life,'" opponent Paul Conover said.[32] Off-road-vehicle users feared they would be ousted from a monument, so they gathered signatures and forced an advisory referendum. Just before the vote, SUWA spoke for the referendum, but Emery County voted it down 53-to-47 percent. Both Governor Leavitt and President Bush said they would follow the will of the voters. Compromise died on the swell.

Utah politicians compromised twice with SUWA, both times on environmentalist terms. In the first deal in 2006, Congress passed a wilderness bill at Cedar Mountain to try to keep nuclear waste from reaching the Goshute Reservation. Utah Republican congressmen wanted just enough wilderness to block the path, but SUWA and an environmentalist coalition stopped that until Utah congressmen agreed to a larger swath of 100,000 acres of wilderness. In the second compromise, Washington County tried to follow Nevada counties that had recently made wilderness agreements. As part of those deals, Congress let the BLM sell large tracts of land and the proceeds went partly to county and state governments. Republican senator Bob Bennett and Democratic representative Jim Matheson sponsored the Utah bill, and it had the blessing of senate majority leader Harry Reid (D–Nev) who had sponsored the Nevada deals. SUWA rallied 120 national environmental groups, and environmentalists sent 100,000 emails to Congress and beat the bill. Then Matheson, Bennett, county commissioners, and environmentalists negotiated. "We got beat up in the negotiations," said county commissioner Ray Gardner, but he agreed to a bill that he did not like in hopes of ending a fight that had gone on for decades.[33] In the final bill, Washington County got three times as much wilderness as had been

---

32. Leavitt, "One Thousand Days," 71; Durrant, *Struggle*, 156.
33. Durrant, 103; email correspondence with Washington County commissioner Alan Gardner.

in the Wilderness Study Areas. Little federal land was sold, and the proceeds went mostly to conservation projects.[34] With its national allies, SUWA could block any Utah wilderness bill and it used that power to drive preservationist bargains.

SUWA believed in waiting for the best wilderness deal. "Political life is short and unpredictable, the Redrock Movement endures," said SUWA leader Scott Groene.[35] Utah environmentalists paid a temporary price for SUWA's patience. While the state had more than its share of Wilderness Study Areas, Utah had less Congressionally approved wilderness than any other federal-land state. SUWA and its allies turned down compromises and believed waiting would eventually pay off, as it did in Washington County.

While environmentalists waited, the law protected BLM Wilderness Study Areas but SUWA Redrock lands lay legally vulnerable to development. SUWA sued miners, drillers, and the government to protect its extra acres. It was something called "Sue Ya." In addition, Democratic Clinton and Obama administrations acted to protect land in Utah. Secretary Babbitt sent a special BLM team in 1996 to re-inventory Utah and find more land for wilderness study.[36] No similar team was sent to any other state. Utah sued to stop the reinventory, but federal judges said the state had no legal standing. State and local officials asked to participate in the reinventory but were rebuffed, and when they asked to see the documents used by the BLM they were similarly refused. The BLM did not hold public hearings or draft an environmental impact statement. The Babbitt team found 2.6 million additional acres for the Wilderness Study Areas, bringing the total to about what SUWA had included in early Redrock bills.

Thus during the Clinton administration, SUWA's Redrock lands

---

34. "Washington County Lands Bills, 2006–2008," *Leavitt Center for Politics and Public Service*, http://leavitt.li.suu.edu.

35. Scott Groene, "Political Life Is Short," *Redrock Wilderness*, summer 2010.

36. "Wilderness Statistics Report," *Wilderness Connect*, www.wilderness.net; SUWA attorneys Bloch and McIntosh, "View from the Front Lines," 487; Blumm and Erickson, "Federal Wild Lands Policy," 39–40, 43.

were "informally" protected as if they were wilderness. Both Babbitt and environmentalists hoped that courts would rule that this additional acreage was like Wilderness Study Areas, so only Congress could end special protection. SUWA could then block any unfavorable wilderness bill in Congress and wait until its opponents agreed to big Utah wilderness. But when Republican George W. Bush became president in 2001, Utah saw its chance and reactivated its lawsuit. Instead of contesting the suit, the Bush administration agreed that Babbitt's action had been illegal and renounced the new reinventory. Angry environmentalists were excluded from the negotiations and sued in federal court. Judge Dee Benson agreed with Utah and the Bush administration; the law forbade any administrative withdrawal of more land into wilderness-style protection. SUWA appealed, and appellate judges upheld Benson but on technical legal grounds, without ruling on his reading of wilderness law.

Despite the court rulings, Ken Salazar, Interior Secretary in the Obama administration, announced he would administratively select more "wild lands," as Babbitt had tried in Utah. But Salazar's plan applied to all states and roused a coalition of Western congressmen who placed a clause in an appropriations bill denying funds to carry out the initiative.[37] Salazar put his general plan on hold but he found ways around the law to preserve Utah land. Early in the Obama administration, he came to Utah to denounce the pro-drilling policies of the Bush years. In an unprecedented gesture, he took back seventy-seven Utah leases that companies already bought and paid for. SUWA challenged those leases in court, and Salazar agreed with SUWA, as the Bush administration had agreed with Utah politicians on the Babbitt reinventory. Salazar said that some of the leases were too close to national parks and the National Park Service had not been consulted.

---

37. Lee Davidson, "BLM," *Deseret News*, Feb. 26, 1994; *Utah v. Norton*, 396 F. 3d 1281 (10th Cir. 2005); "Salazar, Abbey Restore Protections," Department of Interior news release, Dec. 23, 2010; Brumfield, "Birth, Death, and Afterlife," 22; Thomas Burr, "Salazar Reverses Wild Lands Policy," *Salt Lake Tribune*, June 3, 2011.

The leases were made in a hurry, as "midnight actions," rushed to auction under pressure from the Bush administration in its final days. He ordered an investigation of the Utah BLM, and he quietly reduced future leasing, bringing economic trouble to the Uintah Basin.

Under George W. Bush, Utah's oil-and-gas-rich Uintah Basin boomed. From 2000 to 2008, the number of wells rose six-fold to almost 1,000. Natural gas production reached a record high. Drilling jobs more than doubled and the population rose 30 percent; unemployment fell to 1.9 percent. The boom depended on government policy. Only 21 percent of basin land was private. Most was owned by the federal government. The BLM auctioned leases quarterly for the right to drill on federal land, and drilling underlay prosperity. Salazar issued an "informal directive" saying the BLM should not issue drilling leases on lands that Congress was considering for wilderness.[38] SUWA's Redrock Wilderness Act was the only wilderness-expanding legislation pending in Congress, so the directive affected only Utah and made leases harder to get within the 9.7 million acres SUWA wanted for wilderness. Federal policy changed. In 2009 the BLM issued leases for drilling on 278,000 acres in Utah, and in 2010 it leased only 16,000 acres, 6 percent of the previous year's acreage. Under the new policy, the number of wells fell by half, and 4,000 jobs were lost. Unemployment rose above 10 percent and poverty to 11.7 percent.[39] Bankruptcies, foreclosures, and trustee sales filled newspaper pages as basin residents lost jobs, businesses, trucks, and homes.

While everyone saw the basin's impoverishment, environmentalists said that the Obama administration should not be blamed. The economy had collapsed near the end of the Bush administration, oil and gas prices had fallen, and environmentalists said drilling declined because prices fell.

---

38. Downen et al., *Structure and Economic Impact*, 9; interview with BLM representatives Mitch Snow and Teri Catlin, Aug. 30, 2010, by the author.

39. "Economic Data Categories," *Department of Workforce Services*, https://jobs.utah.gov; Collins and Jarvik, "Beneath the Surface," *Deseret News*, Sep. 6, 2009; "Final BLM Review," Oct. 7, 2009, *Marriott Library Digital Stacks*, https://collections.lib.utah.edu.

TABLE 1. BLM (Utah office) oil and gas leases by parcel

	average per year		
years	nominated	offered	leased
1998–2009	594	54.5%	209
2010–2016	491	14.7%	46

Source: "Oil and Gas Statistics," Bureau of Land Management.

Table 1 compares BLM leasing in Utah for twelve years before Obama with seven years of the Obama administration. The leasing process begins when a drilling company nominates a parcel where it hopes to drill. If low prices caused a decline in drilling, it would show in the number of parcels nominated, and in fact that number fell by about one-sixth, as shown in the "parcels-nominated" column. After nomination, the BLM decides which parcels to offer for lease. In the years before the Obama change, the BLM approved about 55 percent of the nominations. Afterward the BLM approved only about 15 percent. So, shown in the last column, the total number of parcels leased fell by more than three-quarters, mostly because of government decisions. Moreover, the reduced chances of a nomination's success likely contributed to the reduced number of nominations. Drilling rigs, unable to work in Utah, were moved to other states where drilling continued successfully on private land through the recession. Basin residents said the Obama administration busted their economy and damaged their lives from hostility to drilling. In the first year of the Donald Trump administration, the number of parcels leased more than tripled, although it was still lower than the average number offered before Obama's election. As drilling increases, environmentalists worry for wildlife, archaeological sites, and wild lands they hope will become wilderness.[40]

In July 2010, Uintah County Commissioner Mike McKee heard

---

40. Interview with Uintah County commissioner Mike McKee, May 2010, by the author.

that the Department of Interior had completed its investigation of the Utah BLM ordered by Secretary Salazar during his Utah visit. McKee and senators Hatch and Bennett asked to see the report. When released, the report showed the seventy-seven leases taken back by Secretary Salazar had been auctioned properly within the rules. The process had not been hasty, but careful. The Park Service had been consulted, although not closely enough to avoid misunderstanding. There was no evidence of pressure from the Bush administration. The charges Secretary Salazar had made during his Utah visit turned out to be false. The date on the report was December 2009. When the *Deseret News* asked why it had not been released until the senators asked to see it in July, Department of Interior officials said it was an oversight.[41]

In January 2017, with only one week left in office, the Obama administration settled a lawsuit with SUWA, agreeing to set aside "lands with wilderness characteristics" using the rules Secretary Salazar had devised for his "wild lands" plan before Congress had refused to fund it. The settlement might result in SUWA's Redrock wilderness lands receiving wilderness-like protection. The State of Utah is asking an appellate court to overturn the settlement, as of this writing.

Utah politicians counterattacked on dirt roads. Old dirt roads crisscross federal land in Utah like spiderwebs. County commissioners claim rights-of-way based on a law passed by Congress in 1866 called Revised Statute 2477: "The right of way for the construction of highways over public lands, not reserved for public purposes, is hereby granted." As Judge Michael McConnell commented, the statute is "short, sweet and enigmatic."[42] Detailed clarity proved unnecessary,

41. "Investigative Report: BLM Utah Lease Sale," Dec. 29, 2009, *Office of Inspector General, US Department of the Interior*, www.doioig.gov; "Enough Dithering" editorial, *Deseret News*, July 18, 2010.

42. "Settlement Agreement in *Southern Utah Wilderness Alliance et al. v. US Department of the Interior et al.*," www.blm.gov; McConnell ruling, Sept. 8, 2005, *Southern Utah Wilderness Alliance v. Bureau of Land Management*, 425 F. 3d 735 (10th Cir. 2005), https://caselaw.findlaw.com.

however, as the statute codified public practice and shaped the West. When Congress passed R.S. 2477, almost all western land was public. Few roads could go anywhere without crossing the federal domain. Roads began as tracks, where people walked, rode horses, drove wagons, or herded stock. Later jeeps and trucks made more roads. Many paved roads began this way, at least over part of their length. Under R.S. 2477 no one had to ask permission or record a road once it was made. Public policy valued roads. Not once had the federal government gone to court before 1976 to challenge the right to travel across unreserved public land. Disputes did arise when an individual acquired a piece of public land and closed it off. Then road users sometimes claimed against the new owner a right-of-way acquired when the government owned the land. The federal government had no interest in these disputes, so they went to state courts and were decided by state law. The Federal Land Policy and Management Act of 1976 repealed R.S. 2477 but reaffirmed valid right-of-way claims for roads "existing on the date of the approval of this act." Later the Department of Interior claimed power to define R.S. 2477 roads and to close those that did not meet their new definitions.[43]

For many rural Utahns, dirt roads gave them access to the land where they lived. Roads enabled grazing and development, and more importantly most of the people who had fun on the land went by dirt road. At many recreation sites, backpackers, hikers, and mountain bikers were outnumbered by families camping with trailers and off-road vehicles (ORVs). In 1998 there were 52,000 ORVs registered in Utah. By 2018 there were 208,000. Environmentalists complained that ORVs frightened wildlife and scarred the land when riders left designated trails or trespassed on Wilderness Study Areas. Some environmentalists looked down on ORV riders. "The fat pink soft slobs who go roaring over the landscape on these oversized over-priced over-advertised mechanical mastodons are people too lazy to walk," Ed Abbey wrote. The BLM closed much of its land to ORVs,

43. Pub. L. No. 94–579, 90 Stat. 2786, 43 USC § 1701 (1976); McConnell ruling, 27.

and SUWA sued to keep ORVs off of even more land and carried its losing case to the US Supreme Court.[44]

Dirt roads symbolized dwindling rural rights against an increasingly bossy federal government. When the BLM began to administer the new Grand Staircase–Escalante National Monument, federal officials offered to discuss road closures with Kane County commissioners. Commissioners agreed to talk, but Kane County citizens wanted to fight. They filled a protest meeting in the high school auditorium and demanded that commissioners defend the roads. Commissioners, supported by Governor Mike Leavitt, said that fighting was futile and that the BLM would negotiate reasonably. "They were more than willing to come past center with us," said Commissioner Joe Judd. But in the next election, one commissioner was defeated and the other two saw voters turn against them and left office when their terms ended. The BLM posted signs closing thirty dirt roads in the monument. The new county commissioners took down the signs and put up their own signs declaring the roads open. The United States Attorney in Salt Lake City took evidence against the sheriff and a commissioner to a grand jury, but jurors did not indict.[45]

Utah's dirt-road counterattack scored in the Tenth Circuit Court of Appeals in *Southern Utah Wilderness Alliance v. Bureau of Land Management and San Juan County*. A unanimous three-judge panel said the Department of Interior did not have legal authority to define R.S. 2477 roads. When the 1976 law went into effect, state law determined rights-of-way. State law said that ten years of continuous use made a road a public highway and the court determined state law ruled. After that victory, state and county officials expanded their counterattack. They travelled on dirt roads with global positioning devices

44. Smith, "Utah Off-Highway Vehicle," 4; correspondence with Utah State Tax Commission spokesman Charlie Roberts, Jul. 11, 2018; Abbey to *Esquire*, Sept. 11, 1976; *Norton v. Southern Utah Wilderness Alliance, 542 U.S. 55 (2004)*.

45. My interviews with Mike Noel, Aug. 2005, former Kane County commissioner Joe Judd, Oct. 2005; Gehrke and Baird, "Kane County," *Salt Lake Tribune*, Apr. 27, 2005; "Kane Raising Cain," *Deseret News*, Mar. 20, 2005.

and compared their findings with old maps and aerial photographs. They found old people who remembered using the roads decades before. And they filed claims for about 10,500 dirt roads extending over about 45,000 miles of federal land, more claims than all other states put together. Utah won title to a few roads in court and lost title to others. Decades of road litigation seem to lie ahead.[46]

In 2016, as he left office, President Barack Obama designated 1.3 million acres as the Bears Ears National Monument. Native Americans and environmentalists cheered. Anglos who lived near the new monument complained, as did Utah politicians. President Obama did not sneak up on Utahns, as President Clinton had. Interior Secretary Sally Jewell came to Utah and discussed the possible designation. She visited the site wearing a floppy hat and a back pack, looking like a hiker. The announcement still seemed sloppy. The White House tweeted a picture to show the beauties of Bears Ears mistakenly of the wrong site 100 miles away from the monument.[47] President Obama acted in the last days of his presidency to secure his legacy as an environmentalist, as President Lyndon Baines Johnson had expanded Utah monuments as he left office. Bears Ears surprised no one.

The surprise came from President Donald Trump. He reduced the size of the Bears Ears Monument by 85 percent and cut Grand Staircase–Escalante by almost half. The last president to cut the size of a monument was Woodrow Wilson in 1915. Trump divided the remains of Bears Ears into two pieces and the Grand Staircase into three. Before Trump acted, Ryan Zinke, his Interior Secretary, travelled to Utah. At the monument sites, he wore a western hat and rode a horse to look like a cowboy. Cheering Utahns filled the capitol rotunda as Trump denounced Democratic monument making

---

46. My interview with Harry Souvall, director of Public Lands Section, Utah Attorney General's Office; *Kane County, Utah v. United States*, 934 F. Supp. 2d 1344 (D. Utah 2014); *San Juan County, Utah v. United States*, 754 F.3d 787 (10th Cir. 2014).

47. Matthew Piper, "Before a Packed Meeting," Maffly and Burr, "Obama Declares Bears Ears," "Reactions," *Salt Lake Tribune*, July 18, Dec. 28, 29, 2016; Carter Williams, "Whoops!" *KSL TV*, www.ksl.com.

in Salt Lake City. "These abuses of the Antiquities Act have not just threatened your local economies; they've threatened your way of life. They've threatened your hearts," he said. Protestors gathered outside the capitol, including Native American Helaman Thor Hale, who was there with his wife and three sons. "It's a historical trauma our people have been through over and over," he said, referring to the loss of native lands. Five tribes sued immediately to overturn Trump's action. At least eleven environmental groups joined them in court. Once again, decades of litigation seem to lie ahead.[48]

REMARKS

Federal land politics resemble Utah territorial politics. In both instances, a minority, unable to win Utah elections, made national allies and controlled policy in Utah through the federal government. For forty years, almost all elected Utah politicians have favored, at most, moderate wilderness. That is about the amount suggested by the BLM and the president after they followed the legal process of surveys, appeals, public comment, reviews, and selection. That process suggested more wilderness in Utah than in most other western states. But environmentalists rejected the results and instead demanded more BLM wilderness than in all other western states combined.

In Congress, the Utah delegation and national environmental coalitions fought to deadlock. In the absence of legislation, the executive branch made Utah land decisions, and those administrative decisions have been partisan. Republican administrations favored Utah's political establishment, for example, when the Bush administration agreed to Utah's suit against the Babbitt reinventory. Democratic administrations favored environmentalists: President Clinton selected Utah for his campaign monument. Secretary Babbitt reinventoried only Utah.

---

48. Darryl Fears, "Zinke Listens," *Washington Post*, May 14, 2017; Romero and McKellar, "Native American Tribe Coalition," *Deseret News*, Dec. 4, 2017; Trump remarks, Dec. 4, 2017, www.whitehouse.gov; Julie Turkewitz, "Trump Slashes Size," *New York Times*, Dec. 4, 2017; *Wilderness Society et al. v. Donald Trump et al.*, US DC Court, 1:17–cv–02587, Dec. 4, 2017.

Secretary Salazar imposed his informal anti-drilling directive only in Utah, and President Obama designated Bears Ears, his biggest national monument, in Utah. Democratic administrations believed that Utahns "would not support the administration under any circumstances," and chose Utah for gestures, demonstrations, and experiments they did not impose on those states where they hoped to win votes.

Democratic gestures sometimes harmed Utahns. Notably, Obama-administration drilling policy inflicted economic hardship on the Uintah Basin and its people. Democratic land actions in Utah sometimes come unexpectedly and unexplained, such as President Clinton's monument or Secretary Babbitt's reinventory. Utahns are not angry. But many rural politicians are an exception to that generalization. They are angry at federal land policy.

Utahns reacted to the gestures: after President Clinton's monument, voters defeated Bill Orton, the state's only Democratic congressman. Utahns claimed more old dirt roads than all other states combined, and legislators attempted a new sagebrush rebellion. Utah, the federal government and environmentalists sued each other repeatedly. Democratic administrations have imposed unpopular federal land initiatives partly because Utahns were recalcitrant Republicans, and Utahns have become more recalcitrant and Republican because of unpopular Democratic land measures.

Democratic administrations acted more boldly than Republican administrations, until President Donald Trump reduced two Democratic national monuments. Uproar and litigation followed, and Utah federal land policy seems likely to become even more contentious.

(In Februray 2019, as this went to press, Congress passed a federal lands act that designated 660,000 acres of wilderness in the San Rafael Sell and 248,00 acres of recreation area. Most Utahns in Congress voted for the bill, which vindicated the SUWA strategy of waiting—in this case for 17 years—for compromise on environmentalist terms.)

11

THE UTAH STATE LEGISLATURE

About twenty older men and women in yellow tee shirts stood among the lobbyists outside the House and Senate. "Mobile Home Owner" was written on the front of their shirts, "I Vote" on the back. They came every day for three weeks asking legislators to pass a bill to make it harder for trailer park owners to raise rents, but legislators voted their bill down in committee. Browning Arms Manufacturer did better. The gun company set up a booth in the rotunda displaying dozens of firearms, including the M1911 handgun, which lawmakers soon voted Utah's official state gun, the first official state gun in America.[1] After victorious Browning left, college students erected science demonstrations showing the effects of acute exposure to ambient air particulates, or bioelectrocatalytic oxidation, of cholesterol. A choir from West Jordan High School in matching formal wear sang patriotic songs. People in wheelchairs carried signs against human-service budget cuts. Teachers and volunteer parents herded busloads of school children through the crowds to the galleries to watch laws made. Roger Turner, his gray hair in a ponytail, handed out sheets of paper explaining how a court had treated him unfairly. Lobbyists, sleek and suited, swarmed through the hallways, waiting to ask lawmakers for their vote. State legislative sessions resemble

---

1. Robert Gehrke, "Utah's State Firearm," *Salt Lake Tribune*, Mar. 17, 2011.

village fairs. People and interests gather to watch, display their work, air their views, and seek advantage.

This chapter and the next five turn from politics to state government. The first four deal with institutions: legislature, governor, bureaucracy, and courts. The last two talk of schools and budgets, historically the most important Utah governmental issues. Utah state government is less distinctive than the state's politics. American federalism makes state governments similar. For a century all state governments have followed federal leadership and federal money. They have taken grants, built roads, made welfare payments, served school breakfasts, and administered Medicaid. Federal courts, wielding the Supremacy Clause, required states to follow national policies. States are like a flock of sheep, some occasionally wayward but all herded along loosely together by the federal collie dog. In addition, governments observe proprieties such as standard accounting, balanced-budget requirements, and merit systems. Similar proprieties and programs make for similar organizations. Even so, all of Utah government, and especially the legislature, has bent to Utah's Republican, Latter-day Saint, conservative, anti-federal politics. Latter-day Saint Republicans win elections, and in Utah's legislature those victories are leveraged.

As an institution, the legislature in Utah is like all the others. In 2016 there were seventy-five representatives who were elected for two years and twenty-nine senators elected for four years, all from single-member districts. After the 2010 census, each representative had about 37,000 constituents and each senator had 97,000. As in other states, legislators divide into Republicans and Democrats. A speaker of the house and a president of the senate directed business under formal rules.[2] Utah's legislature has four chief characteristics: (1) Latter-day Saint Republicans exercise control. (2) Lawmakers are embedded in a community of special interests. (3) Utah's legislature

---

2. Brown, *Utah Politics*, has a full treatment of Utah's legislature, chapters 4–5.

TABLE I. Percent of Latter-day Saint legislators

year	legislature	population
1896	64	56
1981	81	72
1997	86	62
2011	89	60
2019	88	62

Sources: *Drumm's Manual of Utah*; Croft, "Influence of the LDS Church"; Dan Harrie, "Utah's Legislature," *Salt Lake Tribune*, Jan. 19, 1997; 2011 survey by author; Lee Davidson, "LDS Lawmakers rule on the Hill," *Salt Lake Tribune*, Jan. 21, 2019. Population estimates: 1981, 1997, 2011, from Governors Office of Planning and Budget; 1896, Poll, *Utah's History*, 692.

is non-professional. (4) The legislature has gained power within the government and continues to gain power over the state.

Members of the dominant church seem always to have been in the majority. Results from five surveys of religion taken since 1896, are shown in table 1. In all five instances there were Latter-day Saint majorities, and their share of the legislature has always been larger than their share of the population. Their legislative majorities have increased since 1981, even though their population share has declined.

Most Latter-day Saint legislators are devout. In the 1981 legislative survey, 79 percent of the lawmakers said they attended church once a week or more often. In 2011 only one Latter-day Saint senator and two representatives said they were not regular church goers. In fact, voters disproportionately elect local Church leaders. In 2011 at least thirty-five male lawmakers had served in bishoprics or stake presidencies. "There are more bishops here than anywhere," Senator Terry Spencer said of the senate. Of twenty Latter-day Saint women, sixteen had served in Primary or Relief Society presidencies.

Republicans are the party of Latter-day Saint men. Democrats are more diverse. Of the eighty Republicans in the 2011 legislature, seventy-seven (96 percent) were Latter-day Saint and seventy-three (91 percent) were men. Of the twenty-four Democrats, half were women and half were non-Mormon, including two Catholics, two Methodists, two Jews, an Episcopalian, a Protestant, a Christian, and one who said she had no religion.[3]

Latter-day Saints win elections partly because they are known and liked by their neighboring co-religionists. To be known through Church is an advantage in Utah's simple legislative elections in which no candidate uses radio or TV and victory often hinges on who is known, who can persuade neighbors to display lawn signs, and who knocks on the most doors. A story told in capitol hallways recounted a Republican primary in which district boundaries happened to include all of candidate A's stake and only a sliver of candidate B's, so candidate A won because more voters knew him through church.[4] Utah politicians use religion carefully, however. The Church of Jesus Christ of Latter-day Saints asks its local leaders not to mix religion and politics, and a candidate who appeals too blatantly or invidiously to the predominant religion risks offending both non-Mormons and Latter-day Saints.[5]

Students of the legislature ask whether so many Latter-day Saints give the church too much power. The answer to that question appears to be a matter of faith. The Church commissioned a private poll of its members, the results of which were leaked on the internet. It showed that Latter-day Saints believe their church has less influence than all the interests it was compared to in the poll: less power than teachers, voters, the tourist industry, minorities, and the news media. In contrast, political scientists Ronald J. Hrebenar and Clive Thomas surveyed politicians and capitol insiders in the mid-1990s, in 2002, and again in 2007. Their respondents said the church was more influential

3. A 2011 survey by the author.

4. Recounted by Rep. Stephen Rees. A stake is made up of several wards (congregations), which are determined geographically.

5. E.g. Cox, *Utah Politics*, 71; Benjamin Wood, "Controversial Campaign Tactics," *Salt Lake Tribune*, Nov. 5, 2018

than any other interest. The Church has a staff of professional lob-byists, and, though some lawmakers have accused them of "political bullying," most say Church lobbyists are low-key and respectful. They do not loiter in hallways, gossiping with the political crowd, enter-tain lawmakers, or donate to campaigns. Privately legislators call them "home teachers" (now ministering brothers and sisters) in reference to the Church members who visit every faithful household once a month with a gospel message. Whatever influence the Church may have, 84 percent of Utah Protestants and 79 percent of Catholics say it is too much, according to a *Utah Policy.com* poll. The same poll showed 75 percent of Latter-day Saints thought their church has "about the right amount of influence."[6] Political scientist David Magleby found that leaders consciously restrict their politicking to avoid an appearance of being too powerful or controlling. Magleby and Hrebenar–Thomas both noted that most legislators already know the Church position and do not need a lobbyist to tell them. Historically the legislature has been the most favorable forum for the Latter-day Saint side on issues of public morality. But on other issues, the Church sometimes loses, even when leaders take a public stand.[7]

Latter-day Saint legislators themselves deal with the question of Church influence by ignoring it. No lawmaker lists religious affiliation on his or her legislative web page, and religion is rarely mentioned in debate. In a 2011 survey, seven Republican legislators declined to say whether they were Latter-day Saints, though all of them were active members. They say religion is private and not material to legislative business, but they quickly add that religion does supply the values they bring to their office and affects their views on policy and society.

---

6. Davidson and Canham, "Mormon Church Lobbying," Jennifer Dobner, "Leaked Survey," *Salt Lake Tribune*, Mar. 29, 2015, May 11, 2017; Hrebenar et al., "Utah," 119; Bob Bernick, "How Much Influence?" *Utahpolicy.com*, Apr. 20, 2015; also Croft, "Influ-ence of LDS Church," chap. 4–5; email from Hrebenar and Thomas.
7. Magleby, "Religious Interest Group," 195. Church leaders have clashed with the legislature over concealed weapons in churches, illegal immigration, and criminalizing recording of conversations.

TABLE 2. Legislative approval

	approve	disapprove	number
Latter-day Saint	68%	32%	4,861
Non-LDS	36%	64%	2,009

Source: Center for the Study of Elections and Democracy

Citizen approval of the legislature also varies by religion. Latter-day Saints like the legislature and non-Mormons do not. From 2005 to 2011, the Center for the Study of Elections and Democracy at Brigham Young University conducted fourteen polls asking Utahns whether they approved of the job the legislature was doing. Table 2 shows responses. Latter-day Saints liked the legislature by a margin of two to one, and non-LDS disapproved by nearly the same margin. In short, Utah's legislature is dominated by Latter-day Saints, approved by Latter-day Saints, and disapproved by members of other religions.[8]

Overall, Utah's legislature wins lower approval than Utah governors, but higher approval than the legislatures of other states. Besides the fourteen BYU polls, Dan Jones and Associates conducted twenty-six surveys of legislative job approval between 1989 and 2018, mostly for KSL TV and the *Deseret News*. The average of the forty combined polls over twenty-two years shows a 56.1 percent legislative approval, a high rating for a legislature. Two political scientists compared approval ratings of eighteen state legislatures in 2007 and Utah ranked highest. In 2012 another study compared all fifty legislatures and placed Utah fourth, with 58 percent approval.

Utah legislators are embedded in a community of special interests that pay their campaign costs. In the 2016 election, an average winner received $31,006 in campaign donations, 92 percent from

---

8. Squire and Moncrief, *State Legislatures Today*, 239; Richardson Jr. et al., "Public Approval," 99–116.

TABLE 3. Utah House of Representatives campaign money, 2016

candidates	total	per candidate	PAC	spent
winners (75)	$2,325,425	$31,006	92%	78%
losers (39)	$629,535	$13,490	39%	89%

Source: "Campaign Finance," website, office of the Utah Lieutenant Governor.

political action committees (PACs). An average Utah senate incumbent candidate received about triple the amount of a house candidate, also 90 percent from PACs. Of the seventy-five representatives who won election, sixty were incumbents. Many of the incumbents did not ask anyone for campaign contributions because special interests provided the money; all the representative had to do was take it. The PACs supplied more campaign cash than house members needed. On average a winning candidate spent only 78 percent of the campaign money she had, and only two incumbents lost in the final election.[9] Though money comes easily to incumbents, it is harder for challengers to come by. The forty-six Democrats or Republicans who lost in the final election raised on average only $13,490, and $2,000 of that on average was their own money. The PACs donated less than one-fifth as much to an average losing candidate as to a winner.

For many American politicians, fund raising is a dreary, relentless task, but many Utah legislators easily receive more money than they need. This is partly because of PAC generosity, but also because legislative races are comparatively cheap. In 2016 the candidates in Utah's fourth US congressional district raised and spent $7.4 million, an expensive congressional race, and also more than all of the 229

---

9. Lee Davidson, "Special Interests," *Salt Lake Tribune*, Jan. 22, 2018; and articles in the *Deseret News* by Davidson, Feb. 9, 2009, Bob Bernick Jr., Jan. 2, 1991, Davidson and Bernick, Dec. 18, 2004, Dec. 3, 2006, Apr. 25, 2008, and Bernick and Jerry Spangler, Jan. 18, 1997.

candidates for the Utah House and Senate spent altogether in the ninety legislative races during that election.[10]

Realtors, bankers, health insurers, doctors, hospitals, unions, billboard companies, contractors, and other interests donate to legislative elections. Interests have professional lobbyists, who often deliver checks personally. The lobbyists "develop a relationship" with legislators. They treat them to golf, take them to lunch, praise a legislator's wisdom, and laugh at his jokes. Lobbyists use their relationship with legislators—facilitated with campaign cash—to present their client's case. Though similar combinations of lobbyists and PAC money hold sway in many states, a 1998 study showed that Utah legislators received the highest percentage of campaign money from PACs, out of seventeen states surveyed. Compared to other states, Utah's rules regulating contributions and lobbyists are loose, and some Utahns fear that moneyed interests acquire influence at the expense of those who do not contribute to campaigns and do not have a hired voice.[11]

Utah has a citizen legislature, part time and non-professional. Political scientists rank legislative professionalism by three criteria: how much time they spend in sessions, how much they are paid, and how large their staffs are. Congress is America's most professional legislature. Senators and representatives serve full time, draw high pay, and command large staffs. Indeed, the trend in that direction in state houses is sometimes called Congressionalization. Legislatures began as gatherings of local notables who made their living outside of government and came to the capitol for a short time, at low pay, often serving at a loss to themselves. Beginning with California in the 1960s, state legislatures began to "professionalize" in big states,

---

10. "Utah Congressional Races," *Open Secrets: Center for Responsive Politics*, www.opensecrets.org.

11. Cassie and Thompson, "Patterns of PAC Contributions," 164. Utah allows unlimited contributions. In rating legislative financial transparency from 2003 to 2008, the UCLA School of Law gave Utah a D- or F five times out of six. "Grading State Disclosure," *Campaign Disclosure Project*, campaigndisclosure.org.

such as California, New York, and Michigan, they became full time, like congressmen. Utah, along with New Hampshire, the Dakotas, Wyoming, and a few other states, still adheres to the citizen tradition. In nine political-science rankings of legislative professionalism from 1960 to 2015, Utah ranked no higher than forty-second and as low as forty-ninth.[12]

Professional legislators spend most of the year at the capitol. In Utah, time is short. The state constitution limits lawmakers to one forty-five-day general session each year, only about thirty-three working days, the second shortest time of any legislature.[13] Lawmakers also go to the capitol eight-to-eighteen additional days for interim committee meetings, special sessions, and veto-overrides. Legislatures with more time pace their work and meet three or four days a week. Utah lawmakers must meet five days a week on a schedule. Committee meetings usually start at 8 a.m., a floor session at 10, and lunch at noon, when lawmakers often eat together in party caucus. There is floor-time again at 2 and more committee meetings at 4. Early in a session, committee meetings substitute for floor time, and later floor time takes over from committees. While the legislature is in session, legislators work long days.

Unlike all professional legislators, Utah lawmakers have no personal staff. Leaders have staff, and the legislature as a whole hires several hundred workers (discussed below). Legislators work only fifty-to-sixty days each year, not enough to produce a job for a staffer. Each lawmaker has a student intern. The student comes to the capitol during the session and receives class credit instead of money. As they spend less time in session, legislators make less than those in other states. In 2014 they earned $273 per day, which meant $12,285 for a session, plus $4,000 or so for extra days. The

---

12. Squire and Hamm, *Chambers*, 80; Squire and Moncrief, *State Legislatures Today*, 79; King, "Changes in Professionalism," 331–32; Squire, "Theory of Legislative Institutionalization," 1029–30; also "Squire Index Update," 361–71.

13. "Legislative Session Length," *National Conference of State Legislatures*, Dec. 2. 2010, www.ncsl.org.

state also pays health insurance and retirement benefits and provides expenses for legislators who live away from home during a session. In legislative salary surveys, Utah ranked fifth lowest in 2003 and sixth lowest in 2008. If the lawmakers worked full-time at their daily rate, they would earn $71,760 a year.[14] Compensation has improved over a century from when they used to receive $4 a day and no benefits. "You have to be able to afford it," lawmakers used to say of their service.

The scant evidence available indicates that most legislators are well-off. The only survey of incomes, conducted in 1981, showed that the average legislator's income was about $40,400, at a time when the average household income in Utah was $22,797.[15] Besides being richer than their constituents, legislators can take time off from work to go to the capitol. Twenty-eight members in the 2011 session owned their own businesses. Every session a few bankers, more educators, and a few public employees make laws. Their employers and colleagues hope to benefit from a sympathetic lawmaker and sometimes help them serve. Wealthy people, and those with interests behind them are more likely to find time and resources to serve.

Legislators earn their livings in ways that have varied over time, as table 4 shows. The first legislature had the highest percentage of lawyers. Farmers and ranchers predominated in 1941. Educators reached their highest numbers in 1971, and recent legislatures have been dominated by Republican business people.

Occupations matter because lawmakers seems to represent their work almost as much as they represent their districts. A fifth to a quarter of all bills relate to the sponsor's job. In the 2010 session, Ogden police chief John Greiner sat as a senator and sponsored nine bills affecting the police, including "Access to Crime Victim's

---

14. Squire and Hamm, *Chambers*, 73; Squire and Moncrief, *State Legislatures Today*, 81; "2014 State Legislator Compensation," *National Conference of State Legislatures*, Apr. 11, 2014, www.ncsl.org.

15. Croft, "Influence of LDS Church," 280–89.

TABLE 4. Legislators' occupations (percentages)

year	attorneys	farmers/ranchers	educators	business
1896	22	16	0	20
1941	3	50	5	30
1971	12	9	21	19
2011	13	4	10	43

Source: *Drumm's Manual of Utah*; Schleicher and Durham, *Utah: The State and Its Government*; Pace, *There Ought to Be a Law*; and legislators' web pages

Mental Health Records" and "Vehicle Impound Amendments." Real estate broker Gage Froerer introduced "Common Interest Ownership Amendments," while insurance man Jim Dunnigan sponsored "Amendments to Health Insurance Coverage on State Contracts."[16] Most legislators do not know vehicle-impound law or the details of health insurance on state contracts. They rely on the sponsors who understand the subjects from their work and have studied the specifics of the bill. Because sessions are short, committee hearings and floor debate are also short, so deliberating, bargaining, and rewriting often occur in private meetings between the sponsor and affected interests.[17] Most bills are technical, of narrow interest, and are not reported in the news. Ordinary citizens are not involved and do not participate in the give-and-take on most measures. If the affected interests can agree on a bill, lawmakers usually pass it.

Over the past half-century, American state legislatures have become more professional. Scholars tend to believe that growing societal complexity requires professional legislators with professional staffs. And besides, legislators like more pay and help and often vote for those things when the opportunity arises. In Utah, the chief sign

---

16. Lee Davidson, "One of Every Four Bills," *Salt Lake Tribune*, Mar. 6, 2017; Bob Bernick Jr., "Utah Legislature," *Deseret News*, Feb. 21, 2010.

17. Adam Brown, "The 2017 Legislature," *Utah Data Points*, Mar. 15, 2017, utahdatapoints.com.

Both houses of the Utah legislature meeting with visitors from Idaho and Wyoming on January 15, 1901. In the early twentieth century, legislators usually served one term. Today most run for reelection and some serve for decades. *Classified Photo Collection, Utah State Historical Society*

of professionalism is declining legislative turnover. Professor Adam Brown of Brigham Young University counted the freshmen in each session and found that 90 percent of legislators were new in 1900, but only 18 percent were new in 2015.[18] Fewer newcomers win election because more sitting members serve multiple terms. While not a profession, Utah legislating has increasingly become an amateur career. Unlike their non-career predecessors, many long-time Utah legislators believe they understand state government as well as anyone, particularly as well as the governor.

Though scholars and politicians favored professionalization, voters,

18. Both Fordham, *Legislative Institution*, 49–54, and Squire, "Squire Index Update," 361–71, think professional legislatures are better. Brown, "Where Have All the Freshman Legislators Gone?" *Utah Data Points*, Mar. 17, 2011.

at least for a few years, disagreed. From 1992 to 1994, nineteen states imposed term limits to force out veteran politicians and make room for citizens to serve. In almost every state that allowed initiatives and referenda, voters gathered signatures and limited terms. Utah was one of only two states where lawmakers limited their own terms, and Utah limits were tactical. Merrill Cook, "self-proclaimed master of the Utah political initiative process," led a drive to gather 76,000 signatures and force term limits to a vote of the people. In 1994 he appeared likely to succeed. Polls showed 76 percent of Utahns wanted term limits. Speaker of the House Rob Bishop made a deal with Cook. Lawmakers would limit their own terms, and Cook and his colleagues would abandon their petitions. Legislators then passed a twelve-year limit, longer than in most other limited states, and no legislator would have to leave until 2006. Not soon enough, said Cook, and his group resumed gathering signatures. But in the public debate before the vote, lawmakers said Utah already had limits and did not need any more. The referendum failed 65-to-35 percent. Then in 2003, before any member had to leave, legislators repealed the law. According to a poll, 70 percent of Utahns still wanted limits. But lawmakers could see that the energy had gone out of the movement. Cook called the repeal "cynical," but term limits died and few people noticed.[19]

Despite their short time in session, lawmakers have become more productive—passing more laws than they used to, and the laws have become longer and more complicated. Graph 1 shows the number of pages enacted each year since statehood. From 1896 through 1960, lawmakers passed 165 pages of statutes, appropriations, and resolutions per year. From 2007 to 2016, they passed 2,778 pages per year.[20]

---

19. Kousser, *Term Limits*, 3–21; Matthew S. Brown, "Cook Makes History," Jerry Spangler, "Utahns Soundly Defeat Term-Limitations," *Deseret News*, July 12, Nov. 9, 1994; articles by Bob Bernick Jr. in the *Deseret News*, Aug. 29, 1993, Feb. 12, 1994, Jan. 14, 2001, Feb. 5, 2003; and Carey et al., *Term Limits*, 4.

20. Adam Brown found the number of bills and resolutions passed has increased to almost 500 per year, about 20 percent more than the median state legislature. *Utah Politics and Government*, 53.

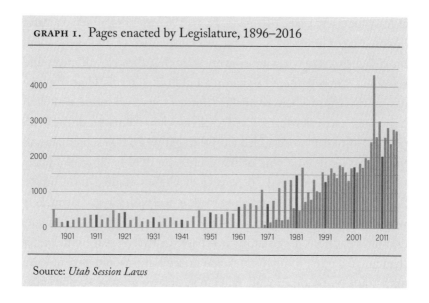

GRAPH I. Pages enacted by Legislature, 1896–2016

Source: *Utah Session Laws*

The legislature has become a law-making production line. In earlier days lawmakers would schedule half a day to debate a bill. Now only a few bills receive as much as an hour or two of floor debate and most are voted up or down in twenty minutes. A conscientious legislator used to be able to read the 330 pages passed in a typical sixty-day session and know what lawmakers had done. Now no one reads more than a fraction of what a legislative session passes. More law is made in each succeeding decade as legislative production accelerates.

So many bills in short sessions may mean less scrutiny for most bills. As table 5 shows, in each of the twelve general sessions from 2000 through 2011, lawmakers introduced an average of 708 bills and passed, on average, 425, or 60 percent. Over time the pass rate has risen. From 1953 through 1973, lawmakers met every other year, although for a longer session. They considered fewer bills and passed only 36 percent of those introduced. Not only are pass rates higher now than they used to be, they are higher than in other states. Two political scientists surveyed the number of bills introduced and passed in the fifty state legislatures in 2005 and 2006. As the line

TABLE 5. Bills introduced and passed

	introduced	passed	percent	requests	percent
Utah average, 1953–73	595	212	36	1038	41
Utah average, 2000–11	708	425	60		
US average, 2005–06	2,150	388	18		

Source: Memmott, *Legislative Workload Summary*; Squire and Moncrief, *State Legislatures Today*; and information from the Office of Legislative Research and General Counsel

labeled "US average" shows, lawmakers in the other states introduced three times as many bills but passed only 18 percent of them. Utah had the sixth highest pass percentage of all the states.[21] The pass rate does not show the whole process, however. Winnowing begins before a bill is even introduced. From 2000 to 2011, Utah lawmakers asked the Office of Legislative Research to draft an average of 1,038 bills per session. As a bill is drafted, the sponsor discusses it with colleagues, lobbyists, and others, who may persuade her that the bill is a bad idea. Circumstances may change, or a lawyer drafting a bill may discover technical problems. For these and other reasons, about a third of the drafts are never introduced. Of all the draft requests from 2000 to 2011, about 41 percent finally became law. Even so, Utah is a comparatively easy place to get a law passed.

Every legislature has committees, caucuses, and leaders. In Utah, leadership and caucuses are strong, and committees are rushed. In some other legislatures, standing committees spend weeks or months considering a bill, debating ideas, and refining language.[22] In Utah, with its short sessions, a chair has to hurry deliberation along. Committees listen to a bill's sponsor, solicit public comment, give their views and perhaps offer amendments, and then hold a vote to kill the

---

21. John M. Memmott, "Legislative Workload Summary," Utah Constitutional Revision Commission, 1978; Squire and Moncrief, *State Legislatures Today*, 161–62; data from *Book of the States*.

22. Rosenthal, *Heavy Lifting*, chapters 4–6.

legislation or pass it to the floor. In Congress and other state legislatures, members serve on the same committee for years and become experts. Utah lawmakers often change committees. Expertise comes less from years on a committee than from work outside the legislature.

The leadership has large formal powers. The senate president and speaker of the house choose committee chairs and assign members of committees. They consult with their leadership team (the majority leader and whips), try to seat members on committees of their choice, allow Democrats to make most of their own assignments, and sometimes they allow senior members to choose first. The speaker and president also assign bills to committees, although they usually follow recommendations of the rules committees. A political science study ranked the formal powers of the speaker in forty-nine states and found Utah's tied for fourth most powerful.[23]

Republican caucuses are Utah's most distinctive legislative institution. In contrast to committees and leaders, whose authority and duties are prescribed by rule, the caucuses are informal groups with no legal standing. As in almost all legislatures, both Republicans and Democrats caucus before each session to elect their leaders, and those decisions are ratified on the floor. But in Utah caucuses continue to meet through the session, and house and senate Republican caucuses may decide other floor votes. Few other legislatures have informal groups that are so powerful. Republican caucuses make big budget decisions, and leadership brings up other important bills to see if there are enough votes to pass them. Republican caucuses rouse suspicion because the senate always meets in secret, while the house usually meets openly but goes into secret meeting whenever members wish.[24] Some Utahns suspect the public legislative process merely reenacts what Republicans have decided secretly in caucus

---

23. Interview with former Democratic whip Rebecca Chavez-Houck, July 2018, and former speaker Greg Curtis, Feb. 2011; Clucas, "Principal Agent Theory," 326.

24. Lisa Riley Roche, "Behind Closed Doors," *Deseret News*, Jan. 23, 2016; Joel Campbell, "Time for Sun to Shine," *Salt Lake Tribune*, June 3, 2011; Francis, "Leadership, Party Caucus," 249, 253.

for secret reasons. Utah may be the only state where major budget decisions are made in closed party meetings.

The legislature is Utah's rising branch. Since World War II, it has gained power in two stages: first, from 1947 to 1985, legislators followed a national, non-partisan program of reform. Second, since about 1980, Republican lawmakers have asserted authority against the governor, the bureaucracy, the judiciary, the voters, and the schools. Reform began in 1947 with the creation of a Legislative Council with a staff of four to conduct studies and plan for legislative sessions. Until 1947 lawmakers met for sixty days in odd-numbered years and then vanished from the capitol. The Legislative Council first cast a slender legislative presence over the long interim, and the staffers were the legislature's first professional analysts. In 1968 lawmakers proposed, and voters ratified, a constitutional amendment allowing a twenty-day budget session in even-numbered years.[25] Legislators created interim committees to meet one day in most months between sessions to study issues and hear from department heads. They hired their own lawyer and authorized an auditor to investigate government. Legislators were getting too big for the constitution, attorney general Phil Hansen said. He sued, contending that legislators could take legal advice only from him. Utah's Supreme Court agreed and abolished the legislative legal counsel. The next attorney general, Vern Romney, went to court and ended the per diem pay for interim meetings. Legislators did not dare to ask the court to reconsider for fear justices would end interim expense money for rural lawmakers who drove long distances and stayed in hotels to attend meetings. Legislators served without pay on interim committees, but complained of "a thinly veiled atmosphere of executive and judicial hostility." In 1972 lawmakers proposed and voters approved another constitutional amendment that authorized staff and interim work. They hired professional staffs for three offices: Legislative Research and General Counsel, Legislative Fiscal Analyst, and Legislative Auditor General.

---

25. Whipple, "State Legislative Reform," 17–50; also Lloyd, "Legislative Council."

By 2015 the legislature had hired 133 permanent staffers and about a hundred temporary workers during legislative sessions.[26] In 1984 legislators obtained a third constitutional amendment allowing them to meet in 45-day general sessions every year instead of alternating sixty-day general sessions and twenty-day budget sessions. Over thirty-eight years, both Democratic and Republican legislatures pursued a goal of sufficient time and staff to do their jobs. They overcame obstacles, acquired independence from other branches, and established a continuous presence in state government.

In the second stage, which still continues, Republican legislators enlarged their power against other parts of government to advance a conservative agenda. Against the governor, they regained the upper hand in budget decisions, gained power to call themselves into veto-override sessions, and gained limited authority to convene special sessions. Over the bureaucracy they asserted oversight, as their interim committees replaced the boards and commissions that had previously supervised government agencies. Against the courts, they tried occasionally to intimidate judges, and after decades of acquiescence they attacked and sometimes rejected judicial nominees.[27] Against voters, they raised additional barriers to stop initiatives and referenda making it harder for citizens to legislate directly, thus protecting legislative ownership of law-making power. In addition, lawmakers redistricted themselves to favor Republican incumbents, to keep electors from voting them out of office. Against schools, legislators seized direction from the elected school board and enacted Republican reforms.[28] The legislature has been a conservative force,

---

26. *Phil Hansen v. Legal Services Committee of the Utah State Legislature*, 19 Utah 2d 231, 429 P. 2d 97a (1967); Pace, *There Ought to Be a Law*, 51–54; "Size of Legislative Staff," National Conference of State Legislatures, Oct. 2, 2018, www.ncsl.org. The national average was 523 permanent legislative staffers.

27. Aaron Falk, "For Judge Hilder," Taylor W. Anderson, "In 45 Days," Lee Davidson and Taylor Anderson, "Utah legislature Overrides Vetoes," *Salt Lake Tribune*, Aug. 21, 2011, Mar. 11, Apr. 18, 2018; Utah Const., Art. VII, § 7, amended 1980.

28. Changes are discussed in subsequent chapters on the judiciary, education, governing, and budget.

enacting more tax cuts, highway spending, and payments to business, while holding down spending for schools and human services.

For most of a century, Utah lawmakers followed the governor. He was a professional; they were amateurs. But lawmakers gained confidence as they hired expert staff and spent more time at the capitol, both in sessions and especially through longer legislative careers. In the second decade of the twenty-first century, some legislators have worked with three governors, and a few have worked with six. They have developed and strengthened their opinions by talking government and politics with each other, that is, with like-minded conservative Latter-day Saint legislators. They form a community of opinion, articulated and reinforced in the Republican caucus. Republican legislators rode Utah's conservative surge. As voters became more conservative and Republican, the legislature responded and gained power as the chief agent of the new majority will.

"No man's life, liberty, or property is safe while the Legislature is in session," Judge Gideon Tucker said in 1866. "We have never really wanted our state legislatures to amount to much. And they have obliged us," said the Citizens Council on State Legislatures in 1973. Across America, state legislatures get little respect. In Utah the legislative seizure of power for conservatism draws anger and ridicule from non-LDS, non-Republicans, non-conservatives. Such citizens predominate in news media, non-profit advocacy organizations, colleges, and universities. Critics say legislators serve money, disdain ethics, impose Latter-day Saint morals, bash gays, act secretly, starve schools, grind the poor, rape the earth, and make insensitive remarks sometimes in bad grammar.[29]

Legislators dismiss most criticism. They see themselves serving three ideals: First, political scientists used to classify states by their

---

29. "Final Accounting," 1 Tucker 248 (N.Y. Surr. 1866); "From the Horse's Mouth" editorial, "Buttars: Gays," "Broken Promises" editorial, *Salt Lake Tribune*, Jan. 4, Feb. 18, Mar. 1, 2018; "Utah Legislature," *Deseret News*, Nov. 16, 1990; "Secret Bills," *Alliance for a Better Utah*, Feb. 4, 2015, betterutah.org; "The State Rock is Coal," *Salt Lake City Weekly*, Jan. 11, 2017; *Getting by with Less*, 14, 18–19.

"political culture," and said that Utah had a "moralistic" political culture, meaning that government office is seen as public service, rather than as seeking personal advantage.[30] Few legislators have ever heard the phrase "moralistic political culture," but almost all would agree that they serve the public, not their own interests. They like to remind citizens how they work long hours for low pay, and say they do the best they can by the state. A second ideal is the citizen legislator. Lawmakers say they remain tied to their communities, where they earn their living and spend their time, unlike professional politicians who earn their living and spend their time in government. Third, many lawmakers have been unpaid leaders in the Church of Jesus Christ of Latter-day Saints, which has no professional clergy, and they think of the legislature as similar service. Most legislators have succeeded in their professions, as well as in their church and community, and have the confidence such success brings. The most often repeated phrase of the 2011 session, for example, was "Utah is the best managed state in America." Legislators believe their decisions, especially their conservative budgeting, contributed to that judgment by the Pew Foundation. Two buildings on Capitol Hill make rising power visible: The four-story House and Senate Office Buildings were completed in 2004. Neither is beautiful, like the Capitol south of them, nor ugly, like the State Office Building to the north. They stand mostly empty most of the time, displaying in bland granite lawmakers' sense of their growing power.

---

30. Elazar, *American Federalism*, 93–126.

12

UTAH'S GOVERNORS

In 1933, Utah legislators met amid calamity. The Great Depression had impoverished Utah even more than other states; one-third of the labor force could not find work. Total personal income had fallen more than half. People rioted when sheriffs seized homes for unpaid taxes. Governor Henry Blood and Latter-day Saint president Heber J. Grant each received hundreds of pleading letters from people with hungry children. In response, legislators passed what they called, without irony, "the dictator bill," giving Democratic governor Blood power to cut or shift spending, hire or lay off workers, reduce salaries, create or cancel projects, abolish departments, and close schools to meet the emergency.

Blood made an unlikely caudillo: slender, gray-haired, with a kind face and weak voice, orderly habits, and a pedantic manner. Republicans charged that he came from the "Dern machine." He had been a small-town banker and businessman who was elected Davis County treasurer and appointed by his predecessor, George Dern, as chair of the State Road Commission, the tenderloin of Utah party patronage. Through his first term, he continued to serve as president of the North Davis Stake of the Church of Jesus Christ of Latter-day Saints. Instead of seeking a third term, he became a mission president in California. Governor Blood nursed Utah with New Deal remedies, by soliciting federal projects, raising taxes to match grants, and participating in every program Washington offered, taking every

TABLE 1. Approval ratings

governor/in office	job approval	number of polls
Calvin Rampton, 1965–77	72%	3
Scott Matheson, 1977–85	78%	12
Norman Bangerter, 1985–93	58%	21
Mike Leavitt, 1993–2003	79%	21
Olene Walker, 2003–05	83%	3
Jon Huntsman Jr., 2005–09	78%	34
Gary Herbert, 2009–	71%	19
Average for Utah Governors	74%	114
263 Governors, 50 states (1948–2009)[a]	50%	5490
Presidents Johnson to Obama[b]	51%	
United States Senators from Utah[c]	59%	49

Sources: *Salt Lake Tribune, Deseret News, Survey USA*; [a] Richard Niemi, Thad Beyle, and Lee Sigelman, "Job Approval Ratings: State Governors 1958–2009 Database"; http://www.unc.edu. [b] Gallup News, "presidential approval ratings, historical statistics and trends." [c] Senators are: Wallace Bennett, 1 poll, 45% approval; Frank Moss, 2 polls, 61.5%; Jake Garn, 18 polls, 68.3%; Orrin Hatch, 41 polls, 62.6%; Bob Bennett, 25 polls, 57%.

federal dollar he could find. He professed Utahns' "complete willingness to support every move undertaken by President" Franklin D. Roosevelt.[1] He is now remembered mostly by scholars and descendants, but his story shows the chief asset of Utah governors: they are expected to lead. People want governors to face problems, propose plans, and take action, and when they do, citizens support them. Expectations and support are hard to measure directly but may be indicated by length of tenure and approval ratings.[2]

Utah governors win unusually high approval in polls of how well people believe their chief executive has performed. Table 1 shows the

1. Quinn, "Governorship of Henry H. Blood," 5–7, 11–12, 32, 137.
2. King and Cohen, "What Determines a Governor's Popularity," 231–32, 235.

results of 114 public opinion polls asking citizens to rate seven Utah governors, 1965–2016: job approval averages 74 percent. In comparison, the national average for eleven presidents who governed during the same time was 51.4 percent. A team of political scientists gathered 5,460 polls with job-approval ratings for 263 governors in fifty states from 1948 through 2009. The average job approval was 50.4 percent. In a direct comparison of governors' popularity in 2005–06, Poll USA conducted sixteen monthly polls for all fifty governors and ended up with Utah's Jon Huntsman finishing second-highest. The *Washington Post* later pronounced Utah's Gary Herbert the nation's most popular governor. A national survey in 2017 ranked him the ninth most popular.[3] As the table shows, governors get higher job-approval ratings than United States senators from Utah.

Political science studies show that high approval ratings bring increased power over the state bureaucracy, more influence in the legislature, and higher electability with voters.[4] While these findings seem intuitive, they are not fully borne out by Utah experience. Governor Olene Walker, an educator and Latter-day Saint grandmother, had the highest overall approval rating of any Utah governor as she finished Mike Leavitt's term. But when she tried to win election on her own, she was defeated in the 2004 Republican state convention. Her highest single rating came after she had lost. Utahns liked her and may have disagreed with the delegates' refusal to let her out of convention. Norman Bangerter had the lowest job approval ratings, but as a former speaker of the state House of Representatives he got along with legislators better than other governors. High job approval makes governors feel good and may help them do their job, but that help is limited.

Political scientists have also studied how governors achieve high

---

3. "Polls," SurveyUSA, www.surveyusa.com; Sean Sullivan and Aaron Blake, "The Most Popular Governor in the Country?" *Washington Post*, Feb. 21, 2014; Dennis Romboy, "Herbert Fares Well," *Deseret News*, Apr. 11, 2017.
4. Dometrius, "Gubernatorial Approval," 254–56; Ferguson, "Chief Executive Success," 160–61

approval, and found that a good economy with low unemployment boosts the ratings and that a governor's approval often goes up and down along with the US president's.[5] Again, those findings do not hold in Utah. It is true that governor Norman Bangerter had the lowest overall approval partly because he presided over a bad economy, but governors Rampton, Matheson, Leavitt, Huntsman, and Herbert governed through hard times and retained high ratings. As for presidents, Utahns approve Republicans and disapprove Democrats, with little effect on gubernatorial approval. The low Utah rating for President Jimmy Carter did little to damage the high approval of fellow Democrat Scott Matheson. Republican governor Mike Leavitt was popular when President Bill Clinton was not, and Utahns approved of Governor Gary Herbert when they disapproved of President Barack Obama. Conversely, Norman Bangerter had low ratings though he governed through terms of Ronald Reagan and the first George Bush, two popular presidents in Utah.

Utah governors float free of presidential approval partly because they win popularity by opposing the federal government.[6] Starting before Cal Rampton, Utah governors fought Washington over federal land, and from Scott Matheson onward all of them have disputed downwinder issues. In addition, Matheson defended the Central Utah Water Project against President Jimmy Carter's "hit list." Bangerter launched a court fight over abortion. Leavitt criticized federal welfare rules and federal imposition of gay student clubs in Utah schools. Huntsman rejected President Bush's No-Child-Left-Behind educational initiative. Governor Herbert opposed President Obama's Affordable Care Act. Utah governors often lose their disputes with Washington but win approval from citizens as they go down fighting.

While legislators seized power as agents of the Latter-day Saint Republican majority, governors won popularity by bridging Utah's

---

5. Hansen, "Life is not Fair," 167.
6. Foy, "Utah," 387.

political–religious divide. Starting with Cal Rampton (1965–77), Utah governors have all acted as moderate conservatives, almost always to the left of the legislature. All of them except Jon Huntsman worked for school funding, often preferring education spending over tax cuts. Huntsman (2005–09) put tax cuts first, reduced Utah's long-term effort for education, and tacitly consigned schools to more years of want. But he wooed non-LDS Democrats with his liberal stance on public morality. He spoke for same-sex civil unions and won liquor-by-the-drink, and with it non-Mormon hearts.

When asked about Utah governors' high approval, Mike Leavitt said, "If you do an okay job, they sort of sustain you."[7] "Sustain" is a word Latter-day Saints use. Congregations are asked to "sustain" their leaders, and they do so unanimously. Leavitt implied that the Latter-day Saint tradition of support for religious leaders may extend to governors as well, if "you do an okay job."

Since statehood, Utah governors have been reelected more often and served longer than governors in other states. There were only fourteen Utah governors from 1896 to the end of the twentieth century, while every other state (except Alaska and Hawaii, which had no state governors until 1959) had at least eighteen, and Vermont had the most at thirty-two.[8] In the twentieth century, the average American governor served 4.03 years; but in Utah, 7.2 years, the longest of any state. Political scientists say that starting about the middle of the twentieth century, the office of governor changed across the country. In 1950, governors in twenty-one states served only two-year terms, and many states restricted gubernatorial powers and expectations. Some states had a largely ceremonial office occupied by what Professor Larry Sabato called "good-time Charlies."[9] Then states reformed, changed their constitutions, enlarged

7. Conversation with the author, 2001.
8. *National Governors Association*, www.nga.org, with the exception of the two most recent states mentioned above.
9. Sabato, *Goodbye to Good-Time Charlie.*

executive power, and looked to their governors for leadership. By 2010 only two states, New Hampshire and Vermont, still had two-year terms. Utah governors, in contrast, have always had four-year terms and were always leaders of state government. The state had strong governors before it became fashionable.

After the mid-century reforms, other states' governors served longer. Two Utah governors, Leavitt and Huntsman, left office to take federal appointments, the first in Utah to fail to complete their terms. Utah still has the longest average overall gubernatorial tenure, outside of Alaska and Hawaii, but it is no longer so unusual. Still, Professor Adam Brown points out, the last Utah governor beaten in a general election was Herbert Maw in 1948, since then only J. Bracken Lee and Olene Walker have lost in the convention or in a primary.[10] A key figure in this modern longevity was Democrat Calvin Rampton (1965–1977), who won a third term after four other governors had tried and failed, breaking what many voters considered an informal two-term limit. He served longer than any other Utah governor.[11] After him, Leavitt and Herbert won three terms. Another reason incumbents win is that since Norman Bangerter (1985–1993), Utah's Republicanism has meant that only candidates from that party have won, so Republican nominees win easily in November elections. Although Utah is no longer an outlier for tenure, incumbent governors still disproportionately win reelection.

Utah governors differ from others in their past histories, in their careers after leaving office, and in personal traits. Eleven of seventeen Utah governors have been faithful Latter-day Saints.[12] Of the others, George Dern and J. Bracken Lee were Presbyterians, Simon Bamberger was America's second Jewish governor, and Calvin

---

10. Brown, *Utah Politics*, 110

11. Wells, Spry, Maw, and Lee had run for third terms. Clyde's chief talking point when he beat Lee in the 1956 Republican Primary was Utah's two-term tradition.

12. In order of their terms in office, the LDS governors were Heber Wells, John Cutler, William Spry, Charles Mabey, Henry Blood, Herbert Maw, George Clyde, Norman Bangerter, Mike Leavitt, Olene Walker, and Gary Herbert.

Rampton, Scott Matheson, and Jon Huntsman were indifferent Latter-day Saints. Most American governors have been lawyers, but in Utah only Maw, Rampton, and Matheson practiced law. Wells, Spry, Lee, Huntsman and Herbert had careers in government and politics. Maw, Clyde, and Walker were educators. Eight governors (Wells, Cutler, Bamberger, Mabey, Dern, Blood, Bangerter, and Leavitt) were businessmen.

Utah has more citizen governors than other states. Only 10 percent of all American governors from 1900 to 2011 were political newcomers.[13] In contrast, six, more than one-third, of Utah's governors had never served in a political office before they became governor, and governor was the only elective office any of them ever held. Six of the others had been state legislators, and five had been locally elected officials. After being governor, only J. Bracken Lee (1949–57) was elected to another office. He became mayor of Salt Lake City. Lee and Spry both ran unsuccessfully for the US Senate. Huntsman ran twice for president and lost. George Dern became President Franklin D. Roosevelt's Secretary of War, Leavitt Secretary of Health and Human Services under George W. Bush, and Huntsman Ambassador to China and Russia; Wells and Spry took lesser federal posts. Ten Utah governors returned to private life when their terms were over. In summary, Utah governors are more likely than others to be elected as private citizens and to leave politics after serving as governor.[14] Political scientists look to institutions and state culture to explain why governors succeed, but it also seems likely that Utahns have been fortunate in the people they chose for the job. They have won approval from their peers. Seven Utah

13. Governors with no previous political experience were John Cutler, George Clyde, Calvin Rampton, Scott Matheson, Mike Leavitt, and Jon Huntsman. For a general discussion, see Ferguson, "Governors and the Executive Branch."

14. Those who fall into this category are John Cutler, Simon Bamberger, Charles Mabey, Henry Blood, Herbert Maw, George Clyde, Calvin Rampton, Scott Matheson, Norman Bangerter, and Olene Walker. For comparable national data, see Ferguson, "Governors and the Executive Branch," 211.

Simon Bamberger, fourth governor of Utah, at his desk in the newly completed capitol, August 4, 1917. Bamberger owned a hotel, several railroads, the Lagoon amusement park, coal mines, and was part-owner of a successful silver mine. *Photograph by Harry Shipler, Peoples of Utah Collection, Utah State Historical Society*

governors have chaired the National Governors Association.[15] Only Virginia has had more governors elected chair by their colleagues.

Political scientists compare formal gubernatorial powers granted in state constitutions, and Utah governors are among the stronger.[16] The governor proposes a state budget to the legislature, which makes final decisions; he appoints department heads, subject to the consent of the senate (the governor's appointment power is limited in education and the judiciary); and the governor fires top administrators at

15. William Spry, George Dern, Herbert Maw, Calvin Rampton, Scott Matheson, Mike Leavitt, and Gary Herbert.

16. Thad L. Beyle, "Gubernatorial Power: The Institutional Power Ratings for the Fifty Governors of the United States," unpublished paper, 2007.

UTAH POLITICS

will. The governor can veto legislation she disagrees with, including line items in budgets. It takes two-thirds of the legislature to override a veto. The framers of Utah's constitution sought to restrict governors by dividing the executive power among several elected officials, including the attorney general, treasurer, auditor, and secretary of state. Starting in the 1970s, Utahns changed their government so that elected officials remained, but restraint on the governor lessened. Most importantly, the Secretary of State was changed to a Lieutenant Governor, who became the governor's running mate and a member of his administration.[17]

Some governors are stronger on paper than in practice, but in Utah the executive has informal advantages that enlarge official sway. Utah has had no scandals involving governors, in contrast to the twenty-three American governors from 1970 to 2011 who were impeached, resigned in the face of imminent prosecution, or left office for prison.[18] The late Thad Beyle, a professor at the University of North Carolina–Chapel Hill, showed that such scandals not only tainted the evildoer, but eroded public regard for the office. The high sustained approval of Utah governors reflects, in part, the historical record of probity they inherit. Most government professionals outside the judicial branch work for the governor, so they often have better information, understanding, and staff work than part-time legislators and board members. Utah's media are convenient for governors, and they get more attention than many of their peers in other states. Because the main television stations and newspapers in Salt Lake City reach the entire state, the governors command statewide coverage and can marshal news to present their views and project their personalities.

Professor Margaret Ferguson of Indiana–Purdue University ranked governors by personal and institutional power in 2011, and she listed Gary Herbert as the third-most powerful governor in the country.

---

17. These changes are discussed in the next chapter.
18. Ferguson, "Governors and the Executive Branch," 240.

Based on their formal powers and reelection record, Professor Adam Brown says that Utah governors are the country's most powerful. Two other political scientists, Thad Kousser and Justin Phillips, estimated power by reading the state-of-the-state speeches of twenty-seven governors in 2001 and twenty-five for 2006. They counted proposals the governors made and legislation passed to produce a kind of gubernatorial batting average. In 2001 the sixth most successful governor was Utah's Mike Leavitt, who persuaded the legislature to pass two-thirds of his proposals. In 2006 the ninth most successful was Jon Huntsman, who saw 60 percent of his proposals become law. The researchers also estimated the importance of each proposal to give each governor an "impact score." By that measure Leavitt ranked tenth and Huntsman seventeenth.[19] That would indicate that they were more powerful than average, but less powerful than Ferguson or Brown believe.

Gubernatorial power will remain debatable. But evidence shows that Utah governors are comparatively popular and successful. Reminiscences, journalistic accounts, and academic studies of top executives in other states have reported rancorous politics, inability to rally public opinion, lack of control over the bureaucracy, conflict with legislatures, and disappointment in the realities of office.[20] Utah governors are less beset by those troubles. As Norman Bangerter said, governors "swing a hammer hand" in daily state business and often get their way. Of the eight Utah governors I have interviewed, every one of them confessed to being happy on the job.

---

19. Brown, *Utah Politics*, 110–122; Kousser and Phillips, *Power of American Governors*, 109–12; also "Governors and the Executive Branch," 208–51.

20. See, for example, McCall, *Power of the Texas Governor*; Salmore and Salmore, *New Jersey Politics*; Cronin and Loevy, *Colorado Politics*; Medler, "Governor."

TABLE 2. Utah governors

name	party	years
Heber M. Wells	R	1896–1905
John C. Cutler	R	1905–09
William Spry	R	1909–17
Simon Bamberger	D	1917–21
Charles R. Mabey	R	1921–25
George H. Dern	D	1925–33
Henry H. Blood	D	1933–41
Herbert B. Maw	D	1941–49
J. Bracken Lee	R	1949–57
George D. Clyde	R	1957–65
Calvin L. Rampton	D	1965–77
Scott M. Matheson	D	1977–85
Norman H. Bangerter	R	1985–93
Mike Leavitt	R	1993–2003
Olene Walker	R	2003–05
Jon M. Huntsman Jr.	R	2005–09
Gary R. Herbert	R	2009–present

13

GOVERNING

This chapter tells how Utah moved from institutional squalor toward a reformist idea of good government. The state began with a nineteenth-century constitution and bad habits. The government ran deficits, the administration served the political party in power and other special interests; wily politicians seized fiefdoms, and government lacked coherence. No one knew what the government was or what it did. This chapter tells stories of the old ways and of improvements made in public administration and constitutional practice. Unlike other aspects of Utah politics, the improvements had little to do with religion. Rather, Utah struggled to impose order on faction, interest, and sprawl.

After Latter-day Saints renounced polygamy in 1890, Congress passed an enabling act inviting the state to try again for statehood, the seventh attempt but the first by federal invitation. In 1894 citizens elected 107 delegates to a constitutional convention: sixty Republicans and forty-seven Democrats; seventy-nine were Latter-day Saints and twenty-eight non-LDS. Of the latter, all but five were Republicans.[1]

At the 1895 convention, delegates agreed on basic institutions almost without discussion: a declaration of rights, a bicameral legislature, a separate executive of several elected officers, an independently

---

1. Ivins "Constitution for Utah," 100–01.

elected judiciary, and free (tax-supported) public schools. Delegates copied most of the provisions from other state constitutions. Conventional political wisdom at the time saw some states mired in legislative corruption and bankrupting debt, and advised restrictions. Although the territorial legislature had not shown evidence of corruption and had left a manageable debt of $750,000, delegates followed the conventional wisdom and imposed restrictions.[2] For instance, the legislature could meet only once every two years for a sixty-day general session, and only the governor could call a special session. Lawmakers could do less damage if they met fewer days, the framers calculated. But that meant that after each session, the governor would rule alone for twenty-two months, which was too much power for one person. As a check on the governor, the delegates created five additional elected executive officials, more than were needed to do the work, they believed, but they would divide power and watch each other.[3] As another check, the constitution created boards to make policy, oversee administration, and ensure deliberative government while the legislators were away. For example, the Board of Insane Asylum Commissioners comprised the governor, auditor, and treasurer. The Board of Pardons included the supreme court justices, governor, and attorney general. Most formidably, the Board of Examiners (governor, secretary of state, and attorney general) was required to approve all claims for money except for salaries set by law.[4]

A few issues roused disagreement: urban delegates wanted one-person-one-vote but lost to rural delegates who insisted on at least one representative from every county. Republicans wanted to pay

2. Hickman, "Constitutional Law," 75; White, "So Bright the Dream," 328, 333–35; also Hafen, "Legislative Branch." In Alexander, "Utah's Constitution," we learn that the 1849, 1856, and 1862 drafts borrowed from the Iowa constitution; the 1872, 1882, and 1887 drafts borrowed from Nevada; and the final version drew from several state constitutions.

3. The executive positions were attorney general, secretary of state (later changed to lieutenant governor), treasurer, auditor, and school superintendent (later a Board of Education appointee). White, *Utah State Constitution*, 90; Utah Const. art. VII, § 12–14.

4. Other boards included Equalization, Labor Conciliation and Arbitration, and State Prison Commissioners. See "Separation of Powers."

"bounties" to lure businesses to Utah, but Democrats were opposed. In a compromise, the constitution forbade the state from buying stock or lending its credit, but not from offering other subsidies. Most Latter-day Saints wanted women to vote as they had in Utah Territory until Congress disfranchised them. Non-Mormons feared woman suffrage would enlarge Latter-day Saint electoral advantage, and some Saints joined them, fearing that female suffrage might imperil ratification. The delegates debated for a month, citizens petitioned, and editorials advised, and then the Latter-day Saint Relief Society called for suffrage. With that, the franchise became part of the constitution and Utah became the third state where women voted.[5]

Statehood could have failed in two ways: either Congress or voters could have rejected the proposed constitution. To satisfy Congress, the framers followed the enabling act and included article III saying that "polygamous or plural marriages are forever prohibited." To woo voters, delegates tried to show that statehood would not raise expense. The convention met during an economic depression, so delegates feared that high salaries or the prospect of higher taxes might incite voters against ratification. Next to suffrage, government salaries provoked the longest debates. To show that the new state would not overtax people, and to follow the policy of restrictions, the constitution limited state and local taxation and debt.[6] Delegates drafted a document of about 15,800 words, which was two-and-a-half times longer than the United States Constitution but shorter than the average state constitution.[7] Voters ratified it by 78 percent. Most of the opposition came from non-Mormon communities.

After the constitution was adopted, scholars of public administration changed their views and proposed a four-part ideal for government: a unified executive under an elected governor who hired

---

5. Ivins "Constitution for Utah," 107–08; White, *Charter for Statehood*, 52–55.

6. White, *Utah State Constitution*, 148; also Moseley, "Constitutional Restrictions," 462–90; Morrill, "Property Tax Assessment," 491–516.

7. For the length of the constitution, I rely on Brown, *Utah Politics*, 13. It is now about 18,000 words.

and fired department heads; executive agencies grouped by function; government workers hired by merit and protected by rules; and all spending appropriated by the legislature, spent under control of the governor and independently audited. Experts came to view Utah's multiple elected officials, administrative commissions, and elaborate but ineffective fiscal controls as so much Victorian bric-a-brac. The short, simple US Constitution returned to fashion as a model for state reform.[8] Utah's six failed constitutional attempts then appeared as a decline. The best constitutions (most like the US Constitution) had come first, and later documents degenerated as Utah abandoned simplicity, borrowed from other state constitutions, and pandered to Congress. Governors and legislators sometimes believed Utah's form of government, including its constitution, statutes, decisions, habits, and institutions, impeded good government. Utah's constitutional history is one floundering attempt after another to overcome the nineteenth-century constitution and early habits and change the way of governing.

The first problem was that Utah could not pay its bills. The state had enough revenue, in theory, but it arrived at the wrong time. The fiscal year began in January, but property taxes, which provided most state revenue, were not collected until November, so the state usually ran out of money about May. Governor Heber Wells complained that the state paid with warrants, which could be presented to the state treasurer, but if he does not have any "cash ... the warrants are registered and marked 'not paid for want of funds' and must then be hawked about for perhaps ten or twelve months before the taxes provide sufficient funds in the treasury to redeem them." Wells asked to divide property taxes into two collections. Lawmakers turned down that plan, but allowed the state to borrow money to pay the warrants and appropriated money to pay interest on the loans.[9]

---

8. Flynn, "Constitutional Difficulties"; Flynn, "Federalism and Viable State Government."
9. *Journal of the House of Representatives*, 1897, 14; Young, "Utah Public Debt History," 5, 10.

Governors wanted more control over the budget. Departments often spent more than their appropriations, and the state usually spent more than its revenues. Governors said that if they had more control, they could impose thrift and end the deficits. As he was selling bonds to cover his predecessor's deficits, Governor Simon Bamberger (1917–1921) proposed a new "scientific" plan that would give the governor power to propose and enforce a budget. The legislature gave him part of what he requested. As he was selling bonds to cover Governor Bamberger's deficits, Governor Charles Mabey (1921–25) persuaded legislators to create a Department of Finance and Purchase, enlarging the governor's control over departmental spending. Mabey also began an enduring theme. Legislators had created new agencies, created commissions to govern them, and left them unconnected to the rest of government. Government became a pile of boards and bureaucracies. To organize the pile, reformers grouped agencies by function. In Mabey's case, over the course of twenty-five years, the legislature had created a Livestock Commission, Crop Pest Commission, Apiaries Commission, and Board of Horse Commissioners. All these were reorganized into a new Department of Agriculture, with a new Board of Dairy Commissioners added.[10]

Governor Mabey's new Department of Finance and Purchase took power away from the Board of Examiners, the gray eminence of Utah government. The constitution said "the Governor, Secretary of State and Attorney General shall ... constitute the State Board of Examiners, with power to examine all claims against the state." Initially, the board examined claims by people who said Utah Territory had owed them money, and the examiners recommended which claims the state legislature should pay. In addition, the legislature had given the board power to authorize "deficit appropriations," allowing a department to overspend its budget in an emergency. The examiners

---

10. "Appropriations Bill," *Salt Lake Herald Republican*, Mar 11, 1917; *Journal of the House of Representatives*, 1917, 26; Layton, "Governor Charles," 16; *Laws of Utah, 1921*, chapter two.

also approved some purchases of desks and supplies, and the hiring of clerks, but mostly departments spent money without any outside approval. Under Governor Mabey, the new Department of Finance took from the examiners the power to approve spending and took from the departments the power to spend on their own. After reform, all expenditures were approved by the Department of Finance, under the control of the governor, before purchases were made and then approved again after billing but before payment by the examiners. Reformers liked this system, but legislators did not, and they cut the salary of the director of finance and refused finance requests.[11]

In 1924, Democrat George Dern (1925–33) ousted Republican Charles Mabey, while Republicans retained control of the legislature and other elected offices. The Department of Finance, galling in the hands of a Republican, proved intolerable when controlled by a Democrat. Lawmakers abolished the department in 1927. Governor Dern vetoed the bill, but the legislature overrode him and returned to the old system of less control over departmental spending. The Board of Examiners became the Board of Finance and Purchase, with authority to approve proposed expenditures.[12] Thus Republican legislators moved control from a Democratic governor to a board of two Republicans and one Democrat.

There was more than partisan difference, however. The politics showed rivalry among the elected executive officers, the governor versus the attorney general and secretary of state. Reformers believed the governor should control executive-branch spending. But the attorney general, backed by the secretary of state, theorized that "claims against the state" included not just bills or claims presented for payment but any proposed expenditures, which the examiners could approve or block as they chose. If that view prevailed, the attorney general and secretary of state would each equal the governor

---

11. Utah Const. art. VII, § 13; Snow, "Triumvirate Rule," 75.

12. *Journal of the House of Representatives*, 1927, 537; "Tangles Occur as End Nears," *Salt Lake Tribune*, Mar. 11, 1927.

UTAH POLITICS

in their ability to control state spending. No one else paid much attention to that theory, however.

Democrat Herbert Maw ran for office in 1940, promising to re-organize the government to end the "astonishing waste" and to save "great ... vast" sums of money. When he submitted his plan to the legislature in 1941, he pointed to a report by political scientist G. Homer Durham, who in 1939 found that the legislature had appro-priated a budget of $8.6 million for two years. But Utah had spent $26.5 million in the first year alone. This was because the legislature appropriated for the general fund, but Utah also had 109 special funds, many of which were untouched by legislators. Federal relief grants bypassed legislators and went directly to the Welfare Com-mission, as did state sales taxes. Federal highway grants were spent by the State Road Commission, as were driver's license fees and gas-oline taxes. The Banking Commission, Department of Agriculture, and Securities Commission all operated on fees they collected from people they regulated. The Land Board kept 20 percent of state leases and sales, and the Fish and Game Department spent income from licenses; none of that was any business of the legislature. Durham counted about 120 state offices, bureaus, boards, or commissions and fifty-to-sixty state departments.[13]

Maw asked the legislature to consolidate these disparate agencies into eleven departments and to bring the budget under the control of the legislature and governor, as the constitution seemed to intend. The house passed a version of his plan, but the senate stalled until the session ended and the bills died. Maw fought on by calling two special sessions in three months solely to consider reorganization. He got the government sorted into fourteen departments and brought a larger share of spending under the legislature, although most spending still escaped its control. Contrary to reformist principles, the lawmakers put boards or commissions in charge of most of the departments. Often commissioners were chosen from interests related to the

---

13. *Journal of the House of Representatives*, 1941, 19; Durham, *Public Administration*.

departments they regulated. For instance, most members of the water commission were irrigators, engineers, or water lawyers; and bankers and bank attorneys sat on the banking commission. Government by commission, coupled with independent revenue, assured that some agencies would be independent from the governor and that some agencies would serve the interests they were supposed to regulate. Though he failed to get full reform, Maw achieved more reorganization than any other Utah governor. Afterward, when scholars studied the results, they could not tell whether reform had saved money.[14]

As part of the 1941 reform, the legislature recreated the Department of Finance, empowered to approve all state spending under a three-person Finance Commission. Then attorney general Grover Giles staged a coup. He issued a legal opinion saying the act was unconstitutional, that the powers of the Finance Department infringed the constitutional powers of the Board of Examiners. But the Finance Department might be saved by making it the *agent* of the Board of Examiners. Governor Maw, careful not to risk his hard-won reforms, agreed to Giles's coup. This meant that the Department of Finance controlled expenditures, and the examiners controlled the department, and the largest interpretation of examiner power governed Utah.[15]

For forty years, the Board of Examiners swept across Utah government like a raiding party. They controlled hiring, firing, salaries, raises, promotions, purchases, and travel. The law in 1953 said the Board of Education would set the salary of the State Superintendent of Schools between $6,000 and $8,000. The Board of Examiners intervened and cut the salary to $6,000. At their next session, the legislature raised the salary to $8,000 and revised the law to emphasize that the Board of Education would set the superintendent's salary. Nevertheless, the Board of Examiners cut the superintendent's

14. Anderson, "History of the Reorganization," giving a full account of the Maw reorganization

15. Snow, "Triumvirate Rule," 79; Rawlings, "Utah Board of Examiners," 350–61.

salary again in 1957, 1959, 1960, and 1970 without legislative reaction. The school superintendent and the University of Utah both went to the Utah Supreme Court seeking freedom from the Board of Examiners. Both failed.[16]

Besides cutting salaries, the examiners spent money. The University of Utah wanted a new theater and suggested it should commemorate the old Pioneer Theater built by Brigham Young and cherished in Latter-day Saint memory. Near the end of 1956, university officials said if they could get just $500,000 from the state immediately, they could raise the rest from private donors. Latter-day Saint president David O. McKay, an alumnus of the university, endorsed the plan. The day after Christmas, when no one was looking, the Board of Examiners made a deficit appropriation to the University of Utah of $500,000. Legislators from outside Salt Lake City were shocked. They muttered about a conspiracy between the university, the Church, and the examiners. When the legislative session began three weeks later, senate president Orval Hafen from St. George introduced a bill to repeal the deficit appropriation. President McKay asked to meet with legislative leaders, the only such meeting ever applied for by a Church president. He stood and smiled. "I have come," he said, "to confess my sins." Theater opponents were first charmed, then routed. President McKay's portrait now hangs in the lobby of the Pioneer Memorial Theater on the University of Utah campus.[17]

The board also provided a stage where secretaries of state and attorneys general could court public attention and impose policy. In the late 1970s, as Americans were debating the Equal Rights Amendment, professional organizations of nurses and social workers said they would not hold conventions in states, such as Utah, that refused to ratify the amendment. The attorney general Robert Hansen and secretary of state David Monson, both Republicans,

---

16. Snow, 121–24; *Bateman v. Board of Examiners*, 7 Utah 2d 221, 322 P. 2d 381 (1958); *University of Utah v. Board of Examiners*, 4 Utah 2d 408, 295 P. 2d 348 (1956).

17. Hodson, *Crisis on Campus*, 196–222.

announced a counter boycott: the Board of Examiners would not pay for state workers to attend conventions of any organizations boycotting Utah. Democratic governor Scott Matheson was outvoted and chagrined.[18]

There was one constant: political victories brought political spoils. When Democrats first came to power in 1917, they quadrupled the state debt to build roads. The Democratic legislature abolished the State Road Commission and substituted a new commission of five statewide elected officials, all of them Democrats. Road building stopped for a year while the new commission fired road agents, highway engineers, and workers and hired Democrats in their stead. Commissioners then made up for lost time by promoting "practical road building," unhampered by "a purely technical engineering standpoint." But they discovered that those roads failed to meet federal specifications, and the Federal Bureau of Public Highways refused to pay matching grants, throwing Utah into a fiscal crisis that was relieved only by more borrowing in the subsequent Republican administration of Governor Mabey. Even as they borrowed to fund Democratic road debts, Republicans imitated the Democrats by abolishing the road commission and replacing it with another. Once more road building stopped, this time because Utah had no money, and Republicans used the pause to fire highway workers and hire Republicans. Construction resumed mostly because of generous new subsidies from Washington.[19]

In 1939 there were at least twelve separate ways to be hired by state government. Different agencies paid much different wages for the same work. Professor Frank Jonas wrote in 1940 that "the chief source of revenue in the Democratic Party is the 1 to 5 percent of the salaries of state employees collected each month by a party agent." A worker who refused to pay could be fired, and there was no recourse in law.

---

18. Roger Pusey, "Board Says Boycott," *Deseret News*, Mar. 23, 1978.
19. *Biennial Report of the State Auditor*, 57; Knowlton, *History of Highway Development*, 168–79, 195–207, 220–29.

The federal government forced Utah to adopt some merit protection. Congress said grants for health, unemployment, and welfare could go only to agencies under merit. So in 1937 and 1939, Utah enacted a merit system for only those three departments. A merit system meant hiring based on established criteria so that the best qualified worker was picked over the politician's friend. Raises and promotions were based on rules and performance, not the politician's choice. Workers could be fired only for cause. Reformers liked merit, but party leaders did not, and Utah lagged. A 1961 study showed that 65 percent of state employees nationwide worked in a merit system, but only 23 percent in Utah. After the 1958 election, federal officials charged that three Republican state road supervisors had asked employees for a percentage of their pay as a Republican donation. "Employees may not deserve pay raises if we don't contribute to the Republican Party," one supervisor said. The federal Civil Service Commission demanded that Utah fire the three supervisors, which Republican governor George Dewey Clyde refused to do. Washington then fined Utah $42,000, twice the combined annual salary of the three, and deducted the money from Utah's federal highway grant. Utah sued in federal court and lost. Utah's highway historian Ezra C. Knowlton said that road workers had been pressured to pay political money for as long as there had been state roads. "It was covered up as much as possible," he wrote.[20]

Utah's constitution and supreme court blocked reform. A law passed in 1963 took the Finance Department from the Board of Examiners and made it answerable to the governor. Secretary of State Lamont Toronto sued to preserve examiners' power. He hired outside counsel, while the attorney general's office defended the law. But the attorney general sat on the Board of Examiners. Though the lawyers

---

20. Knowlton, 660–62; Report of the Investigating Committee of Utah Government Units, 25; Jonas, "Utah: Sagebrush Democracy," 31; *State of Utah et al. v. United States*, 286 F.2nd 30 (10th Cir. 1961); cert. denied, 366 U.S. 918; also Gordon et al., *Personnel Management*, 133.

opposed each other in court, the interests of both would be best served if the law were declared unconstitutional, as, in fact, it was.[21]

Since statehood, public officials, including state treasurers, had deposited public money in select banks at no interest. Grateful bankers had given these officials a "nominal job" and salary while they still held office. In the administration of Governor William Spry, the treasurer made large interest-free deposits in a bank where the governor was a director. Democrats joked of *Sprynancial* concerns, but the governor still won reelection. Later banks confined their gratitude to campaign contributions and jobs only after a treasurer had left office, but state money was still deposited at no interest. In 1965 the legislature created a Money Management Council to improve earnings. Treasurer Lee Allen sued, saying the council usurped his duties. Utah's supreme court agreed. The justices reasoned that the treasurer had taken care of funds in territorial times, and territorial practices were tacitly adopted by the state constitution, so the money management council was unconstitutional.[22]

Encouraged by the treasurer's victory, state auditor Sherman Preece sued to take back his power to write checks, which had been given by law to the Finance Department. Again the court noted that the auditor had issued checks in territorial days, and therefore ruled the law assigning the task to the finance department was unconstitutional.[23] Since the Maw reforms in 1941, the auditor had performed post audits, that is, he checked to see that records were properly kept and expenditures were properly made. The supreme court's decision meant that the auditor issued checks then audited his own accounts to make sure he had not stolen any money.

Like Herbert Maw twenty-four years before, Democrat Cal

---

21. *Toronto v. Clyde*, 15 Utah 2d 403, 393 P. 2d 795 (1964).

22. "How Two Officials Switch State Jobs," "Jaycee Sights on Idle Funds," *Deseret News*, Dec. 29, 1948, May 16, 1968; *Allen v. Rampton*, 23 Utah 2d 336, 463 P. 2d 7 (1969). Governor John Cutler mentioned favors from bankers in his State of the State address, *Journal of the House of Representatives*, 1905, 16. Stauffer, "Utah Politics," 58.

23. *Preece v. Rampton*, 27 Utah 2d 56, 492 P. 2d 1355 (1972).

Rampton ran for governor on the promise of government reorganization. At his request in 1965, lawmakers created the "Little Hoover Commission" to propose a plan. A consultant said the government had grown to 156 separate agencies. Like Maw, Rampton asked lawmakers to combine the agencies into eleven "super departments." Legislators created three departments, but left the rest in sprawl. The commission also recommended the abolition of administrative commissions, which headed 120 of 156 of state agencies. The governor should be able to hire and fire agency heads, the commission said. Lawmakers rejected that suggestion and created additional commissions for the super departments, on top of the commissions that directed the agencies.[24]

The Little Hoover Commission also recommended broad constitutional changes. Legislators responded by proposing seven amendments for a vote of the people in 1966, including one to abolish the Board of Examiners. Legislators went further and added to the ballot a vote to call a convention to address all the troubles at once by drafting a new constitution. The secretary of state and attorney general fought to save the Board of Examiners. Attorney general Phil Hansen explained that the examiners were like the First Presidency of the Church of Jesus Christ of Latter-day Saints, three men given authority to guide matters aright. The amendment to abolish the Board of Examiners failed by a two-to-one margin, and every other proposed constitutional amendment was also voted down. The call for a constitutional convention failed six-to-one, making it one of the biggest defeats ever for a ballot proposition.[25]

Utah seemed incorrigible, mired by habit, constitution, and popular preferences, spoils, and disorder. But over the next forty years, Utah gradually changed its constitution and ways of government.

---

24. Foremaster, "Little Hoover Commission," 30–31. The original Hoover Commission created by US president Harry S. Truman in 1947 reorganized the executive branch of the federal government.

25. Snow, "Triumvirate Rule," 185; "All Propositions Soundly Defeated," *Deseret News*, Nov. 9, 1966.

After the 1966 defeat, lawmakers created a Constitutional Revision Commission to study government and suggest constitutional amendments. Voters approved a "gateway amendment" allowing whole articles to be changed at once. The commission then rewrote the legislative, executive, judicial, education, taxation, and corporate articles, and proposed many small changes. Both lawmakers and voters approved most of their work, and government quietly became more like the reformist ideal.

Legislative limits were eased first. Lawmakers met every year instead of every other year. A 1972 amendment allowed committees and professional staff to operate between sessions, and a legislative auditor's office was created to investigate government at legislators' direction. Executive amendments replaced the secretary of state with a lieutenant governor, who runs in tandem with the governor and becomes part of his administration. The duties of the auditor and treasurer were made subject to law. Finally, the Board of Examiners was abolished.[26]

Constitutional change, especially continuity in the legislature, led to statutory changes that ended government by commission. Early legislatures met only once every two years, so they were not at the capitol enough to oversee government. Commissions palliated an absentee legislature. They held public meetings, in contrast to the governor's private meetings with advisers. Commissioners' terms of office were different from the governor's, and they were hard to fire, so if they chose, they could protect workers from being replaced for political spoils. But after the legislature became a year-round presence, legislators could oversee departments themselves. Department heads came to interim meetings and talked with legislative committees. Legislators no longer wanted a commission to hold separate meetings and to make competing policies. From the 1960s through the 1990s, lawmakers passed a dozen bills reorganizing one

---

26. On the amendments, see White, *Utah State Constitution*. The reduced responsibilities of the Board of Examiners were spelled out in 1980, and the subdued board was quietly abolished by another constitutional amendment twelve years later.

department at a time, grouping agencies by function and replacing the administrative commissions with executive directors responsible to the governor.[27]

Gradually Utah ended spoils. Republican governor George Dewey Clyde, embarrassed by the charge of taking money from workers for his party, asked for a merit law near the end of his term. Democrats, who controlled the legislature, suspected Clyde of wanting to make his Republican hires permanent, so they refused to pass his bill. Clyde then imposed a merit system by executive order. When Democrat Cal Rampton won the next election, he did not overturn Clyde's order, to the disgust of Democratic party leaders. Instead, the legislature replaced Clyde's order with a statute that kept merit but exempted some 2,000 jobs near the bottom of the pay-scale, saving those for spoils. Not until 1979 did Utah clearly adopt merit principles into law and extend protection to all state workers.[28]

In a series of acts beginning in 1947 and extending to the Revenue Procedures Act of 1992, lawmakers took control of state revenue and spending. After statutory and constitutional changes were approved, they created a Money Management Council to invest idle funds for the best, safest return.

Utah's original constitution, courts, statues, and political practices reinforced each other in interlocking barriers to change. But when reforms were finally made, they had an effect larger than the sum of the individual measures. Utah's government changed its style. Once a government of spoils, brawls, and deals, it took on proper forms and orderly habits, and won national recognition for good

---

27. The departments were Natural Resources, 1969; Transportation, 1975; Agriculture, 1979; Health, 1981; Commerce, 1983; Corrections, 1985; Human Services, 1988; Environmental Quality, 1991; and Workforce Services, 1997. The Liquor Commission, Higher Education, Public Education, and Tax Commission continue to be controlled by boards, and Public Safety is led by a commissioner who serves a fixed term.

28. Jonas, "Utah: The Different State," 290–91; "Personnel Management Act," *Laws of Utah, 1979*, chapter 139. Robert Huefner, an emeritus professor of political science at the University of Utah, was a Rampton staffer. He remembers Democratic Party leaders berating Rampton because he had not hired enough Democrats.

management.[29] The alteration was gradual, quiet, and muddling, with no goals announced or agenda items checked off. Even scholars and people in government have all but forgotten Utah's old ways and scarcely realize how different state government has become.

29. Stebbins and Comen, "The Best and Worst Run States," *Wall Street 24/7*, Dec. 6, 2017, available at 247wallst.com; "Grading the States 2008 Report," *PEW*, www. pewtrusts.org; "Money Management Act" and "Revenue Procedures and Control Act," *Laws of Utah*, 1974, 1992, chaps. 27, 259.

14

COURTS AND PUBLIC LAW

JUDICIAL ADMINISTRATION

Utah's judiciary was a "put-down, depressed" branch of government in 1973 when Richard Peay became the first state judicial administrator. The judges' salaries were the lowest in the nation. The state trial courts, called district courts, depended on counties for courtrooms and clerks, and some of them met in shabby facilities with unqualified staff. Procedural rules differed from court to court. Information and statistics were haphazard. Jurisdictional boundaries overlapped in geographical disorder. The judiciary lacked staff to prepare budgets, make plans, or advocate for itself. Peay became part of a reform movement to improve justice and "enhance the status of the judiciary,"[1] two goals scarcely distinguishable in the judicial mind.

The first target of reformers was the justice of the peace (JP), a court descended from medieval England, adopted in Utah Territory, established in the state constitution, and disdained by bench and bar. Justices of the peace were not lawyers and were limited to small cases They rose to the bench by election in the locality they served. In 1989 twenty-five of Utah's 140 JPs had not graduated from high school. They kept no court records, so no litigant could appeal based on the record. But a defendant had a right to a new trial in district

---

1. May, *Utah Judicial Council*, 7–12.

court if requested, though few such requests were made. The JPs provided their own courtrooms, often their own homes. Many of them made themselves available at all hours, so if a traveler got a speeding ticket at night, an officer could bring him to the magistrate, who would get out of bed, hear the case at his kitchen table, collect bail, and send the traveler on his way. Justices accommodated because they were paid fees instead of salaries. In 1960 a JP got ten cents for filing a document, fifty cents for a final decision, and three dollars for conducting a trial. A few made a lot of money. One earned $66,000 in 1974, which was more than the salary of a Utah Supreme Court justice. To earn so much, a JP had to win the favor of law officers, who brought defendants to the justice of their choice—often a strict judge, likely to convict and impose a high fine.[2] Utah leaders acknowledged the JP conflict but excused it, saying that a dissatisfied defendant could always ask for a new trial.

In 1901 legislators allowed cities to replace JPs with city courts, more for money than for justice; the city that supported the court kept the fines. City judges were attorneys who sat in proper courtrooms, but like JPs their impartiality was suspect. They were appointed by politicians who wanted the court to generate money. A judge who did not bring in enough revenue might be replaced by someone who did. Amid loud claims of improving justice, Utah replaced all twenty-five city judges with thirty-three circuit court judges who were attorneys, paid a salary by the state, and conducted courts of record. Circuit court fines were shared by city and state: 40 percent to the city if the defendant had broken a state law, 70 percent to the city if the defendant had broken a city ordinance. Cedar City and Saint George enacted the entire state misdemeanor and traffic codes as

2. "Utah Details Fees" and "JP in Utah," "County Attorneys Differ," "Why Utah Should Improve" editorial, *Deseret News*, Jan. 11, 23, 1960, Mar. 11, 1975; "Senate Votes," *Salt Lake Tribune*, Jan. 26, 1989; Utah Const. Art. VIII, § 8 (repealed in 1984). In 1997, Utah justice courts heard about 300,000 cases, and in only 501 instances did defendants request a new trial (Bates, "Exploring Justice Courts," 791). An income of $66,000 in 1974 would be over $300,000 today.

city ordinances so they could keep 70 percent of all fines.[3] In 1996, Utah quietly abandoned circuit courts and turned their officiators into district judges. Circuit courts had been limited to small cases. Turning them into district courts eased judicial administration and the need to hire more judges. Traffic and other small cases were returned to JPs and local courts, both renamed "justice courts," all of them sponsored by a city or county, which kept money from the fines. Though limited to small cases, justice courts carry the caseload. In 2008 they heard 587,000 of 860,000 matters brought before the state's courts, about 70 percent of all cases.

Justice courts extract money from squalor. The defendants typically have no lawyers, and prosecutors are able to bend the rules. Enforcement is haphazard. As of June 2018, justice courts had 61,455 outstanding warrants, many for people who had failed to appear in court. These fugitives are often not pursued. Some of them are eventually caught violating traffic laws or in other encounters with police, but others escape. Even at that, justice courts brought in $71.2 million in 2017. For some local governments, fines were their second largest revenue source after property taxes. In a memorandum, Salt Lake City's chief administrative officer praised the city courts for their 97 percent conviction rate and for the money they brought to the city. Some justice court judges were bullies, and critics charge that the courts pursue money as much as justice.[4]

Lawyers and judges studied justice courts and made recommendations, and the legislature enacted some of them. The power to hire and fire judges was taken from local politicians. Instead, justices are chosen by committees to six-year terms, followed by a

3. Vance Bishop, "History of the Judicial System in Utah," *Annual Report: Utah Courts*, 1977–78, 3; Dunn, *Performance Audit*, 17, 27.

4. Christine M. Durham, "State of the Judiciary," Jan. 21, 2008, digitallibrary.utah.gov.; "Fugitives," "The Trials," *Deseret News*, July 6, 1999, Aug. 30, 2011; "Nickeled and Dimed," *City Weekly*, May 27, 2010; "Performance Measures," 2017–18, *Utah Courts*, www.utcourts.gov; Newton et al., "No Justice," *UtahOnLaw*, 2012, dc.law.utah.edu"; Mike Martinez, "Utah's Justice Court," *Utah Bar Journal*, Mar./Apr. 2009, 27.

retention election without an opponent; voters choose whether to keep a sitting judge or fire him and have the committee pick a new one. Cameras were installed to make a record of proceedings. Justice courts were brought under the supervision of the Utah Judicial Council. Almost all justices are now lawyers.[5]

While reform was imposed on justices of the peace from without, judges themselves led the reform of other courts. Juvenile courts reformed first. They were created by the legislature in 1907 and placed in the State Welfare Department in Governor Maw's 1941 reorganization. While the pay of state judges was low, the pay of juvenile judges was even lower. They organized and asked the legislature to take them out of the Welfare Department and put them in the judiciary. Welfare officials objected, saying the move would turn juvenile judges toward legalism and away from sympathy for children, and lawmakers narrowly rejected the move. Afterward, welfare officials refused to reappoint juvenile judges until they promised they would not go to the legislature again. But then juvenile judge Regnal Garff sentenced a boy to the Industrial School and privately suggested to the defense attorney that he might appeal, arguing that the juvenile courts lacked judicial power because they were not part of the judicial branch. The appeal was made, and the Utah Supreme Court agreed, ruling that all courts must be in the judiciary. In 1965 the legislature complied and moved the juvenile courts. Free at last, juvenile court judges formed their own judicial court with a council of judges that made administrative decisions and uniform rules of procedure.[6]

The example of a unified, self-governing court appealed to other judges who wanted a judicial council for all courts and administrators to see to their judicial needs. Not all judges agreed. Supreme court justice A. H. Ellett said that he could administer the courts

---

5. *Salt Lake Criminal Justice System Assessment,* 6.3–.8; "Justice Court Study Committee Interim Report," Dec. 1997, www.utcourts.gov; S.B. 72, 2008 General Session; S.B. 200, 2011 General Session; H.B. 160, 2016 General Session.

6. Bradley, "Reclamation of Young Citizens"; *In Re Woodward,* 14 Utah 2d 336, 384 P. 2d 110 (1963); Garff, "Emancipation of the Juvenile Court," 269, 275n8.

with "a telephone on a Saturday afternoon." Most of his colleagues on the high court agreed. District judges took their plan to the legislature anyway and obtained a council and administrator for district and city courts. The supreme court remained aloof, juvenile courts had their existing council, and JPs were not invited. From 1973 to 1992, the Judicial Council formed a dozen committees, commissions, and task forces to suggest improvements. Utahns rewrote the judicial article of the constitution; juvenile courts, justice courts, and the supreme court were all brought into the judicial council; a new court of appeals was formed; court boundaries were regularized; procedures were enacted for disciplining judges; statistics were compiled, and uniform rules of practice promulgated.[7] The council and administrator lobbied for better salaries, benefits, and tenure.

Utah judges began as a political afterthought, chosen and dismissed on party and religious affiliation. Until 1952 district judges and supreme court justices were nominated by political parties and elected by voters. Utah originally had three supreme court justices who served staggered six-year terms, so that one was elected every two years in the general election. Until 1916 parties balanced their tickets between Latter-day Saints and non-Mormons. Every nominee for governor was a Latter-day Saint, and for balance every supreme court nominee was non-Mormon, so until 1917 every Utah Supreme Court justice was non-Mormon.

In 1917 when Democrats took power for the first time, legislators enlarged the court from three to five justices and lengthened their terms from six to ten years, so that one justice would still run for office every two years. It took Governor Simon Bamberger "approximately thirty seconds" to sign the bill and appoint two Democrats to the court, the *Salt Lake Tribune* reported. One of the new appointees, Samuel Thurman, was the first LDS justice. A Democrat won election in 1916, so the court had a Democratic majority for the first time. After Jewish Simon Bamberger was elected governor, religious

7. May, *Utah Judicial Council*, 3, 5.

balance fell from fashion. Twelve of the next sixteen supreme court justices were Latter-day Saints. Party affiliation, however, remained decisive. From 1895 to 1950, every one of thirty justices who won elections came from the party that won the House of Representatives that year.[8] Party-line voting staffed Utah's highest court.

Beginning in 1950, Utah moved in steps to retention elections, so judges ran unopposed and voters decided to retain or dismiss them. Few ever lost—only one supreme court justice, and that was after police said they had caught him in a motel with a prostitute. Some legislators, envious of the ease of judicial reelection, complained that the judges were not responsible to the people. But Utah has avoided the trouble that judicial elections bring in other states where judges' campaign donors appear before them and justice appears purchased.[9]

The court administrators lobbied for judges, and salaries rose from lowest in the nation to just below the national average. Twenty-five new court houses were built from 1986 to 1998. Still, the judicial branch remains lean. In 2010, Utah had the second-fewest judges for its population of any state.

Democratic governor Scott Matheson (1977–1985) changed Utah's supreme court. He appointed more justices than any other Utah governor. His appointees changed constitutional law and sought a larger voice for courts in Utah government.[10]

ASSERTING UTAH'S CONSTITUTION

Much of the constitutional law that limits and guides Utah government came from federal judges applying the US Constitution and federal procedures. Even in state cases, Utah lawyers often argue and

---

8. Alley Jr., "Samuel R. Thurman," 233–34; Julien, "Utah Supreme Court," 280. In 1948 the two parties elected equal numbers of representatives. The Democratic nominee won the justice seat.

9. May, *Utah Judicial Council*, 8; "Callister Should Resign" editorial, *Deseret News*, May 27, 1965 (the justice was not convicted); Robert Barnes, "Court Ties Campaign Largess to Judicial Bias," *Washington Post*, Jun 9, 2009.

10. Moncrief and Squire, *Why States Matter*, 70; Crockett, "Remembering Justice A. H. Ellett," 256–57.

Utah Justices A. H. Ellett (1967–79) and Christine Durham (1982–2017) were of a different type. Ellett called himself a "redneck judge," and used salty language that embarrassed his colleagues. Durham, in contrast, was decorous and church-going—the first woman on the court. She received national honors as she sought to reform and enlarge the state supreme court's role in Utah policy making. *Utah State Historical Society*

judges decide on the basis of the federal constitution. Utah's constitution is but raggedly clothed in precedent and learned comment. For a time some state supreme court justices sought to "strengthen Utah's Constitution." Chief Justice Christine Durham called for a "rich and complex body of state constitutional law," and she championed Utah's basic law from the bench and in scholarly articles.[11] To strengthen a constitution is to empower a court. A rich and complex body of constitutional law provides justices with a basis to critique and modify policy decisions made by other branches. But Republican governors and legislators thought Utah had more than enough guidance from judges and that the space remaining after federal judicial enclosures

---

11. See Gardner, *Interpreting State Constitutions*; Marsden, "Utah Supreme Court"; State v. Earl, 716 P. 2d 803 (1986); Durham, "Employing the Utah Constitution."

should be saved for popular self-government through elected repre-sentatives. Strengthening Utah's Constitution had small success.

Efforts to strengthen state constitutions rose from the history of federal constitutional law. Until the 1920s the Bill of Rights did not apply to the states, which saw to the rights of their own citizens. Then, as part of the Rights Revolution, the US court imposed parts of the Bill of Rights nationally, to the dismay of legislatures, to reform of public morality and to vindicate individual rights. Beginning in the 1950s, justices developed a new model of court leadership. Jus-tices found a new constitutional interpretation, sometimes opposed by a majority of Americans. At first only the power of law compelled obedience from some citizens, but over time people got used to the new judge-made ways and embraced the wisdom of court. The court was said to be the schoolmaster to the republic, teaching Americans new morals with respect to race and sex, women and gays, and the meaning of justice.[12] The justices applied the new model to perfec-tion in civil rights cases, which brought prestige to the court and discredit to states' stewardship of civil rights. The Supreme Court also led America on abortion, criminal rights, equality for gays, por-nography, and cases involving religious rights.

As they followed the Supreme Court, federal judges changed Utah on abortion, pornography, criminal rights, gay rights, and religion; fed-eral courts ruled in ways Utahns would not have chosen. The justices also mandated reapportionment of legislative and congressional dis-tricts nationwide. In Utah federal courts ended cable TV censorship, enabled teens to get birth control without telling their parents, devised a detailed code for Latter-day Saint seminaries in schools, banned prayer in public schools and at graduations, and overturned the rules for the Church-owned Main Street Plaza. Federal cases under federal statues forced schools to accept gay student clubs; child protection ser-vices were for a time placed under a special court-appointed committee; judges liberalized welfare rules; the Utah State Prison was ordered to

12. Bickel, *Least Dangerous Branch*; Franklin and Kosaki, "Republican Schoolmaster."

provide a sweat lodge for Native American inmates and a diagnostic unit for the mentally ill; state road projects were delayed; and federal courts decided public land issues.[13] At times Utah's effective political opposition seemed less the minority Democrats than groups such as the American Civil Liberties Union, Planned Parenthood, Sierra Club, Society of Separationists, and Southern Utah Wilderness Alliance, which brought federal law suits to overturn state government decisions.

Conservatives nationwide disagreed with federal judicial leadership, contested judicial appointments, and slowed court-led change. An invitation then went to state courts to employ their own constitutions to advance rights. The invitation was one-directional. State courts could enhance protections of rights, for instance, on abortion or pornography, but could not diminish federal protections.[14] Beginning in the 1980s, Utah made modest steps toward its own independent protection of rights, starting with the right of police to conduct searches in the case of *State v. Larocco*.

Phillip Larocco came to State Auto, Salt Lake City, in 1981, saying he wanted to buy a Mustang. He took a Mach I for a test drive and never returned. Dave Luce, the salesman who let Larocco take the car, later left State Auto for Valley Ford, where four years later he again saw Larocco asking to test drive another Mustang. When the police were contacted, detective Linda Robison went to Larocco's house, saw the Mach I parked on the street, opened the car's unlocked door, and found the vehicle identification number on the inside door frame. Larocco was arrested, charged, and convicted by a jury. He had recently been released from prison for test driving a truck and never bringing it back.[15]

---

13. *Petuskey v. Clyde*, 234 F. Supp 960 (D. Utah 1964); *Linnet et al. v. Wimmer et al.*, 662 F. 2d 1349 (10th Cir. 1981); *David C. et al. v. Leavitt*, 242 F. 3d 1206 (10th Cir. 2001); *Utahns for Better Transportation v. U.S. Department of Transportation*, 305 F. 3d 1152 (10th Cir. 2002); also Sillitoe, *Friendly Fire*, 90–93, 192–99.

14. Brennan, "State Constitutions," 491, 495; *Right to Choose v. Byrne*, 450 A. 2d 925 (New Jersey 1982); *State v. Henry*, 732 P. 2d 9 (Oregon 1987).

15. I have followed the account in Cassell, "Mysterious Creation of Search and Seizure," 751; also *State v. Larocco*, 665 P. 2d 1272 (Utah 1983).

On appeal to the Utah Supreme Court, Larocco's lawyer noted that detective Robison had not obtained a warrant. The US Supreme Court allowed the search of a car for identification. Utah's constitution (art. I, § 14) is almost the same on searches as the US Constitution, but Utah justices ruled that the same words had a different meaning in Utah and required a warrant unless there was a threat of danger or of evidence being destroyed. Larocco went free.

To give independent meaning to Utah's constitution, the Utah court freed other criminals too. Two owners of a security firm who successfully bribed an employee of Utah Power and Light were convicted of anti-trust violations and racketeering. The evidence against them came partly from their bank accounts, which federal law allowed the police to search. But Utah's justices cited *Larocco* and overturned the convictions.[16]

The Utah constitution did provide independent guidance in public prayer cases. A staffer for the Salt Lake City Council recruited people of various faiths to pray at council meetings. The federal constitution allows such prayers, but article I, paragraph 4, of the Utah State Constitution reads, "No public money or property shall be appropriated for or applied to any religious worship, exercise or instruction." The Society of Separationists argued in a law suit that paying a staffer to arrange for prayers applied money for religious worship. They won in district court, and the city appealed to the Utah Supreme Court. While the court deliberated, Republican legislators said that even if the court ruled for prayer, the separationists would come back to stop schoolchildren from singing Christmas carols or prevent legislators from praying, or imposed some other restriction on faith. They convened a Religious Liberties Committee that proposed nine amendments to remove guarantees of church–state

---

16. *State v. Larocco*, 794 P. 2d 460 (Utah 1990); *State v. Thompson*, 810 P. 2d 415 (Utah 1991); cf. *New York v. Class*, 475 U.S. 106 (1986); *United States v. Miller*, 425 U.S. 435 (1976); *State v. Thompson*, 751 P. 2d 805 (Utah Ct. App. 1988); *In Re Criminal Investigation*, 754 P. 2d 633 (Utah 1988); *State v. Fletcher* 751 P. 2d 822 (Utah Ct. App. 1988).

separation put in the Utah constitution to prevent Latter-day Saint control of the government. The Republicans said they were not seeking to enlarge Church power, only to secure the traditional place of religion in public life. The amendments narrowly failed to get the required two-thirds majority in the legislature, as Democrats voted as a bloc to put them off until the court ruled. The court ruled for prayer, and Justice Michael Zimmerman spent fifty-two pages reassuring legislators that public religion was safe in Utah, as long as all beliefs were treated equally. Pleased with the opinion, legislators abandoned their constitutional amendments.[17]

Citing the rule that beliefs must be treated equally, Tom Snyder, of the Society of Separationists, asked to pray at a Salt Lake City Council meeting and submitted his prayer in advance. "God, if there is a God," it read, give officials wisdom to "never again perform demeaning religious ceremonies," and the prayer continued at length. Rather than listen to Snyder, council members voted to stop praying. Thus, although Snyder was an atheist, his prayer was answered.

Next he asked to pray at the Murray City Council meeting. When Murray refused to allow the prayer, he sued in federal court, and appealed to the US Supreme Court, losing all the way. Federal judges said Snyder's prayer was "more like a political harangue." He then took his case to Utah state courts. "One man's political harangue is another man's prayer," supreme court justice Leonard Russon said as he ruled that governments may not choose prayers on the basis on content.[18] Rather than listen to Snyder, Murray City also stopped praying. In the two prayer cases, the Utah Supreme Court calmed the raging legislature, found a stance independent of

---

17. "S. L. Council Sued," "Two Amendments," "Prayer Amendment," "Utah Supreme Court," *Deseret News*, Sept. 27, 1991, Feb. 16, Mar. 3, Dec. 17, 1993; Kouris, "Kyrie Elaison: A Constitutional Amendment"; Smith, "Be No More Children"; *Marsh v. Chambers*, 463 U.S. 783 (1983); *Society of Separationists v. Whitehead*, 870 P. 2d 916 (Utah 1993)

18. Brooke Adams, "S. L. Council," *Deseret News*, Feb. 9, 1994; *Snyder v. Murray City Corp.*, 124 F. 3d 1349 (10th Cir. 1997), 159 F. 3d 1227 (10th Cir. 1998); *Snyder v. Murray City Corp.*, 73 P. 3d 325 (Utah 2003).

the US Constitution, allowed prayer at public meetings, but kept the majority from excluding others.

An example of the rise and fall of a state constitutional assertion concerned tort law. The legislature imposed limits on suits brought by injured people against the government, building contractors, doctors, and manufacturers. Democratic supreme court justices appointed by Governor Matheson invoked Utah constitutional rights against those limits. But the constitutional assertion faded away as Republican governors appointed justices who were more inclined to follow the Republican legislature. The legal limits on law suits began in 1965, with the Utah Governmental Immunity Act. Soon thereafter, builders, contractors, and architects persuaded the legislature to limit suits against them as well. Doctors won the Utah Malpractice Act in 1976, and Utah passed America's first product liability statute in 1977, including a statute of repose ending a manufacturer's liability six years after a product was sold.[19]

Matheson appointees began knocking down the legislative limits when they overturned the statute of repose in 1985. Alan Berry died in a plane crash, and the Beechcraft Bonanza he was in was twenty-three years old, well beyond the statute of repose. But when Berry's widow sued the manufacturer, Justice Daniel Stewart cited Utah's Declaration of Rights (Art. I, § 11): "All courts shall be open, and every person, for an injury done to him in his person, property, or reputation, shall have remedy by due course of law." The statute of repose had unconstitutionally closed the courts to Mrs. Berry, Stewart ruled as he struck it down. In subsequent cases, the court cited *Berry v. Beech* and overturned time limits, damage caps, and immunities for builders, architects, doctors, hospitals, and government. Judges cited the "open-courts doctrine" to invalidate a three-month time limit on *habeas corpus* petitions by Utah prisoners as well. Almost all the votes for the open courts doctrine came from Matheson appointees. But

19. I follow Roberts and Shaw, "What is Left"; Magleby, "Utah's Medical Malpractice"; Carma Wadley, "Utah Copes," *Deseret News*, July 26, 1977.

after Matheson left office, Utah had only Republican governors. Justices they appointed said that courts were, in fact, open. Anyone could bring suit, but litigants and judges must follow the law as written by the legislature. As Republican appointees became the majority, the court abandoned the open-courts doctrine. For example, five-year-old Athan Montgomery came to court in 2005 with brain damage, seizures, and trouble balancing, all caused by obstetrician Gregory Drezga, who had fractured his skull at birth. The jury awarded Athan $2.7 million, but the judge cut the amount to $1 million in accordance with the Utah malpractice statute. Three justices appointed by Governor Mike Leavitt upheld the reduced damages. Chief Justice Christine Durham, the last Matheson appointee, wrote a sharp dissent. Hardly anyone but judges, scholars, and tort lawyers noticed the rise and fall of the open-courts doctrine.[20] If any governors knew of the issue, they never mentioned it in any prominent way. Yet in the ordinary course of government, governors found appointees with congenial views, and over decades justices produced a constitutional assertion and its demise.

To assert a constitution, a court needs "independence," that is, enough public support so that politicians cannot cow the justices. The US Supreme Court has independence, but Utah's court has been pressured by the legislature, as happened in Judge David Young's case. In 1994 a twelve-year-old brought a "rusty, trigger-less gun" to the Treasure Mountain Middle School in Park City. District officials invoked their "zero tolerance" policy and expelled him for the rest of the school year. When his family sued, judge David Young issued a temporary restraining order allowing the boy back in class during litigation. The school year ended before the case was decided. Then school superintendent Don Fiedler

---

20. See *Berry v. Beech Aircraft*, 717 P. 2d 670 (Utah 1985); *Currier v. Holden*, 862 P. 2d 1357 (Utah Ct. App. 1993); Justice Michael Wilkins dissent in *Laney v. Fairview; Judd v. Drezga*, 103 P. 3d 135 (Utah 2004); also Verbica, "Medical Malpractice"; Weinacker, "Judd and Jury." Matheson appointees who provided the votes for open courts are Gordon Hall, Richard Howe, Daniel Stewart, Christine Durham, and Michael Zimmerman.

said publicly he might punish the boy when school began again in the fall. Young called the school-district lawyer and threatened to award lawyer's fees to the plaintiff if punishment were reimposed. The boy escaped punishment, but the superintendent accused Young of "direct extortion" and filed a complaint with the Judicial Conduct Commission. A panel of six commissioners recommended that the Supreme Court reprimand the judge. At the Supreme Court, Young's lawyer pointed to Article V, Section 1, of the Utah constitution that divides government into legislative, executive, and judicial branches, and says that "no person charged with exercise of powers properly belonging to one of these departments, shall exercise any functions appertaining to either of the others." Three legislators had sat on the Judicial Conduct panel in Judge Young's case. The justices ruled unanimously that that violated the separation of powers, so they refused to reprimand Judge Young. The decision enraged legislators. They want power to check judges. The constitution empowers legislators to remove a judge by impeachment or address, but lawmakers have never attempted either cumbersome process. To impose workable discipline, a law in 1971, followed by a constitutional amendment in 1984, created the Judicial Conduct Commission with ten members, including two senators and two representatives. Legislators said banning them from the commission negated their power to check judicial abuse, and they plotted retaliation. "One thing we can do is start impeaching," said Representative Lamont Tyler. Legislators began to change their rules so that most impeachment work could be done by committee instead of by the whole House. They had a judge in mind, too: district judge Leslie Lewis. Some citizens had complained about her, and maybe legislators would try out their new process on judge Lewis.[21]

---

21. *In Re Inquiry Concerning a Judge, the Honorable David S. Young, District Judge*, 916 P. 2d 918 (Utah 1999); Kristen Moulton "Is a Move Afoot?" and Jerry Spangler and Bob Bernick, "Lawmakers Step toward New Rules," *Deseret News*, Aug. 22, Nov. 18, 1998.

Facing legislative anger, the supreme court backed down. At their own initiative, the court reversed itself and said that legislators could sit on the commission after all. Gracious in victory, lawmakers abandoned impeachment plans, and the supreme court reprimanded Judge Young.[22]

Religious freedom might seem a field for action by an independent Utah court. In contrast to the laconic First Amendment, Utah's constitution contains many clauses on religion. Moreover, the US Supreme Court no longer defends the free exercise of religion when in conflict with other laws. That leaves protection of religion for Utah justices if they want it, and some justices would like to be defenders of the faiths.[23] But a principled protection of religion entails protection of unpopular religion, and in Utah unpopular religion means polygamy. In recent decades Utah has only prosecuted polygamy as a secondary charge to sex with underage girls. In dealing with such cases, Utah justices have not protected religious liberty but rather stretched the law to punish polygamy, for example in Tom Green's case.

Green became a polygamist after he served an LDS mission and married a Latter-day Saint wife. When he took Beth Cook as a second spouse, his first wife divorced him, and the Church excommunicated him. Cook had a twelve-year-old daughter, Linda Kunz, from a previous polygamous marriage, and Green wanted to marry her as well. As the family traveled the western states selling magazine subscriptions, Green betrothed his stepdaughter in Nevada with her mother's consent. Tom, Beth, and Linda then went to Mexico, where Tom and Linda were married in a spiritual ceremony. She was thirteen and he thirty-seven. She gave birth after they returned to the United States.[24]

Bespectacled, balding, pot-bellied, and poor, Green still found

---

22. *In Re Young*, 961 P. 2d 918 (Utah 1998); *In Re Young*, 976 P. 2d 581 (Utah 1999). *In re Richard Worthen*, 926 P2d. 853 (1996), gives a history of judicial discipline.

23. Durham, "What Goes Around," 358–59; *Employment Div. v. Smith*, 494 U.S. 872 (1990); concurring opinion of Justice Durrant in *State v. Green*, 99 P. 3d 820 (Utah 2004).

24. Edward L. Carter, "Green Ordered to Stand Trial," *Deseret News*, June 30, 2000.

more wives: sisters Shirley and Leann Beagley and their mother, June Johnson; sisters Cari and Hannah Bjorkman; Allison Ryan; and Julie Dawn McKinley, all married Tom Green. In 1995 the whole family moved to Greenhaven, a cluster of mobile homes in the Juab County desert, far from anyone else. They schooled their twenty-five children themselves and held their own church services. They sold magazine subscriptions by telephone, but the wives and children also took about $100,000 in government assistance over several years. Green enlisted as a "soldier for religious freedom." He and his wives appeared on television shows to explain their religion.[25]

Juab County Attorney David Leavitt saw the Greens on *Dateline* and investigated. Birth certificates showed that Linda Kunz had sex before she was fourteen, rape under Utah law. He charged Green with rape of a child, five counts of bigamy, and one count of welfare fraud. Tapes of Green's TV appearances provided evidence. But Green had been sly. Before he married a new wife, he always divorced his current legal wife so that he was never legally married to more than one woman at a time. Equally sly, prosecutors said Green and Kunz, though divorced, had by living together remarried at common law, making the other marriages bigamous. The jury convicted.

The Utah Supreme Court complained that Green's lawyer had failed to properly brief the common-law-marriage issue. Utah law says that bigamy occurs only if the defendant knew he was legally married when he took the second wife. Chief Justice Durham said it was "at least unfair" to retroactively apply a civil statute in a criminal case and find that Green knew he was still married though he had divorced his other wives. But the brief was improper, so the conviction was upheld. As for child rape, no evidence proved sex outside Mexico, where Utah law does not reach. The court said Green's betrothal showed a conspiracy to rape. The opinion did not mention that the betrothal occurred in Nevada. Prosecutors argued that the

---

25. Judge Donald Eyre, Memorandum in decision *State v. Green*, July 10, 2000, case number 001600036; *Utah Supreme Court Briefs* v. 1770; Tenney, "Tom Green," 143.

Greens had been in Utah, and being in Utah after betrothal in Nevada extended Utah conspiracy law into Mexico. The justices did not accept that argument, but they could find no other explanation for their decision. Loath to let a child rapist go, the court ignored legal technicalities and just sent Tom Green to prison for six years.[26]

Four of his wives, including rape victim Linda Kunz, moved their children to Provo, lived in the same house together, and waited for their husband. Parole officers said Green should not be allowed to live with his family after his release. After all, he was sent to prison for living with them before. The state parole board, however, said it was their policy to encourage parolees to live with their families, and that included Tom Green. "We won't be doing bed checks," spokesman Jack Ford said. Prison failed to rehabilitate Green's polygamy, but it did cure his advocacy. On the advice of parole officers, he refused all interviews.

In another polygamy case, Utah Supreme Court justices admitted that they lacked sufficient independence to treat polygamy as an issue of constitutional rights. Rodney Holm was a police officer in the polygamist town of Hilldale when he married sixteen-year-old Ruth Stubbs as his third wife. She left polygamy and complained to authorities, who convicted Holm of sex with a minor and bigamy. He spent nine months in jail, with work release. At the supreme court, Justice Ronald Nehring wrote in a concurring opinion that the case "probes a particularly sensitive area of our state's identity." He had "not been alone," he wrote, "in speculating what the consequences might be were the highest court in the state of Utah to become the first in the nation to proclaim that polygamy enjoys constitutional protection." Nehring added, judges could not be deterred by public opinion.[27] He noted that Utah's constitution contains an ordinance that forever bans polygamy (art. III), and a bigamy statute makes it

---

26. *State v. Green*, 99 P. 3d 820 (Utah 2004); *State v. Green*, 108 P. 3d 710 (Utah 2005).
27. *Reynolds v. U.S.*, 98 U.S. 145.

a crime. Polygamy had not been protected even back when the US Supreme Court guaranteed freedom of religion.

But the laws against polygamy are old, and times have changed. When the anti-polygamy ordinance was adopted, adultery, fornication, pornography, sodomy, and abortion were crimes. The purpose of the law then was to uphold traditional morality and traditional families. Now all those formerly criminal acts are protected by the US Constitution. The purpose of the law now is to protect an individual's right to choose sexual conduct. Polygamy differs from legal sex only in that it involves religion and marriage. But Justice Nehring concluded that protecting polygamy from criminal prosecution would be "so much at odds with widely and deeply held cultural values that it would not only undermine the legitimacy of the ruling but call into question the legitimacy of the court."[28] In short, Utah justices saw the anomaly of polygamy prosecutions but lacked the independence to treat it as other sexual acts between consenting adults, even if they had believed that was what the constitution required.

Federal judge Clark Waddoups acted where state courts had not dared. Kody Brown and his wives, Meri, Janelle, Christine, and Robin, and seventeen children, starred in *Sister Wives*, a reality cable-television show. Utah County Attorney Jeff Buhman had said he would not prosecute otherwise law-abiding polygamists, but citizens complained, and his office opened a criminal case file. The Browns struck first and asked a federal court to rule that criminal laws against polygamy were unconstitutional. Buhman quickly issued a written statement reinstating his non-prosecution policy. Nonetheless, in 2013, Judge Waddoups struck down the state polygamy statute anyway. For thirty years Utah had prosecuted only "religious cohabitation," he wrote. The law punished polygamous cohabitants who claimed religious sanction but left other cohabitants alone. Polygamy is like adultery, the judge said, and the Utah Supreme Court last

---

28. See *Berg v. State*, 100 P. 3d 261 (Utah Ct. App. 2004); concurring opinion in *State v. Holm*, 137 P. 3d 726 (Utah 2006).

heard an adultery case in 1928. While conceding that his opinion broke precedent, he pointed to the US Supreme Court's reasoning when it struck down anti-sodomy laws. His reasoning in this case was similar, he said. Utah could refuse to license polygamous marriages but could not prosecute them as a crime. At the Tenth Circuit Court of Appeals, however, a three-judge panel overruled Waddoups. They said Buhman's non-prosecution statement should have ended the case.[29] But the judges added that any future polygamy prosecution might result in overturning the statute.

Everyone agrees that a high court should decide cases, but people argue about whether a court should redirect government and change society. The US Supreme Court has made decisions as important as any by Congress or the president, decisions that have changed America. Courts in other states have also changed policies and governments, but the Utah court has made no comparable decisions. The US court acts in a government divided between progressives and conservatives. When the court decides, neither side usually has a large enough majority to contest judicial leadership. In contrast, Utah has a large LDS-Republican majority that can amend the state constitution, threaten retaliatory impeachments, or pass mitigating statutes against judicial decisions. In addition, the duration of conservative power has produced a more conservative court that defers to the legislature. The US Supreme Court sets an example of judicial leadership that some justices in Utah sought to follow. But the Utah reaction against federal court decisions and Utah's conservative electorate and government have prevented the Utah court from emulating the national model.

---

29. John Schwartz, "Polygamy as Lifestyle Choice," *New York Times*, Jan. 8, 2014; *Brown v. Buhman*, 947 F. Supp. 2d 1170 (D. Utah 2013); *Brown v. Buhman*, 822 F. 3d 1151 (10th Cir. 2016); cert. denied, 137 S. Ct. 828 (2017); cf. *Lawrence v. Texas*, 539 U.S. 558 (2003).

15

BUDGETING, SPENDING, TAXING, REVOLTING

State budgets remind Utah politicians of family stories from their formative years. When he talked of state budgets, Governor Norman Bangerter told how his father taught him the homebuilding business and how to plan spending, control costs, and pay bank loans promptly. His successor, Mike Leavitt, often cited his farmer grandfather, who, when his neighbor bought farm equipment on credit, said, "We'll be here when he isn't," and time proved him right. In Utah government, fiscal discipline is an ancestral virtue.

Budget officials don't mention ancestors, but they like the word *discipline*. "Revenue estimates bring discipline to the process," one says. "There's a discipline issue. If you had a $7 billion dollar budget and you didn't say where the money goes, you'd have a kind of amorphous blob," another said. "You've got to have discipline," a third summed up.[1]

Taxing and spending are the chief business of state government. Budgets direct how money flows and have been made regularly since before statehood, always in dollars, so they are roughly comparable both over time and to other states. Budgets help outsiders, especially legislators, understand and influence government. This

---

1. My interviews with budget officers Leo Memmott and Lynn Ward of the governor's office and Mark Ward of Human Services.

chapter talks first of the state's budget values, especially discipline and balance; second, the budget process; third, how spending shows changes in the size and purpose of government; and fourth, an account of taxes, including Utah's tax revolt. Budgets show both change and enduring values, for in state government, where your treasure is, there will your heart be also.

Utah's constitution is one of forty that require a balanced budget (see Art. XIII, § 9). But the state is unusual in the care it takes to fend off deficit. Bond ratings show Utah's habitual discipline. Along with forty-four other states, Utah borrows funds by selling general obligation bonds. Three financial service companies regularly examine and report the creditworthiness of each state, and Utah is one of six states with only the highest bond ratings since 2000. In fact, Utah has had only top bond ratings since 1965.[2] A number of financial publications and studies have called Utah the most fiscally disciplined state.[3]

Disciplined budgeting reflects a policy choice that brings gains and losses. The losses are immediate: spending money makes politicians popular, and there is never enough money for everything they want to do. Fiscal discipline means that government chooses not to stretch itself or take risks, but to tax more or spend less to reduce the risk of red ink. Utah politicians and bureaucratic leaders embrace discipline on their own. Lobbyists and interest groups, who swarm about the budget, ask for more spending or lower taxes. Voters prefer a balanced budget, but that preference is abstract, supported by no immediate interest Yet Utah politicians believe governors and legislators should insist on balance, even against the inclinations of constituents and pleas of pressure groups. For Utah's governing

2. *Budget Processes in the States*, 33; "State Credit Ratings," *Ballotpedia*, ballotpedia. org; David Damschen, "Utah Maintains AAA Credit Rating," June 14, 2017, *Utah State Treasurer*, treasurer.utah.gov.

3. *Financial World*, May 12, 1992, May 11, 1993, Sept. 6, 1995; *Governing* magazine, Feb. 1999, 2001; *USA Today*, June 23, 2003; Pew Trust Foundation, Feb. 1, 1999, www. pewtrusts; *24/7 Wallstreet*, Apr. 13, 2018.

class, fiscal discipline is an internally imposed standard of good practice, a way to structure part of their work, and an ethic of collective resistance to demands from outside government.

Utah Republicans, however, apply discipline selectively. Republicans come in two fiscal types: budget balancers and tax cutters. Utah Republicans are budget balancers in their state, but tax cutters in Washington. Though Republicans like state tax reduction, they do not vote for cuts if they put the state in deficit, and they support tax hikes when needed.[4] In Washington they say they favor balanced budgets, but all of Utah's congressional Republicans voted for the Ronald Reagan, George W. Bush, and Donald Trump tax reductions.[5] None of them *said* they were voting for deficits. They said that spending should be cut to balance the budget, but they all knew the tax cuts would enlarge the deficits, and voted for them anyway. One difference is ownership. State government is ours and should be kept strong. The federal government is theirs, and its strength may soon be used against us. Utah voters support the division; they vote Republican: balance for their state and deficits for their nation.

Legislators and governors point to fiscal habits as a chief difference between themselves and Washington. They cite their own carefully balanced budgets, point to the big federal deficits, and taunt Washington for profligacy. "It is not sustainable," spoken in solemn tones of national fiscal policy, may have been the most repeated phrase of the 2012 and 2013 legislative sessions. Nonetheless, Utah accepted increasing amounts of money from Washington. Federal grants rose from less than 20 percent of Utah state spending in 1985 to just over 30 percent in 2011, as Utah took federal stimulus funds during the recession. The federal share of spending declined after

---

4. For two examples, see the tax increases of 1987 and tax hike of 2015, discussed below.

5. Reagan cuts: Senators Jake Garn and Orrin Hatch and Reps. Jim Hansen, Dan Marriott, David Monson, and Howard Nielson. Bush cuts: Senators Robert Bennett and Orrin Hatch and Reps. Jim Hansen, Chris Cannon, and Rob Bishop. Trump cuts: Senators Orrin Hatch and Mike Lee and Reps. Rob Bishop, Jason Chaffetz, Mia Love, and Chris Stewart.

the economy improved. In total Utahns get back about $1.50 for every $1 they send to Washington, which is about the average state return.[6] Federal politicians believe it is more blessed to give than to receive, and they borrow the difference.

Legislators designed the budget process to keep themselves from spending too much money, rather as Odysseus had himself tied to the mast when his ship neared the sirens. For example, to make a budget for the coming fiscal year, the government must estimate how much revenue there will be. In most states, experts estimate a likely range of revenue, then governors and legislators choose a number along the range in accordance with their "appetite for risk."[7] The larger the number, the more money they have, but the more likely they are to fall into deficit if revenues fail to meet expectations. But in Utah, experts provide only one number. Governors and legislators give themselves no choice because they do not trust their own appetite for risk. Nor do politicians enlarge the number later to give themselves more money. "They play games, but they don't play games with revenue estimates," former budget director Brad Barber said. Politicians also follow another unwritten rule: They rarely spend one-time money for ongoing programs. When income exceeds estimates, money is left at the end of the year, called "one-time" money, that legislators apply only to one-time expenditures such as a road project that will be finished when the money is gone, rather than as a raise to teachers, for instance, since the teachers will still be there needing salaries after the surplus is spent.

Utah's budget process is seasonal, participatory, top-down, and contested between the governor and legislators. Budgeting follows the seasons as closely as farming. The seasons are summer, fall, and the legislative session. Each summer the departments compile

---

6. Hanson, "Intergovernmental Relations," 41; Utah State Auditor, "A Graphical Analysis of Utah's Reliance on Federal Funding," Feb. 18, 2014, auditor.utah.gov. A decline in federal grants to 23 percent of total state expenditures is shown in *Single Audit Report: State of Utah*, 2016. See also Huefner, "Utah 2010."

7. Forsythe, *Memos to the Governor*, 22–25.

spending requests that are passed on to the governor in the fall. Two analysts, one working for the governor and another for the legislature, work in a leisurely amicable way with each department and learn its budget. In the fall the governor meets with his analysts and department heads to hear their requests. Throughout the year, a committee from the governor's office, along with the Legislative Fiscal Analyst and the Utah State Tax Commission, forecast future revenue and produce quarterly estimates.[8] The governor takes the most recent revenue estimate and cuts department spending requests to fit the estimate. Each December he publicly announces a budget proposal with a suggested sum for each agency. Legislative analysts make a competing proposal with a sum for each appropriations subcommittee, although the legislative proposal is kept secret.

Every legislator participates in making the budget and has a seat on one of eight appropriations subcommittees—an unusual arrangement that resulted from history. Before 1970, when the legislature met only in odd-numbered years, an appropriations committee drafted the budget, as is done in most legislatures. In 1970 Utahns amended their constitution to allow for short sessions in even-numbered years limited to making a budget. The question arose: What will other legislators do while the appropriations committee meets? The prospect of idle hours raised alarm. The answer was to put every legislator on an appropriations subcommittee, with senators and representatives sitting together so there would be work for all.[9] Though the short budget sessions are gone, the appropriations subcommittees endure.

When legislators convene in January, each appropriations subcommittee begins with an assigned sum of money from the proposed rough budget prepared by legislative analysts. Subcommittees meet and listen to department heads, interest groups, analysts, and the public, and then divide the sum into budget line items about as they choose, as long as

---

8. Huefner, "Utah Living," 7.
9. F. Ted Hebert, "Utah: Legislative Budgeting," 103–14

they stay within their assigned sum. Utah budgeting is top-down. It begins with revenue estimates, then major decisions divide available revenue among competing programs, and down to smaller line items. An Executive Appropriations Committee comprising budget chairs and Democratic and Republican leaders oversees this process, but the Republican caucus exercises control. "We make all the big decisions, in caucus," explained former House Speaker Marty Stephens. "We take money off the table for raises, or tax cuts, or whatever we want." A team of political scientists said Utah has the most transparent budget process of any state, but one wonders if they knew Utah makes big budget decisions in secret party caucus.[10]

Governors and legislators struggle for control over the budget, and each branch has an institutional style. Though they write their proposals in private, governors reveal them with fanfare in messages delivered in schools or workplaces to show how their plans will improve education and help young people find jobs. The governor employs themes, ideas, and slogans to enlist public support.[11] In contrast, legislators themselves see their first rough budget only if they ask to see it, and few of them do. If the public and special interests know preliminary numbers, it becomes harder to cut items later. Keeping the early figures secret preserves freedom to make decisions after discussions and hearings when legislators know better what they want. Legislative secrecy is partly a counter to the governor's advantage in publicity. In recent decades legislators have gained power over budgets, at the expense of the governors.

As the end of the forty-five-day legislative session nears, final budget negotiations proceed amid rumor, alarm, and a looming deadline. Governors threaten veto. Appropriations subcommittees plead for more money. Lobbyists and legislators try to find money for their

---

10. My interview with Martin Stephens; James E. Alt et al., "Causes of Transparency," 19.

11. Bob Bernick and Lucinda Dillon, "GOP Isn't Applauding Leavitt's Budget," *Deseret News*, Dec. 13, 1998.

causes. In the final days, legislators pass several budget bills, usually completing the task hours before the final midnight when they lose their power. It often takes several days for the analysts and legislators to understand the details of what has been done. "Budgets begin very rationally and end very irrationally," one staffer summarized.

Looking at the budgets over time shows growth, new government purposes, and changed relations between federal, state, and local governments. In 1897 when the state was young, it collected $1,350,014 in revenue and spent a little more than that. In 2015, Utah collected and spent more than $15 billion. Of seventeen governors, only one, Charles Mabey, left office (1925) with a smaller state budget than when he entered. He was also the only elected governor to lose his bid for a second term. Though spending has grown, spending in other states grew more and so did federal spending. From 1915, when the US Census Bureau began tracking state budgets, to 2012, Utah's expenditures grew at a compound rate of 8.75 percent a year. At the same time, the combined spending of all states grew at 8.93 percent, and federal spending increased 9.13 percent. The growth is partly illusory because of inflation. It took government about seventeen dollars to buy in 2010 what a dollar purchased in 1915. The population has grown, too. But Utah's budget has grown less in spending per person than other states. Utah spent $11.07 per capita in 1915, more than double the average of all states. By 2011 Utah's per capita spending had grown to $4,591, less than the state average of $5,385 and less than half the federal $11,559.[12]

State government has grown more than local governments. The spending by all local governments together was more than the state and federal governments combined before 1927, except in wartime.

---

12. Rasmussen, *History*, 13; Ball et al., "Utah State Budget Report," 1; Layton, "Governor Charles Mabey"; *Annual Survey of State Finances*, 1915, 1921, 1925, 2011, 2012; Office of Management and Budget, "Historical Tables," www.whitehouse.gov; "Spending Details," *US Government Spending*, www.usgovernmentspending.com.

A Census Bureau study showed that the combined spending of Utah's municipalities until 1932 was more than what the state spent. By 1941, after the state government had grown during the Depression, the State of Utah outspent its local governments by about one-third, and has outspent local jurisdictions ever since. The Census Bureau reported that Utah spent $17 billion in 2012, compared to $12 billion by Utah's local governments (29 counties, 242 municipalities, 288 special districts, and 41 school districts).[13] In the twentieth century, all governments grew, but states grew more than local governments, and the federal government grew the most of all.

In its first half century, Utah's state government grew mostly because it took jobs away from local governments including road construction, welfare, and schools. At statehood Utah paid little attention to roads. Dirt roads for wagons were a county concern. Then well-off people—the kind who influence state government—began buying automobiles and demanding highways. All over America states borrowed money to build roads. World War I postponed construction, so money accumulated in Utah's road fund. Banks profited because politicians continued to deposit funds at no interest with bankers who had made campaign contributions to winning candidates. When the war ended in 1919, Utah had a road fund of more than $5 million and a total state budget of $10.8 million. Amid patronage and fiscal disorder, Utah spent money and built roads.[14]

Graph 1 shows the flurry of construction spending at the end of World War I. Congress began highway grants in 1916, and seven years later Governor Mabey obtained a gasoline tax to build roads and pay off highway bonds. Gas taxes, federal grants, and highway bonds still pay for most Utah road construction. Highway

---

13. Gray, *Financing*, 108, 128, 132, 135; *Annual Survey of State Finances*, 2012. Care must be taken not to triple-count funds that pass from the federal, through state, to local jurisdictions.

14. Balmforth, "Good Roads Roberts," 65; Petersen, "Lincoln Highway," 192; Teaford, *Rise of the States*, 29–35. See also the early chapters of Knowlton, *History of Highway Development*.

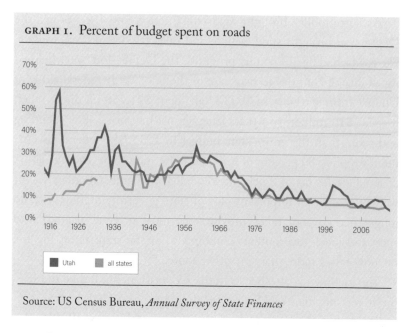

GRAPH 1. Percent of budget spent on roads

Utah | all states

Source: US Census Bureau, *Annual Survey of State Finances*

expenditures, in keeping with the national pattern, was at 33 percent of all state spending in 1959 when America was building the
interstate highway system. Then transportation declined to 6 percent of state spending in 1994–95. In the twenty-first century, Utah
has spent a higher percentage for roads than the average state, with
wide variations from year to year as the legislators have periodically
issued road bonds and used highway spending as a sponge to sop
up money and keep it from education and human services. In the
1990s legislators created a ten-year Centennial Highway Fund to
absorb surpluses in prosperous years and hold down other spending.
In 2012 lawmakers earmarked 30 percent of all sales tax growth for
roads, but Governor Gary Herbert vetoed the bill, saying it would
mean "decreased ability to fund other budget priorities." "Wow," said
House Republican leader Brad Dee, "I think he has stated our case."
Legislators overrode the veto.[15]

15. Bob Bernick, "Paving the Way," *Deseret News*, Aug. 30, 1998; Robert Gehrke,
"Veto Override Session," *Salt Lake Tribune*, Apr. 26, 2011.

As automobiles brought road construction and the gas tax, the Depression brought state welfare and sales tax. Until then, welfare, like roads, had been a county program. The Depression overwhelmed the ability of counties to take care of the poor. Only federal aid kept Utahns from starving. In 1933 Utah spent $11,750 on direct relief; it spent $16 million two years later, almost half of all state spending and more than the entire state budget in 1933. The federal government supplied 80 percent of it. To raise the state share, the legislature enacted a sales tax of 2 percent. Federal grants and state matches for welfare remain an important part of state government. Sales tax, no longer tied to poor relief, provides the most revenue of any tax to state and local governments combined. For the state alone, income tax now raises more than any other source.[16]

The income tax also began in the Depression, but unlike the sales tax it was not tied to Depression programs. The Utah constitution required that all property be taxed at a uniform rate. But stocks, bank deposits, and other financial wealth were rarely taxed. Farmers thought it unfair that they paid taxes on their farms, while people who lived on dividends or interest paid nothing. After decades of debate and maneuver, Utah amended its constitution to exempt financial wealth from property tax and to substitute a tax on personal and corporate income, with proceeds eventually dedicated to schools.[17]

As graph 2 shows, Utah welfare spending fell from 49 percent of state expenditures in 1935 to 8 percent in 1968 and rose again in a new form. The old Aid to Families with Dependent Children, which had dominated welfare, became less important. In its place, Medicaid, which the Census Bureau includes in its welfare accounting, drove spending growth. Though federal grants paid about 70 percent of Utah Medicaid costs, state legislators enacted strict eligibility

---

16. *History of the Utah Tax Structure*, 13; *Auditor General's Annual Report*, 1933–35. Utah had eighteen separate sales taxes in 2016 bringing $3.5 billion to state and local governments, compared to $3.37 billion from the individual income tax.

17. Rasmussen, *History*, 27–28.

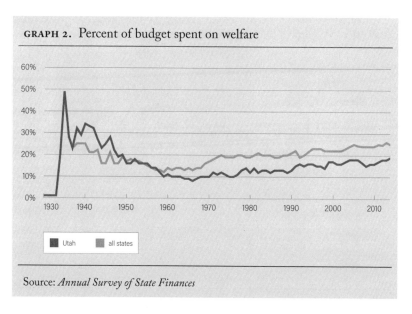

GRAPH 2. Percent of budget spent on welfare

Utah   all states

Source: *Annual Survey of State Finances*

requirements to restrain the growth of the caseload. The program still grew faster than any other part of Utah's budget in the twenty-first century, and in recent years welfare, Medicaid, and other human services surpassed public education to become the state's chief expense. Although the federal government paid most of the costs, Republican legislators felt they were being pushed by federal decisions into larger human service commitments than were prudent for the state. They opposed the expansion of Medicaid under President Obama's Affordable Care Act and rejected other programs to bring more help to poor people.

Over the decades, spending on roads and welfare rose and fell, but education has been a budget constant. Every year for which the Census Bureau reported state finances, starting in 1915, Utah spent a higher percentage of its budget on education than the average state. But as graph 3 shows, the school share of state spending for all states declined over time. It peaked in 1925 for Utah with 69 percent of the budget going to schools, which was over 30 points higher than the average for all states. In the 1920s Utah was often the state that spent

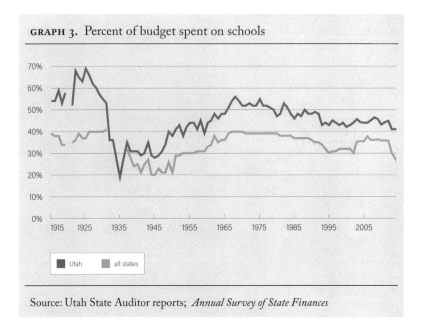

GRAPH 3. Percent of budget spent on schools

70%
60%
50%
40%
30%
20%
10%
0%

1915   1925   1935   1945   1955   1965   1975   1985   1995   2005

■ Utah   ■ all states

Source: Utah State Auditor reports; *Annual Survey of State Finances*

the highest percentage of its budget on schools. When the Great Depression struck, federal money poured in for poor relief, and other state revenues fell with the economy, so that in 1935 only 19 percent of state spending went for education. It recovered to peak at 56 percent in 1968, after the Rampton tax increases that are discussed below. Thereafter it fell to between 43 and 46 percent. This represents about 10 points more than the US average. Note that the census includes colleges and universities in education spending, while the state counts higher education separately. That means that the federal census calculations show education spending higher than welfare, while the state shows welfare higher than public education alone. Utah's share of education is comparatively high because Utahns have more children and rely more on the state, and less on local governments, to fund schools. In dollars spent per student, however, Utah has spent less than the national average almost every year.

A historical view of Utah taxes shows more change during the Depression than at any other time, followed by three decades of calm, three decades of increases, a tax revolt, and thirty years of cuts. Sales and income taxes both began in the Depression, then remained steady for almost thirty years. The income tax brackets and rates of 1935 lasted to 1965. The 2 percent sales tax of 1933 was the same in 1961. In those years politicians spoke of state finances as a stable three-legged stool of property, income, and sales taxes. Then beginning in 1959, five of six successive legislatures raised taxes. In twenty-two years, income tax was raised four times. Democratic governor Calvin L. Rampton (1965–77) raised taxes most. His first year in office, he persuaded a Democratic legislature to raise income, corporate, and sales taxes and to grant more authority to towns to raise property taxes, though he cut state property tax.[18] A political child of the New Deal, he was the last governor to speak well of the federal government. He won office with the big national majority that elected President Lyndon Johnson in 1964, and as Johnson expanded government in Washington, Rampton did the same in Utah. But while Johnson declared a War on Poverty and enlarged government to help the poor, Rampton raised taxes for schools and colleges. School funding had fallen from about the national average in 1944 to 25 percent below the mean. Rampton tried to keep it comparable to the norm in other states. He had followers, all advocates for tax hikes, since Rampton said that schools need more money. However, in the next election, voters turned out the tax-raising Democrats. But Rampton was midway through his term and immune to the anti-tax anger. By the time he faced the electorate again in 1968, the anger had lapsed. He stayed in office three terms and coaxed big increases in sales tax and income tax from later Republican legislatures.

His successor, Democrat Scott Matheson (1977–85), obtained a tax increase for schools, once again from Republican lawmakers. The

---

18. *History of Utah Tax Structure*, 9, 156; Office of Management and Budget, "Key Budget Drivers," gomb.utah.gov/budget-policy/budget-drivers (Nov. 2016); Lowe Rudd, Stephen Kroes, and Janice Houston, "Utah's Tax Situation," *Utah Foundation*, 2004; O. N. Malmquist and Jerome Full, "Big Income Tax Hike," *Salt Lake Tribune*, Mar. 12, 1965.

An interchange nearing completion on I-15 for access to a new road in Davis County, the Layton Parkway, part of a larger project that included widening ten miles of freeway and partly funded by a $1 billion grant from the federal government. *Photograph Utah Department of Transportation, November 2010*

next governor, Norman Bangerter (1985–93), a Republican, faced a bad economy and falling state revenues. He cut spending, including school funds, but then proposed raising taxes to mitigate further cuts. Tax protestors filled the capitol rotunda chanting "Teachers yes, taxes no; Bangerter's plan has got to go." Radio station KTKK (pronounced K–talk) summoned a few thousand protestors, whose angry shouts carried into the chambers where legislators deliberated. Despite the protest, the Republican legislature passed the biggest tax increase in Utah history. Tax rebels followed up by gathering signatures for a popular vote in 1988 on propositions to roll back the increases and to limit future taxes and spending. They formed the Independent Political Party that nominated anti-tax candidate Merrill Cook for governor. Early polls showed a two-to-one majority in favor of the anti-tax propositions, making Cook a contender in his race as well. Under attack, the political establishment united against the rebels. Republican and Democratic candidates appeared together and spoke against the propositions. The Parent Teacher Association held meetings in schools to denounce the ballot measures. The AFL–CIO, Chamber of Commerce, Salt Lake Health Department, Utah Bar Association, and Utah Medical Association followed suit. Major news media donated to the campaign against tax cuts, and the news coverage was biased again them.[19] Though asked to speak against the propositions, the Church adhered to its policy of avoiding politics and remained silent. When the vote was held, the anti-tax propositions failed three-to-two. Bangerter won reelection; the anti-tax candidate Cook finished third.

The tax revolt that year was the third and largest of four waves of protest that broke over Utah from 1975 to 1990. Protests came as legislators raised sales and income taxes, but protestors complained most about property taxes. The Utah revolt coincided with tax revolts in many other states, and part of the Utah protest followed a California example. But revolt began in Utah before the national movement started and continued after it ended. Property taxes, which caused most anger, had on average declined. In 1965 people had paid $50 in property taxes for every $1,000 in personal income, and ten years later it had fallen to $32.[20] Governor Rampton raised taxes on sales and income but eliminated the state property levy, except for the portion that went to schools. Though the average fell, the tax went up on many homes.

Property tax had long defied public administration. The state constitution said that all property must be taxed at an equal rate on its fair-market value. But home assessments, the official estimate of fair-market value, were actually 10 to 70 percent of real value, and home taxes fluctuated haphazardly, so that some homeowners paid

19. Rasmussen, *History*, 130–32; Bob Bernick Jr, "Tax Initiative," Jay Evensen, "Fighting Tax Initiatives," Lee Davidson, "Rivals Get Together," "Support for Tax Initiative," "List of Opponents," *Deseret News*, Sept. 2, 7, Oct. 5, 9, 28, 1988.

20. "Utah's Property Tax Burden," *Utah Foundation*, www.utahfoundation.org.

more than their share and others less. Legislators enacted reforms in 1915, 1947, 1953, and most stringently in 1969 when they put county assessors under supervision of the Utah State Tax Commission and mandated a five-year rolling reassessment of all property.[21] Order would come to property taxes at last, lawmakers said.

Fate then struck from afar. International oil prices rose, inflating the price of everything, including property values. As a minor energy producing state, Utah fared well and people moved in to take jobs, driving home prices even higher. When rising home prices hit rolling reassessments, some tax bills jumped ten-fold. Angry homeowners held meetings and gathered signatures to force a referendum in 1976 on the Budgetary Procedures Ceiling Act, but voters turned it down. A new model for tax revolt came from California where tax rebels won passage of Proposition 13 in 1978, forcing big cuts on property taxes. California inspired imitators, and by 1984 at least thirty-nine other states had seen tax-cutting or spending-control initiatives reach the voters.[22] Utah's tax rebels brought a near copy of Proposition 13 to a referendum in 1980, but again, voters defeated the proposal.

Politicians acted to assuage the rebel anger. Every legislative session from the mid-1970s through the mid-1990s debated property taxes. Legislators repealed the rolling reassessment and enacted rebates for homeowners, statutory limits on government spending, "circuit-breaker" laws that allowed older people to put off property taxes, and "truth in taxation" to pressure local governments to lower rates when home prices rose.[23] For Republicans, the revolt pitted their middle-class homeowner constituency against their business supporters, and they sided with homeowners. Politicians wanted to

---

21. "Historical Overview of Utah's Property Tax," *Utah State Tax Commission*, propertytax.utah.gov; Rasmussen, *History*, 18, 54, 56, 84; Teaford, *Rise of the States*, chap. 3; Morrill, "Property Tax Assessment," 491–516.

22. Steve Wayda, "Davis Taxpayers," Douglas L. Parker, "Some Extol, Others Castigate," *Salt Lake Tribune*, June 11, 1975, Oct. 10, 1976; Citrin, "Legacy of Proposition 13," 13.

23. Rasmussen, *History*, 96, 106; Lisa Riley Roche, "State Tax Rebate Checks," *Deseret News*, Sept. 3, 1988. Examples are the Appropriations and Tax Limitation Act of 1979 and the Tax Increase Disclosure Act of 1985.

cut home taxes to pacify the rebels but maintain property taxes on businesses to pay for schools and local government. They fixed the home assessments to their 1978 values, while allowing business assessments to go up. They enacted an additional 20 percent cut in home assessments, but not for businesses. Businesses sued in court, pointing to the equal-taxation clause of the state constitution, and the Utah Supreme Court struck down both legislative enactments.[24] Lawmakers then proposed a constitutional amendment allowing homes to be taxed at 45 percent less than businesses. This time (1982) voters approved the measure.

The tax rebels came from outside government and deprecated the establishment. They said taxes were high because politicians were entrenched, wasteful, and uncaring. They spoke of widows driven from their homes by high taxes, though such victims proved hard to find. In the most typical exchange, a politician would ask a tax rebel what government services should be cut if taxes were reduced. The rebel would say that there would be no need to cut services, that government could just waste less.

In all, signatures were gathered to bring six tax-cut or spending-limit referenda to the ballot, in 1976, 1980 (two), 1988 (two), and 1990. Voters rejected all six propositions in all four waves of protest. In other states, such as California, Massachusetts, and Oregon, tax activists passed referenda, imposed tax cuts, and brought difficulty to government. Utah voters believed their establishment politicians when they said big tax cuts would harm schools and services, so they voted for established policies and people and against the insurgents.

Though the protests failed, big tax increases ended in 1987. The improved economy yielded more revenue without higher rates. Republicans governed and avoided ambitious spending. Utah's long-term

---

24. In *Rio Algom Corp. v. San Juan County*, 681 P. 2d 184 (Utah 1984), the court struck down a plan to fix home assessments. In *Amax Magnesium Corp. v. Utah State Tax Commission*, 796 P. 2d 1256 (Utah 1990) and 874 P.2d 840 (Utah 1994), the 20 percent reduction for homeowners was ruled invalid.

TABLE I. Taxes as a percent of personal income

	1959	1988	2014
individual tax burden	10.8%	12.5%	11.1%
Utah's rank	17	9	31

Source: *Statistical Review of Utah Government*

trend reversed from increases to tax cuts. Table 1 shows Utah's state and local tax burden as a percent of total personal income compared to other states. From 1959 to 1988, the tax burden rose as Utah's sales tax rates more than tripled, with both state and local increases. Income tax rates increased more than 40 percent, and levies on corporate earnings, gasoline, mining, cigarettes, and liquor also rose. In contrast, since 1988 state sales and income tax declined (local sales taxes continued upward). The gas tax rose slowly, and only cigarette taxes soared. Taxes rose for twenty-nine years. Then, for thirty years, to this writing, they have fallen. In 2015 the legislature raised gasoline taxes and property taxes. The latter regularized education budgets between school districts because legislators feared a law suit if spending remained unequal.[25] The Republicans who govern Utah believe in tax cuts and will likely enact more when opportunities come.

Because tax-rebel shouts still echoed in their heads, politicians cut property taxes first. In 1995 Republican legislators secretly plotted to take property taxes away from schools altogether. They did not even tell Republican governor Mike Leavitt of their plan. "It's time the state of Utah got out of the property tax business," House Speaker Mel Brown said. The secret plan would have cut property tax bills 25 percent and reduced school funding by $280 million. Legislators said they would replace part of the school losses. The secret scheme soon fell apart, but lawmakers and the governor did agree to cut $140

---

25. Morgan Jacobsen, "House Approves $75M Property Tax," *Deseret News*, Mar. 11, 2015.

million from property taxes, lowering the rate for schools by about one-third. And they followed with another cut of $100 million in 1996. Since then, Utah property taxes have been comparatively low: in 2011 Utah ranked thirty-fifth in property tax rate, compared to eighteenth highest in income tax and nineteenth in sales tax.[26]

A bigger round of reductions came in 2005 with the election of Governor Jon Huntsman, who ran on a promise of lowering taxes. He believed that business leaders look for states with low taxes, so by lowering rates Utah could attract corporations and thereby improve its economy. "I'm not just a kind of senseless tax-cutter," he said. "I really do believe in our competitive posture longer-term." In his first year in office, he proposed ending Utah's corporation tax, the source of $200 million annually for Utah schools. Republican legislators feared cutting school revenues so much and refused to go along. But at a special session in 2006, they cut $70 million from personal income taxes. "A good first step," Huntsman said. In 2007, Utah's economy flourished, revenues overflowed, and Huntsman argued that extra state revenues should be used to "buy down" the tax rate; he persuaded legislators to cut $220 million, mostly by cutting incomes taxes for wealthy people by lowering the top rate from 6.98 to 5 percent. Spokesmen explained that chief executive officers choose company locations in part to reduce their personal tax bills, so a lower top rate would attract them and their companies. Huntsman had intended to eliminate deductions to protect state revenue. But the Church of Jesus Christ of Latter-day Saints publicly asked the state to keep the deduction for charitable giving and legislators chose to keep the deduction for home mortgage interest. Thus school revenues suffered long-term harm, although the prosperity of 2007 hid this effect for a year or two. Huntsman also talked lawmakers

---

26. Dan Harrie and Tony Semerand, "Tax Limbo," Harrie and Semerand, "Legislature Cuts Taxes," Semerand, "A 3-Way Tax Cut," *Salt Lake Tribune*, Jan. 18, Mar. 2, 1995, Feb. 24, 1996; "How Utah Compares," *Utah Taxpayers Association*, Oct. 2013.

into reducing the sales tax on food, mostly as a benefit to poor and working people who spend a large portion of their income to eat.[27]

Huntsman's beliefs lingered after he left. His successor, Gary Herbert, believed the state's business climate was the chief ingredient of economic growth and favored lower taxes. In contrast to the anger of the tax rebels, he and Huntsman talked optimistically in business-school vocabulary, and said careful economic management—including moderate taxes for businesses and business leaders—would bring prosperity. Some economists questioned this theory, but Utah fared better before and after the Huntsman tax cuts than most other states.[28] Republican politicians who supported lower taxes claimed their policies contributed to that success.

REMARKS

In early statehood, Utah took programs from counties, partly because roads and then welfare became too big and expensive for counties, but also because federal grants for those functions came to the state. Both are now "marble cake" programs with federal, state, and local participation intermixed.[29] Education also became an activity shared by all three levels of government, though federal participation is less than in the other two. Over its first seven or eight decades, Utah state government became more orderly and acquired a habit, still in effect, of disciplined budgeting and careful fiscal management.

From a long perspective, Utah's fiscal history divides into two regimes, before the Great Depression and after. Before the Depression, state money came from property tax. Sales, income, and

---

27. "Huntsman Pushes Tax Change," "Huntsman's Tax," *Salt Lake Tribune*," Jan. 11, Oct. 16, 2005; "Utah Ponders Flat Tax," "More Tax Cuts?" "Utah's Lawmakers," "Huntsman Signs Tax-Cut," *Deseret News*, Mar. 27, 2005, Sept. 13, 2006, Mar. 11, 15, 2007; "Getting by with Less," *Utah Foundation*, www.utahfoundation.org; *History of Utah Tax Structure*, 11.

28. Ahmari Sohrab, "How Utah Avoids the National Economic Funk," *Wall Street Journal*, Aug. 17, 2012.

29. Grodzins, *American System*, 8, contrasting the "layer cake federalism" of Europe to the "marble cake federalism" of America.

corporate taxes were adopted in the downturn and now pay most of the state's bills. Before the Depression, the combined spending of local governments surpassed the state budget, but afterward state government spent more than combined local governments. Utah added welfare to state expenditures during the Depression, and by official state count welfare, Medicaid, and other human services are the largest state expenditures today.

After the big changes of the Depression, taxes stayed quiet for thirty years. However, Utahns have more children than other Americans and a middling economy to pay for education. The enduring question of Utah budgets is how much effort should be made for education. By the late 1950s, spending for schools was well below the national average. Four governors—two Republicans and two Democrats—pushed for tax increases, and both Democratic and Republican legislatures passed them. The increases over a quarter of a century aimed only to keep Utah within the range of national school spending.

Tax revolts came to three-fourths of the states, and Utah was among the first. Petitions, controversies, and referenda extended over fourteen years (1976–90). Every tax-rebel proposition failed at the ballot box, but after the peak of the revolt in 1988 Utah politicians stopped raising taxes and began reducing them. Since then, Utah's tax burden has gone from among the top ten to below average. Governors Leavitt and Walker tried to mitigate tax cuts to preserve school money. Governor Jon Huntsman, in contrast, led the biggest cuts, saying this would lure businesses to Utah and help the economy. Both before and after the Huntsman cuts, Utah had a better economy than most states. During the thirty years or so of cuts, Utahns have elected only Republican legislatures, and despite the qualms of some Republican governors, the lawmakers continue to cut taxes. Utah schools have been the loser, as shown in the next chapter.

16

UTAH SCHOOLS

Utah schools have been a policy battleground between educators and Republican politicians since the 1980s. Educators believe in well-funded programs run by professionals, and most Utah Democrats and school experts nationally agree. Republicans, on the contrary, believe that schools are not as good as they need to be and that more money is not the answer. Rather, schools must focus more on math, English, and science, and each student must work harder.[1] Educators control the schools, and politicians control the money. Both sides talk politely. Educators hope to coax money from the legislature. Politicians hope to persuade educators to reform. Educators campaign in politics to bring pressure on politicians, and politicians pass laws to force educational change. Both fail, and Utah education policy is not successful.

Utah has the poorest schools in America. Every year since 1987, Utah has spent less money per child than any other state. Utah has many children and a middling economy, and therefore less money to pay for each child. But in addition, low school spending has become state policy. In the 1990s and 2000s, the Republican legislature cut taxes and diverted money away from education. In 2014, Utah spent less than 60 percent of the national average in dollars per student,

---

1. Ravitch, *Death and Life*, presents the educators' view; Peterson, *Saving Schools*, is from the perspective of a reform advocate.

and less than one-third as much as the top spending state.[2] Education spending seems like an experiment in how little the state can pay and still maintain acceptable schools.

The schools perform better than their poverty would predict. Students graduate at higher than national rates and score above their peers on standardized tests, though both differences are small. Republican politicians, who are defensive about their low spending record, point to those results and say Utah gets a bargain. But in truth, demography should destine Utah students to success: They are less likely to be poor, more likely to live with two parents, and their parents are better educated than the American average, all auspicious indicators. In 2007 the Utah Foundation compared Utah standardized test results with five demographically similar states and Utah scored much the worst. The comparison was repeated in 2014, when Utah tied for next-to-worst.[3] In fact, Utah schools fail to live up to their demographic potential.

It was not always so. For decades Utahns made strong efforts and had good schools. Graph 1 shows relative school prosperity as a crooked line falling from a high point around the end of World War II. The black line shows the years Utah had the lowest spending of all states. Note that the graph compares spending to the national average. In total funding, or in dollars per pupil, Utah spending has risen along with other states. But until about the end of World War II, Utah schools led other states', and since then they have lagged behind.

Utah's first schools were begun by Latter-day Saints, mostly in ward houses. Non-Mormons founded their own private schools. The territorial legislature appropriated small sums and authorized local districts to levy a limited property tax. Pupils still had to pay tuition.

---

2. "Getting by with Less," *Utah Foundation*, www.utahfoundation.org. Utah spent $6,500 per student, against a US average of $11,009 and the New York amount of $20,610 per pupil.

3. "Single-Year Dropout Rate Report, 2016–17," *Utah State Board of Education*, www.schools.utah.gov; "School Testing Results," *Utah Foundation*, www.utahfoundation.org; Morgan Jacobsen, "Report," *Deseret News*, May 12, 2015.

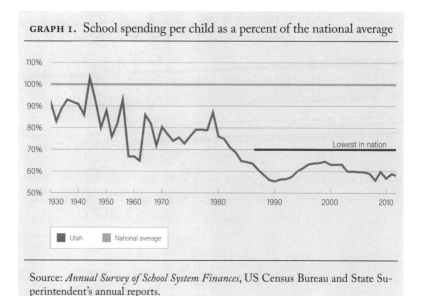

GRAPH 1. School spending per child as a percent of the national average

Source: *Annual Survey of School System Finances*, US Census Bureau and State Superintendent's annual reports.

Free schools came only as part of the deal that reduced Latter-day Saint control in return for statehood. Utah's constitution (Art. X, § 1, 3) provides that the legislature will establish free schools and a board of education and superintendent of public instruction will supervise them. Utah has forty-one local school districts created by law, each with an elected board that hires a superintendent.

After statehood Utah improved schools in three ways, by providing financial help, consolidating small districts, and making attendance compulsory. From 1910 through 1936, lawmakers proposed, and Utah voters passed, five constitutional amendments to raise school taxes and spending. A 1910 amendment allowed state funding of high schools. In 1920 voters approved an amendment for another school tax, and legislators promptly passed the "twenty-five-dollar fund" that aimed to bring state aid to twenty-five dollars per child. In 1930 voters passed two amendments, a "state equalization fund" to help poor districts and a state income tax to support the schools. In 1936 voters approved a Uniform School Fund that eventually paid most education costs. Through the first half of the twentieth century, American school finance moved from local districts to states, and Utah was near the front of that movement.

In the territorial period, most Utah districts had only one school. The need for high schools prompted educators and legislators to consolidate into districts with several elementary schools and eventually a high school. In 1915 the legislature combined many small districts into forty districts statewide. Forty was then the smallest number of district in any state, and Utah continues to have fewer districts than most.[4] After a compulsory attendance law passed in 1919, enrollment jumped from 81 to 97 percent, the highest percentage of children enrolled in any state.[5] Utah children were also more likely to attend school than children elsewhere.

Two professors from Iowa published a study in 1946 that concluded: "Utah easily outclasses all other states in overall performance in education." They noted that Utah was only average in school spending, but as Utahns had more children they had to tax themselves more to achieve average spending. Utah children were more likely to attend school and stay in school longer than students of any other state. Utah had the second-highest completion rate for eighth grade, the highest graduation rate from high school, and the highest percentage of college graduates. Half a century of taxpayer effort and pro-education policy had resulted in good schools.[6]

Success did not last. Other states adopted measures that had improved Utah schools, and they had more money and fewer children. Utah did not keep up. Since the middle of the twentieth century, Utah education has had chronic underfunding and shown long-term decline.

Utah responded to underfunding in two ways: militant politics by teachers and demands for reform by Republican politicians.

---

4. Moffitt, *History of Public Education*, chaps. 9, 12.

5. Cowles, *Organization and Administration*, 34.

6. Hughes and Lancelot, *Education*. The study was made in 1944, the only time Utah's spending per child exceeded the national average. See also Allen, *Still the Right Place*, 33

Teacher activism began in the 1950s. Labor unions had gained strength during the New Deal but had seen their ambitions postponed during World War II. When the war was over, big unions went on strike and won wage increases. Teachers believed that they should get raises too. Moreover, funding for buildings and books had been scant during the Depression and war. In a genteel way, careful of professional dignity, the teachers emulated coal miners and steel workers, organized, and threatened collective action. Utah's constitution makes state government responsible for schools. The state had provided an ever larger share of school money, and the legislature and governor held the most power over school finance. In Utah, school politics are state politics, and teachers targeted the state.

Throughout his tenure, Governor J. Bracken Lee (1949–57) drew national attention for opposing school spending. He was the only governor to veto an entire education budget. In 1953 a committee of sixty citizens recommended an increase, but Lee rejected the proposal. The Utah Education Association (UEA), representing 90 percent of Utah teachers, threatened to keep schools closed the next school year. The school boards, superintendents, and Parent Teacher Association all supported the UEA. Beleaguered Governor Lee finally summoned a special legislative session that met some of the teachers' demands.[7]

Eleven years later Utah had America's first statewide teachers' strike. The UEA pointed to the growing gap between Utah and national spending and demanded that the state catch up. Lawmakers raised spending, but not enough, said the UEA. Governor Clyde (1957–1965) appointed a study committee, but when they agreed with the teachers, Clyde still refused to call a special legislative session to address the issue. In the spring of 1964, teachers staged a two-day, statewide "recess" and voted to shut the schools in the fall. To support them, the National Education Association declared the first national

---

7. E.g. Allen, "Utah's Public Schools," 323n7; Lythgoe, *Let 'Em Holler*, chap. 10.

sanctions again a state, as they asked out-of-state teachers not to take jobs in Utah. Nonetheless, after bluster and recrimination, the teachers went back to their classrooms in the fall on Governor Clyde's terms.[8]

To fight on, the UEA created America's first education political action committee to raise money for friendly candidates. Though teachers had lost the strike, they won the 1964 election. Democrat Calvin Rampton was elected governor, partly on the charge that Republicans had harmed education. Democrats won the legislature, and they raised income taxes, corporate taxes, and school spending. Fortunes then reversed again, as voters threw out the tax-raising Democrats, but their Republican replacements left the higher taxes and school spending in place.[9]

In 1989, near the end of an economic recession, teachers staged a one-day "wildcat" strike and threatened a bigger walk-out later. Governor Norman Bangerter (1985–1993) offered raises of 6 percent, which the UEA rejected. But when the legislature passed Bangerter's program, the teachers stayed in the classrooms. At first, 1989 repeated 1964, with a mini-strike followed by an ineffective threat. But from there, events differed. In 1964 Utahns voted out Republicans and raised taxes and school spending. After the 1989 strike, Republicans stayed in power, but the teachers voted out their strike-threatening UEA leadership and replaced them with a more conciliatory slate.[10]

The last strike to date was in 2000 when the UEA called a one-day "job action" to persuade legislators to make a "long-term financial plan" for schools. Instead, angry Republican lawmakers retaliated by forbidding paycheck deductions for the UEA political action committee. The teachers union sued, and after eight years of litigation

---

8. "Teachers' Big Weapon" editorial, *Wall Street Journal*, May 13, 1963; Evans, *Utah School Crisis*, 13–15, 22–25, 70. Evans was executive director of the UEA.

9. Rampton, *As I Recall*, chap. 4.

10. Twila Van Leer, "Utah Students Cheer," "84 Percent of UEA Members," *Deseret News*, Sept. 26, 1989, Feb. 25, 1990. Write-in candidate Lily Eskelsen won the UEA presidency in 1990, beating Beth Quist Beck, vice president during the strike.

the US Supreme Court ruled that the ban violated teachers' First Amendment rights and struck it down.[11]

Teacher militancy subsided, Utah teachers no longer strike, but they politic continuously. For decades the UEA quietly paid teachers in the legislature the difference between their salaries as teachers and lower pay as legislators. The practice stopped in the 1990s when legislative pay rose. The UEA sometimes donates more than anyone else to legislative elections, contributing to candidates in both parties. They opened a line of credit for legislative leaders to use in campaigns and report as donations only what the leaders spent. Unfriendly Republicans were targeted within their party. Teachers recruited pro-education Republicans, organized neighborhood party caucuses, and elected friendly delegates to the Republican nominating convention. UEA politicos estimate that they beat about twelve anti-education legislators. But Republicans have become more conservative, and more Republicans attend caucuses. That tactic no longer works. The UEA sends a staff of professional lobbyists to the legislature who ally with superintendents, principals, the PTA, and other education groups. Decades ago, political science surveys showed that the teachers' union was the most powerful interest at Utah's capitol, but more recent surveys rank the UEA as second or third, behind the Latter-day Saint Church. All those results seem suspect: if teachers really were so powerful, Utah would spend more on education. The UEA affiliates with the National Education Association and follows a national model. Similar teachers' unions advocate in every state, and surveys show many are among the most powerful interests with their respective legislatures. The national association and UEA leadership lean Democratic, while Republicans run the legislature. The national education political model has not

11. "Teachers Send Utah a Message," "House Action," *Salt Lake Tribune*, Dec. 6, 2000, Jan. 28, 2001. Utah prevailed in the Tenth Circuit Court with *Utah Education Association v. Shurtleff*, 565 F. 3d 1226 (2009), but later in *Ysursa v. Pocatello Education Association*, 555 U.S. 353 (2009) the US Supreme Court overruled the Tenth Circuit and decided for teachers.

worked well in Utah, but neither has anything else. The UEA acts with energy, and has tried different tactics, but has yet to find a way to get education spending off the bottom.[12]

While educators sought money, conservative politicians sought reform. Utah reform began after the 1983 publication of *A Nation at Risk*, a report from the US Commission on Educational Excellence, called by Ronald Reagan's education secretary Terrel Bell. Before he went to Washington, Bell had been Utah State Superintendent of Schools and Utah Commissioner of Higher Education. To chair his commission, Bell recruited David P. Gardner, former president of the University of Utah. The report cried alarm: "The educational foundations of our society are presently being eroded by a rising tide of mediocrity that threatens our very future as a nation and as a people." It promoted the triple premises of reform: (1) Schools must succeed for America to succeed; (2) Schools are not succeeding: test scores have fallen and foreign students outperform Americans; and (3) America must improve its schools. It seized public attention and incited reform attempts in every state.

At the time the report was released, Utah ranked near the bottom in school spending. Democratic governor Scott Matheson (1977–85) had tried to persuade the Republican-controlled legislature to raise taxes for schools, without success. Now the Reagan administration, revered by Utah Republicans, was calling for improvement in a report with Utah connections. Matheson saw his chance: he called a Utah Commission on Educational Excellence to echo the national findings and then called for higher school taxes when the legislature met in 1984.

Republican lawmakers were now willing to raise taxes, but they wanted better schools in return. The new money should raise teacher

12. My interviews with UEA political consultants David Irvine and Jim Eldredge, June 2002; Jerry Spangler and Bob Bernick, "UEA Has Expensive, Big Roar ... No Teeth," *Deseret News*, 3 Feb. 2001; Zeigler and Baer, *Lobbying Interaction*, 61; Hrebenar and Thomas, *Interest Group Politics*, 119–20.

pay, but better teachers should get bigger raises, lawmakers said. The UEA had long opposed merit pay. New funds should be applied to the general salary schedule, to raise the pay of all teachers, they said. Teachers and lawmakers negotiated the Career Ladder Program that would raise taxes, give all teachers a raise, and offer additional money to teachers who did special projects or worked to improve their skills, thus climbing the career ladder. Details were left to each school district. In 1998, fourteen years after the program began, the Legislative Auditor General studied Career Ladder and found that it infused about $45 million extra into teacher salaries, raising each teacher's pay about $1,900. But all merit pay or performance incentive had disappeared.[13] Career Ladder had become the general salary increase the UEA had wanted. Legislators and educators had made a tacit deal on Career Ladder: legislators would raise taxes and educators would make changes to improve schools. The taxes lasted, but not the changes. After the Career Ladder Program, legislators never again raised taxes to improve schools. (They did increase tax collections in 1987 to soften spending cuts in hard times and in 2015 to avoid a lawsuit.) Legislators directed many more reforms in Utah schools, but they were paid for with existing revenues.

Reformers called more commissions, made more plans, and enacted more rules. There have been ten special commissions to study schools, most called and led by Republican politicians. They took ideas from other states, and from scholars, and applied them to Utah schools.[14] Governors and legislators, business and community leaders, for the most part Republicans, were in favor of reforms and recommended them to educators or enacted them into law. When

13. LaVarr Webb, "Lawmakers," *Deseret News*, Jan. 30, 1984; Amsler et al., *Utah Career Ladder System*, 4–5; Malen and Murphy, "Statewide Decentralized Approach," 261; "Survey of the Utah Public Education Career Ladder Program," Nov. 12, 1998, le.utah.gov.

14. Utah Statewide Education Planning Commission, Utah Commission on Educational Excellence, Utah Education Reform Steering Committee, A Shift in Focus, Education Strategic Planning Committee, Governor's Blue Ribbon Panel, State Task Force on Learning and Accountability, The 21st Century Workforce Initiative, Employers' Education Coalition, and Governor's Commission on Excellence in Education.

A Nation at Risk said schools were failing, it implied that professional educators were also failing. Reformers believed that educators were unable to solve school problems, but reformers, with their new ideas, would soon produce excellence. "We shall change the course of education in Utah," said one commission. Another said it would "assure Utah the best educated citizenry in the world."[15] Utah reformers, almost all non-educators, believed they understood better than educators what needed to be done, and they would push change on unenthusiastic professionals and improve schools.

Education is a professional establishment, founded in Utah's constitution, supported by taxes, and buttressed by state and federal law. Admission comes with a degree from a college of education, so educators share a similar outlook and vocabulary, reinforced by their professional training and experiences. Most are tenured. Principals and superintendents rise along established career paths that begin with teaching. Friends of education dominate the elected school boards. Educators believe Utah's school problem is underfunding, and if politicians wanted to help, they should raise adequate resources and leave education to professionals. Educators who have sat on the commissions have mostly cautioned that reforms might not work, and when outvoted have negotiated the least disruptive reform they could and then altered the programs from the inside—just as they did with Career Ladder—so that new measures have become less like the reformers' ideas and more like educators' preferences. Among other reform attempts, educators defeated or blunted site-based management, redirection of efforts, school accountability, tests for graduation, No Child Left Behind, and school vouchers.[16]

Some early reforms called for "site-based management." Each school would create a committee of "stakeholders" to develop a "strategic plan" to improve the school. Reformers had been accused of

---

15. *Education in Utah*, 3; *Utah State Public Education*, 13.
16. Allen, "Utah's Public Schools," 330–33, discusses other attempted reforms, in addition to those mentioned here.

imposing unwanted changes from the "top down," but this would be "bottom-up," they boasted. Governor Mike Leavitt initiated "Centennial Schools" in 1993 and "Schools for the Twenty-first Century" in 2001. In each program, schools won grants by setting goals, involving parents, partnering with business, and other approved innovations. But what many stakeholders wanted, it turned out, was less school. Using site-based management, some schools closed on Fridays or cut an hour off each school day, so teachers would have time to plan, they explained. Students liked that strategic plan, but at the urging of Governor Leavitt, the state school board issued a top-down directive ending extra time off.[17] By 2004 a few schools displayed tattered canvas banners proclaiming them Schools of the 21st Century, but otherwise site-based management had disappeared.

Many high school students completed their graduation requirements before their senior year and then spent their last year at leisure, taking only one or two classes. As far as any student could remember, seniors had always lo.....d, but students admitted that they often wasted twelfth grade. The Employer's Education Coalition, called by Governor Leavitt, said "senior year should be made meaningful again." In addition, the businessmen said schools should redirect efforts away from extracurricular activities and base credit on competence instead of class time. In 2003 legislators asked for those reforms, and the Utah State Board of Education put them into a plan called "Performance Plus." But educators feared that many students would fail the more rigorous standards. Students and parents protested the de-emphasis of football and pep club. Board members heard the complaints, abandoned Performance Plus, and left students to enjoy wasting their twelfth-grade year. Throughout Utah school reform, it proved as difficult to get more work from

---

17. Burns, "History of Development," 63–66; Twila Van Leer, "Twenty Schools," Marjorie Cortez, "State Board," Cortez, "Reluctant S. L. School Board," *Deseret News*, May 27, 1991, May 11, July 19, 1995.

students and support from their parents as it did to get more money from politicians. Utahns wanted students to learn more, but were reluctant to pay more or to work more.[18]

Reformers took a tougher tack. They would use standardized tests to hold schools, teachers, and students accountable. Tests in English, math, and science would direct attention to those subjects, and test scores would show outsiders, including legislators, which schools were doing well and which needed improvement. For decades Utah school children had taken standardized tests, but the scores were kept secret. Such tests were not designed to judge schools, and educators said they would not allow non-educators to misuse them for that purpose. In 1990, Governor Bangerter proposed more money for schools, but, in return, he wanted one set of standardized tests for the whole state, with each school's results made public.[19]

The State Board of Education bought a commercial test called the Stanford Achievement Test for fifth, eighth, and eleventh graders. Utah's eighth and eleventh graders scored better than their national peers, but fifth graders scored below average in reading. That worried educators, who believe that in the upper grades students who cannot read books cannot succeed in school. They asked for help. In 1998, Governor Leavitt lured news cameras to an elementary school where he read children a story and proposed a program to improve reading. Republican lawmakers were at odds with Leavitt that year and voted his plan down, leaving school districts free to set up their own reading programs. A scholar studied how schools tried to improve reading and found that many teachers were not told of the reading problem nor of any plan to correct it. Plans from the top did not reach the classroom, and troubles persisted. In 2004, Governor Olene Walker asked for a special fund to address reading, but

18. "Many Students Goofing Off," *Salt Lake Tribune*, May 12, 2001; "Measure to Boost Number," "An Honest Look" editorial, "Performance Plus," "Plus a Minus for Most Pupils," "School Plan," *Deseret News*, Jan. 31, 1992, Dec. 21, 2002, Oct. 14, 16, 30, 2003; also Kirst, *Overcoming High School Senior Slump*, viii, 4, 12–13.

19. Twila Van Leer, "Bangerter's Education Proposals," *Deseret News*, Dec. 28, 1989.

lawmakers turned her down, too. Walker, a grandmotherly Latter-day Saint, threatened to veto the whole budget, and lawmakers quickly gave her a reading program, then changed their budget process so that no governor could ever do that again. Reading problems and ways to address them slipped from public attention.[20]

In 1998 and 1999, lawmakers enacted a program called the Utah Proficiency Assessment System for Schools, or Upass (pronounced "you pass"). The spelling was changed to U-Pass after students started to call it "Up ass." Lawmakers held students accountable by requiring every tenth grader to pass the Utah Basic Skills Competency Test, or UBSCT (pronounced "you biscuit"), showing their ability to read, write, and do math on an eighth-grade level. Students who failed the test could take it again up to five times, but they had to pass in order to graduate. So failing students might not be admitted to college, or get a job, or enter the military. "Tough love," legislators called it. When the test was given to the class of 2006, 24 percent failed, mostly in math. A father wrote that his daughter was a good student who planned on college until she failed UBSCT math. She took remedial classes and retook the test but "froze up" and failed again. Her father said she was ashamed of her failure and despairing of her future. The State Board of Education acted to help such students, ruling they would graduate after all. Test failures would be noted in fine print on their diplomas but would not appear on transcripts sent to colleges and employers. Such lenience angered legislators, who wanted consequences. As they feared, diminished consequences brought diminished effort. When Jordan School District offered classes to help students on their second or third try, only fifteen of some 300 failing students came. (Educators invited all 104 legislators to take UBSCT, and only one of them came.) In the recession of 2009–10, the state office of education provided lawmakers a helpful list of suggested

20. Jennifer Toomer–Cook, "Better Reading Skills," Jerry D. Spangler, Stephen Speckman, and Bob Bernick Jr., "Lawmakers Settle," *Deseret News*, Dec. 7, 1998, Feb. 28, 2004; Beck, "State-Mandated Test," 200–04.

budget cuts to meet the lean times. Only after they had enacted the cuts did legislators learn that U-Pass and UBSCT had been hidden in the list. Afterward Representative John Dougall, who sponsored the cuts, said he was happy he had ended U-Pass, even though he had not known that was what he was doing. "It pretended to provide accountability but didn't," he said.[21]

The federal No Child Left Behind law, advocated by President George W. Bush, passed Congress in 2002 and overtook state reform. Each state was required to give standardized tests and set a passing score. Each year, more students had to pass than the year before, until 2014 when all students had to pass with no child left behind. Moreover, the scores were to be "disaggregated," that is, counted separately for Caucasians, African Americans, Hispanics, Islanders, Asians, and Native Americans, as well as for non-English speakers, poor children, and the learning-disabled. If any group failed, the whole school failed, and increasingly harsh penalties fell on failing schools: a school that failed five times could be closed. The first year almost one-third of Utah's schools failed, mostly because not enough English learners and students with disabilities passed. Lawmakers rushed to the defense. Though they sometimes mistreated schools themselves, they objected to federal mistreatment. State representative Margaret Dayton introduced a bill to take Utah out of the program. Legislators backed down when Washington threatened to withhold $106 million in federal education funds, but lawmakers said they would be back next year.[22]

In 2005, Representative Dayton introduced an amended bill, designed to flout the law but keep the money. Federal officials said they were not fooled and warned that Utah might still lose its funding. State School Superintendent Patti Harrington repeatedly called US

---

21. See articles by Jennifer Toomer–Cook in the *Deseret News,* Aug. 2, 6, Sept. 11, Dec. 7, 2005; also "Skill Test Failures," *Deseret News,* June 19, 2008; "Thousands of Kids," "State Suspends School Accountability," *Salt Lake Tribune,* May 5, 2005, Apr. 9, 2010.

22. Jennifer Toomer-Cook and Tiffany Erickson, "A Third of Schools Fail," *Deseret News,* Dec. 16, 2003; Rudalevige, "No Child Left Behind?"; Brunelle, "Political Education."

Jon Huntsman Jr., was popular with tax payers and teachers, though he cut long-term school spending. *Photograph US State Department*

Secretary of Education Margaret Spellings, looking for compromise, but she never reached Spellings and her calls were not returned. As legislators considered Dayton's bill, Governor Jon Huntsman was invited to Washington to talk with Spellings. Legislators postponed their vote to wait for talks. Speaking anonymously, federal education officials told reporters that Governor Huntsman had been "summoned" to Washington to "get him and Utah in line." But Huntsman and Spellings failed to agree. Spellings then sent Utah legislators a letter saying that passage of the Dayton bill could cost Utah $76 million in federal money. Undaunted, Huntsman called a special legislative session, and lawmakers passed the anti-No Child Left Behind bill. "A stinging rebuke to the Bush Administration," said the *New York Times*.[23]

23. Sam Dillon, "Utah Vote," "Soccer Mom Ed Chief," *New York Times* Apr. 20, 28, 2005; George Archibald, "Spellings Presses Utah," *Washington Times*, Mar. 18, 2005.

After lawmakers defied the feds, educators resolved the fuss. To placate federal officials, they submitted "disaggregated" scores that focused on minority performance, and they took other steps to comply with federal rules. But educators complied artfully. First, the state board of education lowered the passing score from 65 to 60. Then they created an appeals committee, so that a failing school could appeal, and the committee might grant a passing score. Finally, educators imposed a "confidence interval." If a large number of students take a test many times, their scores will vary. Statisticians can calculate what the high and low scores are likely to be. Suppose a school had ten learning-disabled students, six had to pass for the school to pass, but only five did. Statisticians might then be able to calculate with a "confidence interval" of 90 percent that if the students took the test many times, on their best attempt six disabled students would pass. The school would therefore receive credit for six students passing. Though no one but statisticians understood the confidence interval, it enabled schools to pass. For example, in 2004, 760 Utah schools passed No Child Left Behind, but only 264 (35 percent) actually passed the test. Another 456 (60 percent) passed using the confidence interval, and thirty (4 percent) passed on appeal.[24] After educators adjusted No Child Left Behind, Utah schools fared well. Nationwide more than 3,500 schools were closed or restructured because they repeatedly failed. Only one of them was in Utah.[25]

The pattern of school politics was broken by the introduction of charter schools, which cut across the usual coalitions for and against reform. Charter schools are public schools, privately sponsored, and granted a charter by the state, which means that they have more freedom than regular schools. Minnesota created the first charter in 1992, and Utahns adopted the approach after hearing anecdotes of

---

24. In addition, 290 Utah schools took advantage of the federal Safe Harbor exemption.

25. Stephenson, "Evading 'No Child Left Behind,'" 159–61, 172–74, 187; "84% of Utah Schools," *Deseret News*, Dec. 7, 2004; "Utah Releases School Scores," *Salt Lake Tribune*, Sept. 16, 2009. The school that failed was West Middle School on the Uintah–Ouray Reservation, which soon became a charter school to teach academics and Ute culture.

success from other states. Governor Leavitt proposed a "pilot program" of eight schools in 1998. His plan required faculty to certify as public school educators, and so won cautious support from the UEA and state superintendent. But district superintendents and school boards foresaw charters taking money and students from public schools, and opposed them. On the conservative side, the Eagle Forum feared that some charters might teach permissive morality, and rallied conservative senators to nearly defeat the bill. After seeing the schools in practice, however, conservatives came to like them and sponsored legislation to increase their number and the share of public money they received. By 2010, Utah had seventy such schools teaching 30,000 students. The Jean Massieu School taught in American Sign Language, the Dual Immersion Academy taught in English and Spanish, Uintah River High School promoted Ute cultural pride, Hollywood High taught performing arts, and Success School taught students who were on criminal probation. The Karl G. Maeser Charter School had the largest proportion of students taking Advanced Placement tests of any school in 2009, but some other charter schools scored below average on standardized tests.[26]

Reformers said charters succeeded because they offered students a choice, and partially escaped the educational establishment. School-reforming Republican legislators sought to give every student a choice outside the establishment by issuing a voucher or tax credit to pay tuition so that all parents could choose their child's school, public or private. Public schools would then have to improve, or students, captive no longer, would leave them. Utah had only to value an individual's right to choose over the government's power to compel, and the market's invisible hand would work a salutary transformation—a story to make a Republican smile. But educators feared such choice. They saw private schools taking tax money from public schools, hiring cheap, unqualified teachers, and skimming off

---

26. Jennifer Toomer-Cook, "Charter Schools," *Deseret News*, Feb. 28, 1998; Burns, "History of Development," 66–113.

the best students and most supportive families. Public schools would be left underfunded and disrespected, less able to help the poor students who would be left behind.

Lawmakers rejected the first tax credit bill in 1997, and every session for the next ten years, they debated a voucher or tax-credit bill and voted it down. Governor Leavitt said he would veto any such bill that passed, and Governor Olene Walker did veto a voucher for autistic children, mostly to show that she opposed vouchers of any kind. But in the election of 2004, Republican Jon Huntsman Jr. promised to support school choice and was elected governor. Four years later, by a single vote in the House, Utah passed the most comprehensive voucher plan in America, offering wealthy children $500 toward private-school tuition and a poor child $3,500. That was still less than would have been spent on the child at a public school. No student already attending private school was eligible. No voucher money came from education funds. Lawmakers appropriated $9 million from the general fund, leaving public schools with more money and fewer students. "We are literally buying off the education system," said Senator Greg Bell as he voted yes.[27]

Educators, however, were not to be bought. Within a day of the bill's passage, the UEA began gathering signatures to force a popular vote. Within forty days, as set by law, they gathered 120,000 signatures, the most ever for a Utah ballot measure. Alarmed legislators rushed to the state supreme court and asked justices to enjoin the referendum on legal technicalities. Attorney General Mark Shurtleff issued an official opinion supporting the lawmakers. He also came to a summer meeting of the State Board of Education and told them that they must issue vouchers in time for students to use them in the fall. Board members withdrew into a secret meeting, where they found an "imminent threat to the safety and welfare of the people

---

27. Marjorie Cortez, "Two Weeks Left," *Deseret News*, Feb. 16, 1998; Dan Harrie, "Walker Flunks Bill," Nicole Stricker, "Utah Legislature," *Salt Lake Tribune*, Mar. 24, 2004, Feb. 9, 2007; also Noel, "Utah Education Vouchers," 397.

of Utah." Public danger, they said, compelled them to set aside the law, declare an emergency, and refuse to issue the vouchers. Supreme Court justices convened quickly and ruled that the referendum would go forward and that voters would decide the issue. The National Education Association spent $4 million to stop vouchers, while rich men on the other side spent even more to save school choice. Utahns voted against the vouchers by 62-to-38 percent. Democrats tried to exploit the Republican voucher failure and replace Republican legislators, but most failed.[28] Voters killed vouchers, but then reelected the Republicans who had supported vouchers.

This left Utah schools to continue as before, unreformed and the worst-funded in America. For decades the funding was low because Utah had so many children and a middling economy. In the mid-1990s, legislators quietly made low funding of schools state policy. In 1996 they proposed, and voters approved, a constitutional amendment ending the dedication of income tax to public education. Then legislators shifted income-tax revenue away from schools to other government purposes. Lawmakers also detached schools from the growth in property tax. In the past, school revenue automatically increased when the value of property rose. In 1996 the legislature "floated" the tax, that is, each year they fixed the amount schools would receive and then technicians calculated the rate needed to produce that amount. School property tax eventually fell about one-third as a result. In 2007, a year with record revenue, legislators cut state income taxes and $150–200 million from annual school revenues. None of these measures had a large immediate effect. All were technical, the gradual, long-term reductions were scarcely noticed by the public. By 2006 the Utah Foundation estimated that the changes together cost schools $1.3

---

28. Wendy Leonard, "Will Voters Decide?" Tiffany Erickson, "Spending on Voucher Battle," *Deseret News*, Mar. 2, 2007, Jan. 8, 2008; Nicole Stricker, "Utah Legislature," and "Board Deals," Donald Meyers, "After Voucher," *Salt Lake Tribune*, Feb. 9, May 30, 2007, Feb. 5, 2008; *Snow v. Office of Legislative Research*, 167 P. 3d 1051 (Utah 2007).

billion, one-third of school spending. In 1996, before the changes, Utah had been fifth among the states in percentage of total personal income devoted to public schools. By 2014, Utah had fallen to thirty-seventh.[29] After the mid-1990s, Utah's economy grew more than the American economy, but Utah school spending fell further behind spending in other states. Republican politicians never say they hold down educational spending on purpose. They always say they spend as much as Utah can afford.

REMARKS

Historically, Utahns valued education. From statehood to World War II, they raised taxes, required attendance, and gave their children a good start in life. In the Reagan years, Utahns led the commission that wrote *A Nation at Risk* and persuaded every state to try to improve its schools. Utah launched thirty years of commissions, studies, and reforms and presented each new plan with fanfare and promises. But educators were unenthusiastic. They doubted schools were really so bad and resisted direction from non-educators. Most of all, educators saw that politicians were free with talk but stingy with money. Almost every year since the *Nation at Risk* report, Utah spent less on education per child than any other state.

Only school vouchers provoked open confrontation between educators and politicians, and educators won. With other, less radical reform, educators went along but quietly blunted each plan in implementation. Within the educational establishment, the Career Ladder turned into a general salary increase and site-based management became more time off. Educators granted diplomas around U-Pass and UBSCT, then gulled lawmakers into ending the tests. They defanged No Child Left Behind with statistical hocus pocus. Legislators, governors, the federal Department of Education,

---

29. "Paradox Lost: Utah's Public Education Funding Effort," "Getting by with Less: Two Decades of K–12 Education Revenue and Spending," *Utah Foundation*, Apr., Nov. 2006, www.utahfoundation.org.

Congress, and US presidents all tried to change the schools, and educators outwaited and outwitted them all.

As educators acted quietly to defeat reform, politicians acted quietly to pilfer education money. Republicans pointed to the failure of reform and said they did not want to "pay more for the same old thing." They removed the education earmark from income tax, floated the property tax, founded the Centennial Highway Fund, diverted sales tax, and cut income tax, all, in part, to keep rising revenues away from schoolchildren. Legislators and educators both acted in technical ways the public neither noticed nor understood, and the result has been underfunded, unreformed schools. Utahns wanted better education for their children, but in the three decades of attempted reform, schools were scanted, reforms foundered, and test scores remained mediocre. Utahns were unable to realize their hopes for better schools.

17

RECAPITULATION

Utah is like a control group, preserved, in part, from American change as if to show by comparison the effects of those changes. As in a controlled trial, the difference was focused. Utahns live under the same federal government as other Americans, and their economy and state government institutions are similar. The difference focused on religion, morals, and families. Utah may be the enclave where traditional morality and families best survived social change, and so highlights by contrast the course America has taken, and indicates what a more socially conservative America might have looked like.

Latter-day Saints led the resistance to social change. They held out for traditional families and traditional morality. Their preferences barely affected America, but in Utah their beliefs influenced the way people voted and acted. Utah demography displays the effects of Latter-day Saint family behavior. Traditional family living affects state economic indicators and perhaps its social troubles. Utah politics became religiously divided, conservative, and Republican because Latter-day Saints resisted the American sexual revolution with its new morals and new family norms.

Until World War II, most Americans married and had children in traditional families. To promote such families, laws prohibited sex outside of marriage, gay sex, abortion, pornography, and sometimes birth control. The arts were censored and speech restricted. Religion preached that illicit sex displeased heaven. Men and women had different roles. Men married, worked, supported families. Women married, had children, and took care of families. A woman who chose man's work might face social disapproval, workplace discrimination, sexual harassment, and legal barriers. Laws, habits, expectations, and opinions formed a public morality in support of traditional families. The old morality could be messy, unplanned, changing, oft-evaded, hypocritical in practice, and rarely seen whole, but it kept traditional families as the ideal and the norm, and thus harnessed sex to raising children.

After World War II, birth control improved and enabled women to postpone or avoid babies, earn degrees, pursue careers, and overcome dependence on men. Thus empowered, they demanded opportunity and equality. Young people saw sex without pregnancy and seized their chances. When reproached with old rules, they said sex was private. But if sex were private, why were gays and lesbians so put upon? They, too, demanded acceptance and equality. The old morality came to seem irrational, discriminatory, sometimes even cruel.

Traditional morality conflicts with the American ideals of freedom and equality. If traditional families are the norm, women will be pushed toward marriage and motherhood, and gays are excluded. Neither receives equal treatment. The old morality diminishes the freedom of young people and others to have sex. In a series of conflicts extending over decades, Americans pointed to liberty and equality and dismantled the old morality. They adopted a libertarian solution. Anyone could choose a traditional family, but abortion, gay sex, single motherhood, and other choices became equal before the law. America also enacted new laws—against workplace discrimination or hate crimes, for example—to protect new liberty and equality against lingering old ways and unreformed behavior.

Evangelicals, Latter-day Saints, and others of strong religious belief adhered to the old morality and became political conservatives. Latter-day Saint leaders preached the importance of families more as traditional families became more beleaguered. After *Roe v. Wade* struck down laws against abortion, the American electorate realigned. Strongly religious voters tended conservative, and those of moderate or no religion tended progressive. In America, conservative religious voters are one-quarter of the electorate, but in Utah, Latter-day Saints are two-thirds of all voters, so the change that realigned national politics affected Utah with greater force and wrought a conservative transformation in state politics.

While America chose liberty and equality, Utah chose traditional families, or tried to; federal judges struck down many of Utah's choices. Latter-day Saints led in Utah's pro-traditional-family policies and continued to dissent after national decisions were made. Latter-day Saints became Republicans, by some measures America's most Republican group, because Republicans are more favorable to the old morality and more opposed to enlarged federal power. Utah non-LDS, in contrast, were less attached to the old morality. They saw efforts to retain it as attempts to impose Latter-day Saint morals on non-Mormons, and they preferred government from Washington to government by the Church. They became Democrats and a permanent Utah minority. Utah became America's most religiously divided state.

The new religious division follows the pattern of Utah political history: Agreement on families brings political agreement, while family difference brings political difference. In Utah territory, Saints and Americans disagreed over polygamy. Ever harsher punishments were inflicted and statehood was withheld until Latter-day Saints renounced polygamy and accepted the nineteenth-century, pro-traditional-family morality then dominant in America. After Latter-day Saints became like Americans in their families, statehood was granted, and for eighty years Latter-day Saints and Utahns became like Americans in politics. Utah political parties no longer aligned with religion, so the state had strong, two-party competition. State government usually swung Democratic or Republican as voters chose between parties in national elections, and Utahns usually voted with national majorities. Politically, Utah was an ordinary state in the

American mainstream. But as federal courts imposed a new public morality beginning in 1973, Latter-day Saints withdrew from the political mainstream and became Republicans, almost immovable by issues and trends. Utahns had a second separation into a Latter-day Saint political party and a non-LDS political party as they had in territorial time. Party competition withered as the Latter-day Saint party almost always won. Utah state government no longer changed parties as America changed parties, instead voters gave Republicans a seemingly permanent ascendancy. Utah political history divides into the territory, a mainstream period, and a Republican ascendancy, and the character of each period is determined by whether Latter-day Saints and Americans agreed about sex and families.

As Americans cast off their old morality, families changed. People remained free to choose a traditional family, but fewer did. Americans married later, married less, cohabited more, and had fewer children, and more of those children outside of marriage. Families divided by economic class with a college degree used as a convenient dividing line by social scientists. Upper-middle-class young people typically postpone marriage for college and career, have sex before marriage, but postpone children until after marriage. Poor and working Americans increasingly have children outside of marriage. By 2010, 40 percent of American children were born to unmarried parents. Research shows those children often suffer disadvantage.

Most social scientists who study families say families changed because of economics, not because of morality. New technology that brought women to the workplace brought other changes detrimental to working men. Manufacturing declined in America, as did other jobs that paid family-supporting wages. Returns rose for capitalists, wages rose for the college educated, women found work and earned more, but uneducated men could not find good jobs and could not support a family. Social scientists say the cause of family change is the dissolution of the economic base of working families. The economic diagnosis suggests an economic remedy: the government could subsidize poor and working families so that no one goes without. Progressives point to some European countries, where an even higher share of babies are born outside of marriage, but generous government programs ameliorate poverty and social trouble. Progressives, including almost all social scientists who study families, say America should increase welfare programs and become more like Europe.

Although economics explain part of the decline in marriage, low incomes cannot be the entire explanation. Poor and working people had even lower incomes through most of the past, but they still married before they had children. During the Great Depression, for example, fewer than 5 percent of babies were born outside of marriage, perhaps one-tenth of the current percentage. Economic changes for poor and working people partly caused the rise in out-of-marriage births, but changes in morals and attitudes were also a factor.

Nor does Utah fit the progressive economic explanation. Utah's economy followed the nation as it lost mining and manufacturing jobs. Average wages fell by one-third in comparison to the country as a whole. Per capita income is 18 percent below the national average. Yet Utahns marry more, cohabit less, marry younger, and have more children, with fewer outside of marriage than the national average. Utah and America experienced similar economic change, but Utah had less family change.

Changes in families bring changes in society. For example, married men, especially if they live with their children, are more likely to work than other men. Utah men marry more and have more children than other Americans and are 11 percent more likely to be in the labor force. Utah women are also more likely to be in the labor force, though the difference is smaller. Partly because of family differences, Utah has one of the largest gaps of any state between men's and women's wages. Utah women marry younger and have more children than their national counterparts, and children reduce a woman's income. Partly because they marry young, Utah women are less likely to finish college than Utah men, in contrast to the national preponderance of women graduates. As traditional families persist in Utah, so the old division of men in the workforce and women less attached to careers also seems to persist, and Utah women continue to suffer larger workplace disadvantages than American women.

Work and families keep Utahns out of poverty. Since 1979 when annual statistics became available, Utah's poverty rate has averaged 24 percent less than the national rate. Less poverty means less dependence on government. From 1960 through 2015, Utah participation in federal welfare was just over half the national average. Utahns were one-third less likely to be on Medicaid or food stamps, and Utah often had the lowest federal disability rate of any state.

Traditional families keep children out of poverty. Utah is the state with the smallest percentage of children living in lone-parent families and the largest percentage living with two married parents. Children in lone-parent families are four times more likely to be poor than children living with two married parents. As a result, Utah has averaged 38 percent less child poverty than the nation since 1986. Poor children, social scientists have found, have worse health, do worse in school, are more likely to take drugs, and to get in trouble with the law. The troubles of poor children affect communities, increasing crime, drug use, health troubles, and dependence on government.

For half a century the American rich have become much richer while the poor have stayed just as poor. Progressives say widening inequality has worsened social troubles and threatens democracy. Utah incomes are among the most equal of any state, partly because of less poverty, and Utahns are more likely than other Americans to be middle class. Their middle class lives fit their middle class morality of traditional families and work.

As progressives might predict, Utah, with less poverty and inequality, also has fewer social troubles: lower rates of violent crime, illegal drug use, homelessness, teen pregnancy, abortion, and incarceration, though more property crime and prescription-drug abuse.

Social science shows married men are less likely to be arrested for violent crimes, and children from traditional families less likely to be delinquent or drug users. Traditional family members are less likely to be homeless. Latter-day Saint morality may partly account for lower teen-pregnancy and abortion rates. Utah has a middling economy, stingy social programs, impoverished schools, and conservative government. Yet Utah has less poverty, less inequality, and fewer social troubles than other states, partly because Utahns choose traditional families and work, and those choices affect their lives, children, and communities.

To deal with the tangle of poverty and social troubles, America could try European-style taxes and social programs if voters approved. Utah, however, seems inimitable. Latter-day Saint differences depend on habit, culture, and religion, which are hard to instill and not good tools for government. Moreover, Utah families—and so, maybe, its habits and culture—are changing in the American direction. Demography shows the trend: Utahns marry later, fewer people marry, fertility falls, the population ages, and more babies are born outside of marriage. Religion also declines especially among the young. The difference between Utah and America was not that they moved in different directions, but rather that they moved in the same direction at different speeds. America moved faster, but Utah slowly becomes more like America in sex and family ways.

Although demography moves in the American direction, Latter-day Saint political solidarity seems to have strengthened over the past ninety years. In the Great Depression, Church leaders urged members to shun federal help and practice thrift. They politicked against the New Deal and established a church welfare program to help the poor and to keep members from federal relief.[1] Despite those efforts, Latter-day Saints took more federal help than other Americans, and Utah voters rejected apostle-senator Reed Smoot, chose Franklin Roosevelt four times, and voted to repeal Prohibition.

1. Darowski, "WPA versus Utah Church," 167–85.

In 1940, Utah political scientist Frank Jonas wrote, "The Church membership has not obeyed its leaders on any important issue or candidacy for the past ten years."[2]

As Depression-era Church leaders preached against dependence on government, contemporary Church leaders preach for traditional families and morals. But in contrast to the Depression, Latter-day Saints now adhere to traditional ways more than other Americans, and they vote their moral beliefs. Latter-day Saints see a traditional family as part of a good life, and adhering to that belief, they seem more willing now than they have been at times in the past to stand together with their leaders against national trends.

The politics of social resistance were reinforced by Utah's land and climate. Most of the state is arid, empty, and federally owned. Until about 1970 the federal government, with defense jobs and water projects, appeared the best hope for prosperity in a hard land. But attitudes changed, and Washington came to seem bossy, threatening, and uncaring. Utahns first changed their thinking on defense. During and after World War II, defense work was the engine that pulled Utah out of Depression into a larger share of national prosperity. But the Downwinders' Tale told how nuclear fallout brought cancer to Southern Utah, and defense officials were careless of the risk and untruthful in their response. The story was exaggerated, but partly true, and it led Utahns to fear they might be harmed again by MX missiles, nerve gas, biological weapons, or nuclear waste. All those unsavory things were drawn to Utah's vast, empty, federally-owned lands. In every controversy, Utahns retold the Downwinders' Tale to remind themselves of their vulnerability and of federal perfidy. But opposition to defense was impure. While Utahns fought against MX or nuclear waste, they also fought to keep Hill Air Force Base, and the Tooele truck repair shop because they provided good federal jobs.

From first settlement, Utahns believed irrigation was their answer

2. Jonas, "Sagebrush Democracy," 34.

to the desert. Through most of the twentieth century, they believed only the federal government could build the big projects they wanted. They won the Central Utah Project, but it disappointed in execution, and now near completion, it is not clear that the biggest part of the project was needed. Water no longer ties Utah to Washington.

As the anxieties of the second-driest state receded, the frustrations of the second-most federally-owned stood forward. The federal government tightened its management of federal land and shifted influence from those who lived near the land to environmental groups with lawyers in court and lobbyists in Washington. Utah was affected because the federal government owns two-thirds of all Utah land, and changes in policy can bring local shocks, as in the Uintah Basin. Federal land administration was partisan. Democratic administrations favored environmentalists, while Republicans favored Utah's political establishment. Because Utah was so Republican, Democratic administrations knew they could not win in Utah and selected the state for gestures, demonstrations, and experiments they did not impose in states where they hoped to win votes. So President Bill Clinton picked Utah for his campaign monument, Secretary Bruce Babbitt reinventoried only Utah, and Secretary Kenneth Salazar picked only Utah for his informal directive to limit drilling. Democrats acted more boldly than Republicans, until President Donald Trump, who cut the size of two of Utah's national monuments. Litigation, as always, is underway, and land conflict seems likely to intensify. Utahns were once tied to the federal government by defense jobs and water-project hopes. Now federal land policy, exacerbated by actions of Democratic administrations, reinforce Utah Republicanism and estrangement from Washington.

Every session of the Utah State Legislature sees large majorities of Republican Latter-day Saint men who have enacted their public morality, forbidding abortion, pornography, indecency, providing birth control to teens without notifying parents, and gay marriage. Legislators did not just defend old laws, but passed new ones to accomplish old ends. Many of those laws surely represented the considered preference of most Utahns. For forty-five years, Utahns have debated morality in their legislature and reached decisions that have been thrown out by federal judges. In addition, Utah legislators cut taxes, balance budgets, scant schools and social programs, and complain about federal control. They are among the most popular state legislatures. Latter-day Saints approve them two-to-one. Non-LDS disapprove by an almost equal proportion.

While Utah legislators gained power as agents of a new Republican-Latter-day Saint majority, Utah governors gained popularity by bridging the religious-political divide. For forty-five years of public opinion polling, they have been among America's most popular governors. Except for Alaska and Hawaii, Utah has the longest-serving governors. Both Democrats and Republicans have been moderate conservatives, almost always to the left of the legislature, especially on the intertwined issues of schools and taxes. Starting with Democrat Scott Matheson in 1977, all gained popularity by opposing Washington, even though they often lost their battles.

Utah administration became tidy. State government used to overspend its revenues, fill jobs by patronage, deposit money at no interest, extort political donations from state workers, and lack coherence. After decades of fitful struggle, Utah now wins recognition for the way it conducts business on principles of good government.

Federal courts have been the government agency that most shaped Utah society and history over the past half century with their decisions on public morals. Many Americans were abandoning the old morality even before federal judges struck it down, and more progressive laws would likely have come to most states without judicial intervention. But Latter-day Saints clung more tenaciously to the old ways, and without court rulings progressive change would have been less likely in Utah. As important as the decisions themselves was the Latter-day Saint reaction. They withdrew from the American political mainstream and Utah became Republican, conservative, and religiously divided. In contrast to the large influence of federal courts, state courts have made little policy difference. Some state supreme court justices, led by Chief Justice Christine Durham, sought to "strengthen Utah's constitution" and enlarge the power of constitutional interpretation in Utah governance. But Republican legislators already squirmed under federal court leadership and did not want more direction from judges. Besides, most of the judges who sought a larger voice were appointees of Democratic governor Scott Matheson, who left office in 1985. Since then Republican governors have appointed Republican justices, less interested in strengthening Utah's constitution, and the court retains a lesser policy role.

Republican legislators cut taxes, and most of the money for their reductions came eventually from schools. The tension between taxes and education funding is the historic crux of Utah budget policy. Republicans blared their lower taxes across the state, but to channel the money from education, they found complicated, long-term paths, which citizens hardly followed or even noticed. As a result, Utah has spent, as of this writing, the least money per school child of any state for thirty-two years. Republicans say their tax cuts have helped the economy, and, in fact, Utah has prospered more than other states during the quarter century of tax cuts. Though they cut funding, Republicans sponsored a stream of commissions, studies, laws, and innovations designed to improve schools. None of their measures found much favor with educators, who resisted most of them passively within the education establishment. Republican reform neither succeeded nor endured. Utah schools remain underfunded, unreformed, and underperforming.

Utahns may not have their ideal state government, but they seem to like the one they have. In the past forty years, two national, populist, conservative movements, the tax revolt and term limits, challenged state political establishments. Utahns voted down both. Governors and the legislature consistently receive higher job-approval ratings than their counterparts elsewhere. More important to happiness, the history of Utah has occurred in fortunate times, when people lived longer with better health amid improving technology. Wealth grew, fewer babies died, and families raised children in peace.

In 1978 historian Richard Poll noted the consensus long view of Utah history: "The state and the nation have become so interlocked that one might ask what meaningful distinction remains."[3] Utah historians agreed the Utah story was assimilation: in pioneer times, Utah was a different society from America, but the federal government forced the Saints to give up their chief differences, and after statehood, remaining differences were gradually rubbed away as Utahns followed opportunities in the American economy. There is "little uniqueness to Utah's history after 1920," wrote historian S. George Ellsworth.[4] That was true when Poll and Ellsworth wrote, but even as they were writing, Utah was changing. In the 1970s Utah was politically similar to America, but as Latter-day Saints left the mainstream, Utah became politically different. Utah demography also became different from the American norm, and those differences ramify through Utah's economy, government, and public order as this book has described. The new Utah differences are not so large as those in territorial times, and Utah remains American, but meaningful distinctions are now clear and numerous. Moreover, while Utahns assimilated because of economics, Utahns became different again because of religion, morals, and families, the same factors that brought disagreement in territorial times. The new changes require revision of the old assimilation story. Through the decades of assimilation, Latter-day Saints retained a capacity for moral difference. Moral difference incited territorial conflict, smoldered through assimilation in the string of Utah quarrels over public morality, and then flared again as Latter-day Saints rejected the American sexual revolution for reasons consistent with their history, habits, and

---

3. Richard D. Poll et al, eds., *Utah's History*, 678.
4. Peterson and Cannon, *Awkward State*, 351–55.

teachings. The new story that includes moral difference explains current Utah politics, while the old story cannot. Besides the new story shows Utah is a more interesting place than it seemed before.

Utah quarrels continue ancient quarrels. The political philosopher Leo Strauss said the West—that is, Europe and its offspring—has two roots: Athens and Jerusalem. The two conflict. For example, biblical religions teach the most important human trait is obedient love. The philosophies of Athens teach independent understanding is most important. The conflict cannot be reconciled. The West cannot find integrity, fulfillment, or repose. Yet Strauss believed that conflicting roots brought vitality to the West.[5] Utah is far from both ancient cities in time, place, and character, but Athens and Jerusalem still contend in Utah. Maybe their quarrel will bring vitality. We can hope.

---

5. Strauss, "Jerusalem and Athens," 147–73.

BIBLIOGRAPHY

Abrams, Douglas M. *Conflict, Competition, or Cooperation? Dilemmas of State Education Policymaking.* Albany: State University of New York Press, 1993.

Abshire, David, ed. *Triumphs and Tragedies of the Modern Presidency: Seventy-six Case Studies of Presidential Leadership.* Westport, CT: Praegar, 2001.

Adams, Greg D. "Abortion: Evidence of an Issue Evolution." *American Journal of Political Science* 41, no. 3 (July 1977): 718–37.

Advisory Committee Report on Drug Abuse: Summations and Recommendations. Salt Lake City: State of Utah, 1969.

Aird, Polly. "'You Nasty Apostates, Clear Out': Reasons for Disaffection in the Late 1850s." *Journal of Mormon History* 30, no. 2 (Fall 2004): 129–207.

Akerlof, George A., Janet L. Yellen, and Michael Katz. "An Analysis of Out-of-Wedlock Childbearing in the United States." *Quarterly Journal of Economics* 111, no. 2 (May 1996): 277–317.

Alexander, Thomas G. "Brief Histories of Three Federal Military Installations in Utah." *Utah Historical Quarterly* 34, no. 2 (Spring 1966): 121–38.

———. "The Economic Consequences of the War: Utah and the Depression of the Early 1920s." In May, ed., *Dependent Commonwealth*, 57–91.

———. "The Emergence of a Republican Majority in Utah, 1970–1992." In Lowitt, ed., *Politics in the Postwar American West.*, 260–76.

———. "Interdependence and Change: Mutual Irrigation Companies in Utah's Wasatch Oasis in an Age of Modernization, 1870–1930." *Utah Historical Quarterly* 71, no. 4 (Fall 2003): 292–314.

———. "An Investment in Progress: Utah's First Federal Reclamation Project." *Utah Historical Quarterly* 39, no. 3 (Summer 1971): 286–304.

———. *Utah: The Right Place.* Salt Lake City: Gibbs M. Smith, 2003.

———. "The Word of Wisdom: From Principle to Requirement." *Dialogue: A Journal of Mormon Thought* 14, no. 3 (Autumn 1981): 78–88.

———. "Utah War Industry during World War II: A Human Impact Analysis." *Utah Historical Quarterly* 51, no. 1 (Winter 1983): 72–93.

————. "Utah's Constitution: A Reflection of the Territorial Experience." *Utah Historical Quarterly* 64, no. 3 (Summer 1996): 264–81.

Allen, James B. "The Great Protectionist, Sen. Reed Smoot of Utah." *Utah Historical Quarterly* 45, no. 4 (Fall 1977): 325–45.

————. *Still the Right Place: Utah's Second Half-Century of Statehood, 1945–1995.* Provo: BYU Charles Redd Center for Western Studies, 2017.

————. "Utah's Public Schools: Problems, Controversies, and Achievements, 1945–2000." In Cannon and Embry, eds., *Utah in the Twentieth Century*, 318–42.

Allen, Richard Cardell. "Governor George H. Dern and Utah's Participation in the Colorado River Compact, 1922–1933." Master's thesis, University of Utah, 1958.

Alley, John R. Jr. "Utah State Supreme Court Justice Samuel R. Thurman." *Utah Historical Quarterly* 61, no. 3 (Summer 1993): 233–48.

Alt, James E., David Dreyer Lassen, and Shanna S. Rose. "The Causes of Transparency: Evidence from U.S. States." Paper presented to an International Monetary Fund conference, Washington, DC, Nov. 2005. Available at www.imf.org.

Amsler, Mary, Douglas Mitchell, Linda Nelson, and Thomas Timar. *An Evaluation of the Utah Career Ladder System.* San Francisco: Far West Laboratory for Education Research and Development, 1988.

Anderson, Desmond L. "History of the Reorganization of Utah State Administrative Government by the Twenty-fourth Legislature." Master's thesis, Utah State Agricultural College, 1950.

Anderson, Nels. *Desert Saints: The Mormon Frontier in Utah.* Chicago: University of Chicago Press, 1942.

Annual Report of Labor Market Information. Salt Lake City: Utah Department of Workforce Services, 2006–present.

Annual Survey of State Government Finances. Washington: US Census Bureau, 1915–present.

Anspaugh, Lynn R., and Bruce W. Church. "Historical Estimates of External Gamma Exposure from Testing at the Nevada Test Site." *Health Physics* 51, no. 1 (July 1986): 35–51.

Arrington, Leonard J. "The Commercialization of Utah's Economy: Trends and Developments from Statehood to 1910." In May, ed., *Dependent Commonwealth*, 3–34.

————. *From Wilderness to Empire: The Role of Utah in Western Economic History.* Salt Lake City: University of Utah Institute of American Studies, 1961.

————. *Great Basin Kingdom: An Economic History of the Latter-day Saints, 1830–1900.* Cambridge, MA: Harvard University Press, 1958.

———— and Davis Bitton. *The Mormon Experience: A History of the Latter-day Saints*. New York: Knopf, 1979.

———— and George Jensen. *The Defense Industry of Utah*. Logan: USU Department of Economics, 1965.

———— and Thomas C. Anderson. "The 'First' Irrigation Reservoir in the United States." *Utah Historical Quarterly* 39, no. 3 (Summer 1971): 207–23.

———— and Thomas G. Alexander. "Sentinels on the Desert: The Dugway Proving Ground (1942–1963) and Deseret Chemical Depot (1942–1955)." *Utah Historical Quarterly* 32, no. 1 (Winter 1964): 32–43.

———— and Thomas G. Alexander. "They Kept 'Em Rolling: The Tooele Army Depot, 1942–1962." *Utah Historical Quarterly* 31, no. 1 (Winter 1963): 3–25.

Artis, Julie E. "Maternal Cohabitation and Child Wellbeing among Kindergarten Children." *Journal of Marriage and Family* 69, no. 1 (Feb. 2007): 222–36.

Ashley, Jeffrey, and Robert L. Jones. "The Central Utah Project." *Journal of Land Resources & Environmental Law* 22, no. 2 (2002): 273–308.

Auditor General's Annual Report to the Utah State Legislature. 1930–present. Salt Lake City.

Auten, Brian J. *Carter's Conversion: The Hardening of American Defense Policy*. Columbia: University of Missouri Press, 2008.

Autor, David H. "The Unsustainable Rise of the Disability Rolls in the United States." Cambridge, MA: National Bureau of Economic Research, Dec. 2011. Available at www.nber.org.

Aydelotte, Loman Franklin. "The Political Thought and Activity of Heber J. Grant, Seventh President of the Church of Jesus Christ of Latter-day Saints." Master's thesis, Brigham Young University, 1964.

Babbitt, Bruce. *Cities in the Wilderness: A New Vision of Land Use in America*. Washington, DC: Island Press, 2005.

Bagley, Will. *Blood of the Prophets: Brigham Young and the Massacre at Mountain Meadows*. Norman: University of Oklahoma Press, 2002.

Bahr, Howard, and Theodore Caplow. *Old Men Drunk and Sober*. New York: New York University Press, 1974.

Baker, Mason. "What Does It Mean to Comply with NEPA?" *Utah Environmental Law Review* 31 (2011), 241–62.

Ball, Howard. *Justice Downwind: America's Atomic Testing Program in the 1950s*. New York: Oxford University Press, 1986.

Ball, Jonathan, Juliette Tennert, and Jennifer Robinson. "The Utah State Budget Report for FY16–17." *California Journal of Politics and Policy* 9, no. 1 (2016): 1–12.

Balmer, Randall, and Jana Riess, eds. *Mormonism and American Politics.* New York City: Columbia University Press, 2016.

Balmforth, Janet R. "'Good Roads Roberts' and the Fight for Utah Highways." *Utah Historical Quarterly* 49, no. 1 (Winter 1981): 56–65.

Baskin, Robert N. *Reminiscences of Early Utah.* Salt Lake City: Shepard Book Company, 1914.

Bate, Kerry William. *Utah's 1992 Homeless Count.* Salt Lake City: Division of Community Development Service, 1992.

Bates, Benjamin Will. "Exploring Justice Courts in Utah and Three Problems Inherent in the Justice Court System." *Utah Law Review* 2001, no. 3 (2001): 731–76.

Beck, Beth Gale Quist. "State-Mandated Test Score Accountability: Its Usefulness and Meanings for School Districts." PhD diss., University of Utah, 1995.

Beck, Harold L., and Philip W. Krey. "Radiation Exposures in Utah from Nevada Nuclear Tests." *Science,* Apr. 1, 1983, 18–24.

Bedford, Daniel. "Climate Change and the Future of the Great Salt Lake." In Crimmel, ed., *Desert Water,* 80–97.

Behind Closed Doors: The Abuse of Trust and Discretion in the Establishment of the Grand Staircase–Escalante National Monument. Report of the Subcommittee on National Parks and Public Lands. Washington: General Printing Office, 1998.

Bennion, Lowell "Ben." "The Incidence of Mormon Polygamy in 1880: 'Dixie' versus Davis Stake." *Journal of Mormon History* 11 (1984): 27–42.

Berry, William D., Evan J. Ringquist, Richard C. Fording, and Russell L. Hanson. "Measuring Citizen and Government Ideology in the American States, 1960–1993." *American Journal of Political Science* 42, no. 1 (Jan. 1998): 327–48.

Bickel, Alexander M. *The Least Dangerous Branch: The Supreme Court at the Bar of Politics.* New Haven: Yale University Press, 1986.

Biennial Report of the State Auditor. Salt Lake City: State of Utah, 1920.

Bigler, David L. "The Aiken Party Executions and the Utah War, 1857–1858." *Western Historical Quarterly* 38, no. 4 (Nov. 2007): 457–76.

———. *The Forgotten Kingdom: The Mormon Theocracy in the American West.* Spokane: Arthur H. Clark, 1998.

———. "'A Lion in the Path': Genesis of the Utah War, 1857–58." *Utah Historical Quarterly* 76, no. 1 (Winter 2008): 4–21.

Bingham, Jay R. "Reclamation and the Colorado." *Utah Historical Quarterly* 28, no. 3 (July 1960): 232–49.

Bishop, M. Guy. "The Paper Power Plant: Utah's Kaiparowits Project and the Politics of Environmentalism." *Journal of the West* 35, no. 3 (July 1996): 26–35.

Bitton, R. Davis. "The B. H. Roberts Case of 1898–1900." *Utah Historical Quarterly* 25, no. 1 (Winter 1957): 27–46.

Bloch, Stephen H. M., and Heidi J. McIntosh. "A View from the Front Lines: The Fate of Utah's Redrock Wilderness under the George W. Bush Administration." *Golden Gate University Law Review* 33, no. 3 (Spring 2003): 473–501.

Blumm, Michael C, and Andrew B. Erickson. "Federal Wild Lands Policy in the Twenty-first Century: What a Long, Strange Trip It's Been." *Colorado Natural Resources, Energy, and Environmental Law Review* 25, no. 1 (2014): 1–58.

Blumstein, Alfred, and Joel Wallman, eds. *The Crime Drop in America.* New York: Cambridge University Press, 2006.

Bluth, John F., and Wayne K. Hinton. "The Great Depression." In Poll et al., *Utah's History*, 481–96.

Book of the States. Lexington, KY: Council of State Governments, 2006–07.

Brace, Paul, Kellie Sims–Butler, Kevin Arceneaux, and Martin Johnson. "Public Opinion in the American States: New Perspectives Using National Survey Data." *American Journal of Political Science* 46, no. 1 (Jan. 2002): 173–89.

Bradley, John, ed. *Learning to Glow: A Nuclear Reader.* Tucson: University of Arizona Press, 2000.

Bradley, Martha Sonntag. "The Mormon Relief Society and the International Women's Year Conference." *Journal of Mormon History* 21, no. 1 (Spring 1995): 105–67.

———. "Reclamation of Young Citizens: Reform of Utah's Juvenile Legal System, 1888–1910." *Utah Historical Quarterly* 51, no. 4 (Fall 1983): 328–45.

Brennan, Amy E. "Grassroots of the Desert: Analysis of the Roles of the Utah Wilderness Association and the Southern Utah Wilderness Alliance." Master's thesis, Utah State University, 1998.

Brennan, William J. "State Constitutions and the Protection of Individual Rights." *Harvard Law Review* 90, no. 3 (Jan. 1977): 489–504.

Brim, Patricia. "The IWY Conference in Utah." Unpublished paper, Utah Women's Issues Collection, 1970s–80s, box 4, fd. 35. Special Collections, Marriott Library, University of Utah.

Bringhurst, Newell G. "The Mining Career of George H. Dern." Master's thesis, University of Utah, 1967.

Brint, Steven, and Seth Abrutyn, "Who's Right about the Right? Comparing Competing Explanations of the Link between White Evangelicals and Conservative Politics." *Journal for the Scientific Study of Religion* 49, no. 2 (June 2010): 328–50.

Brinton, Mark Ashby. "A History of the Unemployed Parent Option of the Aid to Families with Dependent Children Welfare Program in Utah." Honor's thesis, University of Utah, 1984.

Brooks, Clem. "Religious Influence and the Politics of Family Decline Concern: Trends, Sources, and U.S. Political Behavior." *American Sociological Review* 67, no. 2 (Apr. 2002): 191–211.

Brooks, Juanita. *Mountain Meadows Massacre.* Norman: University of Oklahoma Press, 1962.

Brown, Adam R. *Utah Politics and Government: American Democracy among a Unique Electorate.* Lincoln: University of Nebraska Press, 2018.

Brown, Susan L. "Marriage and Child Well-Being: Research and Policy Perspectives." *Journal of Marriage and Family* 72, no. 5 (Oct. 2010): 1059–77.

Brumfield, Olivia. "The Birth, Death, and Afterlife of the Wild Lands Policy: The Evolution of the Bureau of Land Management's Authority." *Environmental Law* 44, no. 1 (2014): 249–84.

Brunelle, Nora. "Political Education: An Analysis of the Policy and Politics behind Utah's Opposition to No Child Left Behind." *Utah Law Review* vol. 2006, no. 2 (2006): 419–37.

Budget Processes in the States. Washington, DC: National Association of State Budget Officers, 2015.

Budig, Michelle J., and Paula England. "The Wage Penalty for Motherhood." *American Sociological Review* 66, no. 2 (Apr. 2001): 204–25.

Bumpass, Larry, and Hsien–Hen Lu. "Trends in Cohabitation and Implications for Children's Family Contexts in the United States." *Population Studies* 54, no. 1 (Mar. 2000): 29–41.

Burns, Marlies. "A History of the Development of Charter School Legislation in Utah." PhD diss., Utah State University, 2010.

Burrington, Debra. "The Public Square and Citizen Queer: Toward a New Political Geography." *Polity* 31, no. 1 (Autumn 1998): 107–31.

Cahn, Naomi, and June Carbone. *Red Families v. Blue Families: Legal Polarization and the Creation of Culture.* New York: Oxford University Press, 2010.

Callister, Ellen Gunnell. "The Political Career of Edward Henry Callister, 1885–1916." Master's thesis, University of Utah, 1967.

Campbell, David E., Christopher F. Karpowitz, and J. Quin Monson. "A Politically Peculiar People: How Mormons Moved into and Then

Out of the Political Mainstream." In Balmer and Riess, eds., *Mormonism and American Politics*, 133–54.

———— and J. Quin Monson. "Dry Kindling: A Political Profile of American Mormons." Paper at the Conference on Religion and American Political Behavior, Southern Methodist University, Oct. 4, 2002.

———— and J. Quin Monson. "Following the Leader? Mormon Voting on Ballot Propositions." *Journal for the Scientific Study of Religion* 42, no. 4 (Dec. 2003): 605–19.

————, John C. Green, and J. Quin Monson. *Seeking the Promised Land: Mormons and American Politics*. New York: Cambridge University Press, 2014.

Campbell, Eugene E. *Establishing Zion: The Mormon Church in the American West, 1847–1869*. Salt Lake City: Signature Books, 1988.

Cannon, Brian Q. "Mormons and the New Deal: The 1936 Presidential Election in Utah." *Utah Historical Quarterly* 67, no. 1 (Winter 1999): 4–22.

———— and Jessie L. Embry, eds. *Utah in the Twentieth Century*. Logan: Utah State University Press, 2009.

Carey, John M., Richard G. Niemi, and Lynda W. Powell. *Term Limits in the State Legislatures*. Ann Arbor: University of Michigan Press, 2000.

Carlson, Marcia J., and Mary E. Corcoran. "Family Structure and Children's Behavioral and Cognitive Outcomes." *Journal of Marriage and Family* 63, no. 3 (Aug. 2001): 779–92.

———— and Paula England, eds. *Social Class and Changing Families in an Unequal America*. Palo Alto: Stanford University Press, 2011.

Carmines, Edward G., Jessica C. Gerrity, and Michael W. Wagner, "How Abortion Became a Partisan Issue: Media Coverage of the Interest Group–Political Party Connection." *Politics and Policy* 38, no. 6 (Dec. 2010): 1135–58.

Cassell, Paul G. "The Mysterious Creation of Search and Seizure Exclusionary Rules under State Constitutions: The Utah Example." *Utah Law Review* vol. 1993, no. 3 (1993): 751–874.

Cassie, William E., and Joel A. Thompson, "Patterns of PAC Contributions to State Legislative Candidates." In Thompson and Moncrief, eds., *Campaign Finance*, 158–84.

Chamberlain, Holly. "A Plan of Action: A New Alternative to Traditional School Trust Land Exchanges in the West?" *Journal of Land, Resources, and Environmental Law* 23, no. 2 (2003): 241–68.

Chambers, William Nisbet, and Walter Dean Burnham, eds. *The American Party Systems: Stages of Political Development*. New York: Oxford University Press, 1975.

Cherlin, Andrew J. *Labor's Love Lost: The Rise and Fall of the Working-Class Family in America*. New York: Russell Sage Foundation, 2014.

Chetty, Raj, Nathaniel Hendren, Patrick Kline, and Emmanuel Saez. "Where Is the Land of Opportunity?" National Bureau of Economic Research, Jan. 2014. Available at www.nber.org.

Chi, Keon S. *Welfare Employment Programs: The Utah Experience*. Lexington: Council of State Governments, 1985.

Chitwood, Mitchell. "Utah and Publicly Funded Contraceptive Services: The Struggle to Prevent Minors from Sponging Off the Government." *Journal of Contemporary Law* 13, no. 2 (1987): 277–99.

Christensen, John E. "The Impact of World War II." In Poll et al., *Utah's History*, 497–514.

Christy, Howard A. "Open Hand and Mailed Fist: Mormon–Indian Relations in Utah." *Utah Historical Quarterly* 46, no. 3 (Summer 1978): 216–35.

Citrin, Jack. "The Legacy of Proposition 13." In Schwadron and Richter, eds., *California and the American Tax Revolt*, 1–69.

Clark, J. Reuben. *The Diaries of J. Reuben Clark, 1933–1961*. Salt Lake City: Privately published from a transcript in the D. Michael Quinn Papers, Beinecke Library, 2010.

Clark, Scott H. "Married Persons Favored as Adoptive Parents: The Utah Perspective." *Journal of Law and Family Studies* 5, no. 2 (2003): 203–22.

———. "Utah Prefers Married Couples." *St. Thomas Law Review* 18, no. 2 (Winter 2005): 215–26.

Clayton, James L. "An Unhallowed Gathering: The Impact of Defense Spending on Utah's Population Growth, 1940–1964." *Utah Historical Quarterly* 34, no. 3 (Summer 1966): 227–42.

Cleary, Edward L., and Allen D. Hertzke, eds. *Representing God at the Statehouse: Religion and Politics in the American States*. New York: Rowman & Littlefield, 2006.

Clucas, Richard A. "Principal Agent Theory and the Power of State House Speakers." *Legislative Studies Quarterly* 26, no. 2 (May 2001): 319–38.

———, Mark Henkels, and Brent S. Steel, eds. *Oregon Politics and Government: Progressives versus Conservative Populists*. Lincoln: University of Nebraska Press, 2005.

Clyde, Edward W. "Institutional Response to Prolonged Drought." In Weatherford and Brown, eds., *New Courses for the Colorado River*, 109–38.

Clyde, George D. "History of Irrigation in Utah." *Utah Historical Quarterly* 27, no. 1 (Jan. 1959): 26–36.

Clynch, Edward J., and Thomas P. Lauth, eds. *Governors, Legislatures, and Budgets: Diversity across the American States.* New York: Greenwood Press, 1991.

Coe, Norma B., Kelly Haverstick, Alicia H. Munnell, and Anthony Webb. "What Explains State Variation in SSDI Application Rates?" Working paper, Center for Retirement Research, Boston College, 2011.

Concerning Gambling: Statements from Leaders of the Church of Jesus Christ of Latter-day Saints. Salt Lake City: LDS Church, 1988.

Coontz, Stephanie. *The Way We Never Were: American Families and the Nostalgia Trap.* New York: Basic Books, 1992.

Corcoran, Brent, ed. *Multiply and Replenish: Mormon Essays on Sex and Family.* Salt Lake City: Signature Books, 1994.

Cornwall, Marie, Tim B. Heaton, and Lawrence A. Young, eds. *Contemporary Mormonism: Social Science Perspectives.* Urbana: University of Illinois Press, 1994.

Council on Community Pediatrics. "Poverty and Child Health in the United States." *Pediatrics* 137, no. 4 (2016). Available at pediatrics.aappublications.org.

Cowles, Leroy. *Organization and Administration of Education in Utah.* Salt Lake City: University of Utah Press, 1946.

Crawley, Peter. "The Constitution of the State of Deseret." *BYU Studies* 29, no. 4 (Fall 1989): 7–22.

Cox, Jon. *Utah Politics: Principles, Theories, and Rules of the Game.* San Bernardino: Rockwell Partners, 2018.

Crimmel, Hal, ed. *Desert Water: The Future of Utah's Water Resources.* Salt Lake City: University of Utah Press, 2014.

Crockett, J. Allan. "Remembering Justice A. H. Ellett." *Utah Historical Quarterly* 61, no. 3 (Summer 1993): 249–57.

Croft, Q. Michael. "Influence of the LDS Church on Utah Politics, 1945–1985." PhD diss., University of Utah, 1985.

Cronin, Thomas E., and Robert D. Loevy. *Colorado Politics and Government: Governing the Centennial State.* Lincoln: University of Nebraska Press, 1993.

Darowski, Joseph F. "The WPA versus the Utah Church." In Cannon and Embry, eds., *Utah in the Twentieth Century*, 167–85.

Dawson, Richard E. "Social Development, Party Competition, and Policy." In Chambers and Burnham, eds., *American Party Systems*, 203–37.

Day, Jayme, Lloyd Pendleton, Michelle Smith, et al. *Comprehensive Report on Homelessness.* Salt Lake City: Department of Workforces Services, 2014.

Decker, Rod. "The LDS Church and Utah Politics: Five Stories and Some Observations." In Sells, ed., *God and Country*, 97–128.

Demographic and Economic Analysis. Salt Lake City: Governor's Office of Planning and Budget, 1981, 1997, 2011.

Denton, Craig. "Bear River." In Crimmel, ed., *Desert Water*, 41–58.

Denton, Sally. *American Massacre: The Tragedy at Mountain Meadows, September 1857.* New York: Knopf, 2003.

Deseret 1776–1976: A Bicentennial History by the Deseret News. Salt Lake City: Deseret Book, 1976.

Dometrius, Nelson C. "Gubernatorial Approval and Administrative Influence." *State Politics and Policy Quarterly* 2, no. 3 (Fall 2002): 251–67.

Donahue, John J., and Steven D. Levitt. "The Impact of Legalized Abortion on Crime." *Quarterly Journal of Economics* 116, no. 2 (May 2001): 379–420.

Donnelly, Thomas C., ed. *Rocky Mountain Politics.* Albuquerque: University of New Mexico Press, 1940.

Downen, John C., Pamela S. Perlich, Jan E. Crispin, and Alan Isaacson. *The Structure and Economic Impact of Utah's Oil and Gas Exploration and Production Industry.* Salt Lake City: Bureau of Economic and Business Research, University of Utah, 2009.

Drumm, Mark. *Drumm's Manual of Utah, and Souvenir of the First State Legislature, 1896.* Salt Lake City: published by the author, 1896.

Dunn, F. Roy. *A Performance Audit of Circuit Court Management and a Review of Circuit Court Revenue Allocation.* Salt Lake City: Office of the Legislative Auditor General, 1980.

Dunstan, Roger. *Gambling in California.* Sacramento: California Research Bureau, 1994.

Durham, Christine M. "Employing the Utah Constitution in the Utah Courts." *Utah Bar Journal* 2 (Nov. 1989): 25.

———. "What Goes Around Comes Around: The New Relevancy of State Constitution Religion Clauses." *Valparaiso University Law Review* 38, no. 2 (2004): 353–71.

Durham, G. Homer. *Public Administration and State Government in Utah.* Logan: Utah State Agricultural College, 1940.

Durrant, Jeffrey O. *Struggle over Utah's San Rafael Swell: Wilderness, National Conservation Areas, and National Monuments.* Tucson: University of Arizona Press, 2005.

Dwyer, Robert Joseph. *The Gentile Comes to Utah: A Study in Religious and Social Conflict.* Salt Lake City: By the author, 1971.

Dyer, Bruce T. "A Study of the Forces Leading to the Adoption of Prohibition in Utah in 1917." Master's thesis, Brigham Young University, 1958.

Eastman, Adam R. *Central Utah Water Conservancy District: History in the Making.* Orem: CUWCD, 2009.

———. "From a Cadillac to a Chevy: Environmental Concern, Compromise, and the Central Utah Project Completion Act." In Cannon and Embry, eds., *Utah in the Twentieth Century*, 343–66.

Eberstadt, Nicholas. *Men without Work: America's Invisible Crisis.* West Conshohocken, PA: Templeton Press, 2016.

———. *A Nation of Takers: America's Entitlement Epidemic.* West Conshohocken, PA: Templeton Press, 2012.

Economic Report to the Governor. Salt Lake City: Utah Economic Council, 1988–present. Available at gardner.utah.edu.

Edin, Kathryn, and Maria Kefalas. *Promises I Can Keep: Why Poor Women Put Motherhood before Marriage.* Berkeley: University of California Press, 2007.

Education in Utah: A Call to Action. Salt Lake City: Office of the Governor, 1983.

Edwards, John. *Superweapon: The Making of MX.* New York: W. W. Norton, 1982.

Elazar, Daniel J. *American Federalism: A View from the States.* New York: Crowell, 1972.

Ellett, A. H. *Forty-four Years as a Redneck Judge.* Salt Lake City: by the author, 1983.

Ellsworth, S. George. *Utah's Heritage.* Salt Lake City: Peregrine Smith, 1972.

———. "Utah's Struggle for Statehood." *Utah Historical Quarterly* 31, no. 1 (Winter 1963): 5–60.

Emenhiser, JeDon. "The 1968 Election in Utah." *Western Political Quarterly* 22, no. 3 (Sept. 1969): 526–535.

———, ed. *The Dragon on the Hill: Utah's 38th Legislature, Analysis and Comment.* Salt Lake City: University of Utah Press, 1970.

———. *Utah's Governments.* Palo Alto: National Press, 1964.

Emory, George. *Report of the Governor of Utah, Made to the Secretary of the Interior.* Washington: Government Printing Office, 1878.

Environmental Dangers of Open-air Testing of Lethal Chemicals: Hearings Before Subcommittee, 91st Congress. Washington: House Committee on Government Operations, 1969.

Epp, Charles R. *The Rights Revolution: Lawyers, Activists, and Supreme Courts in Comparative Perspective.* Chicago: University of Chicago Press, 1998.

Erickson, Jon D., Duane Chapman, and Ronald E. Jonny. "Monitored Retrievable Storage of Spent Nuclear Fuel in Indian Country: Liability, Sovereignty, and Socioeconomics." *American Indian Law Review* 19, no. 1 (1994): 73–103.

Erickson, Velt G. "The Liberal Party of Utah." Master's thesis, University of Utah, 1948.

Espeland, Wendy Nelson. *The Struggle for Water: Politics, Rationality, and Identity in the American Southwest.* Chicago: University of Chicago Press, 1995.

Evans, Gary W., and Rachel Kutcher. "Loosening the Link between Childhood Poverty and Adolescent Smoking and Obesity: The Protective Effects of Social Capital." *Psychological Science* 21, no. 1 (Jan. 2011): 3–7.

Evans, John. *Utah School Crisis.* Salt Lake City: Utah Education Association, 1963.

Evans, John Henry. *The Story of Utah: The Beehive State.* New York: Macmillan, 1933.

Evans, Scott T. "Revisiting the Utah School Trust Lands Dilemma: Golden Arches National Park." *Journal of Energy and Natural Resources* 11, no. 2 (1991): 347–68.

Eyre, Harmon J., Joseph L. Lyon, and Charles R. Smart. *Cancer in Utah, 1966–1977.* Salt Lake City: Utah Cancer Registry, 1979.

Ferguson, Margaret R. "Chief Executive Success in the Legislative Arena." *State Politics and Policy Quarterly* 3, no. 2 (June 2003): 158–82.

———, ed. *Executive Branch of State Government: People, Process, and Politics.* Santa Barbara: ABC–Clio, 2006.

———. "Governors and the Executive Branch." In Gray et al., *Politics in the American States,* 208–50.

File, Thom, and Camille Ryan. *Computer and Internet Use in the United States: 2013.* Washington: United States Census Bureau, 2014.

Firmage, Edwin B. "MX: Democracy, Religion, and The Rule of Law—My Journey." *Utah Law Review* 2004, no. 1 (2004): 13–55.

———. "The Utah Supreme Court and the Rule of Law: *Phillips* and the Bill of Rights in Utah." *Utah Law Review* vol. 1975, no. 3 (Fall 1975): 593–628.

——— and Richard Collin Mangrum. *Zion in the Courts: A Legal History of the Church of Jesus Christ of Latter-day Saints, 1830–1900.* Chicago, University of Illinois Press, 1988.

Fisher, Patrick. *Demographic Gaps in American Political Behavior.* Boulder: Westview Press, 2014.

Flake, Kathleen. *The Politics of American Religious Identity: The Seating of Senator Reed Smoot, Mormon Apostle.* Chapel Hill: University of North Carolina Press, 2004.

Flamm, Michael W. *Law and Order: Street Crime, Civil Unrest, and the Crisis of Liberalism in the 1960s.* New York: Columbia University Press, 2005.

Flynn, John J. "Constitutional Difficulties of Utah's Executive Branch and the Need for Reform." *Utah Law Review* vol. 1966, no. 2 (Sept. 1966): 351–70.

————. "Federalism and Viable State Government: The History of Utah's Constitution." *Utah Law Review* vol. 1966, no. 2 (Sept. 1966): 311–50.

Fordham, Jefferson B. *The Legislative Institution*. Philadelphia: University of Pennsylvania Press, 1959.

Foremaster, Harmon Howard. "The Little Hoover Commission and Consequential State Government Reorganization." Master's thesis, University of Utah, 1970.

Forsythe, Dall W., and Donald J. Boyd. *Memos to the Governor: An Introduction to State Budgeting*. 3rd ed. Washington, DC: Georgetown University Press, 2012.

Fox, James Allen. "Demographics and US Homicide." In Blumstein and Wallman, eds., *Crime Drop in America*, 288–318.

Fox, Sarah Alisabeth. *Downwind: A People's History of the Nuclear West*. Lincoln: University of Nebraska Press, 2014.

Foy, Joseph J. "Utah." In Ferguson, ed., *Executive Branch*, 387–91.

Fradkin, Philip L. *Fallout: An American Nuclear Tragedy*. Tucson: University of Arizona Press, 1989.

————. *A River No More: The Colorado River and the West*. Berkeley: University of California Press, 1995.

Francis, John G. "Environmental Values, Intergovernmental Politics, and the Sagebrush Rebellion." In Francis and Ganzel, eds., *Western Public Lands*, 29–45.

———— and Richard Ganzel, eds. *Western Public Lands: The Management of Natural Resources in a Time of Declining Federalism*. Totowa, NJ: Rowman and Allanheld, 1984.

Francis, Wayne L. "Leadership, Party Caucus, and Committees in U.S. State Legislatures." *Legislative Studies Quarterly* 10, no. 2 (May 1985): 243–57.

Frankel, Zach. "Chicken Little's New Career: How Utah's Water Development Industry Sows False Fears and Misinformation." In Crimmel, ed., *Desert Water*, 98–116.

Franklin, Charles H., and Liane C. Kosaki. "Republican Schoolmaster: The U.S. Supreme Court, Public Opinion, and Abortion." *American Political Science Review* 83, no. 3 (Oct. 1989): 751–71.

Freeman, A. Myrick. "Six Federal Reclamation Projects and the Distribution of Income." *Water Resources Research* 3, no. 2 (June 1967): 319–32.

Fukuyama, Francis. *The Great Disruption: Human Nature and the Reconstitution of Social Order*. New York: Free Press, 1999.

Fuller, Craig W., Robert E. Parson, and F. Ross Peterson. *Water, Agriculture, and Urban Growth: A History of the Central Utah Project*. Orem, UT: Central Utah Water Conservancy District, 2016.

Fuller, John G. *The Day We Bombed Utah: America's Most Lethal Secret*. New York: Signet, 1985.

Furstenberg, Frank F. "Fifty Years of Family Change: From Consensus to Complexity," *Annals of the American Academy of Political and Social Science* 654, no. 1 (July 2014): 12–30.

———. "The Recent Transformation of the American Family: Witnessing and Exploring Social Change." In Carlson and England, *Social Class and Changing Families*, 192–220.

Gallagher, Carole. *American Ground Zero: The Secret Nuclear War*. Cambridge, MA: MIT Press, 1993.

Ganzel, Richard. "Regulatory Management of Multistate Energy Projects: The Case of the Allen/Warner Valley Energy System." In Francis and Ganzel, eds., *Western Public Lands*, 265–81.

Gardner, James A. *Interpreting State Constitutions: A Jurisprudence of Function in a Federal System*. Chicago: University of Chicago Press, 2005.

Garff, Regnal W. "The Emancipation of the Juvenile Court, 1957–1965." *Utah Historical Quarterly* 61, no. 3 (Summer 1993): 269–79.

Gerrard, Michael B. "Fear and Loathing in the Siting of Hazardous and Radioactive Waste Facilities: A Comprehensive Approach to a Misperceived Crisis." *Tulane Law Review* 68, no. 5 (May 1994): 1047–1217.

Glass, Matthew. *Citizens against MX: Public Languages in the Nuclear Age*. Chicago: University of Illinois Press, 1993.

Goldin, Claudia, and Lawrence F. Katz. "The Power of the Pill: Oral Contraceptives and Women's Career and Marriage Decisions." *Journal of Political Economy* 110, no. 4 (2002): 730–70.

Goldsmith, Adrienne. "Limitations Regarding Student Clubs and Responsibilities of School Employees." *Utah Law Review* vol. 1996, no. 4 (Winter 1996): 1374–84.

Goodman, Doug. "The Community Context Approach." In Goodman and McCool, eds., *Contested Landscape*, 236–54.

——— and Daniel McCool, eds. *Contested Landscape: The Politics of Wilderness in Utah and the West*. Salt Lake City: University of Utah Press, 1999.

Goodman, Jack. "Jews in Zion." In Papanikolas, *The Peoples of Utah*, 187–220.

Gooyer, Dan de Jr., and Kerry W. Bate. "State of Utah: Utah's Homeless Count, April 5, 1991." Utah State Archive.

Gordon, Oakley J., Reed C. Richardson, and J. D. Williams. *Personnel Management in Utah State Government*. Salt Lake City: Institute of Government, University of Utah, 1962.

Gordon, Sarah Barringer. *The Mormon Question: Polygamy and Constitutional Conflict in Nineteenth-century America*. Chapel Hill: University of North Carolina Press, 2002.

Gorte, Ross W., Carol Hardy Vincent, Laura A. Hanson, and Marc R. Rosenblum. *Federal Land Ownership: Overview and Data*. Washington: Congressional Research Service, 2012.

Governor's Special Investigation of the Accounts and Records of the State Board of Land Commissioners for the Period from Statehood to September 30, 1920. Kaysville, UT: Inland Printing, 1920.

Gray, E. R. *Financing Federal, State, and Local Governments: 1941*. Washington: US Dept. of Commerce, 1942.

Gray, Virginia, Russell L. Hanson, and Thad Kousser. *Politics in the American States: A Comparative Analysis*. Los Angeles: Sage, 2013.

Griffith, R. Marie. *Moral Combat: How Sex Divided American Christians and Fractured American Politics*. New York: Basic Books, 2017.

Griffiths, David. "Far Western Populism: The Case of Utah 1893–1900." *Utah Historical Quarterly* 37, no. 4 (Fall 1969): 396–407.

Grodzins, Morton. *The American System: A New View of Government in the United States*. New Brunswick, NJ: Rand McNally, 1966.

Grogger, Jeff. "An Economic Model of Recent Crime Trends." In Blumstein and Wallman, eds., *Crime Drop in America*, 266–87.

Guillemin, Jeanne. *Anthrax: The Investigation of a Deadly Outbreak*. Berkeley: University of California Press, 1999.

Haber, Mason G., and Paul Toro. "Homelessness among Families, Children, and Adolescents: An Ecological–Developmental Perspective." *Clinical Child and Family Psychology Review* 7, no. 3 (Sept. 2004): 123–64.

Hacker, Jacob S., and Paul Pierson. *Winner-Take-All Politics: How Washington Made the Rich Richer—And Turned Its Back on the Middle Class*. New York: Simon & Schuster, 2010.

Hafen, Bruce C. "The Legislative Branch." *Utah Law Review* vol. 1966, no. 2 (Sept. 1966): 416–61.

Hainsworth, Brad E. "Utah State Elections, 1916–1924." PhD diss., University of Utah, 1968.

Hair, Nicole L., Jamie L. Hanson, Barbara L. Wolfe, and Seth D. Pollak. "Association of Child Poverty, Brain Development, and Academic Achievement." *JAMA [Journal of the American Medical Association] Pediatrics* 169, no. 9 (2015): 822–29.

Hansen, Susan B. "Life Is Not Fair: Governors' Job Performance Ratings and State Economies." *Political Research Quarterly* 52, no. 1 (Mar. 1999): 167–88.

Hanson, Russell L. "Intergovernmental Relations." In Gray et al., *Politics in the American States*, 30–62.

Hardy, B. Carmon. "That 'Same Old Question of Polygamy and Polygamous Living': Some Recent Findings Regarding Nineteenth- and

Early Twentieth-century Mormon Polygamy." *Utah Historical Quarterly* 73, no. 3 (Summer 2005): 212–24.

Harper, Cynthia C., and Sara S. McLanahan. "Father Absence and Youth Incarceration." *Journal of Research on Adolescence* 14, no. 3 (Aug. 2004): 369–97.

Harvey, Mark W. T. *Symbol of Wilderness: Echo Park and the American Conservation Movement.* Albuquerque: University of New Mexico Press, 1994.

———. "Utah, the National Park Service, and Dinosaur National Monument, 1909–56." *Utah Historical Quarterly* 59, no. 3 (Summer 1991): 243–63.

Haskins, Ron, and Isabel V. Sawhill. "The Decline of the American Family: Can Anything Be Done to Stop the Damage?" *Annals of the American Academy of Political and Social Science* 667, no. 1 (Sept. 2016): 8–34.

Heaton, Tim B., Kristen L. Goodman, and Thomas B. Holman. "In Search of a Peculiar People: Are Mormon Families Really Different?" In Cornwall et al., *Contemporary Mormonism*, 87–117.

———, Stephen J. Bahr, and Cardell Jacobson. *A Statistical Profile of Mormons: Health, Wealth, And Social Life.* Lewiston, NY: Edwin Mellen Press, 2005.

Hebert, F. Ted. "Utah: Legislative Budgeting in an Executive Budget State." In Clynch and Lauth, eds., *Governors, Legislatures, and Budgets*, 103–14.

Hevly, Bruce W., and John M. Findlay, eds. *The Atomic West.* Seattle: University of Washington Press, 1998.

Hickman, Martin Berkeley. "Utah Constitutional Law." PhD diss., University of Utah, 1954.

Hill, Marvin S. *Quest for Refuge: The Mormon Flight from American Pluralism.* Salt Lake City: Signature Books, 1989.

Hilmas, Corey J., Benjamin Hall, and Jeffrey Smart. "History of Chemical Warfare." In Tuorinsky, ed., *Medical Aspects of Chemical Warfare*, 9–76.

Himmelfarb, Gertrude. *The De-moralizing of Society: From Victorian Virtues to Modern Values.* New York: Vintage, 1996.

Hinton, Wayne K. *Utah: Unusual Beginning to Unique Present.* Northridge, CA: Windsor Publications, 1988.

History of the Utah Tax Structure. Salt Lake City: Utah State Tax Commission, 2016.

Hodson, Paul W. *Crisis on Campus: The Exciting Years of Campus Development at the University of Utah.* Salt Lake City: Keeban Corp., 1987.

Holbrook, Thomas M., and Raymond J. La Raja. "Parties and Elections." In Gray et al., *Politics in the American States*, 63–104.

Hombs, Mary Ellen. *American Homelessness.* 3rd ed. Santa Barbara: ABC–CLIO, 2001.

Howard, G. M. "Men, Motives, and Misunderstandings: A New Look at the Morrisite War of 1862." *Utah Historical Quarterly* 44, no. 2 (Spring 1976): 112–32.

Hrebenar, Ronald J., and Clive Thomas. *Interest Group Politics in the American West*. Salt Lake City: University of Utah Press, 1987.

———, Melanee Cherry, and Kathanne Greene. "Utah: Church and Corporate Power in the Nation's Most Conservative State." In Hrebenar and Thomas, *Interest Group Politics*, 113–22.

Huefner, Robert P. "Is Utah Living in the Past or Waiting for the Future?" Paper posted by the Kem Gardner Policy Institute, University of Utah, 2008, gardner.utah.edu.

———. "Utah 2010: Meaning of a Legislative Session, a Budget Crisis, and National Rankings." Paper delivered at the Western Political Science Association, San Francisco, Apr. 2, 2010, available at gardner.utah.edu.

Hughes, Raymond M., and William H. Lancelot. *Education: America's Magic*. Ames: Iowa University Press, 1946.

Hundley, Norris Jr. *Dividing the Waters: A Century of Controversy between the United States and Mexico*. Berkeley: University of California Press, 1966.

———. "The West against Itself." In Weatherford and Brown, eds., *New Courses for the Colorado River*, 9–49.

———. *Water and the West: The Colorado River Compact and the Politics of Water in the American West*. Berkeley: University of California Press, 1975.

Hunter, Milton R. *Utah in Her Western Setting*. Salt Lake City: Deseret News Press, 1958.

Huntsman, Rulon J. "Historical Study of Net Migration for Utah, 1870–1960." Master's thesis, Utah State University, 1968.

Hymowitz, Kay S. *Marriage and Caste in America: Separate and Unequal Families in a Post-Marital Age*. Chicago: Ivan R. Dee, 1996.

Isaacson, Alan E. "Structural Changes in Utah's Metal Mining Industry, 1970–1999." *Utah Economic and Business Review*, Sept.–Oct. 2000.

Ivins, Stanley S. "A Constitution for Utah." *Utah Historical Quarterly* 25, no. 2 (Apr. 1957): 95–116.

———. "Free Schools Come to Utah." *Utah Historical Quarterly* 22, no. 4 (Fall 1954): 321–42.

———. *The Moses Thatcher Case*. Salt Lake City: Modern Microfilm, n.d.

Jack, Ronald Collett. "Utah Territorial Politics: 1847–1876." PhD diss., University of Utah, 1970.

Janzen, Fred V., and Mary Jane Taylor. *An Evaluation of Utah's Single Parent Employment Demonstration Program*. Salt Lake City: Social Research Institute, University of Utah, July 1997.

Johnson, Bruce D., Andrew Golub, and Eloise Dunlap. "The Rise and Decline of Hard Drugs, Drug Markets, and Violence in Inner-City New York. In Blumstein and Wallman, eds., *Crime Drop in America*, 164–206.

Johnson, Carl J. "Cancer Incidence in an Area of Radioactive Fallout Downwind from the Nevada Test Site." *Journal of the American Medical Association* 251, no. 2 (1984): 230–36.

Jonas, Frank H. "The 1956 Election in Utah." *Western Political Quarterly* 10, no. 1 (March 1957): 151–160.

———, ed. *Politics in the American West.* Salt Lake City: University of Utah Press, 1969.

———. "Utah: The Different State." In Jonas, ed., *Politics in the American West*, 327–79.

———. "Utah: Sagebrush Democracy." In Donnelly, ed., *Rocky Mountain Politics*, 11–50.

Jorgensen, Victor W., and B. Carmon Hardy. "The Taylor–Cowley Affair and the Watershed of Mormon History." *Utah Historical Quarterly* 48, no. 1 (Winter 1980): 4–36.

Journal of the House of Representatives. Salt Lake City: State of Utah, 1897, 1905, 1917, 1927, 1941.

Julien, Stephen W. "The Utah Supreme Court and Its Justices, 1896–1976." *Utah Historical Quarterly* 44, no. 3 (Summer 1976): 267–85.

Kalil, Ariel, Rebecca Ryan, and Elise Chor. "Time Investment in Children across Family Structures." *Annals of the American Academy of Political and Social Science* 654, no. 1 (July 2014): 150–68.

Kang Fu, Vincent, and Nicholas H. Wolfinger. "Marriage and Divorce in Utah and the United States: Convergence or Continued Divergence?" In Zick and Smith, eds., *Utah at the Beginning of the New Millennium*, 34–43.

Kearnes, John. "Utah Electoral Politics, 1932–38." PhD diss., University of Utah, 1972.

Keim, Paul S., David H. Walker, and Raymond A. Zilinskas, "Time to Worry about Anthrax Again." *Scientific American*, Apr. 2017.

Keith, Jason M. "The 1998 Utah Schools and Lands Exchange Act: Project Bold II." *Journal of Land Resources and Environmental Law* 19, no. 2 (1999): 325–44.

Keller, Jeffrey E. "Gender and Spirit." In Corcoran, ed., *Multiply and Replenish,* 171–82.

Kennedy, Bruce P., Ichiro Kawachi, and Deborah Prothrow–Stith. "Income Distribution and Mortality: Cross Sectional Ecological Study of the Robin Hood Index in the United States." *British Medical Journal*, May 1996. Available at www.bmj.com.

Kenworthy, Lane. *Social Democratic America*. New York: Oxford University Press, 2014.

Kerber, Richard A., John E. Till, Steven L. Simon, et al. "A Cohort Study of Thyroid Disease in Relation to Fallout from Nuclear Weapons Testing. *Journal of the American Medical Association* 270, no. 17 (Nov. 1993): 2076–82.

King, James D. "Changes in Professionalism in US State Legislatures." *Legislative Studies Quarterly* 25, no. 2 (May 2000): 327–43.

———, and Jeffrey E. Cohen. "What Determines a Governor's Popularity?" *State Politics and Policy Quarterly* 5, no. 3 (Fall 2005) 225–47.

Kirst, Michael W. *Overcoming the High School Senior Slump: New Education Policies*. Washington, DC: Institute of Education Leadership and National Center for Public Policy, May 2001.

Knapp, Harold A. *Observed Relations Between the Deposition Level of Fresh Fission Products from Nevada Tests and the Resulting Levels of I–131 in Fresh Milk*. Washington: Atomic Energy Commission, 1963.

Knowlton, Ezra C. *History of Highway Development in Utah*. Salt Lake City: Utah State Road Commission, 1964.

Kohler, Pamela K., Lisa E. Manhart, and William E. Lafferty. "Abstinence-Only and Comprehensive Sex Education and the Initiation of Sexual Activity and Teen Pregnancy." *Journal of Adolescent Health* 42, no. 4 (Mar. 2008): 344–51.

Kost, Kathryn, and Stanley Henshaw. *U.S. Teenage Pregnancies, Births and Abortions: National and State Trends by Age, Race, and Ethnicity*. Washington, DC: Guttmacher Institute, 2012, 2014. Available at www.guttmacher.org.

Kouris, Mark S. "Kyrie Elaison: A Constitutional Amendment Is No Panacea for the Prayer in City Council Meeting Dilemma." *Utah Law Review* 1992, no. 4 (1992): 1385–1430.

Kousser, Thad. *Term Limits and the Dismantling of State Legislative Professionalism*. New York: Cambridge University Press, 2006.

Kousser, Thad, and Justin H. Phillips. *The Power of American Governors: Winning on Budgets and Losing on Policy*. New York: Cambridge University Press, 2012.

Krueger, Skip, and Robert W. Walker. "Management Practices and State Bond Ratings." *Public Budgeting and Finance* 30, no. 4 (Winter 2010): 47–70.

Lacour, Misty, and Laura D. Tissington. "The Effects of Poverty on Academic Achievement." *Educational Research and Reviews* 6, no. 7 (July 2011): 522–27.

Larson, Gustive O. *The Americanization of Utah for Statehood.* San Marino, CA: Huntington Library, 1971.

———. "Government, Politics, and Conflict." In Poll et al., *Utah's History,* 243–56.

Larsen, Kent S. "The Life of Thomas Kearns." Master's thesis, University of Utah, 1964.

Lasswell, Harold D.. *Politics: Who Gets What, When, How.* New York, McGraw Hill, 1936.

Lawrence, Robert Z., and Lawrence Edwards. "Deindustrialization: Insights from History and the International Experience." *Policy Brief,* Peterson Institute for International Economics, Oct. 2013.

Layton, Stanford John. "Governor Charles Mabey and the Utah Election of 1924." Master's thesis, University of Utah, 1969.

Leavitt, Michael O. "One Thousand Days of Progress: The 2002 State of the State Address," *Hinckley Journal of Politics,* 2002–03.

Leith, Patricia. "The Regulation and Trial of Obscenity in Utah: Questions Raised by *Salt Lake City v. Piepenburg.*" *Utah Law Review* vol. 1978, no. 2 (Summer 1978): 375–88.

Leone, Mark P. *Roots of Modern Mormonism.* Cambridge: Harvard University Press, 1979.

Lesthaeghe, Ron. "The Second Demographic Transition in Western Countries: An Interpretation." In Mason and Jensen, eds., *Gender and Family Change,* 17–62.

LeSueur, Stephen C. *The 1838 Mormon War in Missouri.* Columbia: University of Missouri, 1987.

Levine, Ken. "Constitutional Law: Utah's Cable Decency Act, An Indecent Act." *Loyola Entertainment Law Review* 7, no. 2 (1987): 401–15.

Linford, Orma. "The Mormons and the Law: The Polygamy Cases." *Utah Law Review* 9, nos. 2–3 (1964/65): 308–70, 543–91.

Lloyd, Lewis H. "Legislative Council." In Emenhiser, ed., *Dragon on the Hill,* 121–25.

Lloyd, R. , D. Gren, S. Simon, et al. "Individual External Exposures from Nevada Test Site Fallout for Utah Leukemia Cases and Controls." *Health Physics* 59, no. 5 (Nov. 1990): 723–37.

Logue, Larry. "A Time of Marriage: Monogamy and Polygamy in a Utah Town." *Journal of Mormon History* 11 (1984): 3–26.

Long, E. B. *The Saints and the Union: Utah Territory during the Civil War.* Chicago: University of Illinois Press, 1981.

Lowitt, Richard, ed. *Politics in the Postwar American West.* Norman: University of Oklahoma Press, 1995.

Luker, Kristin. *When Sex Goes to School: Warring Views on Sex—and Sex Education—since the Sixties.* New York: W. W. Norton, 2006.

Lyman, Edward Leo. *Political Deliverance: The Mormon Quest for Utah Statehood.* Chicago: University of Illinois Press, 1986.

——— and Linda King Newell. *A History of Millard County.* Salt Lake City: Utah State Historical Society, 1999.

Lynch, Michael J. *Big Prisons, Big Dreams: Crime and the Failure of America's Penal System.* New Brunswick, NJ: Rutgers University Press, 2007.

Lyon, Joseph L., and Katharina L. Schuman. "Radioactive Fallout and Cancer." *Journal of the American Medical Association* 252, no. 14 (Oct. 1984): 1854–55.

———, Melville R. Klauber, John W. Gardner, and King S. Udall. "Childhood Leukemias Associated with Fallout from Nuclear Testing." *New England Journal of Medicine* 300, no. 8 (Feb. 1979): 397–402.

———, Stephen C. Alder, Mary Bishop Stone, et al. "Thyroid Disease Associated with Exposure to the Nevada Nuclear Weapons Test Site Radiation." *Epidemiology* 17, no. 6 (Nov. 2006): 604–14.

Lythgoe, Dennis L. *Let 'Em Holler: A Political Biography of J. Bracken Lee.* Salt Lake City: Utah State Historical Society, 1982.

Mabey, Charles R. *Our Father's House: Joseph Thomas Mabey Family History.* Salt Lake City: Beverly Craftsman, 1947.

Machado, Stella G., Charles E. Land, and Frank W. McKay. "Cancer Mortality and Radioactive Fallout in Southwestern Utah." *American Journal of Epidemiology* 125, no. 1 (Jan. 1987): 44–61.

MacKinnon, William P. "'Like Splitting a Man Up His Backbone': The Territorial Dismemberment of Utah 1850–1896." *Utah Historical Quarterly* 71, no. 2 (Spring 2003): 100–24.

Magleby, David B. "Religious Interest Group Activity in Utah State Government." In Cleary and Hertzke, eds., *Representing God at the Statehouse,* 177–99.

Magleby, James E. "The Constitutionality of Utah's Medical Malpractice Damages Cap under the Utah Constitution." *Journal of Contemporary Law* 21, no. 2 (Oct. 1995): 217–58.

Mahoney, J. R. "Utah—The Great Landlord." *Utah Economic and Business Review,* David Eccles School of Business, University of Utah, Nov. 1964.

Malen, Betty, and Michael J. Murphy. "A Statewide Decentralized Approach to Public School Reform: The Case of Career Ladder in Utah." *Journal of Education Finance* 11, no. 2 (Fall 1985): 261–77.

Mangum, Garth, Shirley Weathers, Judy Kasten Bell, and Scott Lazerus. *On Being Poor in Utah*. Salt Lake City: University of Utah Press, 1998.

Manning, Wendy D., and Kathleen A. Lamb. "Adolescent Wellbeing in Cohabiting, Married, and Single-Parent Families." *Journal of Marriage and Family* 65, no. 4 (Nov. 2003): 876–93.

Marsden, Milo Steven. "The Utah Supreme Court and the Utah State Constitution." *Utah Law Review* vol. 1986, no. 2 (1986): 319–44.

Marshner, Connaught Coyne, ed. *Adoption Factbook III*. Washington, DC: National Council for Adoption, 1999.

Mason, Karen Oppenheim, and An-Magritt Jensen, eds. *Gender and Family Change in Industrialized Countries*. Oxford, UK: Clarendon Press, 1995.

Matheson, Scott M., with James Edwin Kee. *Out of Balance*. Layton, UT: Peregrine–Smith, 1986.

———, and Ralph E. Becker. "Improving Public Land Management through Land Exchange: Opportunities and Pitfalls of the Utah Experience." *Proceedings of the Rocky Mountain Mineral Law Thirty-third Annual Institute* 33 (1988): 1–41.

Maupin, Molly A., Joan F. Kenny, Susan S. Hutson, et al. *Estimated Use of Water in the United States in 2010*. Reston, VA: US Geological Survey, 2014.

Mauss, Armand L. *The Angel and the Beehive: The Mormon Struggle with Assimilation*. Urbana: University of Illinois Press, 1994.

Mavrin, Judith, and Leslie S. Russell, Task Force for Appropriate Treatment of the Homeless Mentally Ill. "Homelessness in Utah: Utah Homeless Survey/Final Report," 1986.

Maxwell, John Gary. *Robert Newton Baskin and the Making of Modern Utah*. Norman: University of Oklahoma Press, 2013.

May, Cheryll L. *A History of the Utah Judicial Council, 1973–1997*. Salt Lake City: Administrative Office of the Courts, 1998.

May, Dean L., ed. *Dependent Commonwealth: Utah's Economy from Statehood to the Great Depression*. Provo: Brigham Young University Press, 1974.

———, and Leonard J. Arrington. "'A Different Mode of Life': Irrigation and Society in Nineteenth-century Utah." *Agricultural History* 49, no. 1 (Jan. 1975): 3–20.

McCall, Brian. *The Power of the Texas Governor: Connally to Bush*. Austin: University of Texas Press, 2009.

McCool, Daniel, ed. *Waters of Zion: The Politics of Water in Utah*. Salt Lake City: University of Utah Press, 1995.

McCormick, John S. *Salt Lake City: The Gathering Place*. Woodland Hills, CA: Windsor Publications, 1980.

McCormick, Sara, and Brent Osiek. "Weighted in the Balance: The Bureau of Land Management Wilderness Inventory." In Goodman and McCool, eds., *Contested Landscape*, 35–64.

McGivney, Annette. "Return of Glen Canyon." In Crimmel, ed., *Desert Water*, 160–77.

McLanahan, Sara. "Family Instability and Complexity after a Non-Marital Birth: Outcomes for Children in Fragile Families." In Carlson and England, *Social Class and Changing Families*, 108–33.

———. "Fragile Families and the Reproduction of Poverty." *Annals of the American Academy of Political and Social Science* 621, no. 1 (Jan. 2009): 111–31.

Medler, Jerry F. "Governor." In Clucas et al., *Oregon Politics*, 134–51.

Memmott, John M. *Legislative Workload Summary*. Salt Lake City: Utah Constitutional Revision Commission, 1978.

Merrill, Milton R. *Reed Smoot: Apostle in Politics*. Logan: Utah State University Press, 1990.

Miles, Daniel W. *The Phantom Fallout-Induced Cancer Epidemic in Southwestern Utah: Downwinders Deluded and Waiting to Die*. Published by the author, 2009.

———. *Radioactive Clouds of Death over Utah: Downwinders' Fallout Cancer Epidemic*. Bloomington: Trafford, 2013.

Miller, Richard L. *Under the Cloud: The Decades of Nuclear Testing*. New York: The Free Press, 1986.

Miller, Tim Ralph. "Politics of the Carter Administration's Hit List Water Initiative: Assessing the Significance of Subsystems in Water Politics." PhD diss., University of Utah, 1984.

Moffitt, John Clifton. *The History of Public Education in Utah*. Salt Lake City: Deseret News Press, 1946.

Moncrief, Gary F., and Peverill Squire. *Why States Matter: An Introduction to State Politics*. Lanham, MD: Rowman and Littlefield, 2013.

Morn, Frank T. "Simon Bamberger: A Jew in a Mormon Commonwealth." Master's thesis, Brigham Young University, 1966.

Morrill, Dennis R. "Property Tax Assessment and the Utah Constitution—A Taxpayer's Dilemma." *Utah Law Review* vol. 1966, no. 2 (Sept. 1966): 491–516.

Moseley, Frank S. "Constitutional Restrictions upon Municipal Indebtedness." *Utah Law Review* vol. 1966, no. 2 (Sept. 1966): 462–90.

Moss, Frank E. *The Water Crisis*. New York: Frederick A. Praeger, 1967.

Moyle, James Henry. *Mormon Democrat: The Religious and Political Memoirs of James Henry Moyle*. Edited by Gene A. Sessions. Salt Lake City: Signature Books, 1998.

Moynihan, Daniel P., Lee Rainwater, and Timothy M. Smeeding, eds. *The Future of the Family*. New York: Russell Sage, 2004.

Mumola, Christopher J., and Jennifer C. Karberg. "Drug Use and Dependence: State and Federal Prisoners, 2004." *Bureau of Justice Statistics Special Report*, Oct. 2006. Available at www.bjs.gov.

Muñoz, Barbara. *Annual Report on Poverty in Utah, 2016*. Murray, UT: Community Action Partnership of Utah, 2017.

Murphy, Miriam B. "John Christopher Cutler," in Powell, ed., *Utah History Encyclopedia*.

Murray, Charles. *Losing Ground: American Social Policy from 1950 to 1980*. New York: Basic Books, 1983.

Murray, Eli H. *Report of the Governor of Utah, Made to the Secretary of the Interior for the Year 1880*. Washington, DC, 1880.

Musick, Kelly, and Katherine Michelmore. "Change in the Stability of Marital and Cohabiting Unions following the Birth of a Child." Online working paper, California Center for Population Research. Available at princeton.edu/papers.

A Nation at Risk: The Imperative for Educational Reform. Report of the National Commission on Excellence in Education. Washington: US Department of Education, 1983.

Neel, Susan Mae. "Utah and the Echo Park Dam Controversy." Master's thesis, University of Utah, 1980.

Nelson, Elroy. *Utah's Economic Patterns*. Salt Lake City: University of Utah Press, 1956.

Nelson, Larry E. "Utah Goes Dry." *Utah Historical Quarterly* 41, no. 4 (Autumn 1973): 341–57.

Noel, Kate M. "Utah Education Vouchers and the Parent Choice in Education Program: What it Was, Why It Failed, and Suggestions for Future Legislation." *Journal of Law and Family Studies* 10, no. 2 (2008): 397–420.

Obama, Barack. "Remarks by the President on Middle-Class Economics." Address to Lawson State Community College, Birmingham, Alabama, Mar. 26, 2015. Available at obamawhitehouse.archives.gov.

Official Report of the Proceedings and Debates of the Convention Assembled at Salt Lake City on the Fourth Day of March, 1895, to Adopt a Constitution for the State of Utah. 2 vols. Salt Lake City: Utah Territorial Legislature, 1898.

Oldroyd, Richard J., and Michael D. Haddon. *Report to Utah on Crime and Justice*. Salt Lake City: Commission on Criminal and Juvenile Justice, 1993.

————, Michael D. Haddon, Christine Mitchell, and Cliff Butter. *Analysis of Utah's Child Kidnapping and Sexual Abuse Act of 1983*. Salt Lake City: Commission on Criminal and Juvenile Justice and Department of Corrections, 1995.

Olson, Laura R., and John C. Green. "The Religion Gap." *PS: Political Science and Politics*, July 2006.

Osterstock, Tim, Janice T. Coleman, Mark J. Roos, and Pauline Williams. "A Performance Audit of the Central Utah Water Conservancy District." Salt Lake City: CUWCD, July 1999.

Pace, Lorin N. *There Ought to Be a Law, and Why There Isn't*. Salt Lake City: published by the author, 1972.

Page, Allison J., Allan D. Ainsworth, and Marjorie A. Pett. "Homeless Families and Their Children's Health Problems: A Utah Urban Experience." *Western Journal of Medicine* 158, no. 1 (Jan. 1993): 130–35.

Page, Marianne E., and Ann Huff Stevens. "The Economic Consequences of Absent Parents." *Journal of Human Resources* 39, no. 1 (Winter 2004): 80–107.

Pangle, Thomas L., ed. *The Rebirth of Classical Political Rationalism: An Introduction to the Thought of Leo Strauss*. Chicago: University of Chicago Press, 1989.

Papanikolas, Helen Z. "Bootlegging in Zion: Making and Selling the 'Good Stuff.'" *Utah Historical Quarterly* 53, no. 3 (Summer 1985): 268–91.

————, ed. *The Peoples of Utah*. Salt Lake City: Utah State Historical Society, 1976.

Parkinson, David R. "Utah Senate Bill 1003: Prohibiting Specified School Clubs." *Journal of Contemporary Law* 23, no. 1 (1997): 268–79.

Parshall, Ardis E. "'Pursue, Retake & Punish': The 1857 Santa Clara Ambush," *Utah Historical Quarterly* 73, no. 1 (Winter 2005): 64–86.

Payne, Keith. *The Broken Ladder: How Inequality Affects the Way We Think, Live, and Die*. New York: Viking, 2017.

A Performance Audit of the Drug Offender Reform Act. Salt Lake City: Office of the Legislative Auditor General, 2009. Available at le.utah.gov/audit.

A Performance Audit of the Utah Department of Environmental Quality. Salt Lake City: Office of the Legislative Auditor General, 1992.

Perlich, Pamela S., Michael T. Hogue, John C. Downen. *The Structure and Impact of Utah's Coal Industry*. Salt Lake City: Bureau of Economic and Business Research, University of Utah, 2010.

Petersen, Jesse S. "The Lincoln Highway and Its Changing Routes in Utah." *Utah Historical Quarterly* 69, no. 3 (Summer 2001): 192–214.

Peterson, Charles S. *Utah: A History*. New York: W. W. Norton, 1977.

———— and Brian Q. Cannon. *The Awkward State of Utah: Coming of Age in the Nation, 1896–1945*. Salt Lake City: University of Utah Press and Utah State Historical Society, 2015.

Peterson, Paul E. *Saving Schools: From Horace Mann to Virtual Learning*. Cambridge, MA: Belknap Press, 2010.

———— and Martin R. West, eds. *No Child Left Behind? The Politics and Practice of School Accountability*. Washington, DC: Brookings Institution Press, 2003.

Pierson, Paul. "The Rise and Reconfiguration of Activist Government." In Pierson and Skocpol, eds., *Transformation of American Politics*, 19–38.

———— and Theda Skocpol, eds. *The Transformation of American Politics: Activist Government and the Rise of Conservatism*. Princeton, NJ: Princeton University Press, 2007.

Poll, Richard D. "An American Commonwealth." In Poll et al., *Utah's History*.

————. "Political Reconstruction of Utah Territory, 1866–1890." *Pacific Historical Review* 27, no. 2 (May 1958): 111–26.

————, Thomas G. Alexander, Eugene E. Campbell, and David E. Miller, eds. *Utah's History*. Provo: Brigham Young University Press, 1978.

Porucznik, Christina A., Erin M. Johnson, Brian Sauer, et al. "Studying Adverse Events Related to Prescription Opioids: The Utah Experience." *Pain Medicine* 12, no. 2 supplement (June 2011): 16–25.

Poverty in Utah: Report to the Governor. Salt Lake City: Utah State Economic Opportunity Office, 1978–present.

Powell, Allan Kent, ed. *Utah History Encyclopedia*. Salt Lake City: University of Utah Press, 1994. Updated edition at www.uen.org.

Power, Thomas M. "Wildland Preservation and the Economy of Utah." Task force paper, Coalition for Utah's Future Wilderness, 1991. Southern Utah Wilderness Alliance Records, Marriott Library.

Preston, Samuel H. "The Value of Children." In Moynihan et al., *Future of the Family*, 263–66.

Prothero, Stephen. *Why Liberals Win (Even When They Lose Elections): How America's Raucous, Nasty, and Mean Culture Wars Make for a More Inclusive Nation*. New York: HarperOne, 2016.

Putnam, Robert D., and David E. Campbell. *American Grace: How Religion Divides and Unites Us*. New York: Simon & Schuster, 2010.

Quinn, D. Michael. "Exporting Utah's Theocracy since 1975: Mormon Organizational Behavior and America's Culture Wars." In Sells, ed., *God and Country*, 129–68.

————. "LDS Church Authority and New Plural Marriages, 1890–1904." *Dialogue: A Journal of Mormon Thought* 18, no. 1 (Spring 1985): 9–105.

———. "The LDS Church's Campaign against the ERA." *Journal of Mormon History* 20, no. 2 (Fall, 1994): 85–155.

———. *The Mormon Hierarchy: Extensions of Power.* Salt Lake City: Signature Books, 1997.

———. "Prelude to the National 'Defense of Marriage' Campaign: Civil Discrimination against Feared or Despised Minorities." *Dialogue: A Journal of Mormon Thought* 33, no. 3 (Fall 2000): 1–52.

Quinn, Rolfe Thomas. "The Governorship of Henry H. Blood: The Critical Years, 1933–34." Master's thesis, University of Utah, 1967.

Rainwater, Lee, and Timothy M. Smeeding. "Single-Parent Poverty, Inequality, and the Welfare State." In Moynihan et al., *Future of the Family*, 96–115.

Rampton, Calvin L. *As I Recall.* Edited by Floyd A. O'Neil and Gregory C. Thompson. Salt Lake City: University of Utah Press, 1989.

Rasband, James R. "Utah's Grand Staircase: The Right Path to Wilderness Preservation?" *University of Colorado Law Review* 70, no. 2 (1999): 483–562.

Rasmussen, Jewell J. *History of Utah's First Century of Taxation and Public Debt, 1896–1995.* Salt Lake City: Bureau of Economic and Business Research, University of Utah, 1996.

Ravitch, Diane. *The Death and Life of the Great American School System: How Testing and Choice Are Undermining Education.* New York: Basic Books, 2010.

Rawlings, James W. "The Utah Board of Examiners." *Utah Law Review* 5, no. 3 (Spring 1957): 349–64.

Recommendations for the Disposal of Chemical Agents and Munitions. Washington, DC: National Academies Press, 1994.

Regnerus, Mark D. *Forbidden Fruit: Sex and Religion in the Lives of American Teenagers.* New York: Oxford University Press, 2007.

Reimann, Paul E. "Federal Land Grants to Utah for Education and Other Purposes." Master's thesis, University of Utah, 1929.

Report of the Investigating Committee of Utah Government Units. State Planning Board Collection, Series 1168, Primary and Secondary Education. Utah State Archives, 1934.

Report to the Community. Findings of the Justice Court Study Committee. Salt Lake City: Utah Judicial Council, 2008.

Review of Closure Plans for the Baseline Incineration Chemical Agent Disposal Facilities. Washington, DC: National Academies Press, 2010.

Richardson, Elmo R. "Federal Park Policy in Utah: The Escalante National Monument Controversy of 1935–1940." *Utah Historical Quarterly* 33, no. 2 (April 1965): 109–33.

Richardson, Lillard E. Jr., David M. Konisky, and Jeffrey Milyo. "Public Approval of U.S. State Legislatures." *Legislative Studies Quarterly* 37, no. 1 (Feb. 2012): 99–116.

Risk Assessment and Management at Deseret Chemical Depot and the Tooele Chemical Agent Disposal Facility. Washington, DC: National Academies Press, 1997.

Roberts, B. H. *A Comprehensive History of the Church Jesus Christ of Latter-day Saints: Century I.* 6 vols. Salt Lake City: Deseret News Press, 1930.

Roberts, Gordon L., and Sharrieff Shaw. "What is Left of *Berry v. Beech*—The Utah Open Courts Jurisprudence." *Utah Law Review* 2005, no. 2 (2005): 677–94.

Rogers, Jedediah S., ed. *The Council of Fifty: A Documentary History.* Salt Lake City: Signature Books, 2014.

———. "Landgrabbers, Toadstool Worshippers, and the Sagebrush Rebellion in Utah, 1979–1981." Master's thesis, Brigham Young University, 1990.

———. "The Volatile Sagebrush Rebellion." In Cannon and Embry, eds., *Utah in the Twentieth Century*, 367–84.

Roper, William L., and Leonard J. Arrington. *William Spry: Man of Firmness, Governor of Utah.* Salt Lake City: University of Utah Press, 1971.

Rosenthal, Alan. *Heavy Lifting: The Job of the American Legislature.* Washington, DC: CQ Press, 2004.

Rudalevige, Andrew. "No Child Left Behind: Forging a Congressional Compromise." In Peterson and West, *No Child Left Behind?*, 23–54.

Russell, George B. *J. Bracken Lee: The Taxpayer's Champion.* New York: Robert Speller and Sons, 1961.

Sabato, Larry. *Goodbye to Goodtime Charlie: American Governor Transformed, 1950–75.* Lexington, MA: Lexington Books, 1978.

Salmore, Barbara G., and Stephen A. Salmore. *New Jersey Politics and Government: Suburban Politics Comes of Age.* Lincoln: University of Nebraska Press, 1996.

Salt Lake Criminal Justice System Assessment. Report prepared for the Salt Lake County Criminal Justice Advisory Council. Berkeley: Institute for Law and Policy Planning, 2004.

Sampson, Robert J., John H. Laub, and Christopher Wiser. "Does Marriage Reduce Crime? A Counterfactual Approach to Within-Individual Causal Effect." *Criminology* 44, no. 3 (Aug. 2006): 465–508.

Schellen, Marieke van, Robert Apel, and Paul Nieuwbeerta. "'Because You're Mine, I Walk the Line'? Marriage, Spousal Criminality, and Criminal Offending over the Life Course." *Journal of Quantitative Criminology* 28, no. 4 (Dec. 2012): 701–23.

Schleicher, Charles P., and G. Homer Durham. *Utah: The State and Its Government*. New York: Oxford Book Company, 1943.

Schnitzer, Patricia G., and Bernard G. Ewigman. "Child Deaths Resulting from Inflicted Injuries: Household Risk Factors and Perpetrator Characteristics." *Pediatrics* 116, no. 5 (Nov. 2005): 253–56.

School Testing Results, 2006–2007: How Utah Compares to Other States. Salt Lake City: Utah Foundation, 2007.

Schwadron, Terry, and Paul Richter, eds. *California and the American Tax Revolt: Proposition 13 Five Years Later*. Berkeley: University of California Press, 1984.

Sells, Jeffery E., ed. *God and Country: Politics in Utah*. Salt Lake City: Signature Books, 2005.

"Separation of Powers," Report of the Utah Constitutional Revision Commission, Aug. 10, 1970.

Shepherd, Gordon, and Gary Shepherd. *A Kingdom Transformed: Early Mormonism and the Modern LDS Church*. 2nd ed. Salt Lake City: University of Utah Press, 2015.

Shipps, Jan. "Utah Comes of Age Politically: A Study of the State's Politics in the Early Years of the Twentieth Century." *Utah Historical Quarterly* 35, no. 2 (Spring 1967): 91–111.

Sillitoe, Linda. *Friendly Fire: The ACLU in Utah*. Salt Lake City: Signature Books, 1996.

Simon, Jonathan. *Governing through Crime: How the War on Crime Transformed American Democracy and Created a Culture of Fear*. New York: Oxford University Press, 2009.

Simon, Steven L., André Bouville, and Charles E. Land. "Fallout from Nuclear Weapons Tests and Cancer Risks: Exposures Fifty Years Ago Still Have Health Implications Today." *American Scientist*, Jan.–Feb. 2006.

———, John E. Till, Ray D. Lloyd, et al. "The Utah Leukemia Case-Control Study: Dosimetry Methodology and Results." *Health Physics: The Radiation Safety Journal* 68, no. 4 (Apr. 1995): 460–71.

Single Audit Report: State of Utah. Salt Lake City: Office of the State Auditor, 2016.

Skyles, George H. "A Study of Forces and Events Leading to the Repeal of Prohibition and the Adoption of a Liquor Control System in Utah." Master's thesis, Brigham Young University, 1962.

Smart, Lucas, and Amber Ayres. "Don't Cry Out Acreage Figures in a Crowded Theater." In Goodman and McCool, eds., *Contested Landscape*, 81–94.

Smith, Brad C. "Be No More Children: An Analysis of Article I, Section 4 of the Utah Constitution." *Utah Law Review* 1992, no. 4 (1992): 1431–96.

Smith, John S. H. "Cigarette Prohibition in Utah, 1921–23." *Utah Historical Quarterly* 41, no. 4 (Fall 1973): 358–72.

Smith, Jordan W. "Utah Off-Highway Vehicle Owners' Specialization and It's Relationship to Environmental Attitudes and Motivations." Master's thesis, Utah State University, 2008.

Snow, Karl N. "Triumvirate Rule of State Government: The Role of the State Board of Examiners." PhD diss., University of Southern California, 1973.

Sorrels, Charles A. "The Scowcroft Commission." In Abshire, ed., *Triumphs and Tragedies,* 160–63.

Sproul, David Kent. "Environmentalism and the Kaiparowits Power Project, 1964–76." *Utah Historical Quarterly* 70, no. 4 (Fall 2002): 356–71.

Squire, Peverill. "A Squire Index Update." *State Politics and Policy Review* 17, no. 4 (Dec. 2017): 361–71.

———. "The Theory of Legislative Institutionalization and the California Assembly." *Journal of Politics* 54, no. 4 (Nov. 1992): 1026–54.

——— and James Hamm. *One Hundred and One Chambers: Congress, State Legislatures, and the Future of Legislative Studies.* Columbus: Ohio State University Press, 2005.

——— and Gary Moncrief. *State Legislatures Today: Politics under the Domes.* New York: Rowman & Littlefield, 2015.

Stacey, Judith. "Good Riddance to 'The Family': A Response to David Popenoe." *Journal of Marriage and Family* 55, no. 3 (Aug. 1993): 545–47.

Statistical Abstract of the United States. Washington: US Census Bureau/ ProQuest and Bernam Press, 1878–present.

Statistical Review of Utah Government. Salt Lake City: Utah Foundation, 1951–present.

Stauffer, Kenneth G. "Utah Politics, 1912–1918." PhD diss., University of Utah, 1972.

Stegner, Wallace. *Mormon Country.* Lincoln: University of Nebraska Press, 1942.

———. *The Sound of Mountain Water: The Changing American West.* New York: Penguin Putnam, 1997.

———, ed. *This is Dinosaur: Echo Park Country and Its Magic Rivers.* New York: Knopf, 1955.

Stephenson, Evan. "Evading the No Child Left Behind Act: State Strategies and Federal Complicity." *Brigham Young University Education and Law Journal* 2006, no. 1 (2006): 157–88.

Stevens, Walter, Duncan C. Thomas, Joseph L. Lyon, et al. "Leukemia in Utah and Radioactive Fallout from the Nevada Test Site: A Case-Control Study." *Journal of the American Medical Association* 264, no. 5 (1990): 585–91.

Stiglitz, Joseph E. *The Price of Inequality: How Today's Divided Society Endangers Our Future*. New York: W. W. Norton & Company, 2013.

Stout, Wayne D. *History of Utah*. 3 vols. Salt Lake City: By the author, 1967.

Strauss, Leo. "Jerusalem and Athens: Some Preliminary Reflections." In Strauss, *Studies in Platonic Political Philosophy*, 147–73.

———. *Studies in Platonic Political Philosophy*. Chicago: University of Chicago Press, 1983.

Summary and Analysis Report of the Utah Little Hoover Commission. Salt Lake City: Utah Foundation, 1966.

"Survey of the Utah Public Education Career Ladder Program." Audit Subcommittee, Utah State Legislature, 1998. Available at le.utah.gov/audit.

Taylor, Mary Jane, and Amanda Smith Barusch. *Multiple Impacts of Welfare Reform in Utah: Experiences of Former Long-term Welfare Recipients*. Salt Lake City: Utah Department of Workforce Services, 2000.

Teaford, Jon C. *The Rise of the States: Evolution of American State Government*. Baltimore: Johns Hopkins Press, 2002.

Tenney, Ryan D. "Tom Green, Common-law Marriage, and the Illegality of Putative Polygamy." *BYU Journal of Public Law* 17, no. 1 (2002): 141–62.

Terrell, John Upton. *War for the Colorado River*. 2 vols. Glendale, CA: Arthur H. Clark Company, 1965.

Thomas, Adam, and Isabel Sawhill. "For Love and Money? The Impact of Family Structure on Family Income." *Future of Children* 15, no. 2 (Fall 2005): 57–74.

Thomas, George. *Civil Government of Utah*. Boston: D. C. Heath, 1912.

———. *The Development of Institutions under Irrigation: With Special Reference to Early Utah Conditions*. New York: The Macmillan Company, 1920.

Thompson, Joel A., and Gary F. Moncrief, eds. *Campaign Finance in State Legislative Elections*. Washington: Congressional Quarterly, 1998.

Torrey, Rickey Shepherd. "The Public Lands Wilderness Review and Interim Management Policy." Master's thesis, University of Utah, 1997.

———. "The Wilderness Inventory of the Public Lands: Purity, Pressure, and Procedure." *Journal of Energy, Resources, and Environmental Law* 12 (1992): 555–620.

Tuorinsky, Shirley D., ed. *Medical Aspects of Chemical Warfare*. Washington: Office of the Surgeon General, 2008.

Trenholm, Christopher, Barbara Devaney, Ken Forston, et al. *Impacts of Four Title V, Section 510 Abstinence Education Programs: Final Report.* Princeton: Mathematica Policy Research, 2007.

Underhill, Kristen, Paul Montgomery, and Don Operario. "Sexual Abstinence Only Programmes to Prevent HIV Infection in High Income Countries: Systematic Review." *British Medical Journal,* Aug. 2007. Available at www.bmj.com.

Utah 2010: Population and Housing Unit Counts. Washington: US Department of Commerce, 2012.

Utah Senate Journal. Salt Lake City: State of Utah, 1903, 1970.

Utah State Public Education Strategic Plan. Salt Lake City: Office of the Legislative Fiscal Analyst, 1992.

Utah's Tax Situation. Salt Lake City: Utah Foundation, 2004.

Utah's Vital Statistics: Abortions. Salt Lake City: Department of Health, 2013.

Van Wagoner, Richard S. *Mormon Polygamy: A History.* Salt Lake City: Signature Books, 1989.

Vedder, Kurt. "Water Development in Salt Lake Valley, 1847–1985." In McCool, *Waters of Zion,* 28–52.

Verbica, M. W. "Medical Malpractice Caps and *Judd v. Drezga*: The Case That Called Discrimination Reasonable." *Journal of Law and Family Studies* 8, no. 2 (2006): 439–48.

Vincent, Carol Hardy, Laura A. Hanson, and Carla N. Argueta. *Federal Land Ownership: Overview and Data.* Washington: Congressional Research Service, 2017.

Vogel–Ferguson, Mary Beth. "Developing a Profile for Identifying Potential Long-Term Welfare Recipients in Utah: The Changing Face of Welfare, from Welfare to Farewell." PhD diss., University of Utah, 2008.

Walker, Ronald W., Richard E. Turley, and Glen M. Leonard. *Massacre at Mountain Meadows.* New York: Oxford University Press, 2008.

Ward, Chip. *Canaries on the Rim: Living Downwind in the West.* New York: Verso, 1999.

Warrick, Richard. "The Year of Utah Wilderness: Lessons from 1984." In Goodman and McCool, eds., *Contested Landscape,* 217–35.

Wasserman, Harvey, and Norman Solomon, with Robert Alvarez and Eleanor Walters. *Killing Our Own: The Disaster of America's Experience with Atomic Radiation.* New York: Dell, 1982.

Watkins, Arthur V. *Enough Rope: The Inside Story of the Censure of Senator Joe McCarthy.* Upper Saddle River, NJ: Prentice Hall, 1969.

Weatherford, Gary, and F. Lee Brown, eds. *New Courses for the Colorado River: Major Issues for the Next Century.* Albuquerque: University of New Mexico Press, 1986.

Webb, Roy. *If We Had a Boat: Green River Explorers, Adventurers, and Runners.* Salt Lake City: University of Utah Press, 1986.

Weed, Stan E., and Joshua A. Olsen. "Effects of Family Planning Programs for Teenagers on Adolescent Birth and Pregnancy Rates." *Family Perspectives* 20, no. 3 (Fall 1986): 153–72.

Weinacker, Adam. "*Judd* and the Jury: How the Utah Supreme Court Dealt a Blow to the Constitutional Right to a Jury Trial by Allowing a Cap on Pain and Suffering Damages." *Utah Law Review* vol. 2009, no. 1 (2009): 219–40.

Weinberg, Daniel H. "Changes in Neighborhood Inequality, 2000–2010." Paper written for US Census Bureau, Mar. 2016. Available at www2.census.gov.

Weiss, Edward S., Marvin L. Rallison, W. Thomas London, and G. D. Carlyle Thompson. "Thyroid Nodularity in Southwestern Utah School Children Exposed to Fallout Radiation." *American Journal of Public Health* 61, no. 2 (Feb. 1971): 241–49.

Wells, Robert W. Jr. "A Political Biography of George Henry Dern." Master's thesis, Brigham Young University, 1971.

Westergren, Bruce N. "Utah's Gamble with Pari-Mutuel Betting in the Early Twentieth Century." *Utah Historical Quarterly* 57, no. 1 (Winter 1989): 4–23.

Wheeler, Ray. "The BLM Wilderness Review." In *Wilderness at the Edge,* 34–40.

Whipple, Conroy Russell. "State Legislative Reform: Its Impact on the Committee System." Master's thesis, University of Utah, 1983.

White, Beverly J. *In My Opinion: A Twenty-Year Look at the Utah State Legislature, 1971 to 1991.* Tooele, UT: published by the author, n.d.

White, Jean Bickmore. *Charter for Statehood: The Story of Utah's State Constitution.* Salt Lake City: University of Utah Press, 1996.

———. "So Bright the Dream: Economic Prosperity and the Utah Constitutional Convention." *Utah Historical Quarterly* 63, no. 4 (Fall 1995): 320–40.

———. *The Utah State Constitution: A Reference Guide.* Westport, CT: Greenwood Press, 1998.

———. "Utah State Elections, 1895–1899." PhD diss., University of Utah, 1968.

Wilcox, W. Bradford, Joseph Price, and Robert I. Lerman. *Strong Families, Prosperous States: Do Healthy Families Affect the Wealth of States?* Washington, DC: Institute for Family Studies, 2015.

Wilderness at the Edge: A Citizen Proposal to Protect Utah's Canyons and Deserts. Salt Lake City: Utah Wilderness Coalition, 1989.

Wilkinson, Richard, and Kate Pickett. *The Spirit Level: Why Greater Equality Makes Societies Stronger.* New York: Bloomsbury Press, 2010.

Williams, J. D. "The Separation of Church and State in Mormon Theory and Practice." *Dialogue: A Journal of Mormon Thought* 1, no. 2 (Summer 1966): 30–54.

Williams, Terry Tempest. *Red: Passion and Patience in the Desert.* New York: Vintage, 2002.

Wilson, James Q. *The Marriage Problem: How Our Culture Has Weakened Families.* New York: HarperCollins, 2002.

Wilson, William Julius. *The Truly Disadvantaged: The Inner City, the Underclass, and Public Policy.* Chicago: University of Chicago Press, 1987.

Wimberley, Ronald C., and James A. Christenson. "Civil Religion and Other Religious Identities." *Sociological Analysis* 24, no. 2 (Summer 1981): 91–100.

Worthen, Bruce W. "The Runaway Officials Revisited: Remaking the Mormon Image in Antebellum America." MA thesis. Salt Lake City: University of Utah, 2012.

Yankelovich, Daniel. *The New Morality: A Profile of American Youth in the 1970s.* New York: McGraw Hill, 1974.

Young, Edgar Levi. *The Founding of Utah.* New York: Charles Scribner and Sons, 1923.

Young, Kimball L. "Utah Public Debt History." *Utah Historical Quarterly* 75, no. 1 (Winter 2007): 8–21.

Zeigler, Harmon, and Michael Baer. *Lobbying Interaction and Influence in American State Legislatures.* Belmont, CA: Wadsworth Publishing, 1969.

Zick, Cathleen D., and Ken R. Smith, eds. *Utah at the Beginning of the New Millennium: A Demographic Perspective.* Salt Lake City: University of Utah Press, 2006.

Zimring, Franklin E., and Gordon Hawkins. *Crime Is Not the Problem: Lethal Violence in America.* New York: Oxford University Press, 1997.

Ziol–Guest, Kathleen M., and Rachel E. Dunifon. "Complex Living Arrangements and Child Health: Examining Family Structure Linkages with Children's Health Outcomes." *Family Relations: Interdisciplinary Journal of Applied Family Science* 63, no. 3 (July 2014): 424–37.

INDEX

Where a letter follows a page number, it indicates that the information comes from a graph (g), footnote (n), photograph (p), or table (t).

Bangerter, Norman, 23t, 50, 111, 171, 182, 207, 250t, 251–52, 255n, 256p, 297, 310, 324

banks, 272, 286, 304; banking commission, 89, 205, 267–68

Bear, Leon, 171–72

Bears Ears National Monument, 226–28

beer, *see* alcohol

Bennett, Robert, 173, 199, 218–19, 299n

biological weapons, *see* weapons, biological

birth control, 75–76, 118, 138, 284; use by teens, 48–50, 53, 284, 350

birth rate, 77–79, 82, 90–91, 97, 103–05, 117–18, 345, 347

Bishop, Rob, 241, 299n

blacks, *see* African-Americans

Blood, Henry, 91, 249–50, 259t

Blue Grass Arsenal, 165, 168

Bradley, Jim, 23t, 213n

Bryan, William Jennings, 24, 30, 31g, 90

Buchanan, James, 6–7

budget, *see* finances

Buhman, Jeff, 294–95

Bush, George H. W., 17–20, 18t, 19t, 175, 252

Bush, George W., 17–20, 18t, 19t, 84, 173, 214, 218, 220–21, 227–28, 252, 255, 299, 332

C

California, 7, 62, 93, 179, 208, 236–37, 312–13; water, 189–90, 195

Camp Douglas, 7, 8p

canals, *see* water, irrigation

cancer, *see* disease/infection, cancer

Cannon, Chris, 217, 299n

Capitol Reef National Park, 203, 209

Carter, Jimmy, 25, 31g, 32, 156–59, 198, 199n, 204, 209, 252

Catholics, 22, 43t, 56, 61t, 62–63, 232–33, 342

cattle, 174, 185, 199; dairies, 145, 148–49, 265; grazing land, 153–54, 204–05, 209; ranchers, 153–55, 205, 208, 238–39; Taylor Grazing Act, 205

Cedar City, Utah, 278–79

censorship, *see* pornography; public morality; television

Center for the Study of Elections and Democracy (CSED), exit polls, 19t, 21, 26, 29n, 43t, 61t

Central Utah Project, 194–98, 252, 349; Completion Act, 196. *See also* reclamation

Chemical Agent Munitions Disposal System (CAMDS), 164–65

chemical weapons, *see* weapons, chemical

child abuse, 79–80, 116–17, 115g, 125, 138, 291–93; kidnapping, 114–15

child poverty, 78–83, 85–86, 126, 138, 202, 346

children, x–xi, 79–80, 117–19, 132–33; health, 145–47, 149, 150n; kindergarten, 79–80; welfare, 280. *See also* adoption; child abuse; child poverty; Utah Division of Child and Family Services

Church of Jesus Christ of Latter-day Saints, 9, 12–13; apostles, 36–37; bishops, 2–3, 186, 231; endorsements, 26–27; Family Services,

55–56; First Presidency, 158–59, 273; general conference, 12, 36, 72; leaders, 26–27, 38, 57–58, 60, 172, 232–33, 248, 269, 347; local leaders, 50–51; Main Street Plaza, 284; members, ix–x, 17–32, 18t, 19t, 22t, 23t, 31g, 231–34, 343; Public Communications Office, 51; Relief Society, 4, 57–58, 263; schools, 320–21; stake presidents, 231, 249; statements, 65, 158–59, 172, 315; Sunday schools, 40–41; sustaining leaders, 2, 253; welfare program, 91, 347; Young Women's Association, 4, 40–41. *See also* Grant, Heber J.; McKay, David O.; Roberts, B. H.; Smith, Joseph F.; Smoot, Reed; Young, Brigham

cigarettes, *see* tobacco

civil disobedience, *see* political activism

civil rights, 73, 341–43; rights revolution, 138, 284. *See also* American Civil Liberties Union; protests; US Constitution, Bill of Rights

Civil War, 1, 7, 13–14

Clark, J. Reuben, 43–44

climate, change, 197, 208; precipitation, 185–86, 190

Clinton, Bill, 19t, 31g, 32, 84, 113, 134, 179, 252, 349; federal land, 199–202, 207–08, 214, 216, 228

Clinton, Hillary, 19t, 20–21

Clyde, George Dewey, 44, 193, 255, 259t, 271, 275, 323–24

Cold War, 156–59

college, 80–81, 100, 103–04, 344; students, 229, 322. *See also* University of Utah, Utah State University

Colorado, 155–56, 190

Colorado River, 188–91, 193–95, 198, 203; basin, 189–91; compact, 190, 193; storage project, 191, 193

commodities, *see* agriculture; cattle; mining

conservation, 192–95, 200, 209; National Conservation Area, 217; National Environmental Policy Act, 208. *See also* national monuments; National Park Service; US Department of Interior; US Forest Service; wilderness

Cook, Beth, 291–93

Cook, Merrill, 23t, 241

corruption, 160–61, 204–05, 271; bribery, 37–38, 234–36; conflict of interest, 161, 267; kickbacks, 270–72; special treatment, 205, 282, 304, 350; spoils, 270–71, 273, 275. *See also* Envirocare; lobbyists

crime, 107–113; gangs, 111–12; juvenile, 112, 118–19; misdemeanors, 278–79; murder, 7, 108, 114–15; property, 108, 109g, 347; recidivism, 114; theft, 108; violence, 107–08, 125, 129, 138, 346. *See also* federal grants; firearms; law enforcement; Leavitt, Mike; Utah Department of Corrections; Utah Legislature

Cromar, Kevin, 49–50

Cutler, John C., 35, 90, 255n, 259t

D

dams, 187–92, 194–96; Davis 190; Glen Canyon, 192; Hoover, 190; Parker, 190. *See also* Echo Park Dam; reclamation

Davis County, 4, 48, 120, 249, 310p

Dayton, Margaret, 332–33

Democratic Party, 92, 180, 198,
204–05, 231–32, 270, 275, 281, 343;
caucus, 244; morality, 36, 57, 69;
religious divide, 12–13, 17–32, 18t,
19t, 22t, 23t, 31g; tariffs, 89–90

demographics, 6, 90–91, 211m; census
data, 76–77, 88, 102, 201, 211m,
230, 303–04; Utah Foundation, 320,
337. *See also* birth rate; immigration; US Census Bureau

Dern, George H., 90, 203, 249, 259t,
266

Deseret News, 10–12, 20–21, 27, 92,
158, 234; Church News section,
57; public morality, 38, 40–41, 42,
44–45, 46

Deseret Telegraph Company, 11–12

disabilities, 66; individuals with, 110;
rights, 229; welfare, 131, 346

disease/infection, anthrax, 169, 171;
cancer, 142–47, 149, 150n; epidemiology, 143–45, 151; public health,
79–80; Q fever, 168–69; sexually
transmitted disease, 118; US Center
for Disease Control, 166. *See also*
leukemia

Dole, Bob, 17–20, 18t, 19t

downwinders, 141–53, 165, 171,
180–83, 348; downwinder politics,
141–53, 153–55, 159–64, 164–68,
171–77, 180–83. *See also* disease/
infection, cancer; Owens, Wayne;
radiation; weapons, testing

drugs, addiction/treatment, 120, 123–
24, 129; cocaine, 118–19, 121–22;
illegal, 81, 113–14, 118–25, 129,
132, 138, 346; legislation, 120, 124;
prescribed, 124, 347; Ritalin, 124;
seizure of property over, 121–23. *See
also* marijuana

Dugway Proving Grounds, 153–55,
168–69, 169p, 171, 179, 182

Dukakis, Michael, 19t, 20

Durham, Christine, 283, 289, 351

E

Eaton, Mark, 134–35

Ebel, David, 173–74

Echo Park Dam, 191–93

economy, 87–106, 347; effect on families, 126, 345; effect on governor's
popularity, 250–52; effect on law
and order, 112–13; exports, 89, 93;
funding for education, 317, 319,
337–38; government influence,
221–22; growth, xiin; military
spending, 158, 165; nuclear waste,
172; protectionism, 30, 31g, 89;
taxes, 315, 350–52; territorial, 3–4,
13–14, 88–89, 133–34; tourism,
200, 203, 212–13. *See also* Great
Depression

education, *see* high schools; school issues

elections, national, 17–21, 18t, 19t,
24–25, 201; primaries, 92, 325;
redistricting, 181n, 246, 284. *See also*
Utah governor, elections

electronic battlefield, 174–75, 206p

Ellett, A. H., 50–52, 280–81, 283p

Ellsworth, S. George, 187, 351

Energy Solutions, *see* Envirocare

energy sources, coal, 95, 199, 204–05,
208–09; hydroelectric power, 187,
191, 196, 208; natural gas, 202–03,
221–22; nuclear power, 171–74;
oil, 92–93, 202–03, 205–07, 206p,
221–22; utilities, 11–12, 171–74,
180, 208–09. *See also* gasoline; nuclear storage/waste; US Department
of Energy

entertainment, *see* recreation; sports; theaters

Envirocare, 159–64, 180; bribes, 160–61. *See also* Semnani, Khosrow

environmental concerns, 348–49; federal land, 200, 208–15; off–roading, 199, 218, 224; oil drilling, 217, 219–22, 228. *See also* conservation; downwinders; pollution; water; wilderness

environmental groups, 162; Audubon Society, 192; HEAL, 162, 182; Sierra Club, 192, 285; Utah Downwinders, 153, 182; Utah Wilderness Association, 209–10; Utahns Against Spent Fuel, 182; Wilderness Society, 192, 210. *See also* Southern Utah Wilderness Alliance

Equal Rights Amendment, 56–58, 269–70

Europe, 82, 85, 162–63

evangelical Christians, 22, 28–29, 62–63, 342

F

family structure, x, 27, 33, 58, 70–71, 72, 75–86; Family Proclamation, 72; Family Support Act, 133; households, 97, 103; traditional, 105–06, 113, 137–39, 341–43, 346–48. *See also* marriage; middle class

federal courts, ix-x, 11–14, 34–35, 48–49, 60, 64–65, 70, 73, 113, 147–48, 167, 173–74, 271, 277–78, 281, 284–85, 344, 350; appellate, 53, 200, 223. *See also* judicial system (Utah); US Supreme Court, US Tenth Circuit Court of Appeals

federal entitlements, *see* Medicaid; Social Security; Supplemental Nutrition Assistance Program; Temporary Assistance for Needy Families; unemployment compensation

federal land, xi-xii, 95, 142, 157, 199–228, 285, 348–49; Federal Land Policy Management Act, 213–14, 224; Homestead Act, 205; mineral rights, 203; US Bureau of Land Management; US Interior Board of Land Appeals, 214. *See also* land sales (Utah)

federal spending, 91, 187–88, 190–91, 198, 299, 303; defense spending, 87, 92–94, 198, 348; deficits, 299; education, 332–34; grants, 49, 160, 263, 267, 270–71, 299, 306–07; 316; law enforcement, 119–20, 123, 127–28; National Priorities Project, 137; welfare, 134

feminism, 57, 105; International Women's Year, 57–58; suffrage, 12, 263. *See also* Equal Rights Amendment; National Organization for Women; women

fertility, *see* birth rate.

finances (Utah): appropriations committee, 300–02; balanced budget, 298–300, 350; bonds, 196, 263–65, 298; borrowing, 263–65, 270; budget, 246, 256–57, 265, 267, 297–317; Budgetary Procedures Ceiling Act, 312; deficit spending, 265, 267, 269, 298–99; fiscal discipline, 297–300, 304; general fund, 267; infrastructure, 3–4; revenue, 300, 303; Revenue Procedures Act, 275; salaries, 268–69, 282; special funds, 267; spending, 110–111, 111g, 265–68, 275, 303. *See also* banks; budget; federal spending; Utah Board of Examiners; Utah Finance Department; Utah

Legislative Auditor General; Utah State Treasurer

firearms, 110, 111–12, 229, 289–90; concealed, 233n; violence, 110–12, 114

food stamps, *see* Supplemental Nutrition Assistance Program

Ford, Gerald, 17–20, 25

G

gambling, 44p, 60–62; horse racing, 41–43; lottery, 60–62

Garn, Jake, 157–58, 171, 181, 204, 299n

gasoline, 267, 304, 314; gasoline tax, 267, 304, 306, 314. *See also* energy sources

gay rights, 23n, 67–71, 138, 284, 341–42; civil unions, 63–64, 253; Gay and Lesbian Utah Democrats, 69; marriage, 34–35, 62–65, 67p, 350; sodomy laws, 69, 138, 294–95, 295

Goddard, George, 3–4

Gofman, John, 146–47, 149

gold, currency standard, 30, 31g, 90; mining, 88

Goldwater, Barry, xii, 27n

good government, 247–48; fiscal discipline, 298–303; Little Hoover Commission, 273; merit-based hiring, 271, 275; reform, 245, 253–54, 261, 264–67, 272–74; US Civil Service Commission, 271. *See also* corruption; Utah Legislative Auditor General

Goshute tribe, 171–74, 218

Grand Staircase–Escalante National Monument, 200–02, 207, 209, 225–26; secrecy surrounding announcement, 199

Grant, Heber J., 36, 40–41, 249

Great Depression, 30, 31g, 37, 91–92, 125n, 130–31, 188, 249–50, 306, 308–09, 316–17, 345, 347; recession, 221. *See also* economy; New Deal

Great Salt Lake, 188, 195, 197

Green River, 188, 191

Green River, Utah (town), 175, 180

Green, Tom, 291–93

Greiner, John, 238–39

Groene, Scott, 216, 219

Ground Wave Emergency Network, 176–77

guns, *see* firearms

H

Hansen, Jim, 176, 178, 179, 299n

Hansen, Phil, 245, 273

Hansen, Robert B., 50–51, 269–70

Harrington, Patti, 332–33

Hatch, Orrin, 25, 68–69, 173, 200, 204, 299n

health insurance, 64, 136–37, 239. *See also* Affordable Care Act; Medicaid

health issues, *see* disabilities; disease/infection; health insurance; mental health

Herbert, Gary, 21, 23t, 87–88, 250t, 251, 255, 257–58, 259t, 305, 316–17

high schools, 47, 67–70, 69, 103–04, 111–12, 118–19, 119g, 229, 322; student clubs, 67–70. *See also* school districts; school issues

Highway Patrol (Utah), 69, 121–22

highways, 203, 225–26, 267, 270, 304–05, 310p, 316; Centennial Highway Fund, 305, 339; interstate system, 121–22, 305. *See also* road construction

Hill Air Force Base, 93, 141, 179–80, 348

Hispanic–Americans, 82–83

homelessness, 125–30, 137–38, 346; Emergency Housing Assistance Program, 126; housing, 125, 126, 128–29; Housing First, 128–29; McKinney–Vento Act, 127–28; mobile homes, 229, 292; Rio Grande neighborhood, 127, 129–30; task force, 127. *See also* Road Home shelter.

homosexuality, *see* gay rights.

Huntsman Jr., Jon, 21, 23t, 39–40, 163, 173–74, 250t, 251–55, 258, 259t, 315–17, 333, 336

I

Idaho, 12, 21, 61

immigration, 9, 82–83; 160; illegal, 233n; Perpetual Emigration Fund, 9, 11

incarceration, 81, 109–111, 113–15, 137, 114, 116–17, 120, 120g, 123–25, 346. *See also* prisons

income: inequality, 100–02, 105–06, 138, 345–47; minimum wage, 132–33, 203; per capita, 91, 94–97, 104–05, 202, 202g, 238; upward mobility, 100–02. *See also* middle class

income tax, 92, 306, 309, 311, 316–17; for schools, 324, 337, 339

industry, *see* commodities; manufacturing; mining

initiatives, *see* referenda

Intermountain Republican (newspaper), 35, 35n

irrigation, *see* water, irrigation

J

Jenkins, Bruce, 70, 145–48

Jews, 21–22, 61n, 232, 254, 281

Johnson, Carl, 149, 151

Johnson, Lyndon B., 24, 30, 31g, 203–04, 226, 309

Jonas, Frank, 270, 348

Journal of the American Medical Association, 143, 145

judicial system (Utah), 11–12, 48–49, 50–53, 278, 286, 351; appointments, 246, 281–82; city courts, 278–79; councils, 280–81; criminal justice, 284, 286; due process, 44, 121; elections of judges, 282; habeas corpus, 288–89; independence, 257, 289–91, 295; Judicial Conduct Commission, 290; juries, 12, 51, 122–23, 161, 225, 285, 292; justice (JP) courts, 277–80; Justice Reinvestment Initiative, 113–14; juvenile courts, 280–81; open courts doctrine, 288–89; sentencing, 110, 114, 116, 123–24. *See also* legal profession; Utah Attorney General; Utah Department of Corrections; Utah Supreme Court

K

Kaiparowits Plateau, 208–09

Kane County, 208, 225; downwinder politics, 143–44, 147, 176–77

KCPX-TV Channel 4 (Salt Lake City), 68, 111

Kempthorne, Dirk, 173–74

Kentucky, 165, 167–68

Kunz, Linda, 291–93

L

labor, *see* workforce

Medicaid, 181n, 306–07, 317, 346

medical profession, nurses, 269–70; Salt Lake Health Department, 311; Utah Medical Association, 311. *See also* children, health; health issues; Utah Department of Health and Social Services

men, 98–100, 103–04, 108, 109g, 112, 127, 137–38

mental health, 126, 132, 239, 285; Board of Insane Asylums, 262

Mexico, 6, 189, 194, 292

microbiology, *see* Blue Grass Arsenal; Dugway Proving Grounds; weapons, biological

middle class, 78–82, 101–02, 105–06, 346; morality, 105–06

military, 7, 8p, 93, 153–59, 164–70, 169p, 174–80, 205–07, 206p; veterans, 137. *See also* federal spending; military bases; military systems; US Air Force; weapons testing; US Department of Defense; Vietnam War

military bases, 43n, 93, 157, 177–80, 182–83, 205–07, 206p. See also Blue Grass Arsenal; Camp Douglas; Dugway Proving Grounds; Hill Air Force Base; Tooele Army Depot

military contractors, 166, 176–77, 179

military systems, *see* electronic battlefield; Ground Wave Emergency Network

Milliken, William, 110–11

minerals, *see* gold; mining, copper; silver

mining, 9–10, 88–90, 92–93, 95, 102–04, 159–64, 314; copper, 89, 95; federal land, 209, 217, 219

missiles, 93, 94p, 155–59, 167, 175–76; Minuteman, 94p; MX, 156–59,

170, 180, 206p, 348; Strategic Arms Limitation Treaty (SALT), 157. *See also* Thiokol Corporation (rocket engines); weapons, testing

Missouri, 4, 13

Monson, David, 269–70, 299n

morality, *see* public morality

Mormon Church, *see* Church of Jesus Christ of Latter-day Saints

Moss, Frank, 22, 25, 194, 198, 208

Murdock, Abe, 92n, 193n

Murray, Eli, 6–7

N

A Nation at Risk, 326, 328, 338

National Education Association (NEA), 323–25, 337

national monuments, 199–204, 206p, 226–28, 349; Antiquities Act, 200, 227; Dinosaur National Monument, 191. *See also* Bears Ears; Grand Staircase–Escalante

National Organization for Women, 54–55

National Park Service, 191–92. *See also* Arches National Park; Capitol Reef National Park

Native Americans, 42–43, 82–83, 175, 196, 285; land, 5, 110–11, 171–74, 200, 205–07, 206p, 218; Navajos, 175. *See also* Goshute tribe; Ute tribe

Nehring, Ronald, 293–94

nerve gas, *see* chemical weapons.

Nevada, 62, 190, 262n; downwinder politics, 150, 157–59, 177

Nevada Test Site, 141, 144p, 150–51

New Deal, 30, 31g, 91–92, 194, 249–50, 347. *See also* Great Depression

New Hampshire, 237, 254

New Mexico, 175, 190, 197

New York, 46, 237

New York Times, 37–38, 40, 54, 192, 333

Nielson, Howard, 197n, 299n

Nixon, Richard, 27, 28p, 120, 155; Watergate, 57

nuclear power, *see* energy sources, nuclear power

nuclear storage/waste, 171–74, 180, 183, 348; spent fuel, 171–74, 182. *See also* Envirocare

nuclear weapons, *see* weapons, atomic

O

Obama, Barack, 19t, 20, 31g, 32, 104, 174, 252, 307; federal land, 214, 220–23, 226, 228

Obamacare, see Affordable Care Act

obscenity, *see* pornography.

Ogden, Utah, 52, 101

Orton, Bill, 23t, 25n, 201, 228

Osguthorpe, D. A., 153–54, 155n

Owens, Wayne, 23t, 25n, 193n, 214; downwinder politics, 170–71, 180, 182

P

Pacific Islanders, 82–83

Park City, 289–90

Pew Foundation, 21–22, 76, 248

pioneers, xiii, 186–87, 195, 197–98, 351. *See also* Utah Territory

Planned Parenthood, 48–50, 285. *See also* abortion; birth control

police, *see* law enforcement

political action committees (PACs), 235–36, 324–25. *See also* lobbyists

political activism: boycotts, 10, 269–70; conservative, 51–52, 56–57, 59, 182, 192; demonstrations, 56–57, 58p, 67p, 68–69, 150, 174–75, 225, 229, 310–13, 317; tax revolt, 310–13, 317; term limits, 241, 253–54; whistleblowers, 166, 199, 232. *See also* civil rights; religious freedom; Sagebrush Rebellion

political parties: Liberal Party, 9; People's Party, 9, 12–13; polarization, 200–01; regular ticket, 2–3, 12–13, 186–87. *See also* Democratic Party; Republican Party

Poll, Richard D., xiii, 352

polling, *see* Center for the Study of Elections and Democracy; social science

pollution, 141–55, 166–67, 348. *See also* environmental concerns

polygamy, x, 4, 5p, 9, 11–12, 34–35, 72, 263, 291–95, 343; cohabitation, 70–71, 78–81, 294–95; Manifesto of 1890, 12–13, 34–35; *Sister Wives* (tv show), 294

population figures, *see* demographics

pornography, 27, 50–53, 284–85, 294, 350. *See also* cable television, censorship; public morality

poverty, 78–83, 85–86, 100–02, 104–05, 125–37, 221, 346–47; flop houses, 126–27; single parent households, 78–79, 84, 126, 130–32, 134, 138, 344. *See also* child poverty; homelessness; income; welfare; workforce

prayer, city council meetings, 48, 59, 286–87; school events, 45–48, 67–70, 284

Price, Utah, 37–38

prisons, 109–113, 125, 129. *See also* incarceration

Prohibition, 35–37, 92, 347; temperance movement, 35, 72

property tax, 197, 264, 306, 311–16, 321, 337, 339, 339; valuation, 311–12

Protestants, 21–22, 35, 43t, 61t, 63t, 72–73, 232–33

Provo, 101, 293

psychology, *see* mental health

public land, *see* federal land

public morality, 4, 27, 33–74, 139, 247, 253, 341–43, 348, 350; censorship, 50–53, 138; indecency, 59, 349; prostitution, 37, 51, 282; sexual transgression (adultery/fornication), 11, 20, 294. *See also* alcohol; *Deseret News*; Sunday closing; US Supreme Court

R

race/ethnicity, 82–83; segregation, 138. *See also* African-Americans; Asian-Americans; Hispanic-Americans; Jews; Pacific Islanders

radiation, 143, 147–48, 159–64; cesium, 143, 151; dosimetry, 143–44, 146–47, 151; Uranium Mill Tailings Radiation Control Act, 159–60; Utah Division of Radiation Control, 160–61. *See also* disease/infection, cancer; downwinders; weapons, atomic

radio, 176–77, 232; KTKK-AM (Sandy, Utah), 310

railroad, 9, 11–12, 88–89; street railroad, 11–12; transcontinental, 9, 88

Rampton, Calvin L., 30, 31g, 44, 56, 118–19, 131, 154–55, 181, 198, 208, 250t, 252–53, 255, 259t, 273, 308–09, 311, 324

rape, *see* sexual abuse

Reagan, Ronald, xii, 17–20, 49–50, 132, 204, 252, 299, 326; downwinder politics, 159, 168, 181

reclamation: Provo River Project, 194–95; Strawberry Project, 187–88. *See also* All-American Canal; Central Utah Project; dams; US Bureau of Reclamation; water

recreation, Glen Canyon National Recreation Area, 207; golf courses, 160, 197; Utah Fish and Game Department, 267. *See also* entertainment; sports

referenda, 122–23, 241, 246, 273, 310–11, 312, 336–37

Reid, Harry, 218–19

religious divide, 231–33; non–LDS population, 88–89, 232, 263, 281, 343; polarization, x, 17–32, 18t, 19t, 22t, 23t, 31g, 24–25, 26g, 43t, 56, 61t, 63, 63t, 73–74, 103, 343–44, 350; Presbyterians, 254; Utah Territory, 5, 9–10, 12–13, 13–15. *See also* atheism; Catholics; Church of Jesus Christ of Latter-day Saints; evangelical Christians; Jews; prayer; Protestants

religious freedom, 284, 286–87, 291–95

reproduction: teen pregnancy, 117–18, 137–38, 346; Reproductive Law and Policy Center, 54. *See also* abortion; birth control; birth rate; Planned Parenthood

Republican Party, xi-xii, 12–13, 35–36, 89–90, 94–95, 271, 343; ascendancy, 103. *See also* religious divide

Rifkin, Jeremy, 169–70

road construction, 285, 304–05, 310p, 316; dirt roads, 223–26, 228, 304; political patronage, 270–71; Utah Road Commission, 249, 267, 270–71. See also highways

Road Home shelter, 127, 129–30

Roberts, B. H., 34–35

Roberts, Kenny, 110, 111g

Roe v. Wade, 53, 55–56, 112–13, 343

Romney, Mitt, 17–20

Roosevelt, Franklin D., 24, 27, 30–32, 87, 91–92, 191, 203, 250, 255, 347

Runyon, Rachel, 114–15

Russia, *see* Soviet Union

S

Sagebrush Rebellion, 204, 228

Salazar, Kenneth, 174, 220–21, 223, 349

sales tax, 92, 267, 306, 309, 311, 316–17, 339

Salt Lake City, 23n, 64–65, 88–89, 100–01, 126–29, 255, 279; Chamber of Commerce, 41, 311; City Council, 286–87; Redevelopment Agency, 52–53; Vienna Café, 41

Salt Lake County, 48, 64, 119–20, 127; county government center, 65; county jail, 124, 129

Salt Lake Tribune, 14n, 38–39, 40–41, 44, 68, 117, 157–58, 212–13, 281

San Rafael Swell, 217–18

school choice, 334–38; charter schools, 334–35; private schools, 320–21; vouchers, 181n, 328, 330, 335–37, 338

school districts, 47, 321; Alpine, 47; Board of Education, 68, 246, 321, 329–31, 336; funding, 253, 306, 307–10, 314–15, 317, 319–326, 336–39, 350–51; Granite, 46, 69; Jordan, 46–47, 331; Salt Lake City, 46, 67–70; superintendents, 262, 268–69, 321

school issues, xii, 10, 13, 79–80, 117, 122–23, 246, 262, 284, 289–90, 329; demographics, 320; extracurricular activities, 329; graduation, 47, 79–80, 284, 322, 331; sex education, 117, 138; site–based management, 328–29, 338; special education, 332, 334; truancy, 321–22. *See also* college; high school; land sales (Utah); school choice; school teachers; school testing

school teachers, xii, 46, 69, 96, 310, 330, 335; Career Ladder Program, 327–28, 338; commissions, 326, 327–28; Parent Teacher Association, 311, 323; strike, 323–24. *See also* National Education Association; Utah Education Association

school testing, No Child Left Behind, 252, 328, 332–34, 338; performance accountability, 320, 322, 330, 334; standardized tests, 320, 326, 328–30, 334–35; Stanford Achievement Test, 330; UBSCT, 331–32, 338; U–Pass, 331–32, 338

Semnani, Khosrow, 160–64. *See also* Envirocare

sexual abuse, 108, 110, 114–17, 125, 291–93; rape, 108, 108g, 125. *See also* child abuse

sexual revolution, ix, 27, 33, 75–76, 341–42, 352; premarital sex, 83–84. *See also* gay rights; Planned Parenthood

Trump, Donald, xii, 17–21, 299, 349;
federal land, 200, 222, 226–28

U

Udall, Stuart, 203–04

Uinta Mountains, 185–86

Uintah Basin, 191, 194, 221, 228, 349

unemployment compensation, 135,
137. *See also* workforce

unemployment rate, 91, 100, 221, 252

United Nations, 57–58

University of Utah, 64, 68, 126, 170,
178, 269

Upshot–Knothole Harry test, 144, 148

US Air Force, 93, 158, 174–75

US Bureau of Land Management,
206p, 207, 212–16, 218, 221–25

US Bureau of Reclamation, 187–89,
191–92, 195–97

US Census Bureau, 303–04, 306–07

US Congress, 6, 11–13, 21–22, 34–35,
48, 127–28, 133–34, 150, 159–60,
177, 214, 216, 218, 299

US Constitution, 1, 55, 64–65,
263–64, 282, 284, 288, 294; amendments, 1, 56–58, 58p; Bill of Rights,
45–46, 52, 284, 325; constitutional
law, 282–95

US Department of Defense, 155–56.
See also federal spending; military

US Department of Energy, 160–61.
See also energy sources

US Department of Health and Human Services, 100

US Department of Interior, 173–74,
207, 217, 224, 225

US Forest Service, 209–10, 213

US Supreme Court, 121–22, 125,
325; public morality, 45–47, 51–52,
53–54, 60, 65; Utah Constitution,
284–86, 287, 289, 294–95

US Tenth Circuit Court of Appeals
(Denver), 34–35, 60, 64–65, 148,
225, 295

Utah Attorney General, 50–51, 60,
245, 262n, 265–66, 269–70, 271–72

Utah Board of Examiners, 262,
265–66, 268–71, 273–74

Utah Constitution, 41–43, 203, 237,
256–57, 271–72, 277, 282–95;
amendments, 245–46, 273–74,
286–87, 306, 321, 337; budgeting and
spending, 298, 301, 306, 311; constitutional revision committee, 274;
convention, 261, 273; Declaration of
Rights, 261, 288; first draft, 1–2

Utah counties, 120, 147, 202g, 217–18,
303; Millard, 121; Uintah 222–23;
Utah, 188, 294. *See also* Davis
County, Kane County, Salt Lake
County, Tooele County, Washing-
ton County

Utah Department of Agriculture, 265,
267

Utah Department of Corrections,
110–111; pardons, 262; parole, 110,
114–15, 293; rehabilitation, 110–11.
See also incarceration; prisons

Utah Department of Health and
Social Services, 111; social workers,
70, 110, 134, 269–70

Utah Division of Child and Family
Services, 70–71, 116. *See also* adoption; children

Utah Education Association (UEA),
323–27, 335, 336

Utah Finance Department, 265–66,
268, 271–72; commission, 268

floods, 189, 205; irrigation, 185–87, 189–91, 195–96, 348–49; LDS Church, 186; tax on, 186, 195; usage, 185–89, 195–96. *See also* California, water; Great Salt Lake; reclamation

Watkins, Arthur, 192, 193n

weapons, 348; atomic, 157, 169p, 176–77, 180; biological, 154, 168–171, 179; chemical, 153–56, 164–68, 165, 169p, 176, 178–79, 181, 182–83, 348; disposal, 155–56, 164–68; testing, 141–53, 144p, 153–55, 156–59, 168–70, 175–77, 180–83. *See also* Dugway Proving Grounds; missiles; radiation; sheep-kill; Upshot–Knothole Harry test; Weteye nerve-gas bombs

Webster v. Reproductive Services, 54–55

welfare, 84, 91–92, 130–37, 138, 284, 306–07, 317, 346; commission, 267; department, 270, 280; Emergency Work Program, 133; fraud, 132, 292; Personal Responsibility and Work Opportunity Reconciliation Act, 134; reform, 132, 134. *See also* New Deal; poverty; Supplemental Nutrition Assistance Program; Utah Department of Health and Social Services

Wells, Heber, 203, 259t, 264

West Desert, 157, 172, 174–75, 216

Weteye nerve-gas bombs, 155–56, 181–83

wilderness, 209–23; Wilderness Act, 209–10, 213

Wilderness Study Areas, *see* wilderness

Wilkinson, David, 60, 114, 170

Wilson, Ted, 23t, 213n

Wilson, Woodrow, 24, 31g, 32, 191

women, 27, 123, 135–36; employment, 97, 100, 105, 344–45; widows, 130–31, 288, 313. *See also* Equal Rights Amendment; feminism; income; reproduction

Woodruff, Wilford, 12–13

workforce, 99, 221, 346; Job Opportunity and Basic Skills Program, 133; labor-force participation, 97–100, 104; labor unions, 311; part time employment, 97, 104–05; Single Parent Employment Demonstration Program (SPED), 134; Utah Department of Workforce Services, 135; Work Experience and Training Program, 133; Work Incentive Program, 133. *See also* men; Utah Education Association; women

World War II, 30, 31g, 87, 92–93, 96, 164

Wyoming, 190, 237

Y

Young, Brigham, 1, 6, 10, 88, 186, 269

Young, David, 289–90

Z

Zimmerman, Michael, 287, 289n

Zinke, Ryan, 226–27

PRAISE FOR UTAH POLITICS

"There may be no more insightful voice on Utah politics than Rod Decker. With an expert's eye and a journalist's ear for the truth, he takes readers on a deep dive into the political culture of one of the most unique states in the union. And in doing so, he uncovers an age-old truth: No government program—no matter how effective or fiscally sound—can substitute for a strong family and a loving home. This book is a much-needed addition to the canon on state politics, and a fitting capstone to a legendary career."

—**Orrin G. Hatch**, US Senate (R-Utah), 1977–2019; chair of the Senate Finance Committee (2015–19), Judiciary Committee (2003–05), and Labor Committee (1981–87) and Senate President pro tempore (2015–19)

"Rod Decker knows Utah politics inside and out. As a reporter for decades in the Beehive State, he developed an understanding of the inner workings of political matters like nobody else. His years at the center of things are in evidence in this thoroughly researched book. It is a fascinating and engaging read that politicians and laymen alike will benefit from."

—**Jeanetta Williams**, NAACP president, Tri-state Conference, Idaho–Nevada–Utah; former public relations officer, Utah Transit Authority, US West Communications

"Rod Decker has given us a lucid and persuasive account of Utah's institutions both political and religious. Each chapter is clearly written, cogently argued, and data driven. There is a fascinating account of the ascendency of the Republican Party and formidable commitment of the LDS Church to defend traditional marriage and family, one that has led to conflicts with the federal judiciary. His treatment of how government and politics function in a state as religiously homogeneous as Utah is fair, informative, and thought provoking."

—**John G. Francis**, Professor of Political Science, University of Utah; past Associate Vice-President for Academic Affairs; author of *Privacy: What Everyone Needs to Know*

"Rod Decker has been one of Utah's most recognized and notable political reporters for decades. Indeed, he is one of the most respected journalists in Utah history. His tenacity, knowledge, and passion were his trademark as a reporter and are evident in this important work."

—**Gary Herbert**, governor of Utah; past chair, National Governors Association; former staff sergeant, Utah National Guard

"Rod Decker served KUTV and the community for years as a lead Utah political journalist. When he arrived to cover a story, it was a double-edged sword. The good news—Decker was on it. The bad news—it would not be a puff piece!"

—**Jenny Wilson**, mayor, Salt Lake County; MPA degree, Harvard University; documentary producer and director, *The Grand Rescue*

"Grounded in data, interviews, and an extensive canvass of secondary sources, Rod Decker has produced a valuable summary of a broad range of Utah politics. His chapters on church/state relations, demography, the economy, the state's relationship to the federal government, and implications of an arid climate help convey important aspects of the political culture. His years as a reporter enhance his original research on governmental institutions and policy issues."

—**David Magleby**, BYU Professor of Political Science; former dean of Family, Home, and Social Sciences; author of *The Money Chase*

Finally Statehood!
Utah's Struggles, 1849–1896

Edward Leo Lyman

Utah's quest for statehood lasted longer, involved more political intrigue, and garnered more national attention than any other US territory. Edward Leo Lyman carefully traces the key figures, events, and cultural shifts leading to Utah's admission to the union. Reflecting an abundance of careful research, *Finally Statehood!* is a thorough attempt to understand the state's history on local and national levels, with each political roadblock, religious conflict, and earnest attempt at compromise engagingly woven into the narrative.

hardback | $49.95
e-book | $9.99
978-1-56085-273-5

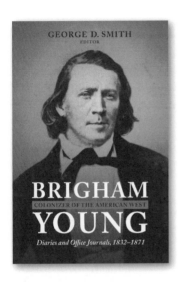

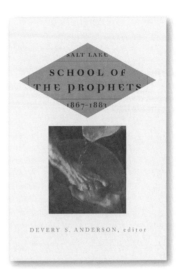

Brigham Young, Colonizer of the American West
Diaries and Office Journals, 1832–1871

George D. Smith, ed.

Brigham Young's diaries and office journals reveal a man dedicated to his church, defensive of his spiritual and temporal claims to authority, and determined to create a modern Zion within the Utah desert. Editor George D. Smith's careful organization and annotation of Young's personal writings, published here for the first time, provide insight into the mind of Mormonism's self-made theologian and frontier statesman.

2 vol. hardback | $100.00
e-book | $40.00
978-1-56085-274-2

Salt Lake School of the Prophets, 1867–1883

Devery S. Anderson, ed.

The priesthood-led institution called the School of the Prophets, first established in Kirtland, Ohio, in 1833, became an integral part of pioneer Utah after Brigham Young revived it some thirty years later. Presented here for the first time are all available minutes for the Utah period, fully annotated. The school discussed theological and doctrinal issues, oversaw local politics, dealt with the influx of outsiders, and gave its members a lasting camaraderie.

hardback | $47.95
e-book | $9.99
978-1-56085-234-6